pedigree

pedigree
THE ORIGINS OF WORDS FROM NATURE

by STEPHEN POTTER *and*
LAURENS SARGENT

TAPLINGER PUBLISHING COMPANY / NEW YORK

AN ARNOLD LENT BOOK

First published in the United States in 1974 by
TAPLINGER PUBLISHING CO., INC.
New York, New York

Library of Congress Catalog Card Number: 73-16964

ISBN 0-8008-6248-1

:   :   :

Pedigree was first published in Great Britain in the New Naturalist series,
edited by:

Margaret Davies, C.B.E., M.A., Ph.D.
Sir Julian Huxley, F.R.S., M.A., D.Sc.
John Gilmour, M.A., V.M.H.
Kenneth Mellanby, C.B.E., Sc.D.
Photographic Editor: Eric Hosking, F.R.P.S.

TO
JAMES MAXWELL McCONNELL FISHER
1912—1970

αἱ δὲ τεαὶ ζώουσιν ἀηδόνες, ᾗσιν ὁ πάντων
ἁρπακτὴς Ἀΐδης οὐκ ἐπὶ χεῖρα βαλεῖ.

CALLIMACHUS

Anth. Pal. VII, 80

Still are they pleasant voices, thy nightingales, awake;
For Death, he taketh them all away, but then he cannot take.

Translation by William Cory in *Ionica*, 1858

contents

CONTENTS

editors' preface

This volume is the combined brain-child of the late Stephen Potter and the late James Fisher, and it is sad that neither is now with us to see it published. The subject of the book is, in a sense, also a dual one – the origin of natural history words (for example the names of animals and plants), and the origin of non-natural history words which have a natural history origin (for example, pedigree, chosen for the title). This combination of two aspects of 'Words from Nature', to quote from this volume's sub-title, makes an original and fascinating book. It will appeal, we are sure, to those generally interested in the English language and its development – as well as to natural history lovers.

When Stephen Potter died, he left the text as a series of notes rather than in a form anywhere near suitable for publication, and the present editors are very grateful to James Fisher for suggesting the Rev. Laurens Sargent, a well-known amateur philologist, as the right person to transform Stephen Potter's notes into a book. He, in turn, as he says in his Preface, has had much help, especially from Professor E. G. Stanley and Mrs Wallace-Hadrill. This combined 'team-effort' has produced a book unique of its kind, and one that we are proud to publish.

author's preface

Among the thousands of readers who delighted in the humour of Stephen Potter, and were saddened by his death, may have been many who (not having read all his books) had not realized that the wit of the creator of *Lifemanship* and *One-Upmanship* was drawn from a deep well of scholarship. He was an artist who could conceal his art, but not his interest in great literature and in Nature – especially, as we know, Human Nature.

For me it is a matter of regret that I never met Stephen Potter in person, but one of happiness that our minds should have eventually made contact through the friendship that we shared with one of the leading ornithologists and nature-conservationists of our times – a scholar, too, and both a lover of poetry and a man of unflagging practical energy – modest, unselfish, and staunch, to whom this book is dedicated. Surely my colleague in the present endeavour would have wished the dedication to be to James Fisher, whose kindly thought it was to suggest the twin-authorship to the friendly minds of Messrs Collins.

Had Stephen Potter lived to see the volume through the press, he would have warmly acknowledged his debt to Mr Eric Partridge for help on various knotty etymological points; as I now acknowledge mine to Mrs Anne Wallace-Hadrill for reading with an expert eye all these pages in typescript and proof, and for her invaluable emendations and suggestions.

Among those to whom I am also very grateful are the late W. B. Alexander, Hugh Gladstone, and J. M. Harrison; Mrs Penelope Heck; Professor E. O. Höhn; the late D. J. N. Lee, I.C.S. (sometime Boden Sanskrit Scholar); and an expert in German and Swedish, my wife Rosemarie.

L. C. S.

abbreviations

A.N.	Anglo-Norman
A.V.	*Authorized Version of the Bible*
Arab.	Arabic
B.B.	British birds
C.E.D.	*Concise Etymological Dictionary*: W. W. Skeat
C.O.D.	*Concise Oxford Dictionary*: F. W. and H. G. Fowler
D.B.	*Domesday Book*
Dan.	Danish
Du.	Dutch
E.D.D.	*English Dialect Dictionary*: J. Wright
F.	French
G.	German
Gael.	Gaelic
Gk.	Ancient Greek
Goth.	Gothic
Hind.	Hindi
I-E.	Indo-European
It.	Italian
L.	Latin
L.G.	Low German
L.L.	Late Latin
M.E.	Middle English
M.E.D.	*Middle English Dictionary*: Kurath & Kuhn
M.L.G.	Middle Low German
med.	mediaeval
N.E.B.	*New English Bible*
N.H.	Natural History
Nor.	Norwegian
O.E.	Old English
O.E.D.	*Oxford English Dictionary*
O.D.E.E.	*Oxford Dictionary of English Etymology*: C. T. Onions

O.F.	Old French
O.H.G.	Old High German
O.N.	Old Norse
O.D.P.N.	*Oxford Dictionary of English Place-Names*: E. Ekwall
Pers.	Persian
Port.	Portuguese
Rom.	Romanic
Scand.	Scandinavian
Skt.	Sanskrit
Slav.	Slavonic
Sp.	Spanish
Swed.	Swedish
Teut.	Teutonic
Turk.	Turkish
*	an unrecorded but historically expected form

pedigree

i

PIED DE GRUE

> ' " Must a name mean something?" Alice asked
> doubtfully.
> "Of course it must," Humpty Dumpty said.'
>   CARROL, *Through the Looking-glass.*

ENGLISH wild-flowers are the best in the world – so we are brought
up to believe. If, later in life, our faith is shaken by the sight of the
foothills of the Alps in early summer, or of the Spanish coast in
spring, we are still convinced that we have the best flower-names:
and these will provide an integral part of our thoughts about names
from Nature.

Wort (as in 'St John's wort') the old name for a plant, pot-herb, or
root, is not the prettiest final syllable in the language; but we may
welcome it because it takes us swiftly back to the roots of our English
language and its relatives. (It is easy to recognize, for example, its
German cognate *Wurtz* in our *mangel-wurzel*.) Of other plant-names
the range is wide, from the earthily forceful to the delicately nostalgic.
As the poet sang, 'Worts and pansies there which grew Have secrets
others wish they knew'.

Many of our bird-names are equally attractive. There is a graceful
dignity about *swan*; *twite* is remarkably apt for a small bird. Whether
the *grey lag-goose* is so called from its feeding more on field-grass, in
the 'leas', than on sea-ware, or from its 'lagging' behind its congeners
on migration, the name may seem better than the German *Graugans*,
simply because it is familiar to us: and, with equal partiality towards
our own tongue, we probably think that 'stormy petrel' suggests the
nature of the bird better than the French *pétrel tempête*, which seems
a little self-conscious as a word, or too pernickety and reminiscent
of the version of Job 40. 15 in the French Bible – *Voici l'hippotame* –
by the side of our 'Behold now behemoth'.

Then there are the names of butterflies and moths. The thoughtful
mind can find something of social history in the pomp of the Purple

Emperor and the Admirals, white and red. What they, or the Camberwell Beauty, would have been named today must be left to the imagination. The Geometer moths would have risked being 'Computers', and having a 'Sputnik' among them.

Some of the names of the moths seem to have been created by a poetical wit who combined the boldness of Browning with the exact word-sense of Tennyson. In point of fact the donors of the names were many, but most of their own names are unknown to us. Their Old Lady and Alchemist, their Feathered Footman and Pugs, might be characters from a play by Molière. The Archer's Dart, the Clifton Nonpareil, the Beautiful Carpet. . . . Who would not be glad to be a lepidopterist and search for these soft beauties?

Much of the inspiration prompting the scientific names in Natural History came from the first and greatest of systematists, Linnaeus (the Swede, Carl von Linné, 1707–1778), whose charming thought it was to embody in his two-term nomenclature for plants and animals names taken from classical myths, legends, and history. *Narcissus, Daphne, Iris*, the *Dryads* and the *Naiads*, and many other gracious beings speak to us through familiar flowers. Our native swallowtail butterfly *Papilio machaon* is called after the son of Aesculapius. *Davus*, the Romans' equivalent of Sambo or 'Rastus, wears the sober brown livery of the marsh ringlet. Among a host of goddesses, nymphs, and heroines of antiquity, *Io*, the beloved of Zeus, becomes the peacock butterfly; *Atalanta* the red admiral, *Sibylla* the white; *Artemis* is a fritillary. The *Pierides*, the Muses, flutter their white wings among our cabbages.

Though birds are not so often distinguished, here and there among them is one bearing a legendary name. We meet *Nisus* and *Perdix*, metamorphosed as they were into sparrow-hawk and partridge, with *Pandion, Athene*, and *Neophron*, whose names became, after the time of Linnaeus, the generic names of the osprey, little owl, and Egyptian vulture. In their company is the prophetic *Picus*, who was changed into a woodpecker by lovesick Circe, and now lends his name to the Linnaean genus which still contains the green wood-pecker, the rain-foretelling yaffle. *Penelope*, the faithful wife of Odysseus, has woven her wool into the soft plumage of the wigeon.

Linnaeus indeed took Nomenclature from the dissecting-room to the Elysian Fields, in which many other great and lesser men have been familiar wanderers. Botanists will agree that the best tribute to this most modest of geniuses lives in the little northern species, the twin-flower, which he selected when asked what plant should be named in his honour. What was thenceforth known as *Linnaea borealis* he chose as being 'lowly, insignificant, unnoticed, and with as short a flowering-season as Linné's'. That he had also a sense of humour is instanced by the tale of the *Browallias*. The first of these blue-flowered plants – originally from Peru – he named *Browallia elata* (upright Browallia) in honour of Browall, a Finnish bishop who had written a tract in support of the Linnaean system of classification. Later, however, Browall attacked a theory advanced by Anders Celsius, Professor of Astronomy at Uppsala and maker of the centigrade thermometer, who had 'discovered' Linné and warmly befriended him in his student-days. Linné counter-attacked by renaming the plant *Browallia demissa* (low Browallia), and, it is said, by calling a second species, now unknown, *Browallia alienata* (unloved Browallia).

An atlas opens out another world of beauty for the philologist, even if he may never visit the scenes which it suggests. It is no wonder that Longfellow, with the echoes of Amerindian names all round him, was moved to write *Hiawatha*. Stevenson drew inspiration from the melodious, almost entirely vocalic, speech of the South Sea Islanders.

Every naturalist is likely to have his own favourite group of nature-words. There is fascination in the language of human anatomy and the names of diseases, and in what can hardly be surpassed for dignity and appropriateness – the nomenclature of Geology. Call the strata *Cambrian, Ordovician,* or *Silurian,* and the words will thunder as if they had come straight out of *Paradise Lost. Eocene* (the Dawn of the New) shows exactly how, by shifting to Greek, to make the right change of key. The gift has not been lost.

This will be a subject to return to; for, though words *from* Nature are our chief concern in these pages, their origins are in man's names *for* Nature.

*   *   *

Not long ago I was bird-watching*, but not quite in the manner of the ornithological editor of the *New Naturalist* series, with telescopic lenses and the right colour-filters, on difficult ground at the end of a

*S.P.

five-mile track 'Impassable to Motorists'. I was watching in the London Zoo, not for courtship-display or nesting-behaviour, but for etymology.

Nearly opposite the Small Mammal House are the Cranes. The name of the 'common' crane is *Grus grus*. In French it is the *grue cendrée*, to remind us that we were formerly allowed to call it *Grus cinerea*, 'the ashy crane'. The Zoo was full of children. Boys like looking at the other sort of crane, on building-sites. Do they realize that the mechanical crane is so called because it cranes its neck like a crane? Probably not.

I took a casual look at the bird's beak, and thought how apt was the botanical name 'cranesbill'. The fruit of that flower is remarkably like the beak of this particular bird. (The careful botanist would not call it 'the fruit', but 'the central persistent axis of the carpel', which remains as a neat decoration while the later flowers of the small plant are still blooming.) In the cranesbill's close relative, the storksbill, the spike is proportionally longer. The O.E.D. says that 'cranesbill' is a translation by 16th-century English herbalists of the Dutch *craenhals*, though the Dutch word suggests 'crane's neck'. What is certain is that the plant's generic name 'geranium' is from the Gk. *geranos*, which itself means 'crane', and is the equivalent of the Latin *grus*.

It was the foot of the crane in the Zoo that focussed my interest. It has three stubby toes, of about equal length and spread out fairly wide. I had been looking elsewhere for the etymological pedigree of *pedigree*: but here it was in nature – *pedigree, pied de grue*, so called because the older genealogical tables used a conventional sign resembling a crane's foot, λ. This, in the words of Professor Skeat, was reminiscent of 'the three-line mark, like a broad arrow, used in denoting succession'.

The earlier form of *pedigree* was a Norman-French word, first known to have been used in an English context by Lydgate, the English Chaucerian, in the early 15th century. The Epilogue to his *Chronicles of Troy* has the phrase.

> 'Who so lyst loke and doe unfolde
> The pee de grewe of these cronicles olde.'

And again:

'The peedegre doth hit specifie,
The figure lo of the genelagye.'

There, in the long leisureliness of Lydgate's Middle English, is a
new word forming, crisp and useful. It has not been altered much
since its introduction – a sure sign that it is speakable. It is all the
more strongly permanent through being based on nature, in this
instance through an amused and quizzical observation by the eye
of a naturalist of the crane's three-toedness.

The story of *pedigree* cannot really be concluded, because the best
word-makers are so often anonymous. No exact date can be given
for its birth; but it takes us back to the time when cranes, now rare
vagrants, were familiar sights in both France and England. Lydgate
would have seen them very often, not only in France, where he used
to go on official business, but also as they flew inland from the
Suffolk estuaries, only half a day's jog-trot from his Benedictine
monastery of Bury St Edmunds.

In *pedigree* we have an example of how, side by side with the
obvious nature-words in our language, is another set of words, at
least equal in number, which owe their origin to some experience
in which Natural History is involved, or to the differences in en-
vironment between the present age and the time when the words
were forming. We can see an earlier and less complicated, less
machine-governed life of a people living in homely contact with
nature.

But *pedigree* cannot have failed to suggest a genealogical tree, even
for a language: and, before plunging into the heart, or the branches,
of our theme, let us delve a little further below the surface of the
ground from which it grows, and try to get at the roots of it.

ii

GROUNDWORK AND ROOTS

'Science is the lamp which man has himself kindled.
It has built him lighthouses on the dark shores of the
unknown; but his dreams, his quests for truth, lead him
beyond the waters which his little lamp of knowledge
illumines.'

s. r. lysaght, *A Reading of Life.*

The names of a great many Englishmen – to say nothing of other
nationalities – may be traced to a physical or moral peculiarity of
some forebear, to a profession, or to a dwelling-place. Similarly, a
large proportion of names for other animals originated in the bodily
characteristics, the habits, or the haunts of the creatures in question.
But straight from Nature – from plants as well as animals – comes
an unexpectedly large number of English surnames. The Stage gave
us the *Trees*; Thomas Hardy gave us *Oak*. *Ash*, *Birch*, and *Beech* are
often met. A *Primrose* became Prime Minister in 1894; a *Heath* in
1970. On a stone in Canterbury Cathedral is carved a *Salmon*, the
signature of a 12th-century Scottish stonemason of that name. Some
at least of the *Lyons* must owe their name to heraldic blazonry, and
some *Leppards* to the 'lion leoparded' variety of the charge. Perhaps,
when *Coward* is not derived from *cowherd*, the name originated in
the *lion coward*, the lion with his tail between his legs, of an armorial
bearing. *Herring* was a painter; *Hogg* and *Crabbe* were poets; *Lamb*
was a man of letters. The notorious 19th-century *Hare* showed no
timidity as a criminal. One *Fox* was a great statesman; and *Bull*
stands for every true Englishman.

Birds provide the closest parallels. Among human beings we find
Whitehead, among birds *Blackcap*. Messrs *Short* and *Little* have counterparts in *Stint* and *Tit*. Men, often dignified by such names as *Noble*
and *Wise*, claim superiority by slighting the *Noddy* and the *Dotterel*.
Swift may write satire in a deanery, or lay eggs in a cranny of the
same building. In one society are *Baker*, *Webster*, and *Taylor*; in

22

another are the *Oven-*, the *Weaver-*, and the *Tailor*-birds. Our *Turner* is paralleled by *Woodpecker*: though our *Fishers*, whether admirals, cabinet-ministers, prelates, headmasters, or ornithologists, never wear uniforms as brilliant as a *Kingfisher*'s. The cock *Kitty Wren* builds no fewer nests than Sir Christopher Wren built churches. Messrs *Fielding* and *Walker* might lead our thoughts to the *Fieldfare*. Even the stately bird which we take as our totem for the sake of *pied de grue* is echoed by *Crane*, the artist. Canon *Raven* was a brilliant theologian, botanist, and author; Kirke *Swann* wedded etymology to ornithology.

We should look in vain among bird-names for the patronymic type so prevalent among the names of men: no bird is a *Johnson*, a *Macdonald*, an *O'Gorman*, or an *ap Evan*. On the other hand a weighty part is played in ornithological nomenclature by a principle relatively unimportant in the composition of the names of Europeans and Americans – the principle found in a few names such as *Singer* and *Whistler* – that of basing the name on the utterance of sound. This is of such vital importance that we may like at this point to risk being 'old-fashioned' and wander a little from our main subject in order to make some endeavour to imagine how human speech started.

At one time the most popular theory was that the origin of all language (which is reciprocally and indissolubly connected with thought, the power to form concepts) was to be found in onomatopoeia – name-making from sounds associated with the objects named. This theory had the blessing of Plato. Primitive man, it was suggested, had made noises imitating sounds produced by, or connected with, his companions, or beasts, or birds, or natural phenomena such as thunder or rushing water or the cracking of a branch; and these noises became the first words. This 'Bow-wow theory', as it was called by Max Müller (1823–1900), the German-born Professor of Comparative Philology at Oxford, has succumbed under the overwhelming weight of evidence that the source of Speech, if it is to be found at all, is not to be found through imitative nouns, but through verbal 'roots' – primitive syllables which are themselves not grammatical words, but the raw material, whatever their hidden origins, of words in a group or family of languages. Our word 'wolf', for example (the Old Norse *ūlfr*, Gothic *wulfs*, Old English *wulf*, Swedish *ulf*, Dutch and German *Wolf*, with the more distantly related Sanskrit *vṛka*, Latin *lupus*, Greek *lukos*, Russian *volk*, etc.), is not derived from the creature's howl, but means 'the tearer'. So also 'owl' is neither a direct imitation of the bird's hoot, nor the source of the verbal notion of howling; but is itself derived from a verb meaning 'to howl' – the root of which was, however, probably influenced by imitation.

All the evidence, indeed, goes to show that primitive man formed his names on a principle entirely different from that adopted by those who encourage children to call a duck *quack-quack* or a dog *bow-wow*. It is doubtful whether many children tend spontaneously to speak of *moos* or *puff-puffs*. If twenty infants were allowed to see and hear dogs without hearing any name for the animals, and, as soon as they could make attempts to speak, were encouraged to imitate the noise made by a dog, it may be assumed that the number of different sounds would approximate to the number of the children. *Bow-wow* might emerge, but not unaccompanied by *oof* and *ro* and *yip*, and other rudimentary sounds containing little or no consonantal element. To these would probably be added imitations produced by those children on whom the dog's whining or snuffling had made the deepest impression. One boy, whose amusement it was to make up a language in which he used to talk to his terrier, used *harn* to represent the noise which he considered typical of his own dog.

'Even if we admit', wrote M. Moncalm in *The Origin Of Thought and Speech* (translated from French by Whitmarsh, 1905), 'that a small number of primitive men set themselves to imitate the murmur of the stream, the rolling of the thunder, the barking of a dog, the groans of the wounded, the only result would have been infinite variations of clamour quite impossible to distinguish or to understand'. Max Müller, in his argument to the same effect in *Lectures on the Science of Language* (1861), had pointed out how differently the same sounds are heard and rendered by different peoples: 'The cock crows *kiao kiao* in Chinese, *dchor dchor* in Mandshu.' This comment is particularly vivid to me,* for one year, while I was staying near *Tintagel*, I was wakened each morning by a cock which seemed clearly and unmistakably to cry, 'O King Arthur!'

Another now discredited hypothesis to account for the origin of language is the Ejaculatory, referred to by Max Müller as the 'Poohpooh theory'. Its advocates held that names began in the sounds forced through the lips of early men at the sight or sound of objects which inspired them with pleasure, fear, disgust, and other emotions.

For practical purposes we may ignore this Ejaculatory theory, and
*L.C.S.

– while respecting the ancillary part played by mimetic or echoic words – posit that only a small percentage of names given to objects represent attempts to copy the noises associated with those objects; and that we can seldom trace a name further back than to a simple syllable containing a verbal meaning, i.e. a 'root' suggesting an action.

There is, however, yet another theory, which calls for a separate chapter.

•••
iii

AND BEFORE ROOTS?

'Modern thought is so confident of where it is
going to that it does not know where it comes from.'
G. K. CHESTERTON, *The Futurists.*

'Man . . . uses, in common with the lower animals,
inarticulate cries to express his meaning, aided by
gestures and the movements of the muscles of his
face.'
DARWIN, *The Descent of Man.*

'IN the science of language,' wrote Max Müller, 'we must accept
roots simply as ultimate facts, leaving to the physiologist and the
psychologist the question as to the possible sympathetic or reflective
action of the five organs of sensory perception upon the motory
nerves of the organs of speech.'

And yet, especially if we are inclined to think that the root is somewhat reminiscent of the 'grin, which remained for some time after
the Cheshire cat disappeared', it may well be urged that the search
for the origin of language cannot stop at the unearthing of roots; and
that those who, though erroneously, believed that the first words
were nouns imitating noises were at least endeavouring to get back
to the beginnings of language, while enthusiasts for roots were
ignoring the main difficulty by refusing to search for what preceded
roots – for what, indeed, might be called the seeds. Surely, having
accepted in principle the Evolutionary theory and traced organic
matter to a single cell, mankind must sometimes speculate about the
origin of that cell: nor will the word-lover long be content to make
no further enquiry when he has reached a root – murmuring, perhaps, 'the insane root that takes the reason prisoner'.

As might be expected, it was Max Müller who, though himself
preferring to leave further enquiry to the physiologist and the
psychologist, held out the hope of a clue by his suggestion of 'sympathetic action': for it would seem quite possible that speech had its

origin in the emission of breath while the tongue and the lips and the other parts of the body which condition speech were striving to imitate action.

To appreciate how natural it is for a man to move his body in sympathy with movement outside him, one has but to observe a crowd watching a cricketer trying to make a high catch, or a high-jumper trying to clear the bar. Even more illustrative is the protrusion of the tongue of a child who is cutting paper with a pair of scissors. When we see such sympathetic movement, and also hear (as we often do) sounds forced out, as it were, by the urgency of the sympathy, we may feel that we are being guided nearer to understanding something about the origin of speech.

This Gesture theory is not new. It seems (like the System of Linnaeus) to have been latent in the minds of many writers, who hinted at it, but never enunciated it. The first serious attempt to examine its possibilities was made a century ago in *The Polynesian* by the famous naturalist and explorer A. R. Wallace. In 1930 Sir Richard Paget, in *Babel*, examined and further exemplified the work of Professor Malinowski, who stated that primitive speech is not an expression of thought, but rather of physical activity – in other words, primitive speech-sounds denote actions. . . . 'Primitive pantomime, being itself a matter of action, is naturally best fitted to describe action; the imitation of objects and the figurative use of action to symbolize qualities and ideas would come later.'

We need not resort to palaeolithic man to appreciate the part played by pantomime in the communication of ideas. Such pantomime, even of the most obvious sort, is not confined today to primitive peoples, or to the more gesticulatory nations of our own times. It is employed every day by the 'stolid' Englishman in the drawing of his arms inwards to reinforce his command 'Come here!'; in the closing of one eye to indicate a veil of mystery; and in a multitude of other similarly suggestive movements. (The contributor of an article on Lebanon in *The Times* of 30.10.1965 stated: 'A dictionary has been compiled of 500 meaningful hand-movements'.)

But, if the Gesture theory is true, we make use of pantomime not only when we wave our arms or wag our heads; we do so also whenever we speak, for the words which we use were born of the sounds made by human breath as it passed organs which struggled to reproduce the movements or the spatial or physical qualities of the objects of man's perception.

It is accordingly not easy to find a name for these words which most clearly illustrate this hypothesis. Few of them are onomatopoetic in the technical sense, although they do 'make names'. 'Echoic' scarcely fits their nature. 'Mimetic' is not far from the mark so long as we remember that we may be trying, in speech, to imitate spatial or other elusive qualities. 'Fitting' would be an apt adjective, since in each of the words we are endeavouring to fit the sound to the sense or sensation.

To illustrate this principle we must fare over unknown ground, stumbling perhaps into many pitfalls. But the journey, though difficult, is worth making. We shall travel back beyond roots; and roots themselves are but generalizations – the common factors of words, not words in themselves.

We might start by considering one of our dialect-words for a hillock, the word *tump*. This is according to the E.D.D. a Celtic word; but modern experts label it 'obscure'. It may be presumed to be cognate with *tomb*, the Greek *tumbos*; and with the Latin *tumulus*, a mound or tomb. *Tumulus* is a derivative, like the English 'tumour', of *tumere*, to swell. Many other kindred words may be cited; and we may not be contented merely with the knowledge that they all spring from the root **teu-* or **tū-*.

Noting that *tū* so often implies a protuberance, a quickwitted child might suggest that *tummy* was accounted for in similar fashion. If we were to rely entirely upon roots, we should have to answer, 'No, for *tummy* is just a way of saying *stomach*, which is from a Greek word, *stomakho* , a diminutive of *stoma*, a mouth; and *tummy* is formed like this just by chance'.

But, true as is the etymology, we should not be correct in giving this answer; nor, indeed, can any word be formed 'by chance'. Such a word as *tummy*, for whatever reason it has gained a secure place in everyday language, if not in our dictionaries, assures us that the oldest influences in language-formation are still alive and active. It is true that the word *stomach* and therefore the childish *tummy* are derivatives, through French and Latin, of *stoma*; but in English they have acquired the sound *um* (which in most of our local dialects, as in other Germanic languages, is pronounced *oom*), because of the primal tendency to imitate by the shape of the mouth the shape of something which swells. Before ever the root *tū- had begun to produce offshoots, the sound *oom* was probably being employed to represent swelling, by mouths which mimicked the swelling even as they uttered the sound.

Only some such hypothesis, in the opinion of its supporters, can cover an array of words which includes *plump, bump, dump, hump, rump, clump,* the Dutch importation *mumps,* the English and Norwegian *lump,* the Danish, Swedish, and Low German *klump* (a lump), the German, Swedish, and Danish *Rumpf, rumpa, rumpe* (the trunk of an animal), the Skt. and Lithuanian *kumpas* (hunched), the Latin *lumbus* (loin), as well as a great many words traceable to the root *tū-, such as those already cited – *tump, tomb, tumour, tumbos, tumulus* – with *thumb* (Swedish *tumme*), the Greek *tulē* (a swelling), and all the other derivatives of the root in the Indo-European tongues.

Considered with all this medley of words betokening something rounded, a protuberance, *tummy,* though a derivative of *stoma,* may be said to have reverted to type.

From a presumed Teutonic base come our word *curl* (metathesized from M.E. *crul,* as the word 'bird' is from O.E. *bridd*), the Dutch *krullen* and the Swedish *krulla,* 'to curl', the Low German *krellen,* 'to turn'. From another presumed base come *cringle, cringe, crank,* and other words such as the Norse *kringla,* 'a circle', and the Low German *kringel,* the parent of our *cringle,* 'a ring'. *Ring* itself, O.E. *hring,* like the Russian *krug,* 'a circle', belongs to a group of words whose original type is presumed as *krenghos. Add to these our *crook* (the Danish *krog* and the Swedish *krok*), *crochet* and *crotchet* (both offshoots of the Late Latin *croccus,* 'hook'), *crisp, crumple, cramp, crimp* (and the Dutch equivalent *krimpen*), Welsh *crwm* ('crooked'), *cross* (traceable to the Latin *crux*), the Greek *kurtos* and the Latin *curvus* ('bent'). Such a selection, say the upholders of the Gesture theory, from a great number of words which, whatever the root or roots may have been, have maintained so perfectly the diagnostic element, should be enough to illustrate the basic connection between *kr-* and the notion of bending or curving. This *kr* (like the sound in 'wriggle' and 'wry') is essentially suitable to denote 'curving', 'curling', and the like, from the fact that its sound is produced against a tongue which has to shape itself to imitate the motion or shape of something curling or curved. (Cf. Chapter XI(a), H. D. Thoreau on *Owls.*)

Sherlock Holmes (or Dr Bell), speaking through Conan Doyle,

remarked on Darwin's supposition that Early Man was able to appreciate musical sounds before he developed the power of speech.

Long was the lapse of time between the earliest attempts at language and the emergence of 'roots'. Innumerable were the modifications of sounds between the time when men communicated by signs mingled with half-articulated noises, and when they were employing real language. Yet still in those syllables which we call roots may often be discerned what appears to be their principle. The cognate Greek *odous* (with its stem *odont-*), the Sanskrit *danta*, the Latin *dent-*, the German *Zahn*, and our word *tooth* are all offshoots of the root *ed- or *ad-, 'to eat'. This syllable has but to be repeated two or three times to declare itself as uttered during an imitation of the motion of biting. The root *es- implies being, existence, life. The connection between breath and life is so close that it would be difficult not to find in *es-, uttered with the mouth in breathing-position, the hiss of respiration. To voice the sound of the root *pet-, 'to fly', necessitates moving the lips in the manner of the wings of a flying bird.

Surely this gesticulatory principle, so hard to pin down, is latent in a host of words which we can neither trace to a common root, nor, in most instances, consider as echoing any sound connected with them. We just find their 'shape', so to speak, satisfying; and, rejecting their competitors, continue to use them, because they and our bodies, as well as our minds, are in harmony. Contemplate at leisure the *puff* group – *pouffe, duff, fluff, huff*, etc. – or *shingle*, which can challenge you not to feel the little pebbles shifting and whishing under your feet, and may even make you see the shine of sea-washed surfaces.

If, at pistol-point, after listening to the contradictory opinions of the expert philologists, one were forced to advance a theory about the word *mother* (of which some cognate words are listed in the next Chapter), one might stammer out, 'Gesticulatory'. We may arrive at a root *mā-, 'to make'. But the root is not the seed.

Now let us boldly face the ridicule of the experts by suggesting that all language began with a form of *ma*.

It would not be far from the mark to guess that all speech started with sounds evoked by Food, Sex, Anger, or Fear (which may be called Anger-in-Reverse). Human beings are apt to shriek with fear – as are hares and many other species of animal. Men are apt to growl and utter various obscure noises – as are other mammals, even the mouse in *Alice in Wonderland* – when they are angry. The phenomenon of sex occasions many different kinds of utterance, voluntary and involuntary. There seems to be no seed of roots in any of these sounds. But who could have had dealings with infants, let alone older children, without remarking that, almost without exception, they move their lips and murmur 'um ... um ... um' when they like their food?

This 'um ... um ... um' when repeated becomes 'mum ... mum ... mum', or, as the syllables would be spelt in most other languages, 'mam ... mam ... mam' or 'ma ... ma ... ma'.

Immediately, as epochs go, the primitive baby's 'ma' would have become associated with food, with the food-giver, with the source of the food-flow – and soon with a large number of associated and subsidiary notions. It is not surprising that *mama* for breast is found among Australian aborigines, and elsewhere, even as *mamma* is found in the languages of the Aryans.

Let us be consistent and go on searching for the root; but let us give the credit to gesticulatory utterance for providing the seed of that root – and quite conceivably of all human speech.

The foregoing examples connected with the Gesture theory may be inadequate or inaccurate. The theory itself may be viewed with suspicion. It may be found to account no better than the Onomatopoetic or the Ejaculatory theory for the existence of roots. Yet it is reasonable to believe that by its aid we may at least attempt to know what was the source of speech, the outward evidence of thought.

But we must now go forward for two or three hundred thousand years to the time when the first pregnant noises had given birth to fully developed languages.

iv

FROM ADAM TO THE ARYANS

'And Noah begat Shem, Ham, and Japheth.'
Genesis 5. 32.

THE Babylonian or other early sage, pondering on the varieties of the human race, came to much the same conclusions as his successors, the modern anthropologists. In one respect at least he was their superior: his theories about the unknowable were expressed a great deal more crisply. Half-a-dozen words – and we have the summary of a 20th-century volume.

The ancient explanation of the existence of the three great groups of mankind known to the Hebrews was that they were the descendants of Shem (the Hebrews themselves and kindred peoples), of Ham (the dark Africans), and of Japheth (their straighter-nosed, lighter-skinned neighbours in the north). We still use the terms Semitic and Hamitic in the same sense as of old; but 'Japhetic' has yielded to 'Indo-European' or 'Indo-Germanic' for languages, and to 'Aryans' for the people from whose primitive speech all those languages have sprung, and for their descendants.

In spite of the still recent misuse of the name 'Aryan' to serve political ends, this Sanskrit word is one which we may be proud to apply to ourselves, without detracting from the dignity of the other great human families. Sprung from **ar-*, quite literally rooted in the earth of antiquity, it affords an excellent example of how a root may branch out into hundreds of words in scores of different languages and dialects.

The root **ar-*, meaning at first 'to go' or 'to move forward', acquired various other shades of meaning, such as 'to move the soil', 'to plough' (e.g. the Latin *arare* and its derivatives such as *arator*, 'a ploughman', *arvum*, 'the place ploughed, a field'). The adjective from *arvum* – *arvensis* – was made by Linnaeus part of the specific name of the skylark. *Armentum* was 'the beast used for ploughing'; *aratrum*, 'the plough'. Greek had *aroun*, Gothic *arjan*, and, eventually, early

32

English *ear* (O.E. *erian*), all meaning 'to plough'. The next stage was reached when **ar-* was used in words having the sense of ploughing the sea: such were the Greek *eretmos* and the Sanskrit *aritra*, 'an oar' (or 'rudder'). Among more modern derivatives are *rudder*, *row*, and *earth* (the German *Erde*). 'Aryan' itself is directly from the Sanskrit *ārya*, 'a man of the soil, a landholder, an aristocrat or noble'.

Ethnologists differ as to the region which probably cradled our remote ancestors, but are generally united in siting it somewhere by the Caspian Sea. The Aryans started, as the Indo-European languages show, as one group of humanity; but in the course of thousands of years two great separations took place. In the first was a migration of some of the folk to the north and north-west, which spread them eventually through what we now call Russia in Europe, Middle Europe, and the lands washed by the North Sea and the Baltic. The second separation took place when some of the remainder trekked on the one hand to the west, on the other to the east and south-east. In course of time these three groups became further divided and sub-divided, with modifications due to climate, new experiences, and other factors continually at work in their speech; until finally the ancient stock and a number of different forms of the primitive language had spread through Persia, North India, and most of Europe. (These migratory movements are evidenced by the agreements and differences in the various languages of the same original family: e.g. in the inflexions of the verb meaning 'to be'; in the numerals; in words for primary concepts such as 'father', 'daughter', 'cow', 'hound', and various plants and wild animals.)

A few European peoples, however, are not of Aryan stock, and speak languages of a much more loosely connected family than the Indo-European, namely the Turanian (known also as Mongolian, Ural-Altaic, or Tataric), which includes Siamese and Malayan, as well as the languages of the Hungarians, Lapps, Finns, Turks, and other non-Semitic nomadic races of Europe and Asia.

There are only a few faint indications (such as grammatical gender) that long, long ago the prototypes of the Indo-European and the Semitic language-families shared their ancestry. For us, the most important Semitic tongues are Hebrew and Arabic.

People may of course be of Aryan origin, and yet not speak an Indo-European language; for instance, the descendants of the Janissaries in Turkey who survived the massacre of 1826. Innumerable non-Aryans on the other hand speak languages developed from that of the early Aryans. Many thousands of Japanese in Brazil, Africans long domiciled in the United States and elsewhere, and Jewish people speaking the tongues of their adopted countries, notably in Europe and America, are obvious examples. The Oxford English Dictionary contains about a quarter of a million different words – about a hundred times as many, perhaps, as an educated Englishman uses in his normal daily speech, unless this happens to be filled with technicalities relating to his profession or some other interest. These words have been shown to spring from a few hundred roots. Some of these roots are peculiar (as far as we know) to one of the more restricted groups, e.g. the Teutonic (Germanic); but many of them are to be found in words of virtually every language in the whole Indo-European family.

If we take the best-loved word in English, we shall have a graphic illustration of the kinship existing among all the Indo-European tongues merely by writing that word in the forms used in a few of the languages, ancient and modern, spoken in a great part of Asia and nearly the whole of Europe.

Mutter, moeder, moder, mote, mate, máthair, mam, mäter, mère, madre, mētēr, mādar, mātṛ, mā: thus is the word *mother* written in German, Dutch, Danish and Swedish, Lithuanian, Russian, Irish and Gaelic, Welsh, Latin, French, Italian and Spanish, Greek (ancient and modern), Persian, Sanskrit, and Hindustani; its principle being rooted in the primitive language shared by all the Aryans before the first great separation, until, dividing and diverging, they were speaking tongue after tongue and dialect after dialect of the great Indo-European language-family. As the old language deviated into a large number of different forms, those forms gradually grew mutually incomprehensible to those who spoke them; until today Welsh, for instance, seems to the casual listener or reader an entirely different language from English, Spanish, or Bengali. Yet below the surface lie the roots that give us the key to understanding – roots such as we have mentioned, with **mar-*, 'to pound'; **ak-*, 'to be sharp'; **ag,-* 'to drive'; **sed-*, 'to sit'; **sta-*, 'to stand'; etc. From each of them hundreds of words may be seen to be derived, and many of them are to be traced in our own English Nature-names for living creatures.

U

THE EMERGENCE OF ENGLISH

'Our language is a great inheritance. It is among
our greatest assets. It is the nearest approach today to
a world-language.'

RONALD STAPLES,
The Alphabet throughout the Ages.

SINCE several dozen different languages help to form our 'English'
nature-names, we should spare a few minutes for considering the
ancestry of the mother-tongue of those of us who call ourselves
'Britons'.

A rhyme of the 19th century schoolroom suggests quite neatly why
modern English is what it is:

'The Romans in Britain first held sway;
The Saxons after them led the way;
And they tugged with the Danes, till an overthrow
They both of them got from the Norman bow.'

For many centuries before the beginning of our era the speech of
almost the whole of Britain was Celtic, various forms of which still
remain as spoken languages in parts of Wales and Scotland, as well
as in Ireland. During the first few centuries A.D. the Latin of the
Roman villas and the popular jargon of the garrisons had considerable influence on the speech of the native Britons, as may be seen
by a student of Welsh: but those who had used this speech were
destined soon to be exterminated from the greater part of the country.
After the inhabitants of southern and eastern Britain who survived
the invasions of the Jutes, Angles, and Saxons in the fifth century
had taken refuge with their kinsmen in Wales, West Wales (Cornwall), and the Isle of Man – and in Brittany – their language became
virtually extinct in that part of Britain which could then justifiably
be called England, with the result that in Old English, Middle
English, and our modern speech is to be found no more of Celtic
than a mere trace of Welsh or Cornish – scarcely more than of the

Gaelic of the Scottish Highlands and the Irish Gaelic or Erse. In the 17th and 18th centuries alone we borrowed many more words from Dutch, the language of our rivals at sea and of William of Orange and the friends whom he brought from Holland, than we had taken from our British fellow-countrymen in more than a millennium.

English has by far the richest vocabulary of all modern languages. After spurning the graces of the Celtic speech, the Anglo-Saxon mother-to-be flirted awhile with the Norse dialects of her next suitors, before finally marrying the Low Latin which the Romans had bequeathed to the Celtic Gauls, the Gauls to the Teutonic Franks who overran them, and the Franks to the 'Northmen' who gave Normandy its name and finally brought their language to England.

But the workaday garments of English have been enriched by embroidery from nearly every language under the sun as a result of the islanders' exploration of every sea and land in search of spices or religious freedom, of men to enslave or to evangelize, of territory, gold, glory, or sheer adventure.

English is near akin to the West Germanic languages which include modern Dutch, Flemish, and Frisian. The most ancient member of the East Germanic languages of which we have a written record is Gothic, thanks to the translation of the Bible into that language made by Ulfilas (or Wulfila), a southern Goth who was sent as a missionary-bishop to his fellow-countrymen by Eusebius of Nicomedia in A.D. 341. All these languages are cousins, so to speak, of (a) German, the descendant of Old High German, and (b) the Scandinavian tongues. All these, the Germanic or Teutonic, are second cousins of the Slavonic and Lettic languages (e.g. Polish, Russian, Czech; Lithuanian); and all in this wider group are kindred of (1) the Celtic languages (e.g. Breton, Welsh, Gaelic – and Cornish, which faded out as a spoken language towards the end of the 18th century, but which right-minded people are trying to restore to life, notably through the medium of West Country newspapers); (2) the Romance tongues, descendants of Latin (e.g. French, Italian, Spanish, and Provençal, the language of the Troubadours); (3) Modern Greek, the child of the Attic Greek of Plato and Aristotle; (4) the progeny of Zend (Old Bactrian) and Old Persian (e.g. modern Persian and Armenian); and (5) the languages sprung from Sanskrit (e.g. Hindi, Bengali, and much of Romany, the dialect of the Gypsies). Romany is still spoken by the two million gypsies on the continent of Europe, and (as 'Anglo-Romany') in Britain, where, however, of the ten thousand of our gypsy-folk only a small number in Wales preserve the pure form of the original tongue. (Dr Donald Kenrick.) Examples from Romany, if George Borrow's word-list was trustworthy, are:

> *choomer*, a kiss (Sanskrit *chumb*, to kiss),
> *chore*, to steal (Skt. *chur*),
> *gil*, to sing (Skt. *gai*),
> *mer*, to die (Skt. *mṛ*),
> *shoon*, to hear (Skt. *śru*),
> *angar*, coal (Skt. *angāra*),
> *manus*, man (Skt. *manushya*),
> *rawni*, lady (Skt. *rājnī*, queen).
> *sap*, snake (Skt. *sarpa*),
> *yag*, fire (Skt. *agni*).

Some sixty years ago the Czech scholar Hrozný showed that another ancient language, Hittite, belongs to the Indo-European family. The Hittites flourished in the Middle East during the second millennium B.C., until their empire was overthrown by the Assyrians. Their cuneiform and hieroglyphic inscriptions are still being intensively studied, simultaneously with the gradual elucidation of the scripts and dialects of the pre-Homeric ('Minoan', 'Mycenaean') civilizations in the Aegaean, conclusively proved by Michael Ventris in 1953 to have been Greek.

*　　*　　*

One way of appreciating the wealth of our inheritance is by imagining the shifts to which we should be put if we had to discard all those things for which we use names from other than Celtic, true English, or Scandinavian stock: i.e. from the languages of Britain-England before the coming of the Normans.

The revision of scientific terms, which are nearly all of Greek or Latin origin, would certainly eliminate mongrels such as *television*, but would cause a set-back to relations with specialists of other nations, even if the change were feasible. *Farspeaker* might be preferable to *telephone* (Gk.); but to rename polysyllabic terms for diseases or for complicated phenomena of quite recent discovery would be a nightmare.

If, however, we were to make the venture, we should not have much trouble with ecclesiastical terms, many of which, such as *Lent*, *Easter*, *Whitsunday*, and *Gospel*, already represent good O.E. words. *Priest*, *bishop* (L. – Gk.), *alms* (L.L. – Gk.), *creed* and *pastor* (L.), for example, could become *elder*, *overseer*, *love-gift*, *belief*, and *shepherd*; though the changes might reopen painful wounds from early battles fought over the translating of the Bible.

We could keep *flummery* (Welsh), but Parliamentary tricks could not revive *guillotine* (F.) or *kangaroo* (Australian). We should in fact bid farewell to politicians (F. – L. – Gk.). Only the *Tories* among present-day parties would survive. The *Queen* or *King* would stand firm, despite the elimination of *monarchy* (Gk.), and so would the *House of Lords*; but the *Prime Minister* (F. – L.), the *Cabinet* (F.), and all the *Commons* (F. – L.) would cease from troubling.

We should still have *games*, but not *sports* (F. – L.), and even some of the games would have to disappear – *cricket* (F. – Du.), *golf* (Du.), and *polo* (Balti – the dialect spoken between Kashmir and Tibet), and some others. We could shoot with *bow* and *arrows*, but not hurl a *boomerang* (Australian).

The arts would suffer grievously. What should we do without *piano*, *violin*, *solos*, *duets*, *basses*, *sopranos*, *arpeggios*, and all the other musical joys which we have from Latin through Italian, and without the *painting* and *sculpture* which Latin has give us through French? Old-fashioned dancers would pine in vain for *polka* and *mazurka* (Polish) and *waltz* (G.).

Happily we could still *make love*.

Owing to Tromp and de Ruyter and the rest of the Dutch sailors our seagoing man would lose his *yacht* and *lighter*, let alone the *orlop* and other *decks* of his ship: he might *run up* his *sail*, but he could not *hoist* it – so many are the nautical terms that he has taken from the Netherlands.

There would be a woeful shrinkage in our foodstuffs and drinkables. The names for these alone would serve to outline the story of British (in the later sense of the word) enterprise. Fortunately we should still have *bread* and *milk*, *water* and *salt*, but no *cheese* (L.) or *butter* (L. – Gk.), though the names of the last two commodities reached England through the Saxon invaders. We could drink good English *ale*, *beer*, and *mead*, but not *cider* (F. – L. – Gk. – Hebrew). Children might be pleased to escape from *cabbage* (F. – L.), but would have also to forgo *chocolate* (Sp. – Mexican). Jane Austen's Mr Woodhouse would no longer be able to offer his guests 'a *nice basin*' (F. – L. and F.) or even a well-made bowl of *gruel* (F.).

We should fare pretty well at breakfast, though deprived of *porridge* (F.), *bacon* (F.), and *marmalade* (F. – Port.); for we could count on *oatmeal, herrings, kippers, kidneys,* and *eggs.* These, however, would not be washed down with *tea* (Du. – Chinese), even if it were not from a *samovar* (Russian), *coffee* (Turk. – Arab.), or *cocoa* (Sp. – Aztec). Any substitutes made from English greenery or berries would have to be sweetened, as in the Middle Ages, with *honey*, for lack of *sugar* (F. – It. – Arab. – Pers. – Skt.).

Those who thirsted for *alcohol* (Med. L. – Arab.) would have to drink English *rum* or Gael. *whiskey* without *soda* (Med. L.); for there would be no *gin* (Du.), *punch* (Hind. – Skt.), *toddy* (Hind. – Skt.), *port, madeira* (Port. – L.), *sherry* (Sp. – L.), or *tokay* (Hungarian) – not to mention *burgundy, moselle, hock, asti,* and all the rest.

As to starchy foodstuffs – Mary Jane, who appeared put out because there was 'lovely rice-pudding for dinner again', could cheer up, for *rice* would not be on the nursery menu, tired of making the long journey from Skt. or Old Persian through Gk., L., Italian, and French. But alas she could not successfully plead for *semolina* or *macaroni* (It. – L.), *sago* (Malay), or *tapioca* (Tupi – more or less the common language of the Brazilian natives). She would have to *batten* or to *bant* on English *shredded wheat* or on English-plus-Scandinavian *cornflakes*, however transatlantic she might think them. It would be fruitless for the housewife to ask for *flour* (F. – L.) or *maize* (Carib.).

O.E. *chicken* and Celtic *mutton* would still be on the board, but never *turkey* (ultimately Tatar) or the *pullet, beef, veal,* and *pork* which will find mention a few pages later on. Gone would be *soup* (F. – L.L.), with *soy* (Japanese), *ketchup* (Malay or Pidgin-Chinese), *chutney* (Hind.), *mustard* (F. with a Germanic suffix), and nearly all the spices: *clove* (F.), the *meg* of *nutmeg* (F. – L – Pers. – Skt.), *cummin* (L. – Gk.), *pepper* (which entered O.F. from Skt. through Gk. and L.), *ginger* (F. – L. – Gk. – Skt.). No skeletal summary can do justice to the vagaries of words travelling along the Spice Routes to Europe. It is not to be wondered at that European adventurers searched more eagerly and bloodily for the Spice Islands than for the Philosopher's Stone which would transmute all baser metals to gold.

Among vegetables we could retain *leeks, peas, beans,* and a few others: we should lose *onions* (F. – L.), *carrots* (F. – L. – Gk.), *spinach* (F. – Sp. – Arab. – Pers.), *asparagus* (L. – Gk.), *artichokes* (It. – Arab.), *shallots* (F. – L. – Gk. – Heb.), *tomatoes* (Sp. – Mexican), *potatoes* – named after the *batata* of Haiti – (Carib), and *haricots* (the *ayacotli* of the Aztec). *Apples, shaddocks,* and various *berries* would have to do duty for the many fruits denied to us, e.g. the *fig* that we had from Latin through Provençal and French; the *apricot* (F. – Port. – Arab. – Gk. – L.), the *cherry* (F. – L. – Gk.), the *damson* (L. – Syriac), the *banana* (Port. or Sp. – Congolese or some dialect of the Guinea coast), and Persian fruits such as *lemon, orange, peach,* and *pistachio,* which have reached us through French; F. – It. – Arab.; F. – L.; and Sp. – L. – Gk. respectively.

For personal decoration we could use *woad* if we wished, but we could not *tattoo* (Tahitian) with it. The dressmaker would have needle and thread, but would be obliged to rely on *thorns,* perhaps, for lack of *pins* (L.). She would have *wool* for *smocks, shifts,* and *shirts,* but not for *shawls* (Urdu – Pers.). There would be broadcloth, but no *alpaca* (Sp. – Peruvian), *muslin* (F. – It. – Syriac), *calico* (F. – Sp. – Arab.), or *silk* (which has shimmered its way from Chinese). We should have *hats,* but not *caps* (L.L.); *trousers* and *kilts* (Scand.), but not *coats* (F. – G.) or *jackets* (F. – L. – Gk. – Heb.). There would be *ties* available, but no *collars* (F. – L.). No one could wear a *blouse* (F. – ?), *camisole* (F. – Sp.), *knickers* (Du.), *suspenders* (F. – L.), or *belt* (L.). *Slips* would still be on the market, with *garters* (for our French suppliers had the word from Celtic), *skirt* (Scand.), and *girdle.* In wet weather we should be well-off with a *cloak* (back to us from Celtic through F.), *macintosh* (Gael.), and *overalls*; and, though we should lose our *boots* (F.), we should have *shoes,* and *leather* for their repair. *Pyjamas* (Urdu – Pers.) would have to be replaced by nightshirts or nothing.

The smoke from the smouldering leaves of English *worts* drawn through a hollow stick would have to do duty for *cheroots* (Tamil) and *cigars* (Sp.) or their French diminutives; *tobacco* (Sp. – Carib) itself being *taboo* (Polynesian).

*   *   *

Many of the exotic languages cited in the foregoing farrago have shared with English and Celtic and Scandinavian tongues in the formation of our modern plant- and animal-names. Less than sixty per cent of the 'English' substantive names of birds (such as *crow*, applied to a number of birds) and individual names (such as *fieldfare*, applied by us to only one species) have a true claim to be called English by derivation. Of these roughly one-third have come down almost unchanged from the O.E. forms, e.g. *ouzel*, *wren*, *hawk*, and *lark*. The remainder are M.E. or modern English words of O.E. stock, e.g. *hawfinch*, *redshank*, and *creeper*. Rather more than twenty per cent of the total number are traceable to Latin, a few having been borrowed directly, e.g. *accentor*; but most of them reached us through French, and a few by way of Italian, Spanish, Portuguese, or Provençal. About five per cent of the *elements* in all the names are of continental Germanic origin; another five per cent of Scandinavian. Gaelic and other Celtic tongues provide about three per cent; Ancient Greek a further three per cent. *Siskin* is of Slavonic origin through Middle Dutch. Other than I-E. languages, namely Arabic and Egyptian, account for about two per cent. A few are difficult to trace with certainty.

So much for an analysis of just the bird-names: if we were to deal with all the adjectives and quasi-adjectives in all our animal names embracing two or more terms, we should find Sanskrit, Hebrew, and many less-known languages playing their parts in the list.

As names for particular species and substantive names used with an epithet for two or more species, with only minor changes in pronunciation and/or spelling, we should find many O.E. names for animals (apart from birds, which we will take separately). Among them are:

bār,	boar	*hund*,	hound
brocc,	brock (badger)	*hwæl*,	whale
bulluc,	bullock	*lamb*,	lamb
catt,	cat	*mūs*,	mouse
cū,	cow	*ottor, oter*,	otter
dēor,	(wild animal), *deer*	*ræt*,	rat
ēowu, ēowe,	ewe	*rā*,	roe (deer)
fox,	fox	*ram*,	ram
fyxe,	vixen	*scrēawa*,	shrew
gāt,	goat	*snaca*,	snake
hara,	hare	*sū, sugu*,	sow
heorot,	hart, (stag)	*wesle*,	weasel
hors,	horse	*wulf*,	wolf

From Norse O.E. took names for some fish, e.g. *hake* – probably connected with O.N. *haki*, 'a hook', from the shape of its jaw. The Latin influence is seen in *trout* (O.E. *truht*, from L. *tructa*), and in O.E. *muscelle* (L. *musculus*), which was later reborrowed from M.L.G. as *mussel*. The Saxons were not entomologists, but we have from them some names for insects, e.g. *ant* and its doublet *emmet* (O.E. *æmette*); *bee*, (*bēo*); *moth* (*moththe*); *fly* (*flēoge*) – *flēoge-nett* standing for a mosquito-curtain, and indicating that little things mattered even to our tough forefathers.

* * *

After a thousand years and more we are still using a great many O.E. names for birds, which include:

amore, omer,	*-hammer*	*līnete,*	*linnet*
ceaffinc,	*chaffinch*	*māse,*	(tit)*mouse*
colmāse,	*coal-tit*	*nihtegale,*	*nightingale*
cran,	*crane*	*ōsle,*	*ouzel*
crāwe,	*crow*	*scrīc,*	*shrike*
cȳta,	*kite*		(mistle-thrush)
dūce,	*duck*	*spearwa,*	*sparrow*
finc,	*finch*	*spearhafac,*	*sparrow-hawk*
fiscere,	(king)*fisher*	*storc,*	*stork*
gandra,	*gander*	*swan,*	*swan*
ganot,	*gannet*	*swealwe,*	*swallow*
goldfinc,	*goldfinch*	*turtla, -e,*	*turtle*-dove
gōs,	*goose*	*thrysce,*	*thrush*
gōshafoc,	*goshawk*	*ūle,*	*owl*
hafoc,	*hawk*	*wrænna,*	*wren*
hlēapewince,	*lapwing*	*wuducocc,*	*woodcock*
hræfn,	*raven*	*bridd,*	(young) *bird*
hrōc,	*rook*	*cocc,*	*cock*
lāwerce,	*lark*	*henn,*	*hen*

Among O.E. forms of names now mainly poetical or provincial are:

agu,	*hagster* (magpie)	*cūscote,*	*cushat* (dove)
culfre,	*culver* (dove)	*earn,*	*erne* (eagle)

hīcemāse,	*hickeymouse* (blue tit)	*mēaw, mǣw, mew,*	(gull)
hwilpe	*whaup* (curlew, whimbrel)	*mūshafoc,*	*mousehawk* (kestrel)
gēac,	*gowk* (cuckoo)	*rudduc,*	*ruddock* (robin)
glida	*glead* (kite)	*stær,*	*stare* (starling)
hæferblæte, =	*goatbleater* (heather-bleater)	*stāngiella,*	*staniel* (kestrel)
(hæ)swealwe,	*(sea)swallow* (tern)	*thros(t)le,*	*throstle* (thrush, mistle-thrush)
hegessugge,	*isaac, haysuck* (dunnock)		

There are also some O.E. bird-names not now in use, e.g. *fina*, 'woodpecker'; *tysca*, 'buzzard'; *wihtel*, 'quail'. There are names too, the meanings of which can hardly be accurately guessed; with others for exotic birds, e.g. *pāwa*, 'peacock' (L. *pāvo*), and poetic compounds such as *guthhafoc* ('war-hawk'), 'eagle'. The existence of a few other names is presumed from the evidence of place-names, e.g. **pinc*, 'finch', in *Pinchbeck*; **speht*, 'woodpecker', in *Spettisbury* (cf. German *Specht*, Swedish *spett*, etc.); *wrōc*, 'buzzard', in *Wraxall*.

Of Celtic origin are our *capercaillie, guillemot, ptarmigan,* and the first element of *dunnock* (the hedge-sparrow) and (possibly) of *dunlin.*

From Scandinavian languages we have *auk, fulmar, snipe, stilt, tern, tit,* with *bonxie* (the great skua), *tystie* (the black guillemot), and parts of other names, such as *sky-, -leg,* and *-wing.*

The O.E. names show traces of direct borrowing from Latin: e.g. *turtla, turtle,* 'turtle-dove', from L. *turtur.* The defeat of the Saxons at Hastings was followed by an influx of words of Latin and Late Latin origin, leavened with others derived from Germanic dialects; but there were some earlier strata of Latin, particularly of the kind brought in by the Christian missionaries.

Of the multitude of plants known to our Anglo-Saxon forefathers (who needed food, firing, timber, medicine, and beauty even as we do) many have kept their names unchanged, e.g. *corn, bean, thorn.* Others are somewhat disguised in today's spelling, e.g. *hrēod,* 'reed';

43

bōc, 'beech'; *hwītlēac* ('white leek'), 'onion'. Many other plant-names will be cited in these pages.

One phenomenon in particular for which we need to be prepared when we are tackling etymology are the changes among the consonants which obscure meanings if we are not ready for them. The words in two or more languages may appear very different one from another; but there are 'laws', i.e. summaries of observed instances, tabulating the changes; and philologists will ever remember gratefully the names of the men who first began to formulate these 'laws'. In this formulation Germany led the way.

The brothers Jakob and Wilhelm Grimm (1785–1863 and 1786–1859) won worldwide fame not only as great scholars but also as the compilers of the *Household Fairy-Tales* collected in their native Hesse. Jakob Grimm was chiefly responsible for a discovery about the relationships of words in the I-E. languages which formulates a system of sound-correspondences in words apparently different but in reality the same. When the same roots or the same words are found in different I-E. languages, their consonants will show variation according to well-marked principles. When, for instance, Sanskrit, Greek, and Latin have *d*, Gothic and Low German have *t*, whereas O.H.G. has *z*. Thus Grimm's Law explains the seeming discrepancies among Skt. *dvau*, Gk. and L. *duo*, English *two*, and the German *zwei*. In the same way it points to the common origin of the Skt. *hyas*, Gk. *khthes*, L. *heri* (for *hesi*), O.E. *geostra* (*daeg*), Modern German *gestern*, and our *yesterday*; and to the common origin of the Skt. *haṃsa*, 'swan', and the various words for 'goose' – *khen*, (*h*)*anser*, *gans*, and *kans*, in Greek, Latin, Gothic, and O.H.G. It should be noted that *the 'law' does not apply to imitative words*, as long as they are felt to be imitative or expressive; for the particular speech-feeling that clings to them makes them resistant to many kinds of change.

vi

NORSE AND NORMAN INFLUENCE

'C'est une des plus incompréhensibles disgrâces de
l'homme, qu'il doive confier ce qu'il a de plus précieux
à quelque chose d'aussi instable, d'aussi plastique,
hélas, que *le mot.*'
    BERNANOS, *Le Journal d'un Curé de Campagne.*

BEFORE we reach chapters dealing mainly with the names of birds,
let us note that the title of *ornithologist* is linked etymologically with
eagles – but not through Norman-French, for *erne* (O.E. *earn*), 'the
soarer', is a word cognate with *ornis*, the Greek for a bird, the stem
being *ornith-*. *Erne* for the white-tailed eagle may for long have been
used only in northern Scotland and the islands still further north;
but Southrons need not turn to their crossword-puzzles in order to
find the word; for thousands utter it, possibly unwittingly, every day,
when they speak of woods, hamlets, villages, and towns such as
Yarner's (on Dartmoor), *Earnley, Earnwood, Arncliffe, Arnold, Arnwood,*
and *Yarnfield,* which, each in a different county, are the names of
no more than a few of the places enshrining the memory of the *erne*:
and to them may be added the surnames, e.g. *Earnshaw,* taken from
them.

The word *bird* cannot with certainty be traced further back than
to the O.E. *bridd.* This may or may not be connected with *breed* and
brood. If it is not so connected, it is without known kindred in other
languages. The Norsemen, the Scandinavians who conquered half
England and left their mark all round the coasts of Scotland, Wales,
and Ireland, called a bird *fugl.* This is still the Danish word, the
Swedish being *fugol.* The Gothic form was *fugls*; the modern German
is *Vogel.* All these are connected with the root **flug-.* The O.E. *fugol*
became *fowl* in Middle English. By the English, prior to the Norman
Conquest, *fugol* was most commonly used for 'bird' and *bridd* for 'a
young bird'.

Place-names, however, embracing *bridd* suggest that it often had a less limited meaning. Since in the later language the *r* tended to be shifted (as in *thirty* for *thritty*), when *Bird-* or *Brid-* appears in the name of a place, it is not always clear whether the syllable refers to *bird*, *bride*, or *St Bridget*: but *Birdham* in Sussex and *Bridgemere* in Cheshire (found in records of 1260 as *Briddismere*) have the respective meanings of 'bird-haunted watermeadow' and 'mere'. *Brid* for *bird* is still used in Staffordshire, and probably elsewhere also. (See under 'Metathesis', Chapter XXIX.) *Fugol* is the base of names such as *Foolow, Foulden, Fulmer, Fowlmere, Fulbourn*, and the Essex *Foulness* – hills, valley, meres, brook, and headland where birds congregated.

Foulney in Lancashire represents the Icelandic (O.N.) *fugl* + *ey*, 'island' – a reminder that the so-called Vikings, the invaders who preceded their 'Norman' kinsmen by two or three centuries, and who named *Lundy* (Puffin island), *Skomer, Skokholm*, and the towns and villages with names ending in *-by* (*-bigh*) and *-wick*, bequeathed to us the names of a few fish, mammals, and plants, and (as we have already noted) more than half-a-dozen bird-names, e.g. *auk* and *tern*, with parts of half a score more, such as the first element of *skylark, titmouse, whinchat*, and the second element of *waxwing* and *yellowlegs*.

Of the many names which came into English after 1066, or through French at any later period, the majority are further traceable to Latin in various stages of its history as, for example, *martin* (from the saint), *cormorant* (*corvus marinus*, 'sea-raven'), and the one mentioned first in this chapter, the *eagle* (L. *aquila*) that ousted *earn*, with a few still further traceable to O.H.G. or L.G., such as *heron*.

Norman thrush, which was used as late as the nineteen-forties on the Northants-Bucks border as a name for the mistle-thrush (D. P. W. McCarthy), is possibly a relic of the Saxons' reaction to the high-handed manners of their conquerers, and not a corruption of *northern thrush* which could be more aptly applied to the redwing or the fieldfare. In the same district the fieldfare is called *falk*, which may be a corruption of *felt*, a common provincial name for the bird.

It was doubtless the mastery of the Normans in England that was responsible for the loss of popularity by the English *fugol*, after that name had become more and more closely associated with the domestic fowl, as *ornis* had become among the Athenians a millennium and a half earlier. As Scott reminded the readers of *Ivanhoe*, it was the part of the conquered Saxons to tend the *sheep* and the *swine*, the *cows* and the *calves*; their Norman overlords ate the flesh – but not under the crude Saxon names. Hence today we speak of *mutton* and *pork*, *beef* and *veal*. In the same way *fowl* was the word for the henwife to use for the bird: the Normans ate it as *pullet* and *capon* (a word which reached them, through L.L. from the Gk. root **kop-*, 'to cut'). For a dove the English kept their *cushat* and *culver*; but the Normans preferred their *pigeon*. As English and Norman-French coalesced into one language, these distinctions persisted; but *bridd* prevailed over any competitor that had worked its way down from the L. *avis* and the L.L. diminutive *avicella* (*aucella*) that provided French with *oiseau*. The comparative unpopularity of *avis* appears in the Spanish use of *pájaro* ('sparrow', L. *passerem*) in common speech in place of the literary *ave*, and in our own use of only a few derivatives such as *avian*, *aviary*, and *aviator*.

Yet we may be cheered by the knowledge that the word *fowl* has kept a secure place in *wildfowl* and some provincial names such as *moorfowl* (the red grouse). *Gairfowl* is now scarcely remembered except by readers of Kingsley's *The Water Babies*, but was preferred to *great auk* by Professor Alfred Newton in his *Dictionary of Birds* (1893–96), where the name is derived from a Gaelic word meaning 'the strong, stout bird with a white spot' (sc. 'on its bill').

Fowl is linked through the root **flug-* with the verb *fly*, which most *fowls* do when they are far enough *fledged* to *flutter* their *plumage* (L. *pluma*).

Another word from the same root is *flight*, a good old term for a number of almost any kind of birds in the air. It is to be found in the 15th-century *Boke of St Alban's*, a treatise on Hawking conventionally attributed to Juliana Berners (or Barnes), the Prioress of Sopwell Abbey in Hertfordshire. In the *Boke* are also to be found other nouns of multitude, e.g. a *watch* ('wakefulness') of nightingales, a *gaggle* of geese, a *herd* of swans, a *muster* (a 'show or display'), from L. *monstrare*, (through French) of peacocks.

Characterizing the Normans' devotion to the chase are also a *sege* or *siege* (i.e. a 'sitting', from root **sed-*) of herons or bitterns, and the word *bevy*. *Bevy* seems to have been applied first to a collection of ladies, and only later to a party of quail. It is a counterpart to what would have normally been a stag-party among the Hellenes, viz. a 'symposium'. It probably springs, like *booze* (M.E. *bousen*) from the root **bi-*, 'to drink', for *bevy* corresponds to the O.F. *bevee*, *buvee*, 'a drinking-party', the equivalent of Gk. *sumposion* (*sun* + *posis*, 'to-gether-drinking'), of which the radical syllable is a product of the Skt. and Gk. root-form **po-*. We may suppose that, in days when a number of quail in company was not such a rare sight as it is today, the neat little birds suggested a picture of a gathering of demure matrons and maids – a hen-party.

The use of a native English word *herd* for a collection of swans, as for a number of sheep, swine, or oxen, is a reminder that the swan has been for centuries a protected, and even a royal, bird. Today the Vintners Company and the Dyers' Company still share with the Crown the right to own the swans between London Bridge and Henley-on-Thames; and the numerous inns bearing the sign *The Swan with Two Necks* bear witness to the two *nicks* cut in the birds' bills at the yearly swan-upping to mark the Vintners' ownership – a practice dating at least from the 15th century.

H. Kirke Swann in his *Dictionary of Names of B.B.* quotes from Nelson's *Laws Concerning Game* (1753): 'Swan is a Royal bird, and by Stat. 22, Edw. IV, c.6, None (but the King's Son) shall have any Mark or Game of *Swans* of his own, or to his use, except he have Lands and Tenements of Freehold worth five marks per Annum, besides Reprises; in pain to have them seized by any having lands of that value, to be divided betwixt the King and the Seizer'. Swans' eggs were also protected, with those of falcon, goshawk, and lanner, by II Henry VII, c. 17: 'in pain of a Year and a day's imprison-ment, and to incur a fine at the King's pleasure, to be divided between the King and the Owner of the Ground'. In 1629 the penalty was reduced to three months' imprisonment, or a payment of 20 shillings for each egg to the churchwardens for the use of the poor. Later the fine was reduced to five shillings for each egg. Today the Game Laws appear to be flouted with impunity.

For his *herd* of swans the Norman lord employed a (presumably Saxon) *swanherd*, side by side with the *shepherd*, *swineherd*, and *neat-herd* for his four-footed beasts. Eventually *herd* came to be applied to collections of other birds, including, somewhat surprisingly, *wrens* (*Boke of St Alban's*). This last convention, whereby the bulky swan was categorized with the diminutive wren, must have sprung, one may think, from the pleasantry of a court-jester – probably not the first of a long line of people who have found interest in and made merry over these nouns of assembly, even as did Sir Arthur Conan

Doyle (in *The White Company*) and the humorous writer Harry Graham, who suggested 'a piffle of wombats'.

Most of the older terms for gatherings of birds reached us through the Normans. Further examples are: for pheasants, a *nye* or *nide* ('nest', from L. *nidus*, through F. *nid*); for partridges, and later for grouse, a *covey* (all the young ones brooded by one bird – O.F. *covee*, from *cover*, 'to hatch', derived from L. *cubare*, 'to lie or sit down'); for coots, *covert* (from O.F. *covrir*, derived from L. *cooperire*, 'to cover'); for geese flying in a long string, *skein* (from a French word possibly of Celtic origin). *Brace*, denoting a couple of game-birds when the association of a conjugal pair is not implied, is from a French form of L. *bracchia*, 'the two arms'. *Charm* (from an O.E. word *cyrm*, 'the blended noise of many voices', associated with another *charm*, through F. and O.F. from L. *carmen*, 'a song or spell'), for a number of goldfinches in company, seems to have increased in popularity during the past few decades, probably owing to the reviving influence of the late Viscount Grey of Falloden's fascinating book, *The Charm of Birds*.

Not beholden to French, for grouse in a larger association than a *covey*, the M.E. *pack* was taken from Middle Dutch; but, though it had relatives in the various languages of mediaeval Europe, its origin is obscure.

English moreover needed no French help in producing a *murder* of crows, a *wisp* (i.e. 'a little bundle', as of hay) of snipe, a *dopping* of sheld-ducks, a *raft* (the word is Scandinavian) of coots, ducks, or other water-birds, a *spring* of teal, and a *trip* of dotterel, with their succession of quick little runs. Another English word, *fall*, applied to woodcock, is a good example of the aptness of the majority of these nouns of multitude, suggesting as it does the sudden silent arrival of the 'cocks when the oaks are shedding their brown leaves: the hint of autumn is there, the season which still in parts of England, as on the other side of the Atlantic, is known by its older name, 'the fall'.

It is hard to believe that such expressions as an *exaltation* of larks, a *clamour* of rooks, and a *murmuration* of starlings were extensively used in everyday speech. There seems to be a flavour of irony even in the wise words of Juliana Berners: 'We say a congregation of people . . ., we must speak of a clatterynge of choughes, a pryde of lyons, a slewthe of beeres . . . a sculle of frerys (i.e. friars) . . . and a superfluyte of nonnes.' The Prioress can hardly have lectured from

49

personal experience her 'superfluyte' of spiritual sisters about 'prydes of lyons' or 'slewthes of beeres'. Let us grant her the 'clatterynge of choughes' (i.e. jackdaws) nesting in the Abbey walls.

The expert use of the earlier collective names, and other terms of the chase, doubtless bolstered up the Norman sportsman's feeling of superiority over the Saxon clod.

Each of the collective nouns, it will be noted, aims at giving a picture of some idiosyncrasy of the animals to which it refers – occasionally a peculiarity of appearance, but most often of some kind of action; and, whether or not we succeed in tracing *bird* to its most primitive form, we may be pretty sure that, from whatever root the word sprang, it indicated something done, some activity. For it is a fact of supreme importance in any enquiry into the origin of a name that what counts most among primitive peoples is activity, not appearance. Colour, size, and other physical characteristics are accidental; behaviour is all-important. It is the panther's rending and biting, not his spots, in which the Gond is most deeply interested. The anaconda can crush a man's ribs whether its scales are black or green. The more man has to battle against Nature, the more utilitarian and practical will be his outlook: and it is easily understood why our remote forefathers took more notice of the shriek of a bird which disturbed their hunting, or warned them that they were being hunted, than they took of the tints of its plumage. Since men (or their womenfolk for them) must carry water from place to place, it is not surprising that desert-peoples should have named the pelican *saqqa*, 'the water-carrier'. It does not matter that they were mistaken as to the main use of the bag beneath the pelican's bill: the point is that they envisaged the bird in action, and not as a mere wearer of an appendage not possessed by other birds. *Pelican* came to O.E. through Latin from Gk. *pelekān*, 'to hew with an axe'. If we were to name the pelican for the first time today, we should probably call it 'pouch-bill', not 'water-carrier'; but we, who turn a tap to fill our bath, can afford a more objective outlook.

This may well be termed significant, for it is an integral part of the evidence pointing to the verb, the name of the action, and not to the noun, as the most primitive form of word. We shall therefore not be surprised to find that, as mammals in general first claimed man's attention and were designated as 'runner', 'cleaner', 'sniffer', or 'render', etc., many birds first gained notice and names by reason of their voices. But though there are a good many names for mammals, insects, and birds which are as purely imitative of sound as is the name of the game *ping-pong*, such as those of the *aye-aye* of Madagascar, the *tuco-tuco* of South America, the *bumble-bee*, and our old friend the *cuckoo*, the number is small by the side of the aggregate of names having a far more general meaning and signifying no more than that the creature is a tearer, a chirper, a screamer, a whistler, or the like.

ʋii

A NET FLUNG WIDE

'I like to be beholden to the great English metropolitan speech, the sea which receives tributaries from
every region under heaven.'

EMERSON, *Books.*

WHETHER or not the epithet 'insular' may correctly be applied to
the Englishman, it would be a flagrant inconsistency to apply it to
the complex organism called 'English'. This was more than suggested in Chapter V, but will bear a little elaboration.

It is characteristic of English to spread its net wide, to fling open
the door to new words, to admit foreigners (provided that we are
allowed to carve the words about to suit our taste), that gives much
of the strength and vitality to our language. Naturally animal- and
plant-names provide a large share of the words from the more
distant foreign countries. Australian words such as *wallaby* and
kangaroo (either of which may have meant 'leaper' to the aborigines)
were enthusiastically accepted, without any attempt to call them
long-legged high-jumpers. They were introduced in 1828 and 1770
respectively. New Zealand sent us the name of the *kiwi* in 1835; and
moa for the extinct *Diornis gigantea* is also a Maori word.

From over the Atlantic we have received numerous Spanish
versions of Carib words – *iguana*, for instance, the *iwana* of Haiti. It
was a Frenchman, the great naturalist and evolutionist Buffon, who
clipped the Mexican name meaning 'field-jaguar', *tlalocelotl*, and
gave us *ocelot* (1774).

Sequoia, for the giant 'redwoods' and their relatives, such as the
tree which we call 'Wellingtonia' and the Americans 'Washingtonia',
perpetuates the memory of Sequoya, the Indian name of George
Guess (*c.* 1770–1842), an educated Cherokee half-breed who composed for his people a syllabic alphabet of eighty-five characters.
Later, further honouring Sequoya, was coined a true-blue nature-
from-nature name for a genus of plants of which only fossil remains

were known to exist. As the unnamed treatise of Aristotle following his 'Physics' came to be known as 'Metaphysics', so the Nomenclature Committee called the fossil genus *Metasequoia*, because it was the next genus to be named after the *Sequoia*. The nomenclators had their reward. Not long afterwards, in 1947, in a hilly district in the interior of China, were found living trees of what had been thought a long-extinct genus. Two expeditions were made by Americans and Britons, fortunately before China became incommunicado. These brought back seeds and cuttings, which proved generously viable; so that tall young specimens of the deciduous conifer *Metasequoia glyptostroboides*, lovely in spring and still lovelier in its bronze-purple dress before the needles fall in autumn, may be seen here and there in selected sites all over Britain.

Hickory is a clipped version of the Virginian *powcahicora* or *powicherry*. The Aztec name for the various species of this type of walnut-tree seems to have been *xicali*, modified by the Spaniards into *jicara*. In Central America your chocolate (the Spanish modification of the Aztec *chocolatl*) may be served, as of old, in cups and bowls made from the hard shells of hickory-fruits of different sizes. Such utensils are also known by the name of *jicara* – a word which appears to have reached Italian as *chichara*, for a tea-cup. (T. Belt.) From the former Portuguese dominion of Brazil we have a few words such as the Tupi *jacaranda*, a species of hardwood tree.

Etymologists differ as to whether *banana* came, through Spanish, from the West Indies or direct from its origin in the Congo; but certainly from Africa came the name of the animal discovered by Sir Harry Johnston in 1900. The *okapi* could be seen, but not for long, a few years later in the London Zoo. The name is Congolese.

Chimpanzee (1738) is the anthropoid ape's name in Angola and came to us through French. *Zebra* (1600) is called a Congolese word in the O.E.D., but some authorities relate it to the Spanish and Portuguese *zebro*, the wild ass, which was perhaps named in the days when it inhabited the Iberian peninsula, from Zephyrus, the west wind, because of its speed. Webster, however, considers that the name originated in Amharic, the language of Abyssinia. *Gorilla* (1853), from a Greek plural *gorillai*, is said to represent an African word meaning 'wild or hairy men' (or women?) acquired during the voyage made down the west coast of Africa by Hanno the

Carthaginian in the 5th century B.C. The species was accepted by Science in 1847, when it was classified as *Troglodytes gorilla*.

Of the words which have reached us from China probably the most popular is *tea*. But the pronunciation has changed since Pope wrote,

'And thou, great Anna, whom three realms obey,
Dost sometimes counsel take, and sometimes tea.'

The word had not been in the language much more than a hundred years when Pope and his contemporaries were calling it 'tay' – a pronunciation that persisted here and there until far into the 19th century. 'Tay' shows the pronunciation echoed by the French *thé* (1664) of the Malayan *teh*; but *teh* is itself an adaptation of the Chinese Mandarin *ch'a*: so the 17th century *cha* is nearer than *tea* to the original name; and 'cha(r)' it has been for generations to the British soldier, who, if he has never himself heard the Hindi word in India, has inherited it from the older generations and passed it on to his civilian friends as a rival to the Cockney's 'rosy'.

Another Malay word, in English since 1623, is *paddy* (*pādī*, 'rice in the straw'); and yet another is *orang-outang* (1699) 'man of the woods' or 'wild man'. (The Malay *hutan* means 'forest' or 'jungle'.)

From the Dravidian dialects of S. India and the E. Indies comes *teak* (1698). This is *tekka* in Malayalam, a tongue allied to Tamil, which gives us, via the Portuguese settlers, *mango* (*man*, 'mango-tree' + *kay*, 'fruit'); *mulligatawny*, 'pepper-water'; *cheroot* (an unpointed roll of tobacco-leaf); and a few other well-known words.

Closer to us geographically, and less remote in language-structure, is Egypt, whence, via Gk. and Latin *ibis*, we have the name of the sacred *ibis*, which has been the totem-bird of the British Ornithologists' Union since its foundation in 1859. The primary meaning of *ibis* for those who used it as a hieroglyph is obscure to us, but Dr R. O. Faulkner says (*in litt.*, 22.1.1965) that it is the determination of the Egyptian word *ḥbī*, which has come down to us virtually unchanged as the name of the bird, having merely lost its aspirate and acquired a Greek ending. 'The sacred ibis', says Sir A. Landsborough Thomson, 'has been extinct in Egypt for nearly a century, but is still a familiar bird south of the Sahara.' Its special sanctity is explained by its having been regarded as the reincarnation of the god Thoth, inventor and patron of arts and sciences, and especially

of speech. We know from Herodotus that in the 5th century B.C.
it was a capital crime to kill, even accidentally, a bird of either of the
two species which he names (Bk. II. 65). The ibis-headed god Thoth
corresponded to the Hermes of the Hellenes.

Cobra is a shortened version of Port. *cobra de capello*, 'snake with a
hood' (1668), in which *cobra* represents L. *colubra*, a word which may
be of Egyptian origin.

A great many English, and notably Biblical, words come ultimately from Hebrew. Among the Natural History terms of this kind
is *camel*, which reached English through L. and F. from Gk. *kamēlos*
(Heb. *gamal*), and which was already established in the O.E.
vocabulary. The gangling neck of the camel shows itself quite clearly
in *gimel*, ג, the third letter of the Hebrew alphabet. Another Gk.
word out of Semitic is the *myrrh* of St Matthew 2. 11. This *myrrh*
(Hebrew *mōr*) is the fragrant resin hardened after its distillation by
the hot sunshine as a white gum from the low thick-trunked tree
Commifera myrrha. The Arabic root implies 'bitterness'; but Gesenius
derives *mōr* from a Hebrew root involving 'distillation'. (The 'myrrh'
of the Old Testament is from a quite different plant, the Hebrew *lot*
– the small bushy rock-rose, *Cistus creticus*, which grows everywhere
among the rocks of Palestine.) From one of these roots springs *myrtle*,
and therefore our *bog-myrtle*, *Myrica gale*. The O.E. *gagel* is still seen
in the alternative name, *sweet gale*. The Arabic division of Semitic
helped us to *saffron*, the autumn crocus (see next Chapter). Through
Turkish *qahveh* we have our *coffee*.

English is indebted to Sanskrit also for many nature-names which
have percolated through a variety of languages. We may cite at
random *mongoose* (1698), the name of the Indian ichneumon,
Herpestes griseus. To get the misleading 'goose', folk-etymology has
been at work on the Marathi *mangūs*, of Skt. derivation.

Rice, an ancient word for a crop cultivated immemorially in the
East, comes trickling through Gk., L., It., and F. either from Skt.
vrĭhi or from Old Persian.

Banyan (better *banian*) is the English name of the Indian fig, *Ficus
religiosa*, of which the drooping branches take root and grow into
trunks, until one tree may become a veritable forest. The name is
ultimately derived from Skt. *vāṇija*, 'a merchant'. An outsize specimen
of the tree near the shore of the Persian Gulf provided under its
canopy of boughs a market-place for itinerant traders, who built a

pagoda there. This tree was nicknamed *vanijo*, which word, passing from Gujarati through Arabic and Portuguese, provided *banyan* as our name for the whole species.

Through French and Low German respectively, we have the Russian *sable*, the furbearing marten or weasel, and *siskin*, the bird. *Steppe* is the Russian *step'*. *Vampire* comes from Magyar through German and French.

Folk-lore as a source of our vocabulary is aided by a dribble of words from Greek mythology. The first *python* was slain by Apollo near Delphi, of which the ancient name was *Pytho*. Our *sweet basil* was originally *basilicum* (Gk. *basilikon*, 'royal' herb), but by some confusion with *basiliscus*, the 'basilisk' or 'cockatrice', a creature reputed to be capable of killing with its gaze, the herb was supposed to supply an antidote against its lethal activities. The words both ultimately derive from Gk. *basileus*, 'a king'.

A rare source is Swiss Romanic – the Romance dialect of the Alps – which hands on to us the L. *ibex* and, via French, *chamois* (mediaeval L. *camox*).

From nearer home are the Celtic words, including the few British words which we have retained: e.g. river-names such as *Ouse*, *Usk*, and *Exe* (all perhaps derived from words meaning 'water') and the name of the fish *wrasse*.

Behind all these are the loan-words which came originally, as *rice* probably came, from some unknown, older language spoken by a race established in Europe before the Aryans invaded the continent. *Ilex*, the L. word for the holm-oak, is said to be of Mediterranean origin. When we ring for the plumber, we are calling for the expert in lead (L. *plumbum*); and evidence suggests (since lead was originally mined in Spain) that *plumbum*, and therefore our *plumb* and *plumbago*, contain a root from the language of those 'shy traffickers, the dark Iberians'. (Cf. *bustard*, Chapter IX(b).)

Let us now attempt to see how Man uses his unique double power of Logos, reason, and Logos, speech, in relation to Nature as he finds it; and let us start with those forms of life which – unless they are bacteria or something else anomalous – are generally, like words, rooted.

·v·iii

PLANT-NAMES FOR PLANT-CHARACTERS

'Vervain, Dittany, Call-me-to-you,
Cowslip, Melilot, Rose-of-the-Sun
  – Anything green that grew out of the mould
  Was an excellent herb to our fathers-of-old.'
                    KIPLING, *Our Fathers of Old.*

ABOUT one third of the plants for which we have English names
were regularly used for medicine, and their names, as we have seen,
reflect this. The word 'herbs' suggests to us nowadays bundles of
rosemary and marjoram hung up in a country kitchen. In Middle
English the word was *erbe*, straight from French, whither it came from
L. *herbam.* The Latin *h* was put back – 'reconstituted' – in both
languages; but even in English the *h* remained silent until the 19th
century – and on into the 20th – on the lips of those who preferred
the elder fashion for 'herb', 'humble', and 'hospital'. (These were
the brave souls who ignored the horrible example of Uriah Heep.
As a schoolboy* I used to wait breathlessly for the then Dean of
Canterbury to trip over such phrases as, 'O ye holy and humble
men of heart': but he never did so.)
  Herbs meant technically plants which were useful for medicine,
food, or scent. Non-herbs were *weeds* – a word of which the root is
unknown, though it had Low German cognates, and its sense of
'unprofitable plant' was strongly established in O.E. Beauty can be
found in both categories, and the changes in standards of floral
beauty. The evolution of the concept 'lovely wildflower' is a phenomenon of a more sophisticated age.
  It was, however, the beauty of their names, rather than that of
the flowers themselves, which attracted Kipling when he penned
Our Fathers of Old. Dittany and *melilot* each came to us from Greek
through Latin and French. The Hellenes named dittany *diktanos*
*L.C.S.

57

from its being found growing on the slopes of Mt Dicte in Crete·
Melilot is virtually unchanged from *melilōtus* (Gk. *meli*, 'honey', and
lōtos, 'clover' or 'lotus'). *Vervain*, through F. from L. *verbena*, signified
in ancient days a bunch of evergreen, such as myrtle, olive, or laurel,
used on festal occasions or in religious rites.

Here, ignoring the other regular medicinal herbs, let us glance at
some examples of plant-names derived directly from the characters
of the plants.

Heath, 'heather', is called after *heath*, 'waste-land', because it
grows there, if the soil is not chalky. *Knapweed* has that hard *knop* or
bud at the top, covered by the minutely patterned and complex
involucre. The *Polygonum* family – the black bindweed and persicaria
and their sisters – is named from the many nodes, the swollen knee-
joints (Gk. *gonu*, 'knee') standing out on the stem. The leaves of two
species of *plantain* (*Plantago*) escape the lawnmower because they can
lie *plānē*, flat on the ground; the word being formed on L. *planta*,
'the sole of the foot'. A *twig* is forked, divided into *tway*. *Gorse*, the
name of the British plant which evoked the special admiration of
Linnaeus when he visited England, is related to Latin *hordeum*,
'spiked barley'. Each plant bristles (L. *horrēre*). The leaves of *mullein*
may sometimes be rough, but they are always thickly soft (F. *mol*).
Another soft plant is *mallow* (L. *malva*); but the name is from the
root **mol-* earlier in its evolution, nearer to its origin in Gk. *malakos*
(see Chapter XV). The Hebrew word *malluach* in Job 30. 4, translated in the A.V. by 'mallows', refers to the *sea-purslane*, *Atriplex
halinus*, a salt-loving plant which is eaten by poor persons in the
East. *Malluach* is derived from Heb. *malah*, 'salt'. Both Arabic and
Hebrew have roots meaning 'to soften' comparable with that of Gk.
meldein (and of *malakos*, 'soft', etc.) and L. *mulcēre*, 'to soothe' and
mulgēre, 'to milk'.

Malva became F. *mauve*, a word which English adopted only in
1859. In this instance the colour is named after the flower; whereas
frequently the plant- or other name has the colour more or less
obviously attached to it, as *whitebeam* and *blackberry*, and *lucerne*, from
the lucidity of its shining grains (L. *lux*, *lucis*, light). Often the sense
of colour is hidden. *Sloe* may be a cognate of L. *livēre*, 'to be lead-
coloured'. The species of dodder parasitic on nettles and hops,
Cuscuta europea, is greenish-yellow in the general appearance of its
threads and leaves; and the word *dodder* resembles the G. *Dotter*,

'yolk of egg' – but the connection is unproven. The Latin name of our meadow-saffron, *Colchicum autumnale* (from Medea's Colchis on the Black Sea which gave the pheasant *Phasianus colchicus* its epithet) reminds us of a famous prescription for gout: its English name is due to its resemblance to the true saffron, *Crocus sativus*, which goes back to Arabic *za'faran*, which may not be connected with an Arab. word for 'yellow', but which has certainly given us a word to describe the dye-colour of its famous and savoury stigmas. *Crocus* itself comes from Gk. *krokos*; and an adjective, *krokōtos*, formed from this means 'yellow, dyed with saffron'. It may be of Semitic origin, the Arab. being *karkam* and the Hebrew *karkōm*.

There are a few taste-names. *Sorrel*, for example, is *sour*-juiced. A few plants are named from their scent. *Gillyflower*, a vanishing name for *Dianthus caryophyllus*, is an extrovert metathesized F. *girofle*, itself a particularly uninhibited version of *caryophyllum*, Mediaeval Latin for Greek *karuophullon*, 'clove', and takes us straight back to the scent of the members of this fragrant family, the *Caryophyllaceae*. To this group also belong many of our native names, such as *sweet cicely*, *meadowsweet* – and *stinking horehound*.

There is wit in many of the names. Those pointing to the most exact observations are some of the shape-names – similes such as *foxglove* and *lady's slipper*. The great *Senecio* genus (L. *senex*, 'old man'), the largest in the family of *Compositae*, gets its name from the rather meagre white-beardedness of the wind-blown fruits, to be contrasted with the long trailing whiskers, in October, of the very different *Clematis vitalba, old man's beard*. Less obvious is *columbine*. Why *columba*, 'the dove'? 'From the fancied resemblance,' as Webster puts it, 'of the inverted flower to a group of five pigeons.' The *delphinium* is so named by Evelyn in 1664 (it had been the Greek for 'larkspur' in the time of Dioscorides), after the resemblance of the shape of its nectary to the shape of a dolphin (Gk. *delphis*).

Several plants are named from their 'habit', as botanists call it – their way of growing. *Cress creeps* along the surface of the water, as is suggested by the German equivalent *Kresse* (from the O.H.G. root of *chresan*, 'to creep' (O.E.D.), *Saxifrage* will break (L. *frangere*) a rock (L. *saxum*). *Pellitory-of-the-wall* (and nothing will destroy this plant's taste for walls) is a change, with *l* for *r*, from M.E. *paritorie*, derived from L. *parietārius*, adjectival form of *paries*, 'a wall'. (This is *Parietaria officinalis* of the Nettle family, with the obscure green flowers. There are several false claimants to the name.) A *turnsole* is a plant which turns towards the sun (from F. *tourner* and *soleil*) – a *heliotrope* (Gk. *hēlios*, 'sun' and *trepein*, 'to turn'), which is correctly pronounced with the long *e* of *hēlios*, and not with the short *e* of *helikos*, 'turning', from *helissein*, 'to roll or twist', which gives us *helicopter*, 'the thing that revolves its wings'.

Helissein is also at the back of *Helminthology*, 'the study of worms', those notorious 'twisters', and of *helix*, a 'whorl, curl, or spiral', adopted as the name of the genus of land-snails: and here we think of the *double helix* that holds the secrets of identity for living things. If we prefix a possibly lost digamma, we have *(w)elissein*, which shows more clearly the relationship to the L. *volvere*, 'to turn', the source of our *convolvulus*. Another cognate is *whelk* (O.E. *weoluc* or *weolc*), the marine gasteropod sold by the dozen, with a pin thrown in, from barrows at our popular seaside-resorts.

Use-names such as *broom* are mostly confined to the medicinal herbs such as *eyebright*, *feverfew*, *fleabane*, and *self-heal*. The once highly useful tree, the *hornbeam*, was, from the Saxon period to 1800, the 'hardbeam'. *Hornbeam* dates from 1577.

Like so many other Natural History words, plant-names offer a great many problems and much etymological interest. What was the origin of *privet*, *Ligustrum vulgare*, recorded first in 1542? It was also called *prim-print*, and at about the same date appears a verb *prime*, 'to prune', which still exists in dialect; but a Scots spelling *privie* suggests *privacy*. Sometimes settling an etymology looks like 'anyone's guess'. It is interesting for instance to think that *sedge* (O.E. *secg*, masc.) might be the same as the rare O.E. *secg*, fem., 'a sword', especially as *secg*, masc., was used to translate L. *gladiolus* (lit. 'small sword'); but there are two words here, and careful attention to the linguistic evidence forbids us to do more than speculate about those sword-sharp blades of sedge-leaves.

The heart of the good English *lettuce* is unexpectedly classical. The milkiness of the tender stems of the wild lettuce was noticed by the Romans. In Greek the word for milk is *gala*, stem *galakt-*, which the Hellenes used in their fine phrase *galaxios kuklos*, 'the milky circle', the Milky Way. The Latin equivalent was *lac*, of which the stem *lact-* appears in the L. name for lettuce, *lactūca herba*. Our word is due to the intervention of the Old French form of *lactūca*, *laitue* (Mod. Fr. *laitue*). English took the plural of *laitue* – or a variant form with -s – and called the plant *lettuce*. It is typical of our respective countries that, whereas French inherits Latin words with sound changes that follow set rules, English is brutally piratical in its treatment of borrowed words. Our *Ypres/Wipers* attitude towards a foreign language colours our whole vocabulary. *Vetch*, ultimately from L. *vicia*, and therefore from the root of *vincire*, 'to bind', treats the French link, *vêche*, with reasonable phonetic respect; but often the Latin in the English derivative is heavily disguised.

Tare or *tares*, the name of one of our commonest vetches, presents a fascinating problem. What does it mean? What is its etymology? Remembering the New Testament parable, we might guess that one of its earliest meanings was influenced by a translation in the early English Bible. In the parable which follows that of the Sower and the Seed in St Matthew 13, verse 25 (A.V.) makes reference to the enemy who came and 'sowed tares among the wheat'. The Wyclif Bible of 1388 has 'sewe aboue taris'. But the word was new then; and we know that in an earlier version it is *darnel*, with *cockil* as an alternative. *Tares* is not recorded before the 14th century. *Darnel* is barely earlier. *Cockle* is O.E. *coccel*. Neither darnel nor cockle is a member of the Vetch family. The bold and beautiful red *corn-cockle*, *Agrostemma githago*, used to be one of the commonest weeds of the cornfield; but the poisonous black seeds have now been eliminated from our flour. In Bentham and Hooker *tares* is *Vicia hirsuta*. I remember that it was a long time, as I am not a farming country-man,* before I first saw the tiny pale flowers of this *papilio*. 'A weed of cultivation,' says the *Cambridge Flora*, which gives the names 'smooth tare' and 'slender tare' (in which the distinguishing adjectives refer to the pods), *Vicia tetrasperma* and *V. tenuissima* respectively.

But what was the meaning of *tares* in Wyclif's Bible? It is a translation of the Vulgate's plural word *zizania*, already established as *zizany* in English by 1300, with the accepted meaning of 'weeds among corn', perhaps 'darnel'. *Zizania* is probably an Arabic word; and *darnel* (*Lolium temulentum*) is a cornfield weed in Asia Minor, as it is in England. *Darnel* it should have remained in the Wyclif Bible; but *tares*, meaning 'strangleweed', somehow fits the parable better.

The subsequent history of *tare*, once it had been established, is so typical that it is worth a note. Once a Natural History word has caught on, it is used with little discrimination. Of the word in

* S.P.

question, first there was an explosion of different spellings, from *thare* to *tor*. Then it was used for 'tare-seed' – all too common among corn-seed in pre-cleaning times, and easily recognized by its small size. Then it became the term for other vetches.

In the time of Gerard and Ray, and later, *tare* and *vetch* were synonymous. From the 16th century onwards *tare* signified a plant of very different appearance, *Vicia sativa*, introduced and cultivated for fodder. It is now often seen, with its beautiful pink and scarlet flowers, naturalized. *Tare* itself became elaborated to 'tare-vetch', 'struggle-tare', 'tare-grass', or 'tare-verding'. Then appeared compound names, such as 'tare-thistle' for the sow-thistle. Finally the etymologists and systematic botanists went to work and cut the word down to size again. Its years of glory were over.

The derivation is obscure. Comparable are Skt. *durva*, a kind of grass; Lithuanian *dirva*, 'a cornfield'; and Old Dutch *taruwe* 'wheat'. This is by no means the only instance of the meanings of related words seeming to be opposites of the same middle; the differentiated offspring of some ancestral word implying in this case, perhaps 'connected with cultivation'.

> 'Loathsome smells,
> And shrieks like mandrakes' torn out of the earth,
> That living mortals, hearing them, run mad.'
> (*Romeo and Juliet*, IV. iii.)

The word *mandrake* takes us straight back to the world of Super-natural History and Folklore, with some genuine Natural History also as part of the scenery. Once again, the first reference is in the Wyclif Bible. In the A.V. the wording of Genesis 30. 16 is: 'And Jacob came out of the field . . . and Leah said, Thou must come in unto me; for surely I have hired thee with my son's mandrakes (Heb. *dudaim*). And he lay with her that night.'

A careful reading of the whole chapter will reveal an almost Strindbergian situation, showing that Jacob's wife Rachel was barren, that Jacob himself was very much the reverse, and that Leah bribed her sister Rachel to allow her to sleep with Jacob. Leah's bribe was some mandrakes found in the field 'at the time of the wheat-harvest'. Somewhere beside or behind this story is the folklore fact that 'mandrakes' (the wholesome *dudaim*) were considered in the Middle East to be an aphrodisiac.

The legend of the plant had long been known in England. The *Saxon Leechdoms* give advice about how to pull up *mandragora* without touching it. In fact Shakespeare's is not the first reference to madness and the shrieking root.

Mandrake is a 14th-century shortened form of the original *mandragora*, which had been taken through L.L. from the Gk. *mandragoras*, presumably the *Mandragora officinarum*, well-known in southern Europe and Palestine. The name might have suggested a connection with the O.E. *māndrinc* (crime-drink) 'poison'. Whatever the meaning of *dudaim*, it became *mandragora* in the Septuagint and the Vulgate. The later *man-drake* in folk-etymology is based on the distinct resemblance of some mandrake-roots, which are usually forked, to the figure of a man from neck to calf.

Obviously it is the more pleasant properties of what was called *mandragora* which were first noticed in the drug which could produce sleepiness and which was used by the ancients as an anaesthetic and an aphrodisiac. The evil meanings came later and were attached to the *mandrake*. Did Shakespeare regard *mandrake* and *mandragora* as two separate words? His references to 'mandragora' are benign. It was one of the 'drowsy syrops' of the world – something which Cleopatra might drink in order that she

> 'might sleep out this great gap of time
> My Antony is away.'

Shakespeare has made *mandragora* all good, *mandrake* all bad: and, as so often, Shakespeare's meanings have stuck.

The *Solanum* family, to which *Mandragora officinarum* belongs, includes many plants of evil repute, such as *dwale* or *deadly nightshade* (*Atropa belladonna*), the poisonous quality of which may have become attached to the mysterious *mandrake*. More baneful still is the *thornapple* (*Datura stramonium*), a naturalized plant which sometimes starts a scare in the daily press. *Henbane* will be mentioned later. Even the fruit and green tubers of the *potato* are poisonous; and for some time after its introduction from Mexico the *tomato* or 'love-apple' was regarded with suspicion and grown only for decoration. Like humanity, the *Solanaceae* are a mixed lot!

So much for a few plants often named from their characters. Now let us deal in the same way, but rather more fully, with the animal kingdom.

ix (a)

ANIMALS NAMED FROM ACTION: TYPICAL HABITS

'Habit is ten times Nature.'
THE DUKE OF WELLINGTON.

THE basis of an animal's name, if found at all, will be found in (a) Vocal Utterance, (b) Action other than vocal, (c) Habitat, normal or occasional, (d) Physical Characteristics, including Coloration, (e) Legend or Fancy.

Among birds, as might be expected, names from their voices predominate. These are not common in other classes of the animal world. What emerges from an examination of the names of all kinds of animal in the Indo-European languages is (as we have already stressed) that the creatures are more often named from what they do, than from their physical features – which in their turn are more important in nomenclature than are habitat and chance-associations. The older the name, the truer will the foregoing statements be seen to be.

Many of the English names for mammals, amphibians, fishes, and insects, both native and exotic, are of obscure origin; but we may take a round score of examples of 'Action-names' for members of these classes.

Deer (O.E. *dēor*, German *Tier*, etc.) denotes not merely *an* animal, as in 'rats and mice and such small deer', but has in many languages narrowed to the sense of *the* animal, the hart, doubtless because it was a favourite quarry for primitive flesh-eating peoples. The word may be derived from the presumed root **deus-*, 'to breathe' (cf. *animal* and L. *anima*, 'breath', 'spirit'); and it is possible that *deer* means 'the panter'. Tate and Brady were good observers when they wrote 'As pants the hart for cooling streams . . .'.

Stag – a name also used provincially for a cock – may well be 'the mounter', from the root **stig-*, 'to climb', 'to go'; but it is hard to identify, because it shares certain phonetic irregularities with those other rather colloquial words in O.E. that give us *pig*, *dog*, *frog*, and even -*wig*, 'a beetle'.

Our *ox* is a cognate of the Skt. *ukshán*; and the verb *uksh* points to its meaning 'the sprinkler', i.e. of sperm. A fine nature-from-nature name is 'ox-eye' for daisy and great tit.

Mole, found in M.E. as *mulle* or *molle*, is clearly connected with O.E. *molde*, 'dust', even if it is not a shortened form of the alternative M.E. *moldwarp*, 'earth-thrower', which in Scotland is found as *mouldiwarp* and in Germany as *Maulwurf*. *Weorpan* and *werfen* are the O.E. and German verbs; our *warp*, 'to twist', 'to bind', earlier meaning 'to throw', is a normal development of the O.E. form. The root of *mould* is the familiar **mel-*, 'to grind', found in *mill*, *meal*, *molar*, and scores of other words.

Earthiness is characteristic also of your *terrier*. He is the French *chien terrier*, the dog sent into the fox's earth or rabbit's bury. F. *terre* represents L. *terram*; *terra*, 'earth', being the later form of *tersa*, 'dry ground', from the root **ters-*, 'to be dry'.

The *wolf*, possibly the beast most dreaded by our Aryan, not merely our Saxon ancestors, was for them 'the tearer'. It was a scourge in England until the reign of Henry VII, and continued to haunt Scotland until the 18th century. The presumed I-E. word for 'wolf' is **wlqwos*. The Skt. *vrach* and the L. *vellere*, *vulsum* (the source of our *convulse* and *revulsion*) signify 'to rend, cut, pluck,' etc.

Ichneumon is straight Greek, via Latin, and means 'tracker' (Gk. *ikhneuein*, 'to track', from *ikhnos*, 'a footstep'). The name is given to the Egyptian mongoose, eater of crocodiles' eggs. We apply it also to the parasitic ichneumon-flies, which persistently follow other species of insect in order to insert their own eggs into the eggs, larvae, or bodies of the host-species, to provide food for their offspring when they are hatched.

Tiger, like the name of the river Tigris, is possibly to be traced back to the Zend *tighri*, an arrow, 'swift attacker'; but the Skt. *vyāghra*, 'keen sniffer' (*ghrā*, 'to smell'), shows that some early men could observe the ways of a wild creature more dispassionately than others who were content with 'swift attacker' for the name of an animal whose invariable habit is shared by his small cousin the domestic cat, and other types of *Felidae*.

The signification of *hare*, with cognate names in other Germanic languages, and in Celtic, is 'the leaper'. The Skt. name is *śaśa* (*śaś*,

65

'to jump'). Apart from its appearance in botanical names such as *harebell* and *hare's-foot*, *hare* gives us at least two good nature-from-nature names – *harebrained* and *hare-lipped*.

Mouse may have meant 'thief'. The oldest cognate word we know is Skt. *mush*, 'to steal'. *Rat* (O.E. *ræt*) we may guess to be from the same root as *rodent*, and call it 'the gnawer'.

Dormouse is often connected with F. *dormeuse*, 'the sleeper' (fem.), but may stand for the provincial *dorm*, 'to doze', + *mouse*, and be 'the sleepy one', in allusion to its long hibernation and somnolent habits even in the warmer weather (cf. Old Dutch *slaepmuys*). Skt. *drā* and Gk. *darthanein* are akin to L. *dormire*, 'to sleep', which, through French, gives us the stem of *dormant, dormer, dormitory*, and *dormition*.

In Aristophanes' *brekekekex koax koax* of the chorus of *The Frogs* we may hear a fine onomatopoetic rendering of the frog's croak. The Gk. word for 'frog' is *batrakhos*, and we may make a guess that this too began by being imitative. All it shares with frog-words in other languages is a lack of history. This is true also for O.E. *frogga*, seemingly a pet-form of O.E. *forse, frose*, a cognate of Modern German *Frosch*. In Britain we are less accustomed to the nightly croaking of frogs than are the people who live on the continent of Europe, as witness our expression 'Dutch nightingales', i.e. frogs.

One might expect the notion of wetness and moist skin to have led our ancestors to call the frog 'the slimy one' or 'the water-dweller'. The last phrase is certainly at the back of *otter* and similar names in cognate languages. Even *hydra*, originally 'a water-snake', is connected with our *water*, German *Wasser*, Gk. *hudōr*, Skt. *udan-*, L. *unda* 'a wave', etc.

Among fish *salmon* reaches us through French from L. *salire*, 'to leap'. No name could be more appropriate than 'leaper' for this champion scaler of waterfalls. It is echoed in our *salmon-leap* for an artificial ladder to aid the fish in their upward struggle.

Shark was taken, by Captain John Hawkins' sailors perhaps, from the use in the 16th century of the verb *shark*, 'to prey upon', derived ultimately from L. *cercare*, 'to circle round', through O.F. *cercer* (the Picard *charquier*), now *chercher*, 'to search'. 'Circling' describes admirably the habit of sharks in pursuit of their prey. Like the hosts of Midian, they 'prowl and prowl around'; and their name is a fitting one for them and for their human imitators.

The *spider* is 'the spinner'. The O.E. *spinnan*, 'to spin' (a web, warp, or woof), gives the feminine noun *spinster* as well as the earlier masculine *spinthra* – later *spithra* – giving M.E. *spithre*, *spither*, modern *spider*. The form *spither* is retained, for instance, in the Wyclif Bible, together with *yreyns* or *areyns* (to which we return for our modern name for the Order *Araneida*) as variant readings. An earlier name was *ātorcoppe* (*ātor*, 'poison', *copp*, 'head', 'top'); *cobweb* was M.E. *coppeweb*.

One foe of the spinner is 'the weaver', the *wasp*. The provincial *wops* or *wopsy* is nearer to the O.E. original *wæps* before the metathesis of the *p* and the *s*. The root of *wæps*, as of *web* and many other words, is **webh-* – a syllable of ill omen to the fly, which, before it is enmeshed, is the *flier*.

The *bee* (O.E. *bēo*) is probably 'the tremulous one', 'the flutterer'. She has cognate names in other Germanic tongues, and the Skt. *bhī* means 'to fear', 'to tremble'.

The *beetle* to our ancestors was *bitela*, 'the biter', from *bītan*, cognate with the G. *beissen*, etc., 'to bite'.

Butterfly seems to unite elements of colour and action, the first implying 'butter-coloured', perhaps because of the yellowish tint of many of our 'whites', the most numerous of the lepidoptera which used to haunt our gardens before the era of horticultural and agricultural poisons.

The *clam* is a bivalve which *clamps* its shells together and *clamps* itself to a rock.

*　　　*　　　*

To preclude any thought that an overwhelming proportion of the Action-names of birds are coined from vocal efforts, let us take as complete a survey as we can from habit-named British birds.

There are very few English bird-names implying action without explicit reference to voice, food, or bodily movement; and in most of these few, as might well be anticipated, the search for food, or the manner of dealing with it, is implicit, as it is in *jaeger* (the German for 'hunter'), the N. American alternative to our *skua*.

Woodpecker is the one conventional English substantive name which, like those of the exotic *tailor-bird* and *hang-nest*, and the provincial *feather-poke* and similar names for the long-tailed tit and other small birds, may contain a reference to home-making. Even *wood-*

67

pecker is as likely to apply as much to the bird's tapping and boring into sickly trees in pursuit of insects as to its more strenuous operations while hewing out its nesting-hole.

Woodpecker is not found prior to Merrett's *Pinax* (1667), Turner having used *hewhole* and *raynbird* for the yaffle (1544).

Whereas the hound called *harrier* is named from the object of its pursuit (the *hare*), the *harriers*, the birds which link the owls and the hawks, derive their name from the verb to *harry* (O.E. *hergian*). The primary meaning of *hergian* is 'to ravage in the manner of an army', *here* (modern German *Heer*). That words with meanings so dissimilar as the O.E. *hara*, 'a hare', and *here*, 'an army', may be confused could be seen by testing the connotation in the minds of local people of the track over the Quantock Hills which is known as the *Hare-Way*, i.e. the Saxon *here-weg*, 'army-road', later 'main-road'.

Vulture, 'the render', is the L. *vultur*, a development of *vellere*, 'to tear', and therefore akin to *vulnerable* (from the stem of *vulnus*, 'a wound'), and the Skt. *vraṇa* and Welsh *gweli* ('a wound'), and other words springing from the root **vel-*.

The Teutonic verbal type **hafjan*, 'to seize', exemplified by O.E. *habban*, 'to hold', corresponds to the L. *capere* and to the origin of Gk. *kōpē*, a *haft* – the handle that one grasps. Hence, by the side of *haft*, we have *hawk*, 'the seizer'. The association becomes plainer when we compare the O.E. *hafoc*, the Dutch *havic*, the German *Habicht*, the Finnish *haukka*, and the Scandinavian equivalents.

Hawk as an element in a place-name is met about as often as *glead* ('a kite'). The oldest record seems to be of *Heafocrycg* (*Hawkridge*, Berks.) in 956. *Hauochesten* (*Hawkhurst*, Kent) is in the Domesday Book. Other names are *Haycrust* (formerly *Hauekehurst*) and *Hawkstone*, Salop; *Hawksley*, Hants.; *Hauxley*, *Hawkwell*, and *Hawkhill*, Northumberland.

Hawks may for a moment take us to *herons*, as happened to Hamlet, who knew 'a *hawk* from a *handsaw*', and who incidentally did not take *handsaw* to mean 'a heronry', as did Randle Cotgrave (1571–1636). In the first French Dictionary compiled in England, Cotgrave, Secretary to Lord Burleigh, not inexcusably defined *heronshaw* (also spelt *heronsew*, *harnser*, etc.) as a *herns' shaw* or wood, i.e. 'a heronry'. The word, in fact, is from the O.F. *heronceau*, 'a young heron'; although in English the meaning was not restricted to young birds, as witness:

68

'Ne of hir swannes, nor of hir heronsewes.'
Chaucer, *Squire's Tale*, 60.
'As when a cast of Faulcons make their flight
At an Herneshaw that lyes aloft on wing.'
Spenser, *The Faerie Queene*, VI. vii. 9.

Heron and *egret*, kindred birds, seem to have dissimilar names; but these are mere variants of the same original. The M.E. *heiroun* was taken from O.F. *hairon* and presumed Low Latin *hagirōn(em)*, from the Middle High German form of the O.H.G. *heigir*. The O.E. name was *hrāgra*.

The parentage of *egret* is now clear, the word *aigrette* being merely a French diminutive of the Provençal *aigron*, 'a heron'. That the primary signification of both *heron* and *egret* is 'seizer' seems certified by the Skt. roots **hr-* and **grah-*, 'to take, to seize'.

The *aigrette* used as a head-decoration, whether a spray of gems, spun glass, or feathers, has its name from that of the little *egret*. In the marshes of the Guadalquivir and elsewhere the filmy plumes worn by Englishwomen had often been torn from the *living* birds in the nesting-season, when the victims were in nuptial dress and the long feathers of the mantle were at their finest. In the millinery trade they were known as 'osprey-plumes'. In 1921, mainly through the efforts of the R.S.P.B., it was made illegal to import them into Britain.

The *egret* or plume of feathers on a hat was named an *osprey* by late 19th-century milliners. It is possible that they meant to call it *a spray* and that another bird-name came in and confused them, as if the story of *osprey* itself was not sufficiently tangled. This word derives from L. *ossifraga*, a bird described by Pliny as feeding on bones and dropping them from a height in order to break them. Modern science identifies this as the lammergeier or bearded vulture. Now the translators of the 1611 Bible used the two names side by side: 'the Eagle, and the Ossifrage, and the Ospray'. (Vulgate: *'aquilam et gryphem, et haliæetum'*; New English Bible: 'the griffon-vulture, the black vulture, and the bearded vulture.') If we allow that the English *ossifrage*, taken in the early 17th century direct from Latin, still represents the same bird, we must admit that *osprey*, in its devious and partly unexplained passage through O.F. **osfraie* (later *orfraie*) also changed birds and became attached to *Pandion haliaetus*,

69

the fish-hawk. So it is in Shakespeare's *Coriolanus*, 'I think hee'l be to Rome As is the Asprey to the Fish'.

In *pochard*, which occurs in Turner's list, appears the ending *-ard*, the Gallicized form of the O.H.G. *hart*, 'hardy', 'bold'. Denoting a male creature, it is found as a suffix in many of the most illustrious German personal names, e.g. *Burkhard, Eckhard*; but in the words which have reached English through French it is nearly always depreciatory, as in *coward, dotard, drunkard*, etc. By the side of *pochard* we have *mallard, buzzard, haggard* (a wild falcon). The local name of *poker* for the pochard-drake (whose mate is the 'dunbird') suggests a bird which 'pokes' about under water for its food; and might derive from O.F. *pocher*, 'to poke'. (Cf. 'buzzard', Chapter IX(a).) The Mod. F. *pochard* is a slang word for a drunkard: the name of the bird is *milouin* or *fuligule milouin*.

The meaning of *turnstone* is well explained by T. A. Coward (1867–1933) in *Birds of the British Isles*: 'In its feeding-habits it shows the value of its short pickaxe bill, using it as a lever to tip up and throw over large stones ... and with an upward sweep jerk the long tangle aside, and quickly pounce on the astonished sandhoppers, small crabs, and molluscs.' One could love Coward for ever, merely on account of that delightfully anthropomorphic 'astonished'.

We can hardly ignore some names made up of two terms.

The first element in *scops owl* is the Gk. *skōps*, a species of owl noted by Aristotle, the name being derived, as are our *bishop* (Gk. *episkopos*), *sceptic, scope*, and various other English words, from *skeptesthai*, 'to use the eyes, to watch'. The Gk. root *skep-* is the equivalent of the Latin *spec-* (as in *spectare*, 'to watch'), which gives us *spectacle, species*, etc. *Skōps* was also the name of a dance in which those taking part mimicked the owl.

The first penduline tit *Remiz pendulinus* recorded in Britain spent at least a week at Spurn Head, Yorkshire, towards the end of October, 1966. The German *Beutelmeise* ('purse-tit') and equivalent names in many other European languages, including Finnish, testify to the bird's wide range of stations across Europe (and Central Asia), and suggest a picture of its nest. This, which is suspended (whence *penduline*) from thin twigs, is globular, with a self-closing tube as a side-entrance, indeed as the sole entrance. The walls are of material so closely woven that Dr David Snow could report from Africa: 'The texture is so tough and durable that old nests are used by the local people as purses' – interesting confirmation of the suitability of the names given in Europe.

* * *

There is a fairly large class of names founded on fancy, folklore, superstition, and anthropomorphism. These, either explicitly or implicitly, point to some habit or characteristic in the species named.

In common with other species of birds – as the red-throated diver, the green woodpecker, and the mistle-thrush – the *plovers* are supposed to be prophetic of rain, their name being an adaptation of the F. *pluvier*, from L. *pluviālis*, 'rainy'; they are locally called *rainbirds*.

Also considered as a harbinger of heavy weather is the storm- or stormy petrel, whose feet dip into the surface of the waves and recall the thought of St Peter walking on the water of the Sea of Galilee. *Storm* is an O.E. word allied to *stir*. 'Sailors', says W. H. Hudson, 'call the petrels "Mother Carey's chickens"; but not, as might be imagined from such a name, on account of any tender regard or feeling of affection for the birds. Mother Carey is supposed to be a kind of ocean-witch, a supernatural Mother Shipton, who rides the blast, and who has for attendants and harbingers the little dark-winged petrels.'

In fact *Mother Carey* is a corruption of *Mater Cara*, the Mother Beloved, Our Lady. Her chickens are not to be classed with the little grebe, the dabchick, that bird of disconcerting appearings and vanishings, which was known in Stirling, according to the Revd. Christopher Swainson, as a witch with the name of *Mither o' the Mawkins*, i.e. 'mother of the hares'. (*Mawkin* and *Greymalkin* or *Grimalkin*, diminutives of *Maud*, *Matilda*, or *grey Maud*, used to signify pussies, whether hares or cats.) And certainly the sprite-like petrels are poles apart from *Gabriel's Hounds* – probably meaning 'corpse-hounds' – that give tongue from the wild night-sky and are identified by prosaic people with gaggles of geese.

That *les oiseaux de Notre Dame*, as the petrels are called in French, do in fact take their name from that of St Peter, who walked on the water (St Matthew 14. 29), and not – however the name may be rationalized – from their *pattering* through the waves, is clearly shown by the history of the word. If we translate the Aramaic name Cephas into Greek, Christ's promise reads, 'Thou art Peter (*petros*, 'a stone'); and on this ledge of rock (*petra*) I will build my church'.

71

From the Gk. form of the name, *Peter* and the word for 'stone' became in French *Pierre*. French could hardly have formed *pétrel* from *Pierre*. Nor did it do so. The F. *pétrel* used by Brisson in 1760 is more likely to have been borrowed from the earlier English *petrel*, formed upon *Peter*, perhaps after *cockerel*, *dotterel*, etc. The Nor. *Peders fugl* and G. *Peters Vogel* are also later than the English word, so that, although they do not confirm the source of that word, they emphasize the ready acceptance of what may have been romantic popular etymology.

A variant of *pierrot* and *pierrette* (French diminutives of *Pierre* and provincial words for 'cock-' and 'hen-sparrow') became the English *parrot*, which supplies the epithet in *parrot-crossbill*.

To the seafaring man who first named the 'sea-swallows' for St Peter, one species, the frigate-petrel *Pelagodroma marina*, also owes part of its name. This fast-flying bird has been recorded only twice in Britain (Lancs., 1890; Colonsay, Hebrides, 1897).

Our *frigate*, the German *Fregatte*, Dutch *fregat*, and the F. *frégate* are all forms of the Italian *fregata*; but this is a word of obscure origin. Its first meaning is 'a light and swift vessel' (1585); later it was applied to a larger ship, and after that (1738) to a bird-genus which includes *Fregata magnificans*, the *frigate-bird*, which may be mentioned here on the strength of one found dead on Tiree, Inner Hebrides, in 1953, and of another, probably of this species, recorded in 1960. With its long hooked bill and wingspan of 75–85 inches, this dark terror of the flying-fish in tropical waters may indeed claim magnificence. The robuster alternative names of 'man-o'-war bird' and 'man-o'-war hawk' smack even more strongly of the seas swept by Nelson's black ships tricked out with white or yellow. It is, however, not their coloration but their wing-power to which both the *frigate-petrel* and the *frigate-bird* owe their trivial names. The latter is said by Fisher and Peterson (*The World of Birds*, 1965) to be 'the most agile of all sea-birds'.

The nightjar holds in its scientific generic name, *Caprimulgus*, the slander of the ancient Greek *aigothēlas*, 'goatsucker', for the bird which pastoral peoples saw in the dusk catching beetles and other insects attracted by the rank smell of the goats. Still known locally in England by that name of 'goatsucker', in Spain as *chotacabras*, in Germany as *Ziegenmelker*, and in other countries by names of equivalent meaning, the beneficent 'fernowl' exemplifies the superstitions connected with so many of the birds – woodpeckers, kingfishers, cuckoos, and others, as well as nightjars – once grouped together as the Order *Picariae*, which in appearance and habits depart from the standards of most birds of similar size. The swift, for instance, is named by the countryman as 'devil-bird', 'deviling', or plain 'devil'.

It would have been as difficult to convince the old-fashioned game-keeper that the kestrel and the barn-owl are far more useful than harmful to man's interests, as it would have been to persuade the ancient Arcadian or the 18th-century English farmer that the nightjar, with its bill so wonderfully adapted for hawking for insects, was quite incapable of milking his beasts.

If Gilbert White did not explicitly attack the absurdity of the name *goatsucker*, as a good naturalist he dissected the crop of a night-jar and found it 'stuffed hard with large *phalenae*, moths of several sorts, and their eggs, which had no doubt been forced out of those insects by the action of swallowing'. That was in, or prior to, 1776. Twenty-eight years later Bewick, in his *History of British Birds*, named the bird *night-jar* and spoke of it as 'a great destroyer of the cock-chafer or dor-beetle, from which circumstance in some places it is called the dor-hawk'. Almost simultaneously Montagu was still writing the libellous name of *goatsucker*, noting *nightjar* as a pro-vincial name. But Bewick's influence prevailed, and from the time of Yarrell's *History of British Birds* (1843) it is 'goatsucker' that has been relegated to the category of provincialisms.

Godwits must have been considered as birds of good omen, if their name represents, as seems possible, the O.E. *gōd wiht*, 'good fellow', a title given also to the kindly sprite, Robin Goodfellow. Attempts have been made, however, to connect the name with the edible qualities of the wader, which was once a favourite tablebird.

The forename of the *harlequin-duck* is of obscure origin, but may have reached English through French from the Italian *arlechino*. Harlequin was the foil to the clown wooing Columbine. Although in theory he was a spirit visible only to his lady, he was conventionally dressed in gay patchwork. Skeat compares the name with the med. L. *familia Harlechini*, the O.H.G. *hella cunni*, 'kindred of hell', the troop of demon horsemen riding by night, known all over Europe. Harlequin's nature, however, was considerably toned down in the Harlequinade, but not his gay dress, after which the bird is named. The generic name of this duck, *Histrionicus*, 'like a playboy', is twice repeated to make up the trinomial. The drake is not so brilliantly

73

coloured as the male of the North American wood-duck, or of the Chinese mandarin-duck with their 'more than oriental splendour'; but his blue legs and his plumage of black, greys, blues, and chestnut, freaked with white, are well suited to a harlequin. The L. *histrio*, 'an actor', the source of *histrionicus*, was taken from *hister*, one of the comparatively few words known to us of the ancient, non-Indo-European, Etruscan dialect.

The wood- and mandarin-ducks (*Aix sponsa* and *A. galericulata*), which may at no long date be admitted to the British list, through birds escaped from captivity, take their generic name from that of a water-bird, presumed to be some kind of goose, mentioned by Aristotle. The primary meaning, however, of *Aix* was 'goat' (cf. *aigothēles*, above). We may like to find a connection between the two genera – *Histrionicus*, the actor, and *Aix*, the duck that plays the goat.

Albatross, considered etymologically, is not a correct name for any of the twelve species of the family of the bird shot by the Ancient Mariner; for it belongs properly (though still inaccurately) to the pelican. The Arabic *al-qādūs* (Gk. *kados*), first 'the bucket', i.e. the trough of a water-wheel, then 'pelican' (from the supposition that the bird carried water to its nestlings in the pouch below its bill), became the Spanish *alcatraz*, which was next borrowed by the Portuguese to denote the cormorant or the albatross. The *b* of 'albatross' has, it seems, crept into the English form of the word made familiar at home by the men who had sailed with the scientifically-minded buccaneer-navigator William Dampier (1652–1715), through false analogy with the L. *alba* (*avis*), 'white' (bird).

But for the most astonishing theory about any of our birds we must turn to the barnacle-goose, which for many centuries was believed to be hatched from the cirriped known to us as the 'barnacle', and in formal French as *anatife* (L. *anas, anatis*, 'duck' +*ferre*, 'to bear'). This 'mystical monster marine' eventually gave the French their *histoire du canard*, or, more briefly, *canard*, for *blague* or 'spoof'. The legend was exhaustively treated by Max Müller in *The Science of Language*, Lecture II, and by Sir Ray Lankester in *Some Diversions of a Naturalist* (1935).

The myth, not found in Aristotle or any other author in classical times, had become current by the 12th century, possibly through a note in one of the books of the Jewish *Qabalah*, which deals with the interpretation of numbers and other esoteric lore. In this treatise, the *Zohar*, it is stated that Rabbi Abba had seen a tree whose fruit produced birds. Giraldus Cambrensis, who had been tutor to Prince John during his visit to Ireland in 1185, and who was familiar also with the coasts of his native Wales, gave his support to the theory, saying that he had seen thousands of these birds hanging down from timber on the sea-shore. He noted that in some parts of Ireland the clergy permitted the eating of the barnacle-goose on feast-days – the *barnacal* 'not being flesh or born of flesh'. In 1215, however, Pope Innocent III forbade the practice, on the grounds that the geese, though produced anomalously, live and feed in the ordinary manner, and were therefore to be considered as birds.

In the 13th century Albertus Magnus and the earliest of our experimental naturalists, Roger Bacon, refused to credit the barnacle-myth. The scepticism, however, was not to become general for some five hundred years.

Although Dutch mariners had already reported their finding the dark-necked geese breeding in Greenland, the gardener-barber-surgeon John Gerard included in his *Herball* (1597) a woodcut depicting a tree bearing large barnacle-shaped buds with little anserine heads peeping from them and gazing at other small geese swimming on the sea beneath the tree. He claimed to have seen the goose-tree on an island off Lancashire.

In 1661, at one of the first meetings of the Royal Society, Sir Robert Moray, the Society's first President, read a paper on the subject, which was printed in *Philosophical Transactions* No. 137, Jan./Feb., 1677/8.

'Being in the island of East,' Moray reported, 'I saw lying upon the shore a cut of a large Firr-tree of about 2½ foot diameter, and 9 or 10 foot long; which had lain so long out of the water that it was very dry: and most of the Shells, that had formerly cover'd it, were worn or rubb'd off. Only on the parts that lay next the ground, there still hung multitudes of little Shells, having within them little Buds, perfectly shap'd, supposed to be Barnacles. ... This Bud in every Shell that I opened, as well the least as the biggest, I found so curiously and completely form'd, that there appeared nothing wanting, as to the internal parts, for making up a perfect Sea-fowl: every little part appearing so distinctly, that the whole looked like a large Bird seen through a concave or diminishing Glass, colour and feature being everywhere so clear and neat. The little Bill, like that of a

Goose, the Eyes mark'd, the Head, Neck, Breast, Wings, Tail, and Feet form'd. . . .'

So compelling is this account that it may be with some regret that we find Sir Robert admitting, 'Nor did I ever see any of the little Birds alive, nor met with anybody that did.'

A more critical age was dawning; but until then the misapprehension was reasonable enough. Flocks of barnacle-geese, which breed in the Arctic, visit in winter Britain and Ireland, especially the northern parts, and the more northerly coasts of other European countries, where barnacle-encrusted timber is liable to be thrown up in any storm. It is not difficult for a vivid imagination to find in the partly protruded proboscis of a barnacle a likeness to the head of a baby-chick. What is harder to find is the etymology of the name shared by the goose and the cirriped.

If, as is probable, the shellfish was named from the bird, and the English dates supporting this view are bird 1227, shellfish 1581, the most plausible explanation is that the M.E. *bernekke* or *bernake* (Mediaeval L. *bernaca*) stood for the Scandinavian *brand* ('burnt', 'dark', as in 'brent', the barnacle's congener) and O.E. *hnecce*, 'the nape of the neck'. But the existence of O.F. *bernoque*, now *bernache* or *bernacle*, hardly lends countenance to this derivation. Could the O.F. name have any connection with *brun*, 'brown', and *nuque*, 'the nape'? If we believe the cirriped's name to have preceded the bird's, we may note that *nuque* is derived from Arabic *nuqa*, 'the marrow of the spine', which the soft substance of the body of the shellfish may have been thought to resemble. A similar picture of the exposed flesh might have produced the name through O.E. *bær*, 'bare', and *hnecce*. But we are unlikely to solve a question which has puzzled all the great authorities.

A quite large part is taken in ornithological nomenclature by names describing character. These must be considered as fanciful, since they indicate not what a bird is, but what its mentality appears to be when judged by human standards.

Let us brazenly introduce the long-lamented exotic dodo as an example of the birds which have suffered from man's cynicism. Thanks to Lewis Carroll and Sir John Tenniel, the poor *Raphus cucullatus* must be better known in England by repute than are nine-tenths of the birds on the British list. *Dodo* is generally taken to be from the Portuguese *doudo*, 'stupid'. The Portuguese sailors may have borrowed this word from the dialect form *dold*, for *dolt*, used by the seamen of Devon who competed with them and with the Dutch (helped by the pigs which they brought with them to the islands) in extirpating the huge flightless pigeon of Mauritius and its relatives the solitaires of Réunion and Rodriguez. With *dold* and *dolt* may be compared such words as the German *toll*, 'mad, nonsensical.'

It is alternatively suggested that 'dodo' is a corruption of the Middle Dutch *dod* or *dodde* + *eers*, 'plug-' or 'lump-rump', which is found in Dutch records of the 17th and early 18th centuries, written during or shortly after the destruction of all the birds in question. The Dictionary compiled by the etymologist J. Franck (1912) says that the original meaning of *dod* or *dodde* is *iets rondachtigs en soepels* – 'something round and supple/soft'. Professor J. Vercoullie's Dictionary (Ghent, 1925) describes *dodde* as *een propachtige dikte* – 'a swelling of the nature of a gag, plug, or wad'. This supports the meaning of the English provincial word *dod(d)*, as in *dodman*, 'a snail', as 'a rounded lump or eminence'.

Those species of gannet known as *boobies* have also been insulted by their persecutors with names imputing stupidity. If the gannet, at the end of its superb straight dive into the sea, breaks its neck on a floating board to which a diabolically ingenious man has nailed a herring, is it more stupid than a performing seal (a highly intelligent mammal) which clashes cymbals tied to its flippers because of an innate tendency to fan itself in that way? What an irrational creature, after all, must man be, who tends to dislike cats because of their incorrigible independence, and to despise animals that are confiding and tame!

The *noddy-tern Anous stolidus*, contemptuously labelled even in its scientific name, is in this slandered category; but after the time of Yarrell it ceased to have a place in the British list. Sailors dubbed it a *noodle* or *noddy* (M.E. *nodden*, 'to nod the head') on account of what they considered stupid, that is trustful, behaviour. In the same way the *dotterel* was rewarded by ungrateful fowlers with a name taken from the same source as the verb to *dote*, 'to be foolish', with the addition of a double-diminutive suffix found also in such words as *cockerel*.

'For as you creep or cow'r or stoop or go,
So marking you with care the apish bird doth do.'
Drayton, *Polyolbion* XXV. 11. 347–8.

'It was believed,' wrote Hudson, paraphrasing in his *British Birds* (as Bewick had done) Willughby's translation of the Latin of von Gesner, 'that when the fowler, on approaching the bird, stretched forth an arm, the dotterel responded by stretching out a wing; that when a leg was put forth, the action was immediately copied; and that the bird, being intent on watching and imitating the action of the man, neglected its own safety and was taken in the net. The origin of the notion, which was credited by everyone, ornithologists included, for two or three centuries, is no doubt to be found in the fact that the dotterel is less shy and active than most plovers, and, like very many other birds, when approached and disturbed during repose, has the habit of stretching out a wing and leg before moving away.'

Even the scientific name of this 'good runner', *Eudromias*, insists that it is a 'little fool' (*morinellus*). If credit for the epithets in scientific names were given to nomenclators before Linnaeus, we should see 'Caius' in brackets instead of 'L.' Caius (John Keyes, 1510–1573) was the royal physician in three reigns. A former student of Gonville Hall, Cambridge, in 1559 he raised it to the dignity of a college, and became its first Master. In one of his many books he named his poor *doterell* by the Latinized form of the Italian *morinello* (L. *mōrari*, 'to play the fool' – Gk. *mōros*, akin to the Skt. *mūrkha*, 'a fool, a *moron*'). More attractive is the standard Italian name of *piviare tortolino*, 'the little turtle-dove plover'.

Personally* I have found few experiences among birds more engaging than sitting on a snow-dappled Lapland fell and gazing at and stroking a dotterel as he brooded his mate's eggs, having eventually to lift him gently from them in order to admire them. But he was back on the nest before it could be photographed. That this parental boldness is not confined to one species or to one sex could be vouched for by any naturalist. I remember repeatedly lifting a hen mistle-thrush from her nest high up in a tree in a country-garden. She, like the dotterel, invariably returned to her eggs within a couple of seconds, as if she were on the end of a rubber cord. Stupidity? Would it be too trite to say that stupidity, like beauty, may be in the eye, or the mind, of the beholder?

If folly be preferable to greed, the *gyrfalcon* is unlucky; for if we use the alternative *gerfalcon* the first part of the name seems to be

*L.C.S.

derived, through French, from O.H.G. *gîr*, mod. German *Geier*, 'a vulture': the root found in O.H.G. *gîri* seems to be the source. Newton in his *Dictionary of Birds* (1893) followed the 13th-century Albertus Magnus (Groot or Albertus of Cologne) in deriving *gyr* from L. *gyrare*, 'to circle', from the bird's flight.

Apart from those birds which we designate as fatheads there are some which suffer the final indignity of having their names used to denote stupid human beings, as witness *goose*, *cuckoo*, and *gowk*, with the German *Wiedehopf* (hoopoe), *Dohle* (jackdaw), and *Gimpel* (bullfinch). An Arabic catchword is 'more stupid than a houbara', because this bustard is reputed to return to its nest and brood substituted eggs. In marked contrast to their pride in Athene's own bird, the little owl, the Athenians showed contempt for the long-eared owl (*ōtos*) by using its name to mean a simpleton. Anyone who has seen the bird sitting erect on a branch close to the trunk of a tree, apparently with eyes closed, yet always facing the observer, will appreciate the ground of the superstition that the owl could be taken if a man walked round and round its perch until it wrung its own neck as it slowly turned its head to watch him.

To these depreciatory names cannot directly be added that of *loon*, which replaces our *diver* in Canada and the United States, and is recorded by Kirke Swann as a local name for the red-throated diver in the Shetlands and Southern Ireland. Poor Jack Point, the 'lovelorn loon' in *The Yeoman of the Guard*, borrowed his sobriquet from the early Mod. Dutch *loen*, 'a clod or lout' – the 'cream-faced loon' of *Macbeth* V. iii. 7; whereas the bird's name is a rendering of a Scandinavian word of which modern forms are the Swedish, Danish, and Norwegian *lom* (pronounced 'loom'). In this instance the *n* of the English word has taken the place of *m* by the converse process to the modern *lime* (tree) for the older *line* (i.e. *linden*). (See Chapter XXV.)

Lumme, compounded in the modern German names for the guillemots, was used by Willughby for the black-throated diver. *Loon* spelt in this way shows more clearly its connection with *lame* and with the awkwardness of the divers and grebes when they are out of the water – a characteristic due to the curious backward position of the ankle-joint. Put technically, 'the tibial segment of the leg is bound to the body by its musculature'. (Cf. names of grebes, Chapter XII (a).)

The derogatory term *loon*, however, has probably achieved greater popularity by being subconsciously associated with the name of the bird. The same may be said of 'gull', of which the origin may have to be sought through the Dutch *gul*, 'easy-going'. Hexham (1658) gives the meaning of the Middle Dutch *gulle* as 'a great wench without wit' – the Dutch word for the feathered gull being *meeuw*, as in our *seamew*.

If anthropomorphism were not so unpopular today, we might say that the birds have at least evened the score by providing, through a fanciful judgment of the habits of the male cuckoo (which was supposed to mate with the females of the small birds which the hen victimizes) the name of *cuckold* for the husband of a faithless wife. Middle English had this word from Old French, which had tacked the German depreciative ending to the name of the bird. Surprising as it is to find a Kentish valley called a combe, the Ordnance Survey map gives evidence of one such pretty spot east of Ashford, 'Cuckold's Combe' – a name which might have offered a salutary warning to the neighbourhood from the time when the thirteenth-century form *Cukkelescombe* was altered to fit a more familiar word until *cuckold* itself became nearly obsolete. By Chaucer the opprobrious term was spelt 'cokewold'; Langland not many years previously had written:

> 'But he be knowe for a koke-wold, kut of my nose!'
> *Piers the Ploughman*, Passus IV. 164.

There is a happier play of fancy in the names of our *goldcrest* and *firecrest* and of their very close American relatives the *golden-crowned* and *ruby-crowned kinglets*, reported in these islands, but not yet officially received. In science each one of the four is a 'little king', *Regulus*; to which name the transatlantic golden-crowned one adds *satrapa*, the name of a viceroy under the old Persian monarchs. We have one record of a *royal tern*; and the *king-eider* wanders occasionally to Britain from the Arctic. Otherwise our regal birds are only those with provincial names (which must be at least four centuries old) – *King Harry Blackcap* and *King Harry Redcap* (the goldfinch).

ix (b)

ANIMALS NAMED FROM ACTION: MOVEMENT

> 'Some birds have movements peculiar to the season
> of love: thus ring-doves, though strong and rapid at
> other times, yet in the spring hang about on the wing
> in a toying and playful manner. . . . Swifts dash round
> in circles, and the bank-martin moves with frequent
> vacillations like a butterfly.'
>
> GILBERT WHITE: 7th August, 1778.

CHARACTERISTIC movement of part of a bird's body seems to be alluded to only in *wagtail* and *wryneck*; for, as we may see later, *lapwing* embraces a more general meaning than appears on the surface.

The wryneck's power to twist its head so that its bill points over its back is, in conjunction with its hissing note, calculated to frighten enemies from its nest. (Our oldest connection with *wry* is the O.E. *wrigian*, 'to turn'.)

The superstition evoked by many of those which used to be called 'Picarian birds' was responsible for the practice among witches of tying a wryneck to a wheel, which was then revolved, to act as a charm on faithless lovers or as a spell against enemies. Thus arose the Greek expression *helkein iugga epi tini*, 'to draw the wryneck against someone'. This is instructive when considered with the uncanny faculty which, helped by the pattern of the neck-feathers, gave the wryneck its English name. In the majority of other European languages the native name has this sense of 'neck-twister'.

Movement of the whole body is the principle behind many names, which often directly imply the agent, as in *diver* (used, if not coined, by Willughby (d. 1672)) and *dipper*, first found in Tunstall's *Ornithologia Britannica* (1771) as an alternative to *water-ouzel* for the bird which both dips from the surface to the bed of the stream and bobs down and up, or 'curtseys', as it stands on a stone. With these two names, which are etymologically connected, may be taken *dabchick*, a common name for the little grebe, earned by its habit, shared with other grebes, of plopping under water and swimming for some distance before re-emerging.

Wader, a general term for shore- and water-haunting birds such as sandpipers, stints, knot, and sanderling, is rich in meaning, and certainly apposite for the birds at the tide-edge. The O.E. *wadan* is cognate with L. *vādere*, 'to go', from a root equivalent to Skt. **gā-* and Gk. **bā-*, the primitive root being said to be **wadh-*. An offshoot was L. *vadum* (Skt. *gādham*), 'a ford, a place where men or cattle might wade through the shoal water'.

Duck is from a Teutonic base represented in modern Dutch and German by *duiken* and *tauchen*, 'to dive or plunge'. The M.E. was *doke* or *duke*, from O.E. *dūce*.

The scarcity of English place-names embracing *dūce* is partly explained by the existence of another O.E. word for 'duck', namely *ened*. It may be that quite early it became the fashion among the Saxons to use *ened* for the wild bird and *dūce* for the domestic kind. *Doughton*, Glos., seems to have been *Ductune* in the 8th century and *Doketon* in the 12th. This name and *Duckinfield*, Cheshire, are certainly the oldest referring to ducks so far found in ancient documents. *Duckpuddle*, Cornwall, and similar names are probably of more recent origin.

Dove, from O.E. *dūfan*, 'to dive', appears to have been extended from water-birds to the pigeons – a variation paralleled by the Gk. *kolumbis*, 'a diver or grebe', from *kolumbān*, 'to plunge', beside L. *columba*, 'a dove'; and perhaps in *dovekie*, the seaman's name for the black guillemot and the little auk, the two notions come together again. This may be accounted for among the pigeons by the family habit of soaring and diving with extended wings in spring and summer.

The O.E. noun-form *dūfe* is found only in the compound *dūfedoppa*, 'a diving-bird of unknown species'; and in a few place-names such as *Duffield*, Derbyshire (*Duuelle* in the D.B.); N. and S. *Duffield*, East Riding (*Nortdufelt* and *Suddufeld* in the D.B.); and *Dufton*, Westmorland.

The *douve* of M.E. had a rival in another word suggesting diving – *culver* (the O.E. *culfre*, perhaps connected with L. *columba*). In the *Legende of Good Women* (line 2319) Chaucer wrote of 'the colver that of the egle is smyten'; though elsewhere he preferred *dove*. Two hundred years later Spenser, with his leaning towards archaisms, used 'culver' at least twice, namely in *The Teares of the Muses* (line 246):

> '(We) like woful Culuers doo sit wayling now;'

and in *The Faerie Queene* (II. 7. 34):

> 'More light then Culuer in the Faulcons fist'.

Dove, or *doo*, has probably always been the more popular name in the Northumbrian speech; *culver* is still heard in Wessex: yet from O.E. *culfre* comes the first element in *Cullercoats*, Northumberland, which is found as *Culvercoats* in records of about 1600.

Yet a third word for the Norman *pigeon* holds the notion of swift movement. The O.E. *cūscēote* or *cūscote* (from the imitative *cū* + *scēotan*, 'to shoot') became the northern *cushat* or *cushat doo*. Thomson in *Spring* (1725) used *dove* and *stock-dove*, but brought out the radical meaning of *cushat* when he wrote:

> '. . . borne on liquid wing,
> The sounding culver shoots.'

The name of *Cushat Law* ('woodpigeon hill'), Northumberland, is found as *Cousthotelau* in documents of *c.* 1200.

In *scoter*, first found in Ray's *Catalogue* (1674), perhaps appears again *scēotan*, or its Old Norse equivalent *skjota*, 'to shoot, to move rapidly'. Its root is found in words of many I-E. languages. It could be the same word as *scooter*, the toy, or the modified motor-cycle. So also the *shearwater*'s name has a parallel in the naval *cutter*'s.

In *merganser* the action is denoted by the first syllable. The name, found in von Gesner's *Historia Animalium* (1555), is composed of the L. *mergus*, some species of diving bird, and *anser*, 'a goose' – *mergus* being derived from *mergere*, 'to dip or dive', which provides English with many words, such as *merge*, *emerge*, and, from its supine stem, others such as *immersion*.

Wall- and tree-*creeper*, birds of different genera, take the common part of their trivial names, through M.E., from *crēopan*, 'to creep'. Turner's list (1544) contains *creeper*. The O.E. equivalent was *crēopere*, 'a cripple'.

The *fieldfare*, 'the traveller over the fields', preserves in its name that derivative of the root **per-* which scarcely lingers in English except in the East Anglian dialect, in which it *fares* ('appears') to have a variety of meanings, and in compounds such as *farewell, warfare, welfare,* and *thoroughfare.* Among many cognates of the O.E. *faran,* 'to travel', are Gk. *poreuesthai* and German *fahren.*

The adjectival element in the name of another traveller, the *peregrine falcon,* is akin to 'fare', the derivation being from the L. *peregrīnus* ('foreign'), which may stand for *per,* in the early sense of 'far', and *ager,* 'land'. From its migratory habits on the European continent *Falco peregrinus* was given its name by Albertus Magnus (*c.* 1250). *Peregrine falcon* was the English version used by Willughby and later writers. The *faucon pélerin, Wanderfalke, pilgrimsfalk, vandre- falk* of French, German, Swedish, and Danish, with equivalent names in other European languages, indicate widespread interest in tbe erratic migratory movements of the species, which has an almost worldwide distribution. These wanderings are no doubt partly accounted for by the parent falcons' fierce intolerance of the young birds, which, like those of many other species, must perforce become pilgrims until they can find territory of their own. *Pilgrim,* used in the Swedish name for the bird, reached English from L. *peregrinus* through Italian *pellegrino,* from which was taken also the M.L.G. *pilegrim.*

Courser, through French, ultimately derives from *curs-,* the supine stem of the L. *currere,* 'to run'. It therefore shares its descent with *current, cursory, excursion,* and a host of other words, including *corridor, courier, course, corsair,* and *hussar.*

'Roller' is accounted for by the amazing aerial acrobatics of the male bird in the breeding-season, and the canary of the same name by the trills in his song.

The name of our most homely bird, aptly called *domesticus* by Linnaeus, is rich in associations with human activities. *Sparrow,* the O.E. *spearwa* and M.E. *sparwe,* has the meaning of 'flutterer' – the one who, in the words of Austin Dobson, 'beateth-to his little wing'. The Teutonic root **sper-* and similar roots in Skt. and Greek, **sphur-* and **spar-,* mean 'to struggle, quiver, or shake'. **Sper-* appears even more plainly in the German *Sperling,* a diminutive form of the O.H.G. *sparo.* Low German and Scandinavian equivalents are Gothic *sparwa,* Icelandic *spör,* Swedish *sparv,* and Danish and Norwegian *spurv. Sparv* and *spurv* are used for both 'sparrow' and 'bunting'. (Cf. *sprosser,* 'sprinkler' of liquid melody.)

84

The Gothic *sparwa* and the O.H.G. *sparo* are kindred forms of the Gk. *strouthos*, the *p* and the *t* being interchanged (as one may see in the roots that branch out into a multitude of words, such as the English *spread* and *strew*). As in Latin *passer* meant 'sparrow', but *passer marinus*, 'the marine sparrow', i.e. the bird from overseas, meant 'ostrich', so for the Hellenes *strouthos* had the meaning of 'sparrow', but *ho megas strouthos* 'the big *strouthos*' or *strouthos katagaios* 'the on-the-ground *strouthos*, the walking bird' meant 'the ostrich'. One must suppose that *passer* and *strouthos* presented to the Romans and the Greeks a much more generalized notion than *sparrow* does to us; or the incongruity could hardly have failed to seem ludicrous. Yet 'spreader' is in fact a suitable name for both the wing-extending, dust-bathing, or love-making sparrow and the huge flightless bird as it raises its wings as sails and runs before the wind. (*Ostrich* in M.E. was *ostrice*, from L. *avis*, 'a bird', and Late Latin *struthio* – Gk. *strouthion*, a development of *strouthos*.)

Restlessness seems to be suggested also in *hobby* (so spelt by Turner, but as *hobbie* by Aldrovandus in 1599), if, as is probable, French had from Low German first *hobet* and later *hobereau* for the name of the little falcon, through the verb *hober*, 'to move about'.

If we could conscientiously attribute the name of the *lapwing* to its habit of flight, we might rest satisfied; but the etymology is not so simple. The M.E. word was *lappewince*; the O.E. *hlēapwince*. The O.E. verb *hlēapan* (our 'leap', German *laufen*) meant 'to run'. The second element in *hlēapwince* is found in *winch*, *wink*, *wince*, and kindred words in other I-E. languages, with the sense of twisting. There is the same suggestion in the slang word *wonky*. Thus *hlēapwince* seems to mean 'twisting as it runs' – a happy description of the pewit when he is feeding or showing off before his mate. The modern spelling is due to popular etymology: 'because he lappes or clappes the wings so often', says Minsheu in his *Guide into Tongues*, 1617.

Ekwall considers that *Winchendon*, Bucks., may make reference to the lapwing.

There are two names of adjectival force, one of which denotes rapid, while the other *may* denote slow, movement. *Swift*, first found in Willughby, is from the O.E. *swift*, an adjective from the weak grade of *swīfan*, 'to move quickly'. *Bustard*, found together with *bistard* in Turner's list, is derived, like the modern French *outarde*, from L. *avis*, 'bird', and a rather mysterious word *tarda*. *Tarda* being the feminine of L. *tardus*, 'slow', the meaning of the compound appears at first sight to be obvious, though not truly apposite. But Pliny (X. 22. 29) makes it clear that *tarda* was a Spanish word for the bustard: noting, '*aves, quas Hispania tardas appellat, Graecia ōtidas*' – 'birds which are called *tardae* by the Spaniards, and *ōtides* by the Greeks'.

Now perhaps a guess may be made at the significance of the debatable word in the scientific *Otis tarda*, and in the Romance languages, for a bird which is *not* slow, except during a few wing-beats after it has risen from the ground. The Portuguese is *abetarda* and the Italian *otarda*. The older Spanish *avetarda* was *abutarda*. In Dutch and Swedish; in Danish and Norwegian; and in German, the bird is (the large) *trap*, *trapp*, and *Trappe*. Four and a half centuries ago Turner gave *Träp* or *Trap Ganss* as the German name. The Finnish (presumably borrowed) is *trappi*. By normal consonant-change, the Russian is *dropha*, the Polish and Czech *drop*.

As *trap* is found in our *trap*, 'the snare' into which a creature may *tread*, and is strengthened or weakened in such words as *tramp*, *trample*, *traipse*, and *trip*, there is little doubt that these *trap* and *drop* names describe, namely the characteristic, dignified walk of the bustard, almost invariably referred to in English as 'stately'. Thus we arrive at 'tramper'. We may conjecture, therefore, that the radical part of 'tread', **trd-*, was present in the ancient Iberian word *tarda*, and that in 'bustard' we are using an ancient name, etymologically connected with *tread* and *trade* and not with *tardy*.

i𝔁 (c)

ANIMALS NAMED FROM ACTION: FOOD-FINDING

'There is no love sincerer than the love of food.'
G. B. SHAW, *Man and Superman.*

OF the birds which are named, wholly or partially, from their diet, the vegetarians are in the minority. There is one which may be classed as a kind of wolf in sheep's clothing. This is the *honey-buzzard*, whose principal diet consists of wasps, wild bees, and their larvae. In 1663, while Francis Willughby was studying the species, during his journey with John Ray from England to Italy, he found the comb of bees on the sides of nests, and coined the name which has unfortunately stuck.

It is a moot point whether the *hawfinch* is so named from its frequenting *haws*, i.e. hedges, or from the fact that the berry of the *hawthorn*, 'hedge-thorn', is a favourite food. There is, however, no ambiguity in *mistle-thrush*, since the first element in the name denotes *mistletoe*, the berries of which are a staple part of the bird's diet in localities where the plant is to be found. This partiality towards mistletoe-berries was known to observers of nature long before the Christian era.

The difference between the methods employed by the *nuthatch* (*Sitta europaea*) and the *nutcracker* (*Nucifraga caryocatactes*) is neatly shown by their names. The *nuthatch* is the 'nut-hacker', the provincial 'nut-jobber', and is so called from its habit of hammering with its bill until it splits the nut which it has previously, if necessary, wedged in a crevice in a tree. The *nutcracker* (a modern formation on *nut* and *crack*) was noted by Turner as *nucifraga* (L. *nux*, 'a nut' + *frangere*, 'to break') from the dialect name of a bird which he saw in the Rhaetian Alps.

The *bean-goose* or *corn-goose* indicates by its name its food-preference, the bulk of the diet of other species of geese being grass and sea-ware. Another grain-eater is the *linnet*. Whether the name is derived from the O.F. *linette* (now *linotte*) or the O.E. *linece*, it originated in the L. *līnum*, 'flax', whence come the O.E. *līn* and our *linen* and *linseed*. The northern *lintwhite* is a descendant of the other O.E. name *līnetwige*, 'flax-twister'. The Germans, Swedes, and Finns also consider the bird as a seed-picker, naming it *Hänfling*, *hämpling*, and *hemppo*, from *Hänf*, etc., 'hemp'. The *chaffinch* may be included in this category, though it is not the *chaff* (O.E. *ceaf*) that interests him, but the chance grains among it.

Of the names of our birds of prey the one suggesting the largest victims is *goshawk*, i.e. *goose-hawk*, Chaucer's *goshauk* or *goshauke*. In the language of falconry *goshawk* is used for the female, the smaller male being called *tiercel* or *tassel*, as is also the male peregrine – more probably owing to the fact that he is about one third smaller than his mate than to the belief that a brood of three consists of two females and one male, though this may often be true. (See Chapter XXXI.) *Goshawk* has parallels in the provincial *mousehawk* (O.E. *mūshafoc*) for the kestrel; in an obsolete name for marsh-harrier and buzzard, *puttock*, which probably represents 'toad-hawk' (M.E. *padde*, 'toad'); and in *sparrow-hawk*, Chaucer's *sperhauk*, the male of which species was formerly known as *musket*. Later this supplied a name for a small fire-arm; as other hawks gave their names to other types of gun, e.g. *falconet* and *saker*. *Musket* has the meaning of 'fly-sized', the M.F. *mosquet* being derived from Italian *moschetto*, diminutive of *mosca*, 'a fly', the L. *musca*.

The name of the *hen-harrier*, which Turner called *hen harroer* or *ringtale*, denotes not sex but robbery in the fowl-runs; that of Chaucer's *merlion*, the *merlin* (to falconers the female of the *jack* or *jack-merlin*), seems traceable through the F. *émerillon* to the L. *merula*, 'a blackbird'. If it is, the initial sound of the intermediate word, the M.F. *esmerillon*, was intrusive. The allusion might be to the size (the jack's being approximately that of a blackbird) or to the prey – though birds of many other species, notably larks and pipits, are more often taken than blackbirds.

The *Boke of St Alban's* details the hawks that might be flown by men of different ranks – and one lady. At the head was the *gyrfalcon*:

'The gentyl faucoun that with his feet distrayneth
The kynges hond.'
Chaucer, *Parlement of Foules*, 337.

After the nobler falcons for prince, duke, earl, and baron came the *saker* for the knight, the *lanner* for the squire, the *merlin* for the lady, and the *hobby* for the 'young man'. The yeoman's bird was the *goshawk*; the 'poor man' had to be content with her mate, the *tiercel*. The priest and 'holy water clerk' (a clerk in minor orders, such as an exorcist) flew respectively the *sparrow-hawk* and the *myrkyte* – probably the musket, rather than the moor-buzzard or harrier. Last came the *kestrel* for the 'knave' or servitor.

Apart from 'herring-gull', 'kingfisher', the 'kynges fissher' of Turner (O.E. *fiscere*), is the only standard name pointing to a fish-diet. Kirke Swann cites it as being also a local name for the common tern on Lough Neagh, and for the dipper in the Scottish Highlands and in part of Ireland.

Although, as we may see, there is some evidence that the name of the *scaup* is taken from its cry, the theory connected with its feeding on small mollusca and crustaceans collectively known as *scaup* or *scalp* may be noted as we turn our attention to the name of the oystercatcher. This was transferred to our bird – previously known as *sea-pie* – from the American species *Haematopus palliatus* named in 1731 by Mark Catesby. (See Chapter XXVII.) R. H. Pough (*Audubon Bird-Book*) includes 'clams and coon oysters' with mussels, cockles, limpets, snails, crabs, and other crustacea in the dietary of *H. palliatus*; but oysters at best, or worst, can be only a small percentage of the food of the European *H. ostralegus*, though the bird makes havoc among the mussels and limpets, which are prised from their rocky seats by its strong bill.

Insect-diet accounts for *flycatcher* and *bee-eater*. The bee-eater (which has equivalent names in many other European languages, including the Modern Gk. *melissophagos*) is so rare a visitor to Britain that the name, except on the lips of an ornithologist, is likely to refer to the great tit, which is regarded with justifiable suspicion by apiarists as a bird which on occasion develops a taste for hive-bees.

Though the *carrion-crow* is far from being the only bird with a taste for high meat, it is reserved for it to bear a name stigmatizing it as a foul feeder.

BIRDS' NAMES BASED ON SOUND

'We must weigh our words as the ancients often
weighed their coins, and not be deceived by their
current value.'

MAX MÜLLER, *The Science of Language.*

THE name of our totem-bird, the crane, can be traced back to the
I-E. root **gar-*. An excellent introduction to this prolific root is to
be found in Max Müller's analysis of some of the bird-names rooted
in **kar-* and **krus-*.

' "Raven" ', says the great philologist (*Lectures on the Science of
Language*), 'which in outward appearance differs from L. *corvus*
much more than "crow", offers much less real difficulty in being
traced back to the same source from which sprang *corvus*; for "raven"
is the Anglo-Saxon *hræfen* or *hræfn*, and its first syllable *hræ* would be
a legitimate substitue for the Latin *cor*. Opinions differ widely as to
the root or roots from which the various names of the crow, the
raven, and the rook in the Aryan languages are derived. Those who
look on Sanskrit as the most primitive form of Aryan speech are
disposed to admit the Sanskrit *kārava* as the original type; and as
kārava is by native etymologists derived from *kā + rava* (making a
harsh noise), *ru*, to make a noise (from the root of *rava*, noise), was
readily fixed upon as the etymon for the corresponding words in
Latin, Greek, and German. If *kārava, corvus, korōnē,* and *hræfn* are
cognate words, it would be more advisable to look upon the *k* as
part of the radical, and thus to derive all these words from a root
kru, a secondary form, it may be, of the root *ru*. This root *kru*, or in
its more primitive form, *ru* . . . is not a mere imitation of the cry of
the raven; it embraces many cries, from the harshest to the softest,
and it might have been applied to the note of the nightingale as
well as to the cry of the raven. In Sanskrit the root *ru* is applied in
its verbal and nominal derivatives to the murmuring sounds of
birds, bees, and trees, to the barking of dogs, to the lowing of cows,

and the whispering of men. In Latin we have from it both *raucus*, hoarse, and *rumor*, a whisper; in German *runan*, to speak low, and *runa*, a mystery. . . . By the addition of final letters *ru* appears as the Sanskrit *rud*, to cry, and as the Latin *rug* in *rugire*, to howl. By the addition of both initial and final letters we get the Sanskrit *krus*, to shout, the Greek *kraugē*, a yell, and the Gothic *hrukjan*, to crow. . . . But, although, as far as the meaning of *kārava*, *corvus*, and *hræfn* is concerned, there would seem no difficulty in deriving them from the root *kru*, to sound, I have nowhere found a satisfactory explanation of the exact etymological process by which the Sanskrit *kārava* could be formed from *kru*. We may say that *kārava* is a regular derivative of the Sanskrit *karu*. This *karu* means literally one who shouts. It comes from a root *kar*, to shout, to praise, to record. . . . Its derivative *kārava* was therefore applied to the raven in the general sense of "the shouter". All the other names of the raven can easily be traced back to the same root *kar* . . . while the English "rook", the Anglo-Saxon *hrōc*, the Old High German *hruoh*, would seem to derive their origin from a different root altogether, viz. from the Sanskrit *krus*.'

Not the least important lesson to be learnt from this careful analysis is that superficial resemblances are often misleading. Too close a resemblance between words in different languages should make the enquirer slow to presume a common origin. The name *raven* as it appears in M.E. and today, and the verb to *raven* may serve as an example; for they are unconnected. That the verb is a derivative of L. *rapere*, 'to seize' (through *rapinam*, 'plunder'), might at first sight seem to point to the origin of the name of a notorious destroyer of weakly lambs and other easy prey; but the application of scientific principles shows, as we have seen, that the search must proceed along other lines. But if we were to connect these two words we should err in good company with Milton, who described Elijah's ravens bringing food 'though ravenous taught to abstain from what they brought' (P.R. II. 69).

Rook holds a similar lure towards false etymology. Some have tried to trace the name to the bird's colour. 'The Old English form *hrōc*,' they say, 'meant "smoky black"; as for smoke or *reek*, the German is *Rauch*, and the form in one north-country dialect is actually *rook*. The archaic adjective *rooky* had the significance of "misty", "darkling". The words from the lips of Macbeth may have had this significance:

> "Light thickens, and the crow
> Makes wing to the rooky wood."

Tennyson, in *The Last Tournament*, used the word without ambiguity, when Tristram,

> "pressing night and day through Lyonesse,
> Last in a roky hollow, belling, heard
> The hounds of Mark." '

How plausible this argument sounds, and how inextricably connected seems the name of our bird with the Dutch *rook* and the *rök*, *rög*, and *Rauch*, which are the equivalent words for 'smoke' in Swedish, Danish, and German! But now we find that the O.N., the O.H.G., and the O.E. forms for the bird-name are *hrōkr*, *hruoh*, and *hrōc*; whereas the verb 'to smoke' is represented in the same tongues by *rjuka*, *reohhan*, and *rēocan*. In short, the names for the bird, such as the English *rook*, the Danish *raage*, and the Swedish *råka*, are sprung from words not beginning with a simple *r* (as are all the words in the *reek* group), but with an *r* preceded by a guttural. The name therefore has nothing to do with *reek* ('smoke'), but is certainly akin to *croak* and *creak*, earlier types of which are to be found in the Gothic *hrūkjan* and the Gk. *krōzein*, whence we are led back to the root cited by Max Müller, namely **krus-*.

The large number of place-names containing some allusion to the raven – *Rainow, Ramsbury, Ramskill, Ravendale, Ravenscar*, etc., through *hræfn*; and *Ranscombe*, and perhaps others, through the alternative form *hremn* – is about equal to the number of names embracing those of the (frequently confused) rook and crow together – *Ruckinge, Rookwith, Craster, Croydon Hill*, etc. The *raven* names will have an even longer lead if the O.E. *hræfn* or the O.N. *hrafn*, often occurring as a personal name, really in some doubtful instances refers to the bird. That most of the *raven* places are inland and distributed all over England is part of the evidence of what is well-known, that the species was formerly far more abundant than it is now.

Before considering *crow*, which differs in origin from both *raven* and *rook*, and which will lead our thoughts to birds of other families, we may examine the names of the chough and the jackdaw, whose various appellations are even more closely connected together than are their possessors.

In M.E. are found *co*, *coo*, also *chogh(e)*, *chough*, taking the place of O.E. *cio* and *ceo*, and the still earlier forms *ciae* and *chyae*, for both chough and jackdaw.

There can be little doubt which of the two birds was referred to as 'the theef the chough' in Chaucer's *Parlement of Foules* (line 345). When, however, we read that King Lear, from the top of Shakespeare's Cliff, west of Dover, spoke of

'The crows and choughs that wing the midway air,'

we need not suspect that 'choughs' did not refer to the slender-billed bird – though the 'crows' may have been jackdaws. The chough, says Dr James Harrison, had ceased to breed in its Kentish home, the Dover cliffs, by 1850; but in Dunkin's *History of Kent* (1857) we read that 'before a war of extermination was ruthlessly waged against the Chough or red-legged Crow, Cornish Chough, Cornish Daw . . . red-legged Jack Daw . . . Cliff Daw, Gesner's Wood Crow, this bird was very plentiful among the Dover cliffs'. The quotation incidentally points to the promiscuous use of 'chough', 'daw', and 'crow'.

Cabourn, *Caville*, *Cawood*, and *Kaber*, in Lincs., Yorks., Lancs., and Westmorland, commemorate stream, field, wood, and hill haunted by jackdaws.

Few birds have been so universally named from their cries as has the jackdaw. In this respect he is a rival of the comparatively few other birds which show that onomatopoeia cannot be entirely ignored – a rival, that is to say of such birds as the cuckoo, cock, and hoopoe. To the Westcountryman he is *chawk* or *chatterjack*; to the Scot *kae*. He is the French *choucas*, the Italian *taccola*. His Spanish names, *grajillo* and *grajo* (from L. *grāculus*, an offshoot of *grācillare*, 'to cackle like a hen') are good examples of names which, however onomatopoetically satisfying, may be traced back to words having a less specialized significance.

The name 'daw' is traceable only as far back as the 15th century. An O.E. **dawe* may be presumed. This would correspond to the O.H.G. *taha*. From a diminutive of *taha*, *tahele*, sprang the L. *tacula* whence came the Italian *taccola* mentioned above. The Shakespearian form was always plain *daw*; but *Iacke dawe* was in use by the first half of the 16th century. Towards the end of the following century Robert Wild, Willughby, and others were writing of 'jack-daws';

but the name had been unhyphened in Lovell's *Panzoologico-mineralogica* (1661) and Merrett's *Pinax Rerum Naturalium Britannicarum* (1667). By the end of the 18th century the modern form of the name was practically always used. Plain *daw*, however, died hard. Thomson, for instance, in *Summer* and *Spring* (1727, 1728) was true to *daw*, though he wrote 'magpie'; and Carlyle still clung to the simple name in 1872. W. H. Hudson showed a preference for *daw*, but used *jackdaw* for variety.

Although a word, so it is said, cannot have two etymologies, its direct course may be influenced by analogy; and an imitative name (which can in any event but poorly reproduce inarticulate sounds) can hardly fail to be conditioned by words already in the vocabulary of the namer; as was suggested by the mention of the Spanish *grajo*, of which the parent word *grāculus* implied a reference to the clucking of a hen. There are moreover other influences which may help to produce an imitative name. Thus, whereas each element of the word *jackdaw* has an imitative basis, the appositeness of the more modern and more directly onomatopoetic *jack* is reinforced by its implication of small size (in comparison with the size of other corvine birds). This depreciative sense of *jack* is common in English. The *jacks* of a pack of cards are the 'knaves', or 'boys'. A multitude of terms can be found to accompany *Jack-a-dandy*, *Jackanapes*, *Jack Straw*, *Jack-in-office*, *jackass*, *cheapjack*, and *skipjack*. By falconers *jack* is prefixed to merlin and hobby to denote the male birds, which observe the general rule that male birds of prey are smaller than their mates. The *jack-snipe* is smaller than the common snipe; the *jack-curlew* (whimbrel) is smaller than its near congener.

In many of the provincial names, such as that last mentioned, *jack* implies familiarity rather than contempt. Thus in some southern counties the once common and now fast-vanishing red-backed shrike was called, not so long ago, *Jack Baker*. (Curiously enough, the more obvious name of *Jack Butcher* does not seem to have been used for the *butcher-bird*.) *Flusher*, i.e. *flesher*, for the same species has disappeared, though recorded in Ray's English translation of the Latin of Willughby (1678). Kirke Swann (1912) listed the following local names from various parts of the British Isles: *Jack Bird* 'fieldfare'; *Jack Doucker* 'dabchick'; *Jack Hawk* 'kestrel'; *Jack Hern* 'heron'; *Jack Ickle* 'green woodpecker'; *Jackie Foster* 'long-tailed duck'; *Jack-in-a-bottle* 'long-tailed tit'; *Jack Nicker* or *Jack-a-Nickas* 'goldfinch'; *Jack*

94

Plover 'dunlin'; *Jack Squealer* 'swift'; *Jack Straw* 'whitethroat'; and *Jacksaw* 'great tit'. Although some of the birds in that list might be accused of harsh utterances, the syllable *jack* could hardly suggest itself as a rendering of the cries of more than a few of them.

In conclusion, it may be assumed that, had *Jack* not been well-known as a proper name – quite apart from any depreciative suggestion – the daw might quite as reasonably have had prefixed to his name a syllable such as *yack* or *chack*. As it is, it would be idle to deny that *jack* is among the best imitations of the bird's staccato cry.

We have seen that *rook* is traceable to the root **krus-*; *raven* to the root **kar-*. From **kar-* comes also the L. *corvus*, which supplies the first element in the name of the cormorant, originally *corvus marīnus*, 'raven of the sea'. *Crow*, however, despite the superficial resemblance to *corvus*, is derived from neither **kar-* nor **krus-*, but from the root **gar-*, 'to cry out, to sound'. The Dutch *kraai* and the German *Krähe* are from *kraaijen* and *krähen*, 'to crow', as the O.E. *crāwe* was from *crāwan*. The modern form is the same as in Middle English. The verb appears in Old Slavonic as *grajati*; and among other kindred words are the Skt. *gir* and Russian *golos*, 'a voice'; the Gk. *gerus*, 'speech'; the Welsh *galw*, 'to call', and *gair*, 'a word'; the Danish *gala*, 'to crow'; and the L. *garrire*, 'to chatter'.

When people call rooks 'crows', they are of course technically correct; but if a gamekeeper mistakes a distant rook for a carrion-crow, the bird is lucky to be out of gunshot. Though countryfolk in some localities use the one name for both species, the confusion may not have existed for more than a few centuries; yet the birds certainly began to be muddled before the beginning of the 17th century, when Shakespeare, speaking through the lips of Lear, while the poor king wandered (where this page is being written) 'in the country near Dover', said, 'That fellow handles his bow like a crow-keeper', that is to say 'a person employed to keep rooks from the cornfields', like Hardy's young Jude.

Names of inhabited places in England which ancient documents show to have been connected with the birds are about equally divided between *hrōc* and *crāwe*. The use of one name or the other did not depend on locality. Northumberland, for instance, has its *Rochester* and *Craster*. Lincolnshire and Norfolk have *Ruckland* and *Rockland*; Cambridgeshire has *Crowdon* and *Croydon Hall*. Devon has *Rockhope*; Somerset has *Crowcombe*. A dozen or more other such names

95

are scattered among as many other counties. The total number is about what one might expect in regard to birds (a) fairly large, (b) familiar everywhere, but not so common as to be disregarded. Since it has been decided that carrion-crow and hoodie are merely regional variants, there is no need to make more complicated this outline-analysis in support of the belief that the crow, when it was still called *crawe* or *craw*, was considerably more numerous, and the rook less common, than they respectively are today. Sir Walter Scott habitually wrote of the *hooded* crow, even when the scene was in the south – e.g. in *Ivanhoe*.

The *rook* (castle) on the chessboard is not a relative of the bird. The original Persian *rukh* may have meant 'a warrior'. The slang 'to rook' indicates someone's acquaintance with the habits of the incorrigible stealer of sticks from the nests of its neighbours while it is building its own nest. Long before English used 'crowbar' for a pointed length of iron, the Romans gave the name *corvus* to the beaked piece of iron hinged to the mast of a warship ready to be dropped as a grappling-hook on the deck of a hostile vessel.

*　　*　　*

The *Corvidae* have by no means exhausted the roots **kar-*, **krus-*, and **gar-* in the names of our birds. *Crane*, the O.E. *cran*, is another offshoot of **gar-*. Cognate words in other Germanic tongues, such as the O.N. *trani* (for *krani*) – in modern Icelandic and Swedish *trana*; in Danish and Norwegian *trane* – the O.H.G. *chranuh*, modern German *Kranich*; with the Welsh, Cornish, and Breton *garan*, the Gk. *geranos*, and the L. *grus* (whence the French *grue*, as in *pied de grue*), indicate the universal attention that the crane has attracted to itself by its voice.

> 'To warmer seas the cranes embodied fly,
>> With noise, and order, through the midway sky.'
>> Homer, *Iliad* III. 3: trans. Alexander Pope.

>> 'Quales sub imbribus atris
> Strymoniae dant signa grues atque aethera tranant
> Cum sonitu.'

> (As cranes by Strymon, when dark clouds arise,
>> Trumpet a warning, while they cleave the skies.)
>>> Vergil, *Aeneid* X. 264.

96

'Like as the birds, that winter near the Nile,
In squared regiment direct their course,
Then stretch themselves in file for speedier flight.'
Dante, *Purgatorio* XXIV. 63: trans. H. F. Cary.

'The crane the geaunt with his trompes soun.'
Chaucer, *Parlement of Foules*, 344.

Ancient and mediaeval literature abounds in such references, which often show that the writers knew a good deal about the life-history of the crane, and not infrequently suggest that, in company with the swift, woodpeckers, plovers (F. *pluvier*, 'rain-bird'), and other birds with notably piercing or resounding cries, the crane has from remote times been considered as a weather-prophet. It is one of the many birds with a highly specialized vocal mechanism. Except in the crowned crane *Balearica pavonina*, whose note is a quite subdued piping, the trachea (windpipe) is not merely long, but is also coiled, the coils fitting into a recess in the sternum (breastbone); and these adaptations so greatly increase the volume and resonance of the bird's cry that it is not surprising that early man should have marked out the crane as a 'crier'.

Britain's loss of the crane as a breeding-bird was certainly not brought about by any lack of vigilance in the mental make-up of this most wary of birds, nor by the disappearance of the type of place where it could breed and feed, but chiefly (whatever other conditioning factors there may have been) by the elimination of tracts *extensive enough* for its way of life. For the crane's desire, when on the ground, is not merely to be out of bowshot, but out of eyeshot of its great enemy, man, who persecutes it because of the damage which it does to his crops.

It may be said that Christianity played a considerable part in hastening the doom of the crane in England. For a thousand years the status of the species will have been inversely proportionate to the success of the temporal activities of the Church. Its numbers must have gone down as land-drainage and agriculture advanced in the neighbourhood of the many monastic settlements in the 7th century. Often the monasteries were in places chosen for their very desolation, as Croyland, Ely, and Thorney-in-the-Fens. The number of cranes may have increased for half a century or so after the Black Death, reaching England in 1348, had carried off more than half of the four or five million people in this country and occasioned the reversion of great areas of land to their primitive swampy state. Then, having dropped for a while, the tally may have risen again during the second half of the 16th century; for the dissolution of the monasteries under Henry VIII, 'when all the institutions of the poor were savagely seized to be the private possessions of the rich', led to another reversion of huge expanses of arable land and pasture into their original condition. Cranes are known to have bred until the end of the 16th century in East Anglia, where large tracts of what is incorrectly called *re*claimed land had again become water-logged, remaining so until the General Draining Act of 1600 began to be implemented in that district. The appearance of surveyors all over their haunts would have been quite enough to drive the shy birds away long before the actual work was put in hand.

In two out of every three English counties are towns and villages with names founded on that of the crane. *Cranbourne*, Hants.; *Cransley*, Northants.; *Cranfield*, Beds.; *Cranford*, Middlesex; *Cranbrook*, Kent; *Cranmere*, Salop.; East and West *Cranmore*, Somerset; *Cranham*, Glos., and several other names are found (in their earlier forms) in records of the 10th to the early 12th century. *Cranwell*, Lincs.; *Cransford*, Suffolk; and *Cranwich* and *Cranworth*, Norfolk, appear in the Domesday Book. The river *Garron* or *Garren* in Herefordshire is the river *Crane* (Welsh *garan*). *Grindalhythe*, E. Riding, stands for 'Crane-valley', with the addition of O.N. *hlidh*, 'a slope'.

Whether a place-name beginning Cor- or Corn- refers to the bird or to grain can almost always be decided by scanning the form of the word in ancient documents and often by the evidence in the documents themselves. Such names from crane are *Cornwell*, Oxon.; *Coreley*, Salop.; *Cornwood*, Devon; *Corley*, Warwickshire; *Cornborough*, N. Riding; *Cornforth*, co. Durham; and *Cornhill*, Northumberland.

What is perhaps of greater significance in what we have now to consider is that in a number of names the O.N. *trana* or *trani* appears as *tran-*, *tarn-*, or *tren-*, as in *Tranmere*, Cheshire (*trani* + *melr*, 'a sandbank'); *Tranwell*, Northumberland; *Tarnacre*, Lancs. (*tarna* + *akr*, 'a field'); *Tranholme*, N. Riding ('cranes' stream').

It is sometimes stated that these names do not go to prove that the crane formerly had breeding-places all over England, on the ground that 'crane' is a provincial name for the heron. Those who have made a study of old documents do not agree to this. Ekwall, from a profound knowledge of all the languages, and a great many of the places, concerned, says roundly in the *Oxford Dictionary of English Place-Names* (1936), 'There is no reason to assume any other meaning for the word, such as "heron". The two birds are always kept well apart in early records'. Both 'crane' and 'heroune' appear, for instance, in Chaucer's *Parlement of Foules*, and frequently in the 'Household Books' of great families, in which the cost of a crane for the table rises sharply year by year in comparison with that of a heron.

It is highly probable that any local transference that there may have been of the name 'crane' to the heron is comparatively recent. What is most puzzling is that it should ever have taken place. In any event it points to the crane's having been once a familiar sight to people living far from the last haunts of the species in England. Only when cranes were no longer to be seen in their former breeding-areas could countryfolk have confused the well-known heron with the noble bird about which their fathers or grandfathers told the tale. It is hardly credible that the name *crane* was used indifferently for crane or heron by men of the Middle Ages. Except that either kind might be seen by the river or out in the marsh, the peasant could not fail to know that their habits were widely different. He would not, for instance, have persecuted the heron (even if he had dared to flout the game-laws*) as a marauder in his barley-fields; nor would he have thought to find cranes roosting in his lord's woods. Certainly from the Norman falconer, with his precise speech about 'herds' of cranes and 'sieges' of herons, the Saxon churl would have had short shrift if he had pointed to a *jack hern* and called it a *cran*. Furthermore, communications in the Middle Ages were too imperfect to make it probable that the name would spread from the crane's unquestioned breeding-places in East Anglia to remote parts of England.

In brief, that after the disappearance of the crane its name should have been used locally for a bird of contrasted habits seems an

*By 19 Henry VII (1503), to kill a heron, except with a hawk or longbow, was punishable by a fine of 6/8d. For poaching a young bird from the nest the fine was 10/-. By 25 Henry VIII (1533) there was a penalty of 20d. for taking or destroying a heron's egg. (For equivalents in 1971, multiply by 40 or 50: for those in 1975, by ———?). One shudders to think what interference with the falconer's finest quarry would have cost a man before the passing of these mild laws; or what would have been the fate of a 16th-century poacher if he had no money to pay the fine.

integral part of the evidence that this giant cousin of the moorhen and the coot was, centuries ago, a summer-resident in suitable tracts in widely separated districts where land-drainage as we know it today was negligible.

It is worthy of note that there are far fewer place-names commemorating the commoner bird – i.e. beginning with 'Heron' or its equivalents – such as the hamlet of *Heronden* in Kent (locally pronounced, except by the pretentious, as 'Harnden'), or somewhat disguised, as in the Essex *Rawreth* (O.E. *hrāgra* + *rīth*, 'stream'). Generally *Herne* or *Hurn* (e.g. near Christchurch, Hants.) has a different significance, such as a bend of a river, or angle; the O.E. *hyrne*, 'corner', passing with slightly changed form into M.E., as in Chaucer's *Franklin's Tale*, line 1121:

> 'yonge clerkes . . .
> Seken in every halke and every herne
> Particuler sciences for to lerne.'

Heronries will have been too common to occasion many place-names.

*　　*　　*

Grouse, first found as *grows* in 1531, is a word of doubtful origin. The plural of Med. L. *gruta*, presumably indicating 'grouse', is used for certain wildfowl by Giraldus Cambrensis in his *Topographica Hibernica*, written towards the end of the 12th century. The word, reminiscent of Gk. *gru*, 'the grunt of a pig', may claim descent from the root **gar-*, despite the retention of the *g*; for it may be, according to Skeat, 'of Celtic origin and allied to "crow" '.

In *gallinule* **gar-* is less obvious, until it is remembered how nearly related are the semivowels *l* and *r*. Everyone knows of the difficulty experienced by some Orientals in pronouncing our *r*, a sound not found in their dialects. An English-speaking Siamese, having strenuously practised the *l* and *r* sounds, was heard to apologize for being 'vely crumsy'. The two liquid letters or trills are often interchanged in the I-E. languages. The change in the F. *rossignol* from the popular Latin *lusciniolus*, 'a nightingale', is paralleled by the difference of the liquids in L. *garrire*, 'to chatter', and *gallus* (originally *garlus*) 'a cock' – both from root **gar-*. From *gallus* came *gallina*, 'a hen', and *gallinula*, 'a chicken' – whence our *gallinule*, a name discarded in English for the moorhen and corncrake (the 'crake-gallinule' of

Willughby and others), but kept for some of the moorhen's relatives in various parts of the world.

As the *nightjar* is the bird that churrs at night, so Chaucer's *nyghtyngale* is the 'night-singer'; though an intrusive *n* attempts to obscure the meaning apparent in the O.E. *nihtegala* (*niht*, 'night' + *gala*, from *galan*, 'to sing'). *Galan* is cognate with *giellan* or *gellan*, 'to yell'. The O.H.G. name of the bird was *nahtagala*, and living Teutonic languages other than English still preserve the purer form of the word, as Dutch *nachtegaal*, German *Nachtigall*, and Danish *nattergal*.

Two ancient names, now used for the most part only locally, keep *nightingale* company;

Yaffle, the commonest provincial name for the green woodpecker, is an imitative name, a 19th-century dialect word meaning to 'bark', 'mutter', or 'make the sound of a green woodpecker'. The bird has also been called *yapping-gale*, as in Tennyson, *The Last Tournament* – which takes the name back to *galan*.

Standgale and *stannel*, with the *staniel* of *Twelfth Night*, II. 5. 126, and other variants, represent the O.E. *stāngella* or *stāngiella*, 'stone-yeller', i.e. the kestrel, for which cliffs and rock-ledges provide typical breeding-places where no woods offer hollow trees or the old nests of crows or the dreys of the fast-vanishing red squirrel. *Standgale* is an etymologizing alteration used through the misconception that it was a synonym for 'windhover' – another provincial name referring to a quite different habit. The O.E. *stāngella* was also used to translate the 'pelican in the wilderness' of Psalm 102 – not a bad shot for a 9th century Englishman!

$\mathcal{XI}$ (a)

'CUCKOO, JUG-JUG, PU-WE, TO-WITTA-WOO'

'The merry larke his mattins sings aloft;
The thrush replyes; the mavis descant playes;
The ouzell shrills; the ruddock warbles soft.'
SPENSER, *Epithalamion*.

HAVING well in mind that articulate language cannot have *originated* in a collection of nouns imitating sounds, before we discuss what was once the trump-card of the old Onomatopoetic school, let us (still, for convenience, limiting ourselves to birds) consider some names which may or may not show themselves to be echoic.

The ancestors of the Hebrews may have been calling the turtle-dove (and the maiden in the next tent) *tor*; and the inhabitants of North America may have been naming tits (chickadees) *ch'-gee-gee*, the raven *ka-ka-gos*, and the horned owl *koo-koo-skoos* – or something of the sort – for thousands of years before the composition of the *Song of Solomon* or the sailing of the *Mayflower*. So also in English, and indeed in all languages, we find a few names of mammals, some of insects (e.g. Skt. *bhramara*, 'humble-bee'), and a multitude of bird-names which are directly imitative, the loveliest, perhaps, being the Persian *bulbul*. North American names include a large number of them, some being primitive, and some comparatively modern inventions of the colonists. A few of these have come to Britain with wanderers such as the *killdeer* (plover), the *bobolink*, and the *bobwhite* (the American quail), which is now known in parts of Britain through birds which have been introduced in order to be shot. These, however, will not give us licence to offer onomatopoeia as the full explanation of even such a name as *crake*.

Imitative as *crake* may be, it is not by chance that it has been formed by the side of words such as *creak*, *croak*, and *crack* (O.E. *cracian*). In the days when one did not have to go far through the fields in summer to find the corncrake breeding, rubbing the finger-nail along a comb reproduced his cry well enough to attract the skulking bird. That was true imitation of inarticulate sound; and it deceived a bird which would not be beguiled by a man's muttering 'crake, crake' until his patience was exhausted. That the name is individual, however, and not one which might be applied to each of a number of species uttering various grating cries, is shown by the common factor in dialect-forms for *crake* is divergent as *rake, drake, scrape, scrack,* and *creek.* In each of these names there is the attempt to reproduce the *rrrr* of the landrail's cry.

The most intriguing of these by-names is the West Country *rape-scrape,* which seems to provide a clue to the debated origin of the alternative name. *Rail,* in *landrail* and *water-rail,* is from F. *râle,* the modern form of the O.F. *raalle,* through the intermediate *rasle.* This *raalle* has been thought to be of Teutonic origin; but German is even more chary than English of a syllable both beginning and ending with a liquid (*r, l*). With two exceptions the odd dozen German words beginning with such a syllable are all borrowed from Latin, or from Latin through French: e.g. *relativ, rollen* (F. *rouler,* from L. *rotula,* 'a wheel'). One of the two exceptions is *Rülps,* with the verbal form *rülpsen,* 'to belch': the other is *Ralle,* 'a corncrake or rail'. We may accordingly begin to suspect that both *Ralle* and *rail* are either imitative or borrowed from Latin – possibly both. Now Latin also tended to shun syllables both beginning and ending with a liquid. (A Latin word beginning *rel-* is invariably a compound of *re-* and some other word; so that in such a word the *l* starts the second syllable.) Apart from the proper name *Ralla,* Latin had only two words beginning with *ral-.* One, seldom used, was *rallus,* a contraction of *rarulus,* from *rarus,* 'thin'. The other was *rallum* (a derivative of *radere,* 'to scrape'). It denoted an instrument for scraping a plough-share, in the manner of the small piece of wood used by some gardeners for scraping their spades and called a 'gardener's man'. In *rallum* we find exactly the word which might be expected to be the source of 'rail', the bird which utters a noise like that made by the tool which scrapes the ploughshare – the bird which was called 'rape-scrape' by the Wessex peasant. Thus *radere,* which gives us *erase, razor,* and *rascal,* could perhaps be also the progenitor of 'rail'. But if the learned etymologists object that we have not accounted for the *s* in the French form, we may have to fall back on their 'Rom. **rascula,* prob. imit.' (Onions).

There is a *Crakemarsh* in Somerset, and in Yorkshire are *Crakehall* and *Crakehill* ('flat by the river frequented by rails').

Another deceptively onomatopoetic name is *murre*. Used only locally in England, it is the standard trivial name in North America for the guillemot, Brünnich's guillemot being called 'thick-billed murre'. Anyone acquainted with the incessant growling of the birds on their breeding-ledges might think it a mere imitation of the noise made by guillemots – and razorbills, which Willughby said had the name of *murre* in Cornwall. That the word is imitative is clear; but we need not go as far back as Sanskrit *marmara* or Latin *murmur* – words meaning rustling, grumbling, murmuring, and so forth – to see that *murre* does not owe its origin to the auks. German, for instance, has *murren*, 'to grumble'; but the nearest modern verbal kindred are Scandinavian, such as Danish *murre*, 'to grumble or growl'. These at once proclaim *murre* as a name imported by the Vikings or later Norse invaders, and having the basic meaning of 'growler'.

Swan, found in the same form in O.E. and M.E., means 'the sounder', being sprung from the root **swen-*, 'to resound', the base of the L. *sonus*, 'a sound', and of an array of English words such as *consonant, sonnet, sonorous, assonance, person,* and *parson*. (See Chapter XXXII.)

> 'Dant sonitum rauci per stagna loquacia cycni.'
> (The hoarse-voiced swans are calling where the
> pools are noisy with frogs.)
> Vergil, *Aeneid* XI 458

Many place-names beginning with 'Swan' are ambiguous, since the O.E. *swān* (the O.N. *sveinn*, 'a boy or servant'; our obsolescent *swain* which holds on in *boatswain*) meant 'a farmhand or herdsman', generally 'a swineherd'. Possibly the Saxons called a swan-keeper **swaneswān*. The place-names, moreover, are all the fewer because another O.E. name for the bird was *ielfetu*, equivalent to the O.N. *elpt*, which is seen in *Elterwater*, the name of a lake in Lancashire. *Swanmore*, Hunts., and *Swanbourne*, Berks. (found as *Suanaburna* in 8th-century records), with possibly *Swanley* and *Swanage*, illustrate the use of one name; the other is found more frequently, as in *Elvet* Hall, co. Durham (in record of 762); *Elveden*, Suffolk; *Iltney*, Essex; and *Altham*, Lancs.

Cognate with *elpt* and *ielfetu* is the Old Celtic *elaio*, from which come the Gaelic *eala*, Welsh *alarch*, etc. From a Celtic source was derived the poetical Latin *olor*, now used as the epithet in the scientific name of the mute swan *Cygnus olor*. The root *al- (*ol-), a variant of *ar-, expresses movement, especially upwards, as in *alauda*, a Latin borrowing from the Celtic word for 'a lark'.

The poets leave no doubt about the suitability of 'upriser' as a name for the swan, as when Spenser wrote:

> 'He, were he not with love so ill bedight,
> Would mount as high, and sing as soote as Swanne.'

Most of such references to the soaring swan are concerned with its singing a death-song – a myth thought by Plato worthy of being put into the mouth of Socrates on the day of his death (*Phaedo*, 85). The legend enshrines both fancy and fact. Probably it started with the sight of the gleaming bird high overhead in the light of the sun. Thus the whooper swan became for the ancients the bird of Phoebus Apollo. Fallen to earth, as life left it, the swan showed its connection with the Inventor of the Lyre who was also the Lord of the Sky by uttering sweet music. Prosaically put, the music is the equivalent of the death-rattle, occasioned by the last slow exhalation through the twists of the bird's long windpipe.

From the names given to the swans and geese in the I-E. languages something may be learnt about the groups into which the Aryans were split by their migrations. The modern Icelandic retains for the whooper the O.N. *elpt* in the form of *alft*, but uses in compounds *svanur* (O.N. *svanr*) for the mute and Bewick's swans. Thus it keeps a variant of the typical northern name in company with Swedish, Danish, Norwegian, Dutch, German, and English – i.e. with the present-day representatives of the common tongue which developed into O.N., O.H.G., and L.G. The descendants of the Slavonic branch of the N.W. European group have a distinct name-type, which may or may not have *al- as its principle. Czech *labut'*, Yugoslav *labud*, and Russian *lebed'* are modern examples.

Among the languages of the progeny of those Aryans who migrated to S.W. Europe, the Greek for swan was *kuknos* ('honker'). Latin borrowed this name as *cycnus* or *cygnus*, which became the parent of the names in the Romance languages, and grandparent of our *cygnet*. The other large group of migrants to S.W. Europe, the Celts, used, as we have seen, names from the stock of *elaio*, 'the rising one'.

From the S.E. or Asiatic group we have *haṇsa*, 'a swan' – corresponding to the words for 'goose' in practically every other I-E. language.

Goose is not so easily invested with a general meaning from a verbal root. The expressive *honk*, applied to the sound of the old type of motor-horn, first represented the cry of wild geese and swans; and it is not surprising that the *ngoh* of Cantonese, which we call 'goose', should be named from its voice in probably the majority of the world's languages.

In *Arctic*, vol. 15, no. 4, Dr E. O. Höhn published lists of the names of birds (and mammals) from five 'Indian' dialects still spoken in the Mackenzie area of N.W. Canada – Loucheux, Hare, Slavey, Dog-rib, and Chipewyan (with Sarcee as well). These, although the percentage of mimetic names is small, all have such names for the Canada goose (*cah*, *cha*, *ha*, and *'ah*) and for the snow-goose (*gukee* or *kukee*, *goga* or *koka*, etc.). But the whistling swan *Olor columbianus*, though named *ga go* in Dog-rib and Chipewyan, is just 'white' to the Slaveys, the Hares, and the Loucheux.

Whether or not the name *goose* can be traced to the root **gha-* to gape (cf. *chaos*, *chasm*, etc.), its *honk* sounds in the names given to it in virtually every I-E. language. If we grant *haṇsa* the meaning of 'goose' as well as of swan', the Skt. name can be cited as representative of the type-name among the S.E. group of Aryans. In the S.W. European group *khēn* was the ancient, as it is the modern, Greek; the L. (*h*)*anser*, found in the name of the merganser or 'diving-goose' has become Sp. *ansar*, Port. *ganso*, F. *oie*, etc. among the Romance tongues. The Irish *goss* was formerly *geis*, 'a swan', the Welsh being *gwydd*. The Slavonic branch of the N.W. European group has such forms as Russian *gus* and Czech *husa*; the western branch includes German *Gans* and Scandinavian *gås*; the Low German type being represented by Dutch *gans* (with similar forms in Frisian, Flemish, and other dialects) and our own name (M.E. *goos*, *gos*; O.E. *gōs*, in which the lost nasal sound of the more primitive **gans* gives a W. Germanic *gās*, from which O.E. *gōs* develops). We have also the diminutive *gosling*.

To these may be added non-I-E. names such as the Finnish *hansi*.

Cognates are *gannet* and *gander*, the O.E. *ganot* and *gandra* (in which the earlier form was eased by an intrusive *d*). Students of

Anglo-Saxon will be familiar with *ganotes bæth* ('gannet's bath') as a 'kenning' for the sea found in very early English poetry.

The *gossander* of Merrett (1667) was given the modern spelling in Ray's edition of Willughby in the following year. No attempt to derive both elements from any one Scandinavian language seems satisfactory. Possibly to the Scand. *gås* was added some form of the O.N. *ǫnd*, 'drake'. No other language appears to use a name anything like it. Even in Icelandic it is called *gulönd*, 'yellow duck'.

Some place-names refer to tame geese, and some to wild: e.g. *Goswick* ('goose-farm'); *Gosport* ('goose-market'); *Goosey* ('goose-island'), found as *Gosei* in the Domesday Book, and *Goseie* as early as 815.

Of single names for ducks in the British list, not more than six, including those of the two sawbills already cited – *merganser* and *goosander* – contain any allusion to the birds' voices. Nor has either *duck* or *drake* any connection with sound-production. Indeed, the *quack* of our childhood's days has a struggle to make itself heard in the names of the British *Anatidae*. It is, in fact, a bird of a quite different family, the quail, whose name is etymologically nearest to that particular sound. The call of the male bird, the 'three castanet-like notes' of Howard Saunders, is reproduced in Scotland and Ireland as 'wet my feet', in Norfolk as 'wet my lip', and in Oxfordshire as 'quick me dick'. *Quayle* is found in Chaucer. The rather earlier *quaille* had passed through French and the late Latin *quaquila* from a Low German source. Modern Dutch *kwartel*, 'a quail', and *kwaken*, 'to quack', represent the earlier forms *quackel* and *quaken*. German *Wachtel* is from O.H.G. *quatala*. Thus the quail has a name related to *cackle* (German *gackeln*) and to the utterances of frogs, represented by Aristophanes' directly imitative *koax* and its derivative the L. *coaxare* (found in Suetonius' *Augustus*) and the German *quaken*, which means both 'to croak' and 'to quack' – and 'to groan'.

We find a sort of *quack* in the name of the *garganey*. In spring the garganey-drake's mating music, described in *The Handbook of British Birds* as 'a peculiar low crackling sound' and by Howard Saunders as 'a jarring noise like a child's rattle', gives the species the name of 'crick' or 'cricket-teal' in East Anglia. This renders plain the significance of the L. *querquedula* and the corresponding Italian *garganello*, 'a book-name', as Alfred Newton (1829–1907) observes, 'for the duck generally known as a summer-teal'. *Querquedula* is met again in *gadwall*, on the assumption that the Kentish physician and ornithologist Latham (1740–1837) was correct in tracing the English name to the syllables *quedul*. This is certainly preferable to the suggestion that 'gadwall' is a corruption of 'gad well', i.e. 'to go about wells' (fishponds). *The Handbook of B.B.* quotes as descriptions of the ordinary notes, 'a chuckling croak', 'a loud, deep rattling *rab*', 'a low *kack, kack*'.

Closely connected with the foregoing etymologies is the history of *kestrel*, which has ousted *staniel* and other forms of the O.E. *stāngale* or *stāngielle*. Like the F. *crécerelle*, it is derived from O.F. *crecele* or *cercelle* (mod. F. *crécelle*, 'a rattle') from an imitative base **krek-* suggested by the kestrel's cry of *kee, kee, kee*.

Scaup is a shortening of Willughby's *scaup-duck*, which is the more correct designation if the bird was named from its feeding habits and not its voice. One meaning of *scaup* (an alternative form of *scalp*) is 'a bed of shellfish'. The word is derived from the O.N. *skalpr*, 'a sheath', and is cognate with *shell* and *scallop* and perhaps the same as the *scalp* of the head. Montagu, in his *Ornithological Dictionary* (1802), says that the duck 'is supposed to take its name from feeding on broken shells, called "scaup" '; and Saunders speaks of its winter-food as 'molluscs, small crustaceans, and sea-plants, obtained by diving over beds of oysters and mussels, known as "scalp".' Saunders, however, also states that the note is remarkably hoarse and discordant, resembling the word *skaup*; and Seebohm's (1832–1895) firsthand account is calculated still further to encourage us to find a substitute for the shellfish theory. 'Of all the cries of ducks,' he says, 'that have come under my notice, I think that of the scaup is the most discordant. None of them are very musical, perhaps; but if you imagine a man with an exceptionally hoarse voice screaming out the word "scaup" at the top of his voice, some idea of the note of this bird may be formed.'

Sceptical as one should be about sound-names, in this instance the mimetic hypothesis is worthy of consideration, and would probably be the more acceptable to modern ornithologists. Pough, for instance, in *Audubon Water-Bird Guide* (1951), speaking of 'this usually silent duck', commonly known in the United States as 'big blue-bill', says, 'Occasionally a flock breaks into a chorus of discordant *scaup* calls.' My own acquaintance* with the species in north and central Sweden is too limited for me to comment; and my close relations with a scaup

*L.C.S.

in England are confined to having nursed a clemmed duck during the hard winter of 1946. During the week which she spent with us, she was quite silent, even at meal-times.

Though it is conceivable that *scaup* is imitative, that it is not inevitable is suggested by the poverty, if not the complete absence, of any imitative element in the names in other European languages for the bird which Germans, Danes, Norwegians, and Swedes unite in considering as the 'mountain-duck' – *Bergente, bjergand,* etc.

The local name of *whistler* indicates the probable meaning of *wigeon* (Turner's *wigene,* Merrett's *widgeon*), the *canard siffleur* of Buffon. Willughby and Ray give *whewer* as an alternative name, especially for the female in Cambridgeshire. *Whew* (a Yorkshire word for a factory-whistle) is another long-standing provincial name which copies the drake's *whee-oo*. Beside English *wigeon* there is a later (seventeenth-century) French *vigeon*; but it must be recorded that the compilers of the O.E.D. regard as very dubious the derivation of *vigeon* and the Italian *bibbio* from the only word which seems to offer a further clue, namely L. *vipio,* cited by Pliny as a species of crane.

It is not uncommon for a name to be shared by two different kinds of bird, especially if it be mimetic; as witness the onomatopoetic *jay* used in Ireland for the mistle-thrush: so that the doubt cast by high authority on the descent of *wigeon* from *vipio* is curious in view of the undisputed descent of *pigeon* from *pīpio*. From *pīpiōn-,* oblique stem of L. *pīpio,* 'a chirper', came the O.F. *pigon,* whence sprang M.E. *pyjon*. The modern French word has the same spelling as our own. A repetition of history is found in the use by our pigeon-fanciers of *squeaker* (and sometimes of *piper*) for the squabs or young. *Pipit,* an imitative word of French origin, has the same basic significance of 'chirper'. The second part of *sandpiper* is of kindred meaning. It is found in O.E., related to the L.L. *pīpare,* 'to pipe', and not the cognate *pīpire*. Yet another variant, *pīpiare,* was used by Catullus in the playful yet moving elegy on the death of his lady's pet sparrow:

> 'ad solam dominam usque pipiabat,
> qui nunc it per iter tenebricosum.'
> (Once ever chirping when our Dear was there,
> Now down the Way of Gloom he needs must fare.)

The *chat* of *whinchat* and *stonechat* is better represented by the provincial *chacker*. Our verb to *chat* is a shortened form of the imitative M.E. *chateren*, 'to chatter'. It has been doubted whether the syllable in *woodchat* (shrike) is the same word, for the bird is far too rare a visitor to this country to have been noticed and named by the ordinary countryman. The origin of *woodchat* is shrouded in mystery. The name was used by Ray in the *Catalogue of British Birds* on p. 21 of the English edition of Willughby (1678), though not in the section dealing with Shrikes. *Woodchat shrike* appears first in Ray's *Synopsis Methodica Avium et Piscium* (1713). Both Willughby and Ray were familiar with the bird, describing specimens found 'near the River Rhene' and 'at Florence in Italy' respectively. Each was struck by the brilliant chestnut-red of the crown and nape which accounts for the 'book-name' in nearly every European language except English; but neither says anything about the note. That the *chat* is imitative is more likely than that the name is a mistake for *wood-cat*, G. *Wald-Katze*, as the O.E.D. states.

Turner used *shrike*, 'the shrieker' (O.E. *scrīc*, 'the mistle-thrush'), and *nine murder* for the great grey shrike, with which he was familiar in Germany, though he had seen it only twice in England; but he seems to have ignored the red-backed shrike (our 'butcher-bird') as a separate species, not mentioning any name derived from O.E. *weargincel*, such as Chaucer's *waryangle* (*Friar's Tale*, 1408), which could cover both kinds of 'felon-bird'.

Shrigley, Cheshire, means 'the wood frequented by shrikes'.

Titmouse well expresses the quick mouse-like movements of the family *Paridae*. To the Scandinavian diminutive *tit*, found also in *titlark*, is added the English *mose*. This *mose* is not connected with the name of the rodent (O.E. *mūs*, 'the thief'), but was affected by it in the sixteenth century when it had lost its identity as the modern form of O.E. *māse*, a name given to various small birds, as *hīcemāse*, *frecmāse*, *colmāse*, and *spicmāse*. All modern Teutonic languages use some form of it. The F. derivative is *mésange*. But only in English does the bird appear so charmingly and appropriately described by a nature-from-nature name.

Macefen, Cheshire (found in 1260 as *Masefen*), being near the border of Wales, may represent the Welsh *maes*, 'a field', +O.E. *fenn*, 'a marsh'; but is possibly 'the marsh of the tits'. If this is so, the birds referred to may well have been, from the nature of the site, bearded tits, which must have had their ear- and eye-attracting colonies in all the fenny districts of Britain. There are quite modern records of the occurrence of the species further North, in Yorkshire, apart from birds unsuccessfully reintroduced into the county. About four miles south-west of Lincoln, on the low ground between the Witham and the Fosse dyke, are North and South *Hykeham* (the *Hicham* of the Domesday Book, later found as *Hiccham* and *Hikham*). The name seems to mean the *hamm*, 'the low-lying meadow by a stream', of the *hīcemāse*; and though 'hickeymal' and variants of that word are provincial names for the blue tit, and sometimes for the great tit, here again seems to be a memorial to the 'bearded reedling'. That *Hickling* Broad, Norfolk, has remained a noted habitat of the bearded tit cannot, one supposes, be set against Ekwall's attribution of the name of the district to '*Hicel(a)'s* people'.

A surprising relationship can be made for *ouzel*, found in *ring-ouzel* and *water-ouzel* (the dipper), but now retained only in the northern counties as a name for the blackbird, which it originally denoted. Bewick (1797) used the name 'black ouzel', giving 'black-bird' as an alternative, as Turner had done 250 years previously. The O.E. was *ōsle*, which, with the modern German *Amsel*, is distantly related to the L. *merula*, whence comes the F. *merle*, adopted in English as a – usually poetical – name for the blackbird. *Merula*, rewritten in its more ancient form, **mesula*, makes clear the bond between *Amsel* and *ouzel*, and tit*mouse*; and therefore between the blackbird's English name and his Latin one. *Ewesley*, Northumberland, represents the earlier *Oseley*. *Nostell*, W. Riding (*Osele* and *Osle* in the D.B.), has the same meaning – 'blackbird-wood'.

The general term *warbler* is a derivative of the M.E. verb *werbelen*, from the O. Norman-French *werbler*, of Germanic origin – 'to sing like a bird'. In Ornithology the name was first used by Pennant in 1773 for the birds of Scopoli's new genus *Sylvia*, transferred from the Linnaean genus *Motacilla*. Of the three dozen warblers in the British list, the *melodious* and the *Orphean* are most honoured in their names. The *melodious warbler* has its epithet through M.F. and Latin from the Gk. *melōidia*, 'a singing', from *melōidos*, 'musical', a compound of *melos* and *ōidē*, each word meaning 'a song'. *Grasshopper warbler* was Latham's name for Willughby's 'titlark that sings like a grasshopper'.

Accentor, 'one who accompanies another in a song', now used only for the Alpine accentor, was borrowed early in the 19th century from the name given by Linnaeus to the hedge-sparrow (which is not a sparrow, except in the primary sense of 'flutterer', most apt for the *shufflewing*). It is a L.L. word derived from *ad + canere*, 'to sing' – the source of *canōrus*, 'tuneful', the epithet added to our cuckoo's *Cuculus*.

From the root **kan-* are derived also the O.E. *hana*, 'a cock', *henn*, a 'hen', and *henna*, 'a fowl' – whence the second element in our *greyhen* and *moorhen* – with *chanticleer*, the M.E. *chauntecleer*, the barnyard cock, such as the proud husband of the 'fayre damoysele Pertelote' in *The Nun's Priest's Tale* of Chaucer. *Hennfuglas* was an O.E. name for the birds which countryfolk call indifferently 'hens' or 'fowls'. ('Moorhen' = 'waterhen': O.E. *mōr*, 'a marshy moor'.)

Hana and *henn* are the keywords in many place-names, sometimes denoting birds of the farmyard, and sometimes wildfowl. To mention only a few – in the Domesday Book are found *Hanechelole* (knoll of the wild cocks) for the modern *Honicknowle* in Devon; *Hanewde* (cock-wood) for *Hanwood*, Salop. East and West *Henney*, Lincs., stand for 'wild cocks' island'. Except in a few names such as *Henwick*, Beds., and *Henton*, Somerset (enclosure and farm where domestic hens were kept), *henna* (pl. of the fem. *henn* and singular of the masculine *henna*, a fowl) is used for wildfowl – probably partridges, moor*hens*, and various waders, as in *Henmarsh*, *Henheads* (hills), *Henhurst* (wood), Great and Little *Henny* (island), in Glos., Lancs., Kent, and Essex respectively, and in many other names.

Whereas *chiffchaff* is an attempt at echoing the note of the 'least willow-wren', *chaffinch*, the O.E. *ceaffinc* denotes the finch that is to be found searching for edible matter in the *chaff* of rickyards. To the chaffinch, the least shy of all our finches, and eye-attracting by its variegated colours, other birds of the family must owe that part of the name which it shares with them. No one familiar with its metallic note could be at a loss to guess the identity of the bird called *chink*, *pink*, or *twink* in various parts of Britain. The even commoner *spink* is found as an alternative to *chaffinche* in Turner's list (1544).

The provincial Welsh name for the chaffinch (more formally *asgell fraith*, 'wing-pied') is *pinc* or *winc*. The Dutch is *vink*. The F. *pinson* and the Spanish *pinzoń* represent the Low Latin *pinciōn(em)*. For *finch* the Norwegian, Swedish, and German is *fink*, the Icelandic *finka*, and the Danish *finke*. Ancient Greek had *spiza* and *spiggos*. Our word is the modern form of the O.E. *finc*, presumably first applied to the chaffinch, and found also in *goldfinc*. That the O.E., however, had also the word *pinca* is suggested by the early spellings of the names of several places such as *Fincham*, Norfolk, and *Pinchbeck*, Lincs., which appear in the Domesday Book as *Pincham* and *Pincebec* respectively. One of the comparatively few nature-from-nature names which we have from birds is due to the fact that from a Lincolnshire village came the ancestor of Christopher Pinchbeck (fl. 1700), the London clockmaker who used an alloy of copper, zinc, and tin – the so-called 'Brummagem gold' – *pinchbeck*. Other places embodying the bird's name are *Finchampstead*, Berks. (*Finchamestede* in the D.B.); *Finchley*, Middlesex; *Finkley*, Hants.; and *Finchale* (*Pincanheale* in the Anglo-Saxon Chronicle, A.D. 788).

Twite is recorded from the 16th century, and is used as a name for the mountain-linnet in Albin's *English Songbirds* (1737). The form taken by this imitation of the bird's note was, we may well believe, suggested by *tweet* and *twitter* (a frequentative form of the unfound verb to *twit* – not the *twit* shortened from the O.E. *aetwītan*, 'to reproach'). Forms similar to *twitter*, such as the Dutch *kwetteren* and the Swedish *qvittra*, are found in many other Germanic languages.

Thrush (O.E. *thrysce*), with *throstle*, L. *turdus*, G. *Drossel* (O.H.G. *drosca*), Russian and Polish *drozd*, and Scandinavian equivalents, offers a seemingly insoluble problem to the radical meaning. The likelihood of the primitive names' having had reference to the thrush as a vocalist is strong in view of such words as Gk. *trizein*, 'to twitter'.

In Chaucer we find *throstle* and *throstel*. Turner lists 'thrusche; thrushe; throssel; mavis or wyngthrush', appending the M.H.G. *Weingaerdsvoegel* ('vineyard-bird') for the redwing *Turdus musicus*, which is today known provincially in Germany as *Weindrossel*, or more formally as *Rotdrossel*. The Danish *vindrossel* seems to be now the only generally accepted European name connecting the bird with vineyards. Willughby, the first writer to use 'redwing', quotes the physician to Charles II, Walter Charleton (1619–1707), who in his *Onomasticon Zooicon* (1668) wrote that the bird was called 'windthrush' (as in Merrett's *Pinax*, published in the preceding year), because the redwings flying to Britain were helped by the winds prevalent in early winter. Willughby himself, however, preferred 'wine-thrush', which he equated with the German *Wyntrostel*.

Nuttall's Standard Dictionary includes *windle*, 'redwing', which

Swann gives as a Devon name. 'Windle' is cited for the county
Dublin by J. Rutty (1772). We have heard a Dorset woman sym-
pathetically comparing a man shivering in a thin overcoat with 'a
poor windledrush'. A *windlestraw* is a bit of dry grass, which is even
more likely to become the sport of the blast; the word being the
modern form of the O.E. *windelstrēaw*, a plant used for binding
(*windan*) cornsheaves and the like.

Turner's 'mavis' we can trace at least to the Norman-French
mauvis. In Scotland *mavis* seems usually to be applied to the mistle-
thrush. In *The Romance of Plant-Life* (1907) a devoted Scotsman,
Scott Elliot, writes of 'the missel-thrush or mavis'. Chaucer perhaps
used *mavys* for the song-thrush, and *thrustle* or *throstel* for the mistle-
thrush, as is the use in East Anglia. Shakespeare, making more use
of *throstle* than of *mavis*, probably did not differentiate between the
species. The M.E. *mavis*, through O.F. *mauvis*, 'a song-thrush',
appears to be of Celtic origin – possibly from the Breton *milvid*. That
the name is from the bird's voice is rendered all the more likely by
the existence of the Cornish (Breton's sister-tongue) *melhues*, 'a lark'.

The origin of the first element in *cirl-bunting* is more elusive than
the bird itself. The name appears in Latham's *General Synopsis of
Birds* (1783), and is said to have been introduced by Latham to
render the Linnaean *Emberiza cirlus*; *cirlus* being a Latinized form of
Aldrovandi's *cirlo*, 'a name applied by the Bolognese to the *zigolo
nero*, probably from *zirlare*, "to whistle like a thrush".' The F. *bruant
zizi*, alternative to *bruant de haie*, indicates the bird's note and points
to the imitative quality of *zirl* or *cirl*, a syllable that has no independent meaning.

Remarkably like *zizi* is *Zeisig*, the German for *siskin*, a name
which seems to have reached us through Middle Dutch from a
Slavonic source. *Siskin*, with the German *Zeysich*, appears in Turner's
list.

We have noted that the *shrike* is 'the shrieker'. The O.N. name,
skrikja was from a similarly spelt verb related to *skraekja*, 'to shriek',
and cognate with M.E. *scritchen*, whence by mimetic modification
came the *screech* of 'screech-owl'.

The owls naturally attract onomatopoetic names to themselves,
such as the G. *Uhu* (eagle-owl) and the Magyar *kuvik* (little owl).
Owl itself, the M.E. *oule* and O.E. *ūle* (side by side with *ūf*) is paralleled, as might be expected, by similar words in cognate languages,

e.g. German *Eule*, Dutch *uil*, Danish *ugle*, and Swedish *ugla*. It is derived from some verbal root meaning 'to howl', as are the kindred forms in other I-E. languages, e.g. Skt. *ulūka* and L. *ulula* (from *ululare*). *Ulula* is found in Varro and Vergil, e.g.,

'Certent et cycnis ululae, sit Tityrus Orpheus.'
(Let owls compete with the swans, and Tityrus be a new Orpheus.)
Vergil, *Eclogue* VIII. 55.

From the most ancient to the most modern times owls have had 'a bad press', both for uttering harsh noises and for doing so under cover of twilight or darkness, when men's nerves are taut and superstition is most powerful. Thoreau in *Walden* makes a suggestive reference to human attempts to imitate the notes of birds; the owl's hooting reminding him of 'the dying moans of a human being – some poor weak relic of humanity who has left hope behind, and howls like an animal, yet with human sobs, on entering the dark valley, made more awful by a certain gurgling melodiousness (*I find myself beginning with the letters gl when I try to imitate it*) expressive of a mind which has reached the gelatinous mildewy stage in the mortification of all healthy and courageous thought.'

The provincial names for the bittern are truly echoic – *boomer*, *bumble*, *bog-bumper*, and the like – and are taken from the weird booming sound uttered by the male in the breeding-season. This may be described as half-way between the blare of a fog-horn and the explosion, in mud, of one of those shells which we used to know as 'crumps'. It is not a beautiful sound; yet it thrilled through my heart like music in the spring of 1911, when, unexpectedly and for the first time, I heard it among the reeds on Hickling Broad, and realized that after the lapse of several decades the bittern was nesting in England once more.* Allowing for the fact that the bittern's bill is raised when he booms, we could say with Thomson (*Spring*, 1728):

'The bittern knows his time, with bill ingulph'd
To shake the sounding marsh.'

It is not surprising that the peculiarly muffled sound of the 'boom' or 'bump' should have given rise to the belief that the bird plunged his bill into the mud before uttering his territory-claim; but by the end of the 18th century the enthusiasm of field-naturalists had
*L.C.S.

cleared away many false notions such as this (found as early as Pliny), and that swallows hibernated in the mud of ponds – though even Gilbert White was loth to accept evidence about their migrating to distant lands.

It is conceivable, however, that *bittern* may have originated in the sharp cry uttered by birds of either sex, not only in the breeding-season. The word is to be traced through French and Late Latin to the L. *butire*, 'to cry like a bittern'. The M.E. was *botor*, the *n* of the modern name being excrescent, like the second *n* in *nightingale*, or that at the end of the provincial *yourn*. Now, 'buzzard' (M.E. *busard* or *bosard*, a French importation which ousted O.E. *tysca* and possibly *wrōc*) represents the L.L. *būsio*. This word, in passing through French, was augmented by the Germanic suffix *-hart*. (See under *pochard*, Chapter IX(a).) *Būsio* stood for the earlier L. *būteo*, 'a sparrow-hawk', which is a doublet of *būtio*, 'a bittern'. Neither the sparrow-hawk nor the buzzard booms like a bittern; but the normal note of the bittern, except in the mating-season, is sufficiently like the mewing cry of both the raptorial birds in question to make it possible of belief that the verb *būtire* may in the first instance have referred as much to the *mew* of all the birds concerned as it did to the *moo* peculiar to the *botor*, to which J. F. Stephens in 1819 gave the generic name *Botaurus*, punning on the L. *bōs*, 'ox', and *taurus*, 'bull' – Pliny having described this or some similar bird (as well as a beetle) under the name of *taurus*.

xi (b)

THE LIMITATIONS OF IMITATION

'Man is a very indifferent imitator of natural sounds, as witness his absurd attemps to represent the barn-door cock. The Englishman says "cockadoodledoo", the German says "kikeriki", while the Frenchman describes it as "coquerico".'

SIR RICHARD PAGET, *Babel*, 1930.

AMONG the compound words of which one element is originally mimetic are *blackcock* and *woodcock* – names best introduced by Max Müller's remarks on that of the cuckoo. ' "Cuckoo",' he freely admits, 'is clearly a mere imitation of the cry of that bird, even more so than the corresponding terms in Greek, Sanskrit, and Latin. In these languages the imitative element has received the support of a derivative suffix: we have *kokila* in Sanskrit, *kokkux* in Greek, and *cuculus* in Latin. "Cuckoo" is in fact a modern word which has taken the place of the Anglo-Saxon *gēac*, the German *Gauch*, and, being purely onomatopoetic, it is of course not liable to the change of Grimm's Law. . . . The same applies to "cock", the Sanskrit *kukkuṭa*. *Kukkuṭa* is not derived from any root: it simply repeats the cry of the bird.' (*Lectures on the Science of Language*.) So Chaucer makes his Chaunteclere cry 'cok cok' (N.P.T. 457).

To *cock* is allied the diminutive form *chicken* (O.E. *cīcen*). Parallel forms are found in other Teutonic languages.

There is, indeed, a close connection between 'cock' and 'cuckoo'. So unusually clear is the consonantal sound in their cries, that few languages fail to reproduce the *k* sound in imitations. To the Malay the cock cries *kukuk* (whence *kakatua*, 'a cockatoo'); '*cūcūrrire solet gallus*' ('*coocoo* is the cock's call'), said the Roman. To the Greek ear the cuckoo's call was *kokku*, from which was formed *kokkuzein*, 'to cry like a cuckoo or a cock'. To the Maori, with his love for musical words, it is the New Zealand pigeon *Hemiphaga novaeseelandii* which calls, and which he names, *kuku*. The long-tailed cuckoo *Urodynamis*

117

taitensis, a summer-visitor to New Zealand alone, with habits similar to those of our *Cuculus canorus*, but with harsher voice, the Maori names *koekoea*.

The O.E. *gēac*, which was ousted after the Norman Conquest by *cukkow* or *cuccu*, representing the F. *coucou*, is still to be seen in *gowk*. This survives as a name for the bird only in Scotland and Northern Ireland, but is retained elsewhere with the meaning of 'dolt' or 'simpleton'. The Teutonic group, exemplified by G. *Gauch*, Icelandic *gaukur*, Swedish *gök*, and our *gowk*, lacks the pronounced imitation of Slavonic, Sanskrit, Greek, and Latin equivalents; the bond of union being audible in the West Country *guckoo* and in the Celtic forms, as Gaelic and Irish *cuach* and Welsh *cog*. But the Welsh also use *cwcw*.

Among nature-from-nature names we have *cuckoo-flower* (of various species), *cuckoo-pint*, *cuckoo-spit*, and *cuckold*.

Possibly the 'Cuckold's Combe' near Ashford, Kent, is a version of 'Cuckoo's Combe', but the early form *Cukkelescumbe* suggests a personal name. The names, however, of built-up areas echoing the bird's cry are few. Yet some four miles south-west of Chester there is a 'Cuckoo's Nest' – a few houses by a double bend in the Wrexham road. Like 'Cuckold's Combe', this name conjures up thoughts of some old-time skimmington-ride past the dwelling of a wayward wife, with the clashing of pots and pans by censorious neighbours. But either or both of these names may merely enshrine light-hearted memories of the bird in spring.

Exbourne in Devon and *Yaxley* in Suffolk stand for the O.E. *gēacesburna* and *gēaceslēah*, the 'gowk's stream' and 'wood'. Earlier forms of the present-day names of these places are found in the Domesday Book or records even older. *Blencogo* in Cumberland represents the Celtic *blaen*, 'top', and *cog*, 'cuckoo', with the addition of the O.N. *haugr*, 'hill'. *Yagdon* in Shropshire and *Yoxham* in Norfolk may be 'cuckoo's hill' and 'meadow'.

'Cock' is found in *Caughill*, Cheshire; *Cogdean*, Dorset; *Cockley*, Northumberland; and a few other place-names. The etymology is not helped by the existence of a second *cocc*, from O.N. *kokkr*, 'a hill'; as in our *haycock*. The species of bird referred to in any particular name is not to be discovered: grouse and woodcock are among obvious and reasonable guesses.

Chicheley, Berks. (*Cicelai* of the D.B.) might have been 'chicken's field'.

To the French we are indebted for another echoic bird-name. The hoopoe's soft call, *hoo hoo* or *bu bu*, is somewhat disguised in the Gk. *epops*. It was imitated also in the L. *upupa*, which became alternatively *pupu* and *huppe* in French. The English rendering of this by Caxton was *huppe*, and variant forms like *houuppe* (as in Turner's list); and *houp* or *hoop*, struggled for supremacy with the present name until the middle of the 18th century. The actual form seems to have been influenced by *hoop* or *whoop*, a word of Germanic origin which reached us with the base of *whooping-cough* and *whooper-swan*.

Curlew is another onomatopoetic name modified from the O.F. *corlieu*. The Modern French *courlis*, alternative to *courlieu*, is perhaps the closest approximation to the bird's cry. The Czech calls it *holiha*, the Pole *kulik*. The name is as much an attempted imitation as *cuckoo*; but the wild cry of the *whaup* (O.E. *huilpe*; Modern Dutch *wulp*) does not lend itself to being copied with such accuracy as do the calls of the cuckoo and the cock. The medial trills reproduce to some extent those in the curlew's cry: but is the initial *k* sound equally true to life? Does not this consonantal sound, which most people hear in the cuckoo's call, seem in the name of the curlew to be little more than a convenience towards making a name easily pronounceable in human speech? In using it we follow the general tendency to employ a guttural (*k*, *g*) or a palatal *ch*, *j*) to imitate what is often a mere approach towards consonantal 'stops' in the utterances of birds.

It may be said that birds have no teeth or lips, and therefore seldom produce sounds which can be accurately represented by the aid of our dentals (*t*, *d*) or labials (*p*, *b*); but neither teeth nor lips are essential for the production of such sounds. This can be learnt from a gramophone-record as easily as from a parrot or from one of those among the passerine birds which are able to copy the human voice.

Darwin, in *The Descent of Man*, noted that 'certain animals do not lack the physical conditions necessary for articulate language, since there is not a letter in the alphabet that a parrot cannot pronounce'. The anatomical explanation of this is that the parrots, like passerine birds, have a larger number of pairs of muscles for contracting and shortening the syrinx (the sound-box) than the majority of birds possess. Some birds indeed, for example the storks, have no muscles for this purpose, and many have only one pair – and accordingly only a limited capacity for modulating the voice.

Here, however, we are considering not the mimicry of human speech by birds, but the imitation of birds' notes by human beings; and in this connection Paget, in *Babel*, remarks: 'The human teeth may be left out of consideration, for all the speech-sounds can, with practice, be produced without them; but the lips are of prime importance. Our lips form the outer door – the ultimate mouth of the instrument – by which the opening-to-air may be completely closed or varied in size. Or the mouth-cavity itself may be momentarily enlarged, viz. by protruding the lips, as when we articulate the vowel *u*, as in "who".'

Incidentally Paget was writing for English people, who in certain forms of 'lazy speech' habitually deceive the ears of their human hearers more successfully than those of birds. Your friend may be reading from *Through the Looking-Glass*. . . . 'There's glory for you!' is what you think you hear: but it is two to one that what your friend actually said was '*dlory*'. Innocently ask him to rattle off the word several times in succession, and he will almost certainly say, 'Dlory, dlory, dlory . . .'

The fact remains, however, that (as one might expect from the possession by birds of throat, palate, and tongue, which they have in common with mankind) of bird-cries which can with any certainty be reproduced by the use of our alphabet, the majority will permit the employment of liquids and of guttural and palatal stops.

Pewit, for instance, seems an essentially close imitation; but strict attention to the sounds involved shows it to be by no means an exact reproduction. All that can be said, in fact, is that it is the best attempt that can be expected from human imitators. Articulate language cannot faithfully copy inarticulate noise. Sometimes *pewee* as a local name replaces the more general *pewit*. The note of a very different pewee, the American flycatcher *Miochanes virens*, is described by Pough (*Audubon Bird-Guide*) as 'a sweet plaintive whistle'. Such is not our lapwing's cry! Of the forms *pewee* and *pewit* which is the more accurate? The answer is that each is far from accurate. *Wee*, unless pronounced by someone familiar with the bird's cry, and able to give an approximate imitation of it, gives no idea of the sharp ending of the lapwing's shriek. *Wit*, pronounced as one would pronounce our word *wit* in a sentence, is equally unsatisfactory. But we do the best we can, and try to suggest the piercing ending of the cry by finishing our imitation with a *t*. That this *t* is not inevitable is shown by various provincial names such as *peeweep, peesweep,* and *peesnips*; and, more pertinently to our present line of thought, by another provincial form, *teeuck,* and by the Westphalian *piwik.*

Similarly, the first letter of *pewit* is a mere makeshift. The best we can say of it is that the sound is not much better suggested if the *p* be replaced by *k*, as in G. *Kiebitz* and Dutch *kievit*. There seems to be no provincial English form of the name beginning with a *k*; but sometimes in East Anglia and the West Country, and generally in Scotland and the North of England, the *p* is replaced by *t*, as in *tewit, teufit,* and the like.

All these variants, with their common factors, indicate the specific nature of the name; but long familiarity with one form must be discounted if the accuracy of the imitation is to be properly tested. Moreover, those forms which make use of the syllable *pee* must be considered in the light of their etymological connection with a group of words which includes 'peevish'. Skeat cites a Danish dialect form *piaeve*, 'to whimper', and the Lowland Scots *peu*, 'to make a plaintive noise'. Even *pewit* therefore, which might be called 'obviously mimetic', cannot be divorced from the general sense of lamentation which may easily be conjured up by the cry of the lapwing.

Of *Iffley*, Oxon., (*Gifetelea* in 1004), Ekwall says that the first element may be an old word for 'plover', or some similar bird, cognate with the M.H.G. *gíbitz* (G. *Kiebitz*); and of *Tivetshall,* Norfolk, that the *tivet* may represent one of the variants of *tuwit,* such as *tufit.*

Other approximations are heard in *kittiwake* and in *killdeer* (plover). *Kittiwake,* found in Sibbald's *Scotia Illustrata* (1684), ousted the form *cattiwake,* used, possibly coined, by Ray a few years previously. The dental sound is present in the *kittiake* heard on the Yorkshire coast; but that the names are all mere approximations is shown by such variants as *killieweeack* and *kishiefaik* used in the Orkneys.

It may be said that the *whim* of 'whimbrel' is an attempt to copy the bird's cry; but it is influenced by, if not directly copied from, a verbal form of more general meaning, i.e. the (dial.) *whimp* which is extended in the frequentative *whimper* and is cognate with *whine* (O.E.

hwinan) and other verbs such as the O.N. *kveina*, 'to wail'. If, as seems likely, *whimbrel* stands for *whimmerel*, it is the diminutive form of the verb *to whimmer*, which is a Lowland Scots form of *whimper*. Curiously enough, that part of the word made up of frequentative and diminutive suffixes is more of a reminder of the bird's rippling call than is the professedly imitative syllable. This is borne out by the *titterel* and *chickerel* of the southern counties.

In a lovely rendering of part of the fragment of early English poetry known as *The Seafarer*, James Fisher (*Shell Bird Book*, p. 43) translates

> *huilpan sweg fore hleahtor wera*

as 'whimbrels' trills for the laughter of men'; and suggests that *huilpe* was a name for both curlew and whimbrel.

By the 16th century, *turtle*, as the name for our turtle-dove, was becoming obscured by the name of the chelonian, which had been corrupted from Spanish *tortuga* or Portuguese *tartaruga* and made familiar by our seamen. To Chaucer the bird was always *turtel*, *turtle*, or *turtil*. By 1544 Turner was writing *turtel dove*, and when we read 'the voice of the turtle is heard in our land' in *The Song of Solomon*, we are reading one of the three instances of the use of *turtle* as a single word in the Authorized Version of the Bible, as against numerous references to 'turtle-doves'.

The O.E. *turtla* (feminine *turtle*) was an adaptation of the imitative L. *turtur*. Perhaps Tennyson's 'moan of doves in immemorial elms' was an echo of the words of Meliboeus in Vergil's 1st *Eclogue*:

> *Nec gemere aeria cessabit turtur ab ulmo.*
> (Nor will the turtle tire of moaning
> > from the elm that woos the sky.)

The original form *turtur* is still used in Wales. Our word is either a diminutive or a form in which the second *r* has been replaced by its sister-liquid *l*. In practically every European language the onomatopoeia is evident, whether the name is a derivative of Latin or has been formed independently. The Portuguese use the charming name *rôla*.

The imitative quality of *partridge* is not so obvious as it was in *perdix*, which Latin borrowed from Greek. When the stem *perdic-* passed into French, an intrusive *r* crept in, and the resultant *perdrix* became the M.E. *pertriche*. (Is there not a hint of a mangled version of this word in the carol which tells of a partridge in a *pear-tree*?) The eponymous Perdix of mythology was the nephew of Daedalus ('craftsman'), the inventor of wings for human flight, who, jealous of the young man's inventive skill, threw him from a tower. Perdix was saved in mid-air by Pallas Athene, who turned him into a bird. After his escape he avoided high places and kept as near as possible to the ground, reminding men of his fate by the repetition of his name. His rasping voice gained him the credit of being the inventor of the saw.

Perdix might well stand for an imitation of the call of our common partridge, if not for that of *Alectoris graeca* (the chukar). It is known that *Perdix perdix* (our bird) was formerly found further south than it is today. It is therefore at least possible that the species best-known in Britain was the one which gave the partridge-family its name. But in any event the etymology is less romantic than the legend; for the source of *perdix* and its derivatives must be sought in the Gk. verb *perdesthai*, 'to make explosive noises', from the root of which, **perd-*, verbs and nouns are to be found throughout the I-E. language-family.

The O.E.D. regards it as impossible that *geai*, the French original of *jay* (one of Chaucer's birds), should be a doublet of *gai* ('gay', 'bright'), a word derived from O.H.G. *wahi*, 'beautiful'. This being so, it is at least worth considering that the F. and English names, and the Port. *gaio* and Dutch *geai*, may have an onomatopoetic origin. But the Late Latin *gaius*, their source, may be just a personal name, like our 'robin'.

Popinjay seems never to have been used as a synonym for *jay*. Chaucer's 'popinjay ful of delicasye' (*Parlement of Foules*, 359) referred either to a parrot or to a green woodpecker, of which 'popinjay' is said to have been a provincial name more recently than the era when shooting at an imitation of a gaudy bird on a pole was popular among archers at rural festivities.

The *n* in *popinjay* is intrusive. M.E. *pape(n)iai*, *pope(n)iay* are from Anglo-Norman *papeiaye*, O.F. *papegay*, from Sp. *papagayo*, from Arab. *babagha*, 'a parrot', with the final syllable assimilated to *jay* by association with the bird's chattering and its bright plumage.

Whooper-swan shares with *whooping-cough* onomatopoetic origin. M.E. *whope*, *whowpe*, 'to utter a cry of "whoop"' was what falconers did, or huntsmen at a kill. The basic element of the verb, the cry *houp*, is found also in F. *houp-là* ('gee up!'), which has been adopted into English as the name of a game. The whooper's congener, our familiar mute swan, is not in fact mute, but merely less vocal, especially in the semi-tame condition, than the other bird.

Of the dodo Hilaire Belloc sadly recorded:

> 'The voice that used to squeak and squawk
> Is now for ever dumb.'

The satisfyingly imitative *squawk*, however, is to be found in 'squacco heron'. Willughby and Ray (1678) gave the name as *sguacco*, which Ulisse Aldrovandi (1527–1605), the Bolognese Professor of Natural History and Botany, said was used in northern Italy, where the bird breeds: but later authors, with the exception of Montagu, have stereotyped the incorrect spelling begun by Latham in the 18th century.

The *knot*, fancifully connected with King *Canute* (O.E. *Cnut*), may have taken its name from its alarm-note.

One or two of our bird-names may be traced to a humble interjectional source. The ejaculation *woe!* is found as *ouai* in Greek, *vae* in Latin and Old Norse, *wai* in Gothic, and *wa* in Old English. Few would deny that *wa-wa* is among the first sounds uttered by a human baby. The next stage is seen in the O.N. *vaela*, 'to wail', which appears in M.E. as *weilen*. The Welsh for the noun *woe* is *gwae*, and the Low Breton for the verb 'to weep' is *gwela*. From this *gwela* is formed *gwelan*, 'the wailer', a gull – the Welsh *gwylan*. From *gwelan* French took *goéland*, in the same way as from Cornish English borrowed the equivalent *gullan*, and clipped it down to *gull*.

Guillemot, which reached us from French, may be *goéland* with the addition of *mouette* or the older form *moette*. *Moette* had a Germanic origin, and is found in modern German as *Möwe*, and in kindred forms in other Teutonic languages. The O.E. equivalent is *mēaw*, which today appears as *mew* in *sea-mew*. *Gull* therefore denotes 'the wailer'; *guillemot* 'the wailing mewer'. At any rate this seems rather more probable than that the first part of the word represents the personal name *Guillaume* – the explanation preferred by some modern authorities. O.E.D. compares *guillem* (Welsh *Gwylym*) for the same bird, and *willock* for guillemot, puffin, and razorbill.

XII (a)

ANIMALS NAMED FROM PHYSIQUE
APART FROM COLOUR

'We see beautiful adaptations everywhere, and in
every part of the organic world.'
DARWIN, *The Origin of Species.*

ENGLISH has adopted a large number of animal-names from all over
the world, notably since the middle of the 16th century. In the older
and the more recent names taken together, physical characteristics,
including coloration, are second in importance only to habitual
action. To illustrate this, let us take a glance at a few mammals and
reptiles, with a fish or two and an amphibian, before making an
enormous task less unwieldy by limiting ourselves to a rather more
detailed examination of the etymology of the names of British Birds.
For the moment we will shelve Coloration.

The *squirrel* is 'shadow-tail', through F. and L. from Gk. *skia*
'shadow' + *oura* 'tail'. The frog's progeny, the *tadpole*, is 'toadhead'
(M.E. *tadde* and *pol*, from O.E. *tādie* 'toad' + Low German *polle*
'head'). An older name was *bullhead*, now transferred to a small
freshwater fish. (Cf. *bullfinch.*) The *stickleback* has a dorsal development of little 'sticks' or prickles.

From overseas we have 'nose-horn', the *rhinoceros*, from Gk. *rhis*
(stem *rhin-*) 'nose' + *keras*, 'a horn'. *Baboon* denotes an animal with
protruding lips, if the etymology is to be found in the F. *babine*, 'a lip'.
The Telegu (S. Indian) words for 'pig' and 'rat' explain *bandicoot.*
Porcupine is derived, through O.F. from L. *porcus*, 'pig', and *spina*,
'prickle'. There we have Kipling's 'Stickly-Prickly', who with his
friend 'Slow-and-Solid', the turtle, became fused into the armadillo
(diminutive of Spanish *armado*, 'armoured', from L. *armare*, 'to
equip' – the generous root **ar-* having swollen from its first significance
to produce the senses of reaching, joining, and furnishing).

'Alligator' is a corruption of Sp. *el lagarto*, 'the lizard': *lizard*
being derived from **lacarto*, a form of L. *lacerta*, the origin of which

word appears to be in the muscular suggestion in *lacertus*, 'the (human) upper arm'.

The anatomical peculiarities of the tortoise affected the Latin and French languages differently. Latin used the resoundingly dignified *testudo*, from *testa*, 'a shell', originally a vessel of baked clay. *Testa*, from the root *ters* (see 'terrier', Chapter IX(a)) came to have a variety of meanings, such as 'brick, tile, shellfish'; and *testudo* became the name of the covering of shields locked above the heads of the legionaries when they advanced to assault a fortified place.

The 'shell' has been retained in French by *tête*, 'head' – *testa*, 'wine-pot', in the Roman soldier's slang. But for *tortoise*, French went back to another Latin word, formed on the verb *torquēre*, *tortum*, 'to twist'. Because the creature had twisted legs, it was called *tortu*, from Late Latin *tortuga*.

In English many variations of these words were used until the second half of the 16th century, when the modern spelling became settled. *Turtle*, the name now usually reserved for the *Chelonidae*, or marine tortoises, is a tough seaman's attempt at the original *tortu*; but *tortu*, turned into the only animal's name which sounds anything like it, *turtle*, is linked to the dove of that name. On the whole this seems one of the most unscientific scientific names in the history of vocabularies. This ingenuous invention appeared in the middle of the 17th century.

In the sea sport the *grampus* (M.E. *graundepose*, through O.F. *grapois*, from L. *crassus*, 'fat', *piscis*, 'fish'); the *porpoise* (through O.F. *porpeis* from L. *porcus*, 'pig' + *piscis*); and the *turbot*, which is the O.F. version of O. Swedish *törnbut* the 'thorny flatfish'.

*   *   *

Turning now to the names of our 'native' birds, we shall find that of the various parts of their bodies the bill, not surprisingly, is the most prominent.

The Late Latin *beccus* represents a Celtic word meaning 'a hook'. This is found in *grosbeak*, the F. *gros bec*, 'fat bill'. The word *bill* itself is the O.E. *bile*, connected with *bill*, 'a sword or falchion' – the *sigēadig bill*, the 'victory-rich sword' of Beowulf. It appears in *crossbill, razorbill, spoonbill*; in *gull-billed tern* and about ten other epitheted names; and in the convenient name of *sawbills* for the fish-catching mergansers, goosander, and smew. These sea-ducks, with the backward-pointing spikelets in their mandibles, take the *saw* in their name from the modern form of the O.E. **sagu*, M.E. *sawe*. Likewise *scythe* and *seax* (the short sword from which the Saxons took their name) is from the root **sek-*, as in L. *secare*, 'to cut', from which we have *sect*, *segment*, etc., and, by way of *secula* and *serra* (= *secra*) 'a saw', the words *sickle* and *serrated*.

The spoonbill was known until the 17th century as *shovelard* or *shoveler*; the shoveler being then called *spoonbill*, a name still in use in East Anglia and Cheshire.

As might be expected, the most arresting characteristic of the snipe, the drumming or 'bleating' occasioned by the vibration of the outer pair of tail-feathers extended sideways, while the bird shoots sharply from aloft, is suggested by names for it in every European country in which it breeds. F. M. Ogilvie, in *Field Observations of British Birds* quotes about forty names culled from more than a dozen languages. The Celtic *gabhar athair*, 'she-goat of the air', may return to our minds when we discuss the possible meaning of *capercaillie*. L. *Capella*, 'she-goat', is the generic name for the common and the great snipe given by Frenzel in 1801. In Welsh are found *gafrwanwyn*, 'goat of the spring', and *dafad-y-gors*, 'sheep of the marshes'. The provincial Danish *hingstefugl*, 'stallion-bird', exists side by side with *horsegøg*, 'horse-cuckoo', and the more formal *dobbeltbekassin*: these and the Norwegian by-name *himmerhest*, 'sky-horse', are reminders of the name of *Hengst*, 'Stallion', the Jutish leader who proved to be a cuckoo in the nest of the Britons who had invited him to help them to resist the Picts. Such names for the snipe are paralleled in England by *heather-bleater* (a corruption of *hæferblǣte*, 'goat-bleater') and the East Anglian *moor-lamb* and *summer-lamb*.

The O.E. for 'snipe' was *snīte*. Snipe itself, the M.E. *snype*, is of Scandinavian origin, representing the O.N. *snīpa*. It has its counterparts in many other Germanic languages, as Dutch *snip* and German *Schnepfe*. The Swedish *snäppa* and Norwegian *sneppa* mean 'sandpiper'. All these, and many kindred words, must refer to the long bill, and have the general sense of 'snipper'. The base is seen in *snap*, *snout*, *snivel*, *snub*, *snuff*, and a great many cognate words in each of the Germanic dialects. In the special vocabulary of falconry to *snite* means to 'sneeze'. There is a connection between all these words and our *neb* (found in the provincial *coulterneb*, 'ploughshare-nose', for the puffin), Dutch *sneb*, and the German *Schnabel*.

Snitterfield, Warwickshire, and *Snydale*, West Riding, are the *Snitefeld* ('snipe-tract') and *Snitehale* ('snipe-flat') of the Domesday Book.

That *puffin* itself is like the by-name of *coulterneb* in alluding to the outsize bill (with or without further reference to the plump appearance of the body) is far from certain. The name may allude to the fluffiness of the young, which have somewhat of the look of young owlets. To this the late W. B. Alexander adds: 'the fact that "puffin" was used for the young of both the puffin and the Manx shearwater, collected from the burrows for food, supports this idea'. (*In litt.*, 1947.) Whimsically enough, of the two species just mentioned, it is the Manx shearwater which bears the scientific name of *Puffinus puffinus*.

If the coulterneb's name had been taken from an attribute even queerer than its beak, it would have been from the horny growths above and below the eyes which are assumed by the adults during the breeding-season. These are doubtless a boon to the short-billed birds when they have to put their eyes dangerously near the sharp beaks of their ravenous young in what would be to us at least the darkness of their burrows.

In the above-mentioned names the references to the bill are explicit: in many others, such as *turnstone*, *woodpecker*, *heron* (see Chapter IX(a)), and *oystercatcher*, its use is implied. For perfection of adaptation one might very well choose the heron's weapon. This does not draw so much attention to itself as do the bills of flamingo, puffin, toucan, and skimmer – to name but a few; yet glance at a heron's skull and beak fused into a six-inch dagger holding, in life, eyes and brain in the very hilt! Birds such as swifts and nightjars can wheel, turn, and pursue their prey until they drive their wide-open gapes against it, whereas the heron will normally stand like a statue until the right moment, when – especially if the intended victim be a fish or even a small mammal – success or failure depends on one lightning movement ending in the bill's becoming a pair of pincers. The human equivalent is a rifleman with his left arm fully extended, so that he hits the object at which in fact he, as well as the rifle, is aiming.

The *griffon-vulture* takes the first part of its name from the heraldic creature popularized as the *gryphon* in *Alice in Wonderland*. The F. *griffon* represents the L. *gryphus*, which was formed from the Gk.

grups, 'curved' – in allusion to the hooked bill of the mythical monster. There is naturally a tendency to associate the hook-billed *grups* with the equally hook-billed *gups*, 'the vulture'.

Some half-dozen of our names contain a reference to the birds' legs, feet, or claws. The common factor of *greenshank*, *redshank*, and *yellowshank* (recently discarded in favour of 'yellow-legs') represents the O.E. *scanca*, 'leg-bone', and is akin to German *Schinken*, 'ham'. *Leg* (O.N. *leggr*) arrived somewhat mysteriously in M.E., without previous history in the language.

The *stilt* is so called from its extraordinary length of leg. *Stylte* in Danish means 'to walk on stilts'; and our word, the M.E. *stilte*, is of Scandinavian origin. It is distantly related to *stalk*, and comparable to the Gk. *stelekhos*, 'a tree-stem', and with various Germanic words of kindred meaning, all from the generous root **stā-*.

The component parts of *phalarope* are the Gk. *phalaris*, 'a coot', and *pous* (stem *pod-*), 'a foot'. The Greek for 'coot', as might be anticipated from the bird's bald forehead, is derived from *phalaros*, 'patched with white'. Together with *phalakros*, 'bald' (whence the L. *fulica*, 'a coot'), *phalaros* is an extension of *phalos*, 'the peak of a helmet', which is itself an offshoot of *phao*, 'I shine'. The Greek root **phā-*, equivalent to the Skt. root **bhā-*, is the parent not only of a multitude of words implying shining, such as *phantom* and *phenomenon*, but also of many which suggest illumination of the mind, such as *phōnē*, 'a sound'; to which may be added the L. *fāri*, 'to speak', which provides us with a series of words connected with *fate* (i.e. 'the thing spoken', *fātum*). The second element in *phalarope* is equally interesting. The Skt. *pāda* (from *pad*, 'to go') means 'foot', and is one of a series of words illustrating one of the regular consonant-changes summarized under Grimm's Law. *Pāda*, *poda*, *pedem*, in Skt., Gk., and Latin, are represented in O.H.G. by *fuoz* (Modern German *Fuss*) and in Gothic by *fōtus* (O.E. *fōt*, our *foot*). Thus the first part of *phalarope* is etymologically akin to *fancy*, *fatal*, *fable*, and *phonetic*: the second part to *tripod*, *pedal*, and *fetter*.

Falcon, the M.E. *faucon*, derives from *falcōnem*, accusative case of the Late Latin *falco*, 'the bird with talons like a sickle' (*falx*). Both *falcon* and *falchion*, 'a curved sword', are thus akin to *reflect* and *reflexion*, and other words directly derived from the present or the supine stem of L. *flectere*, 'to bend'.

Another half-dozen names refer to head-plumage. The *poll* (M.E.

and Middle Dutch) of *redpoll* is difficult to trace further back than
the Low German dialects, and there is no related I-E. word with
this meaning. To draw a bow at a venture, is it a coincidence that
we find in *polo*, a word meaning 'ball' borrowed from the Balti
dialect of northern India, which might itself possibly be a clipped
form of Skt. *kapāla*, 'a skull'?

The *cap* of *blackcap* is to be traced to L. *caput*, 'head', through
Late Latin *cappa*, 'a head-covering'.

The F. *huppe*, 'a hoopoe', has acquired in that language the
secondary meaning of a tuft of feathers, or crest; but conversely it is
to the possession of a crest that several other species owe their names.
The word *crest* (from F. *crête*, L. *crista*) is connected with L. *crinis*,
'hair', and so with *crinet*, the falconer's name for the hairlike feathers
that grow about the cere of a hawk. It appears in *firecrest* and *goldcrest*, and seems to lurk in the name of the *Grebes*, in many species of
which Family the head-feathers are a remarkable feature. On this
assumption we must trace the F. *grèbe* to the Breton *krib*, 'a comb' –
a word probably cognate with 'crest'. Welsh *crib* has the same
meaning.

The *calandra* lark *Melanocorypha calandra*, recorded in England,
1961, owes its epithet to a word found in M.E. for a small bird of
unknown species. In Chaucer's *Romaunt of the Rose* the word is spelt
chalaundre (lines 663 and 914) and *chelaundre* (line 81), using the F.
calendre virtually unchanged. Distinguished etymologists tell us that
the F. and Provençal *calandri* came, with the addition of -*n*- and
dissimilation of *r-r* to *l-r*, from L. *caradrius*, Gk. *kharadrios*,
Aristotle's name (614b, 35–36) for a water-bird which in the daytime
lurked in ravines (Gk. *kharadra*, 'ravine'), where it nested. (We use
Charadrius in the names of some of the *Plovers* of the Family *Charadri-
idae*.) Yet the gulf between Aristotle's bird and Chaucer's seems too
wide to cross. Having a crest in mind, we may at least mention an
earlier theory – that from Gk. *kallos*, 'beauty', through *kallunein*, 'to
beautify', came *kalluntron*, 'ornament' or 'head-dress', which may
have passed, by way of L. *caliandrum*, into Italian as *calandra*, denoting
the Mediterranean lark, even if its 'head-dress' is not as pronounced
as our skylark's. Possibly during his visits to France Chaucer would
have become familiar with the crested lark *Galerida cristata*, though
not with the *calandra*. He often refers to *larkes*; but, although he was a
bird-lover, he is not likely to have distinguished between our sky-

lark and woodlark. Nor would he have cared any more than the author of *The Swiss Family Robinson* cared about poetic licence in the matter of habitats. If the 'head-dress' etymology is correct, the close association of *chalaundre* and *lark* (*R.R.*, 114, 915) and of *chalaundres* and *laverokkes* (*R.R.*, 662, 663) implies that the poet was acquainted with at least two kinds of lark, even if in the case of one of them it was only by name.

The forward-curving crest assumed by the *shag* for the first few months of the year accounts for its name. This seems to be the same as *shag*, 'matted hair' (O.E. *sceacga*, 'hair'), the primary significance of which is seen in the Old Norse *skagga*, 'to jut out'. A glance at the map of northern Europe will show the meaning of this word. A narrow cape at the extreme north of Denmark is called Skagen, as is also a long promontory on the south-west of Iceland. Various Scandinavian languages use forms of the same word to mean a beard. Other kindred words are our *shaggy*, *shag* tobacco, and *shaw* (O.E. *sceaga*), a thicket or copse, which men of Kent, with unconscious irony, term a *shave*.

The *beard* of the *bearded* tit and the *bearded* vulture preserves the O.E. spelling. It is found in similar forms in other Germanic languages, e.g. German *Bart*; and is related to L. *barba*, whence come the modern Romance words such as F. *barbe*. Welsh *barf* exemplifies the Celtic form.

The long black moustachial feathers of the male bird suggest the epithet in *bearded* tit. The *moustached* warbler has a thin white stripe from the nostrils to the eye, and behind it. *Moustache* is to be traced, through F. and Italian, to *mustax* ('the hair on the upper lip'), the Doric form of the Attic Gk. *mastax* 'mouth or jaw'), from *masasthai*, 'to chew'.

The *masked* shrike (one of the birds which lost their places on the British list in 1962 as a result of the enquiry into the suspect 'Hastings rarities') has a white forehead and a broad white stripe above the eye, in contrast to the majority of shrikes, whose 'masks' are black, and foreheads black or grey. *Mask*, F. *masque*, from the Spanish *máscara*, 'a masquerade or mask', is ultimately to be traced to the Arabic *maskharah*, a 'buffoon or a jest'. (The use of *mascara* as eyeshadow is a very ancient practice.)

Established, if not coined, by Pennant in 1766 were the names of the long-eared and short-eared owls, which refer to the longer and shorter feather-tufts on the brows of the two related species.

So apposite does *ruff* seem in view of the breeding-plumage of the male bird, that it is with reluctance that one finds coincidence in the name of a creature with a peculiarity as marked as is the trunk of an elephant or the pouch of a pelican. It should perhaps first be noted that the garment of the same name, the exaggerated collar which became popular in the 16th century, was not named from the bird. *Ruff*, as an article of wearing-apparel, is either a shortened form of, or cognate with, *ruffle*; and is therefore akin to numerous words in the Teutonic group that have a common implication of wrinkling or folding.

Next we might consider the arguments advanced for the bird's having been named from the garment. In the first place it is in the breeding-season that this polygamous species is most easily observed, and therefore named; for the ruffs are markedly less shy when they assemble, usually on some small tump or canal-bank, in order to contest, with characteristic display, for their slim and sober mates. Then, one must admit, the collar, the feathers of which the bird is able to control, draws to itself all the more attention from the fact that the colouring varies from bird to bird. It may be umber, grey, buff, white, or purple-black – plain, streaked or stippled – to name only a few of the common shades. Each bird keeps his own pattern and colour – and the colour of his legs, which may be green, yellow, or pink – seasonally for life.

Yet this 'obvious' explanation of the origin of the name has no etymological support. The name of the bird seems to be older than that of the garment. Another crux is the female's name of 'reeve'. As, by normal vowel-change, the German *Fuchs* has *Füchsin* as its feminine, and the O.E. *fox* had *fyxen* (which became in M.E. *fixen*, or, in the southern counties, *vixen*), so *reeve* may have been formed from whatever earlier word gave birth to *ruff*, or by analogy with similar pairs of words.

The superiority of action over appearance as a prompter of names is exemplified by names for the ruff in other languages: as the Portuguese *batalion*, the German *Kampfläufer*, the F., Italian, and Spanish *combattant*, *combattente*, and *combatiente*, the Dutch *kemphaan*, as well as in the scientific *Philomachus pugnax*, 'the quarrelsome battle-lover'.

Evidence, therefore, both direct and indirect, encourages the belief that the original name of the ruff may have been the same as, or similar to, that from which we have 'reeve', a bailiff – more familiar today in 'sheriff', i.e. shire-reeve. The O.E. *gerēfa*, says Skeat, would earlier have been *gerōfja*, in which the syllable *rōf* meant 'a multitude'. This being so, a title meaning a 'numberer of a host, registrar, or census-taker' makes a strong appeal for its being the origin of the name of the proudly-bedecked ruff parading before his host of potential mates and putting up an angry show of fighting, rather than engaging in serious combat, with his rivals. Certainly 'field-marshal' seems a better title than 'collared dandy' for *Philomachus pugnax*.

The epithet in the name of the *pectoral* sandpiper comes, through the similar French word, from the L. *pectoralis*, an adjective formed from *pectus, pectoris*, 'breast'. In very early Latin the verb *expectorare* was used to mean 'to banish from the mind'. In 18th or 19th-century English it came to have the more literal sense, 'to get it off one's chest' – an expression which describes rather well the display of the pectoral sandpiper in the mating season, as given by E. W. Nelson in *The Handbook of British Birds*: 'In order to utter display-note or "song", male inflates oesophagus into an enormous sac and runs about close to female with head drawn back over shoulders and tail hanging almost directly down.'

The tails of the *redstart* and *wheatear* have earned them names suggestive of their characteristic movements. *Steort* (modern *start*) is the O.E. for 'tail'; *ears* (modern *arse*) for 'rump'. Forms of *steort* are found in other Germanic tongues; and Gk. has the equivalent *storthē*, 'a spike'. All these are rooted in *stā-*. The *stark* in *stark-naked* is not the adjective *stark*, 'strong', akin to the name of the stork, but is a variant of *start*, O.E. *steort* – the phrase meaning originally 'tail-', and therefore 'completely naked'. (Cf. 'Start Point'.) The flame-colour and the white, as redstart and wheatear flitted from bush to bush, or from clod to clod, must have attracted the eyes of our Saxon forefathers as surely as they caught the attention of Gilbert White, who wrote: 'When redstarts shake their tails, they move them horizontally, as dogs do when they fawn; the tail of a wagtail, when in motion, bobs up and down like that of a jaded horse.' The etymology of *wheatear* is more easily seen in its earlier form *wheatears* (later taken for a plural) and in a Cornish version, *whiteass*.

A diminutive of *ears* (M.E. *ers*), *arlyng*, only slightly disguised in *sanderling*, the *arlyng* of the sands', was used as a name for the wheatear by Turner (1544) and by Merrett (1667). Otherwise *ears* seems to have been kept only in names for the grebes. Merrett and Willughby both called the great crested grebe *arsfoot*; *small arsfoot* being Willughby's name for the dabchick. The Gk. form of *ears* was *orrhos* (probably representing an earlier form *orsos*), also meaning 'rump', and akin to another Gk. word, *oura*, a tail, which is found in the second element of the scientific names of many animals.

The *collared* birds – a flycatcher, a pratincole, and a dove – owe their epithet, through French, to L. *collāre*, 'a neckband', from *collum*, neck, cognate with O.E. *heals* and the modern German and Swedish *Hals*.

The name of *waxwing* for the bird that has names meaning 'silk-tail' in German and the Scandinavian languages alludes to the tips of some of the secondaries of the adult. These tips, 3–5 mm. in length, resemble tiny, flat, blunt sticks of scarlet sealing-wax. They are modifications resulting from the fusion of the shaft with the outer vane of the feather. They appear on some or all of the seven outermost secondaries, and occasionally on the eighth. They are sometimes to be seen on the ends of the yellow-bordered tail-feathers. Occasionally a yellow variant of the 'wax' occurs.

Wing came into M.E. as *winge* from O.N. *vængr*, ousting the O.E. *fithere*. *Breast* passed through M.E. *brest* from O.E. *brēost*. *Tail* is the modern spelling of M.E. *tayl*, the O.E. *tægl*.

Goldeneye, the name of the duck with yellow irides, contains yet another offshoot from the root **ak-* – the original sense of the O.E. *ēage*, L. *oculus*, and all similar equivalents for 'eye', 'that which is sharp', being most easily observed in the Skt. *akshi*.

The *skua* with the twisted central tail-feathers is called *pomatorhine*, from its scientific epithet *pomatorhinus*. This might be applied equally to other members of a family notable for the protective plates over the nostrils. The word, made from Gk. *pōma*, stem *pōmat-*, 'a lid', and *rhis*, stem *rhīn-*, 'a nostril', takes us back to an Athenian wine-cup, which might be fitted with a lid, like a German *Bierkrug*.

Xİİ (b)

BIRDS NAMED FROM SEX, SCENT
AND SIZE

'A good ornithologist should be able to distinguish
birds by their air as well as by their colours and shape;
on the ground as well as on the wing, and in the bush
as well as in the hand.'

GILBERT WHITE, August 7, 1778.

Sex plays only a small part in bird-names, but is not quite absent.
Mallard, a derivative of the F. adjective *mâle* (L. *masculus*, diminutive
of *mas*, 'male'), now denotes only one species of duck, irrespective of
sex. The ending *-ard*, referred to under *buzzard* as the O.H.G. suffix
-hart implying male sex, reinforces the meaning of this anomalous
name. The onomatopoetic *cock* (O.E. *cocc*; M.E. *cok*), applied
originally, it is believed, to the male of the jungle-fowl *Gallus gallus*
has become more generalized in a few forms such as *woodcock*.

Drake, meaning 'a male duck', is a baffling word. It has not been
found in O.E. In M.E., a similar word, with the meaning of 'dragon'
(as in *fire-drake*), derives, through O.E. *draca* (as *dragon* itself, from
dracon-, stem of L. *draco*) from Gk. *drakōn*. This is cognate with the
Skt. *dṛś*, 'to see', and the Gk. *derkesthai*, 'to see clearly'; dragons being
notorious for their keen sight and glaring eyes. The name *dorkas*, 'a
gazelle', familiar to us as Dorcas, the Gk. equivalent to the meaning
of Aramaic Tabitha (Acts 9. 36), refers to the creature's large bright
eyes. But there seems to be no bond of union between dragons and
ducks. We must turn to the greater possibility that *drake* is a cur-
tailed version of some word derived from the O.H.G. *antrahho*, which
passed through the intermediate *entrik* to the modern German
Enterich, 'drake'.

This *ant* or *ent* is cognate with the stem *anat-* of the L. *anas*, 'a duck',
and probably with the Skt. *āti*, a water-bird. The Dutch for duck is
eend, the Icelandic *önd*, and the Swedish and Danish *and*. The O.E.

was *æned* or *ened*. The Dutch *andrik* means 'drake'; the Swedish *andrake*, 'mallard'.

The second element in *antrahho*, and therefore in *Enterich*, etc., means 'ruler' or 'king', as do the Skt. *rājan* and the L. *rex* (i.e. *reg-s*). The German Reich means 'kingdom'. The root **reg-* gives English, with a great many obvious words such as *regal*, *regent*, and *reign*, others more or less disguised, as *dress*, *escort*, *sortie*, *surge*, and *dirge* (which is from the opening word in the anthem for the Office of the Departed, '*Dirige, Dominus* . . .').

Drake therefore seems clearly to mean 'duck-ruler'.

         *   *   *

Only one of our birds seems to have acquired its name through an appeal to the human sense of smell. The olfactory sense of the generality of birds is much less acute than it is in mammals; and the scent given off by birds is normally less potent, and certainly far less perceptible by man, than the scent of a great many four-footed creatures. Moreover the importance of scent to the human kind had become considerably diminished by the time when man could give different names to different odours – the poverty of his vocabulary for this purpose justifying the criticism by the dog Quoodle in Chesterton's song:

> 'They haven't got no noses,
> The fallen sons of Eve:
> Even the smell of roses
> Is not what they supposes;
> But more than mind discloses,
> And more than they believe.'

It is not only modern squeamishness that accounts for our lack of names for sensations of evil smells. Nor was the aesthetic development of the rude forefathers of the hamlet, wherever situate, such as to cause us to wonder that no more than one of our birds should be named from the impact that it makes on the human nose. This single exception, the *fulmar*, is paralleled among mammals by the *foumart* (*foul marten*), known also as *polecat* from its former reputation as the terror of the henroost, *pole* representing *pullet* or *poultry*. Another name for this now exceedingly rare animal was *fitchet*, whence came the phrase 'to stink like a fitchet'.

136

Fitchet, 'stinker', is an unpleasant yet interesting word, which reached us through French from Middle Dutch. It takes us back, as *partridge* does, to the ancient root of which the Skt. form was *pard* and the Gk. *perd*. The Gk. *perdesthai* gave rise to *pordē*, 'a smell', and *pordōn*, 'a stinker' – an epithet applied in schoolboy fashion to the philosophers of the Cynic school by their opponents. Cognates are the L. *pēdere*, 'to break wind', and (Grimm's Law preparing us for the change from the unaspirated to the aspirated *p*) the O.H.G. *ferzan*. The O.N. *fisa* meant 'to smell'; and our *fizz*, *fizzle*, and related words are among the many for which pure imitation might appear to account, but which belong to a common stock.

To go back to *fulmar* – this is an Hebridean word made from the O.N. elements *fúll*, 'foul', and *mār*, 'a gull', which corresponds to O.E. *mēaw*, our *mew*. *Foul* and the related Germanic words are offshoots of the I-E. root **pu-*, 'to stink', which gives us *putrid*, *pus*, and other words. *Fulmar* thus points to the strong smell associated with the bird – so clean in plumage, so lovely in its effortless gliding and wheeling flight, and so captivating to see billing and cooing on a cliff-ledge (or on the branch of a tree – see *British Birds*, Feb., 1967), or balanced cork-like on a green roller. The scent is clearly of advantage to the bird, as to the oil-bird and a few other species and genera, though not to the majority of carrion-feeders. It is a musky odour which clings to the nesting-site and eggshells long after they are empty. Additionally the name may refer to the fulmar's habit of ejecting over its captor or pursuer the oil pre-digested for feeding its young.

Birds of various species may become temporarily odorous through eating certain foods: e.g. jackdaws and dabchicks, and wigeon when they have been feeding on *Zostera* (grasswrack). (Dr J. M. Harrison.)

*   *   *

Turning to names which suggest less specialized characteristics, we find a few which unadorned hold the sense of imposing size.

In *stork* there is the same implication of combined stature and strength as is to be found in the probably cognate Gk. *torgos*, a name for both swan and vulture. Similar names for the stork (O.E. *storc*) are found throughout the Teutonic tongues. These are akin to our *stark*, the Persian *suturg*, 'big and strong', and in the last analysis to all words sprung from the root **stā-*, 'to stand'.

Size is the keynote to *capercaillie*, if, as is generally agreed, the word is derived from the Gaelic *capullcoille*, 'horse of the woods'. *Capull* is cognate with the Low Latin *caballus*, 'a horse'; *caballus* itself having probably been taken from a Celtic source: and *coille* (the genitive case of *coll*) is akin to the English *holt*, a word for a wood now almost obsolete except in place-names whose meanings have become dim since the time when Chaucer wrote of the inspiration of the soft west wind 'in every holt and heeth'.

The *capullcoille* derivation was supported by Yarrell (1811): '. . . this species being, in comparison with others of the same genus, pre-eminently large, this distinction is intended to refer to size, as it is usual to say "horse-mackerel", "horse-ant", "horse-fly", "horse-leech", and "horse-radish" '.

J. Harvie-Brown, who went deeply into the question in *The Capercaillie in Scotland* (1879), stated that at that date the name *capull-coille* was still in use in Argyllshire and Lochaber. He referred also, among the many variants, to *capull caolach*, 'horse-cock', and *cabar caolach*, 'branch- or mountain-cock'; but appeared himself to favour *cabhar coille*, 'old man of the woods'. Howard Saunders was of yet another opinion, believing the first part of the name to be derived from *gabur*, the Celtic equivalent to L. *caper*, 'a he-goat', 'with allusion to the elongated chin-feathers of the male, and his amorous behaviour in spring'.

Sir Hugh Gladstone quoted, in *The Meaning of the Names of some British Birds* (1943), a suggestion made in *The Field* of 23.11.1940 that the etymology is *caber coilleach*, '*caber* denoting something clumsy and heavy, as for instance the "caber" used for tossing at the Highland Games'. Gladstone, who preferred the *capull coille* theory, criticized MacGillivray's suggestion of *coileach coille*, considering it a mere translation of the then (1837) current name of the species, 'cock of the wood', rather than an old Gaelic name.

To *cob*, the technical name for the male of the mute swan, the oldest known published reference seems to be in *The Order, Laws, and Ancient Customs of the Swannes* by John Witherings, the Royal Swan-Master (1632); but the O.E.D. cites 'cob-swan' from a record of 1570. As with *blob*, *dob*, *gob*, and Kipling's *flob* ('Gleason's old horse . . . tore down simple flobs of the bank'; *Puck of Pook's Hill*), the shape of the word 'cob' brings to one's mind something round and rather heavy for its size. This is true of corn-cobs, of the big hazelnuts such as Kentish cobs, and of the animal between pony and full-sized horse. The word is akin to *cobbler*, if a cobbler is a man who *repairs boots with thick pieces of leather*, and not one who hits (*cops* or *cobs*) with a hammer.

O.E. *copp*, 'top'. That *cob* refers to the knob or berry at the base of the mute swan's bill would seem obvious if the excrescence on the forehead of the adult were confined to the male. His adornment does in fact become considerably swollen in the spring, at which time the difference in size is sufficient for a moderately practised eye to distinguish the sexes without difficulty. This might be enough to point to the name of the cob-swan, apart from the fact that his mate is called *pen*, if indeed the latter term can be thought to refer to the slightly more pointed look of the head and bill of the female through some connection between *pen* and the M.E. *pinne* (O.E. *pinn*, from L. *penna*), 'a pin or peg', for which the Low German type was *penn*.

Where *cob* is applied to the black-headed gull, it presumably stands for *cop*, i.e. *black cop*, *cop* being our colloquial equivalent to the German *Kopf*, 'head'. An alternative possibility is that the name was given to the great black-backed and other large kinds of gull in allusion to the formidable use of their beaks. M.E. had *copen*, 'to strike', from O.F. *coper*, a verb (like the modern F. *couper*, 'to cut'), from *colp* or *cop*, 'a buffet'. Hence we have the elegant expression, 'I'll cop you one'. The parent of this was the L.L. *colaphus* or *colpus*, from Gk. *kolaphos*, 'a box on the ear', which one may take to be the source of the F. slang *une belle calotte*, 'a jolly good clout'. The Gk. verb *kolaptein* which produced *kolaphos* meant primarily 'to peck', used, e.g. of the eagle or vulture which pecked the liver of Prometheus.

It is possible, therefore, that the cob-swan is the *copper*, the striker or pecker, earning his name from the ready use of his wings and beak against intruders near his brooding mate.

We meet *bull* in *bullfinch*, a name accounted for by the bird's stocky neck and powerful head, the suggestiveness being aided by the short black bill, the black, glittering eye, and the ruddy plumage of the cock's neck, breast, and belly.

Būcephala, 'bull-headed', the generic name of the buffel-headed duck and the golden-eye, is the feminine form of the name of the famous charger of Alexander the Great, made by combining the

Gk. *bous*, 'ox', and *kephalē*, 'head'. But whoever named the little duck 'bufflehead' or, as we say, 'buffel-headed', must have had in mind the huge-headed American bison, the so-called 'buffalo'. *Buffalo* is a word with a long history. The Gk. *boubalos* seems to be a variation of *boubalis*, the name used by Herodotus and other authors for, presumably, the animal now known as *Boubalos boselephas*, the large antelope with massive neck and long head. The Greek word adopted into Latin as *būbalus* or **būfalus* passed into Italian as *buffalo* and Portuguese as *búfalo*, reaching English in the Italian form. *Būbalus*, again presumably for the hartebeest, was used by Pliny and in the Vulgate version of Deuteronomy 14.5, where it is mentioned as lawful food with a number of other beasts which 'part the hoof and chew the cud'; *cervam et capream, bubalum . . .*

Both *būcephala* and *bufflehead* make allusion to the globular appearance of the duck's big head, which is intensified by the diminutive size of the bill. One could compare the schoolboy's use of 'beefy'.

Buffle is an admirable word to illustrate suitability of sound to sense. *Buffoon* (It. *bufone*) is the clown who *puffs* out his cheeks. *Buffet* is a satisfactory word for the muffled type of blow which it implies, as contrasted with the whistling background to *whipping*, the heavy sound of *flogging*, or the quick sound of *smack*. The old prizefighters called their more or less padded gloves *mufflers*. These *ooph* words, with others such as *tuft* (colloquially *tuffet*, like the one which provided a pouffe for Miss Muffett), and *duff*, stodgy pudding, might be put side by side with the *oom*-sounding words in Chapter III.

The etymology of *bunting* is doubtful. The Lowland Scots *buntlin* is the equivalent of M.E. *buntyle* (*buntel*), alternative to *bountynge*. Since the name originally applied only to the corn-bunting, the Scots *bunt*, 'gay or lively', can hardly provide a clue, the corn-bunting being both sober-hued and lethargic. But there is another Scots word, *buntin*, 'plump'. Newton (*Dictionary of Birds*, 1893) suggests that *buntin* is derived from the name of the bird, and not vice versa. Referring to *Buntingford* in Hertfordshire, spelt *Buntingeford* in 1183, Ekwall makes the comment that *bunting* is first found in M.E., but may very well be older. The M.E.D. offers no new relevant information.

The *stint* takes its name from its *stunted* or *stinted* growth: (O.E. *stynten*, 'to stupefy', has a cognate adjective *stunt*, 'dull'). 'Less than two ounces is my weight,' wrote a poet in *Punch* in 1909, contrasting Louis Blériot's flight over the Channel with the prodigious night-journey of the tiny immigrant from the Arctic, with 'heart no bigger than a shilling' for its engine. Bill and all, this fairy wader, the little stint, is hardly larger than a sparrow.

Stinsford, Dorset (Stincteford of the Domesday Book) and *Stinchcombe*, Glos. (the 12th-century *Stintescombe*) still hold the bird's name, which the O.E.D. says was a dialect-word used for sandpiper and dunlin, first found in standard English after 1485.

Of the four ducks of the genus *Mergus* in the British list, the smallest, the *smew*, is named from its comparatively small size. Skeat derives the Dutch equivalent *smient* from Middle Dutch **smehi anud*, and compares the German *Schmalente*, thus bringing out the connection with such cognate words as the Swedish *små* ('small'), *smal* ('narrow'), and our 'small'. These are all offshoots of the root **mar-* (**mal-*).

We have already mentioned the *mouse* of *titmouse*. The first element in the word, found also in *titlark*, the provincial name for a pipit, came into M.E. perhaps from Scandinavian. The O.N. *tittr*, alluding to diminutive size, is found in the Icelandic *tittlingur* for 'bunting', 'pipit', and 'redpoll'. Norwegian uses *tita* for a small bird or a small trout. Swedish uses *mes* for every species of its resident tits except *entita* and *talltita* (lit. 'juniper-' and 'pine-tit') for 'marsh-' and 'willow-tit'. 'Tit' was formerly used in English to denote various other small things, including a small horse; the sense being preserved in *tit-bit* and in the colloquial and nursery word *titty* for 'tiny'. *Tit* for *teat*, 'a nipple', has a different derivation; but here is quite possibly some assimilation of mental imagery.

The diminutive or depreciative form of *jack* has been discussed under *jackdaw*. The jack-snipe, called in some districts 'half-snipe', betrays by his name that he is smaller than the 'full snipe'. It is only a few years ago that I met* a highly educated man who steadfastly stuck to his belief that the rustic superstition was founded on fact and that the wryneck was indeed the 'cuckoo's mate', i.e. the hen-cuckoo; and one would not be surprised to find in country-districts the belief that the 'jack' is the mate of the common 'jill-snipe'.

Avocet is derived from the F. *avocette* taken from the It. *avosetta*, a derivative of L. *avis*, 'a bird', which springs from the root **vay-*, 'to go'
*L.C.S.

–which one must trace back past the simpler Skt. root *ay- (also meaning 'to go') to the simplest of all roots, *ei-. *Ei- is the source of the Gk. *ienai* and the L. *ire*, and the common factor of such superficially dissimilar English words as *ambition, county,* and *trance,* however much they have been expanded and again mutilated.

The diminutive ending of *avosetta*, so characteristic of Italian, indicates grace rather than small size. English, however, is not deficient in true diminutive names. *Whimbrel* has already been noted: it is probably a double diminutive. Other names formed by the addition of one or more of the diminutive-making particles *-er, -el,* and *-ing* are *cockerel, dotterel, brambling, sanderling, starling, duckling, gosling,* and *dunlin. Siskin* is also a diminutive, and possibly *bunting.*

XIII (a)

ANIMALS NAMED FROM APPEARANCE: COLOUR

> 'It is a puzzle to understand how the splendid pagan
> poets of antiquity managed to get their effects with
> such few and vague ideas about colour.'
>
> G. K. CHESTERTON, *Generally Speaking*.

LET us pursue the plan of beginning with a few substantive names (in this case colour-based) from different groups of the animal and vegetable kingdoms. The names of the colours themselves will fit more conveniently into the analysis of the single and epitheted names of our birds.

The Algonquin (Amerindian) name of *wapiti*, a species of deer, is of equivalent meaning to our *wheatear* – 'white rump'. The *collie* (*coaly*) is so called because the Scottish sheepdog was usually black.

Grilse, the young salmon, says Partridge, represents the F. *gris*, 'grey', in the form of O.F. *grisel*, our *grizzle*.

Among variegated creatures the perch, *Perca fluviatilis*, 'the speckled fish', has its name ultimately from the Gk. *perkos*, 'dark or spotted'.

The Indian 'spotted one' is the *cheetah*, which, with *chintz*, is derived from Skt. *chitra*, 'bright, variegated'.

Fritillary, the butterfly, *Argynnis paphia*, is named after *fritillary* the flower, which is speckled like dice (*fritillus*, 'a die'). We have already noticed the *butter* of 'butterfly'.

If we know where to look, we find the *badger*. Skeat says that the origin of the name is unknown, adding, 'spelt *baggard* by Sir Thomas More, a nickname for the brock. Dr Murray shows that the badger = animal with a badge or stripe'. The O.E. *brōc*, taken from Celtic, refers to the white stripe down its face; and there is a provincial word, 'grey', for the shy creature which has given his name to *Brockenhurst* and other woodlands, and which Grahame's Badger says will still inhabit England when Man has passed away.

The *r*-metathesized form of the F. *brun* is found in the *burnet* (great and salad) in the *Rosaceae*. The 'burnet moth' shares the name, although it is its dark and cryptic red, with the dusky green, which is the unforgettable character of its colouring. We shall meet *beaver*, *bear*, and *Bruin* later on.

The lynx (Gk. *lugx*, via Latin) takes its name from the intense gaze and shining light of its yellow eyes. Light, (root **leu-*, 'to shine') is the base of the word. The Gk. *leukos*, 'white', which gives medicine half of *leukemia*, with *leussein*, 'to see', and numerous other words in the I-E. languages make this plain.

* * *

The colour of a bird in the hand provides such an obvious means of recognition that it is not surprising that a large number of English names of comparatively recent invention make use of some adjective of colour. *White* is reinforced by *snowy* and *ivory*; *black* by *sooty*, *coal-*, and *dusky*. The suggestions of redness include *pink*, *scarlet*, *roseate*, *ruddy*, and *rufous*. *Purple*, *tawny*, *cream-coloured*, and even such exotic epithets as *glaucous*, are all impressed into the service of nomenclature.

Colour plays a part in more than thirty per cent of the currently accepted English names, simple and compound, including such designations as 'grey lag-goose' of which it supplies one-third of the meaning, and 'brown flycatcher', of which it supplies half; yet it provides the main principle of hardly sixteen per cent of the individual and substantive names, if we exclude the very recent *bluetail*, *vireo*, and *yellowthroat*. If we spoke merely of names in use in England five to six hundred years ago, we should have to divide this percentage by three. In Chaucer's *Romaunt of the Rose* and *Parlement of Foules*, as against the one *ruddok* (our redbreast) and the vague *pye*, are mentioned more than forty birds whose names give no clue to their coloration. Shakespeare added no coloured birds except the then fairly recent coinage *robin redbreast* (in addition to *ruddock* and the puzzling *redbreast teacher* (? bullfinch).

Provincial names often include an epithet of colour, as *blue hawk* (merlin), *white owl* (barn-owl), *yellow-wren* (wood- and willow-warblers), *green plover* (lapwing), *copperfinch* (chaffinch), and *black martin* (swift). Most of these, however, like the multiple names more generally accepted, are comparatively modern, having been given when life began to grow slightly easier for folk in general, and when leisured people began to take more interest in nature for its own sake.

This comparative ignoring of colour by men of past ages is partly due to the fact that aesthetic appreciation tends to be less highly developed in the more primitive peoples. This is paralleled by the disregard, not to say distaste, for majestic scenery shown by even highly civilized people in old times. Wild grandeur which might move a modern author to ecstasy was abhorrent both to the average Roman of the Ciceronian age and to almost every writer who travelled in the British Isles before the Romantic Revival. Now it is the city-dweller, not the nomad or the tiller of the soil, who tries to find names for all the tints which his – or, more probably, her – eye can distinguish. Modern milliners search the universe for names to describe their subtle shades; and their vocabulary embraces *tangerine, shocking-pink, oyster, lime, melon, glacier, oatmeal, elephant,* and innumerable other niceties. This thirst for accuracy is quite foreign to the spirit of those who live closer to nature. By 'colour' your gypsy means colour – not shades or tints, but brave red, yellow, green, and blue. The plumage of a bird must therefore have been more than normally striking before there would have been much likelihood of its wearer's receiving a name from it, if that name were given in the pre-scientific age.

In the second place, the brightness of a bird's plumage is usually discounted by the distance separating it from the observer, and thus the chances of its being given a popular colour-name are further diminished. Any one of dozens of our smaller birds might be described by the casual observer as a 'little brown bird'. How 'obvious' brown seems is betrayed by the fact that in our odd 500 names (including some forty alternatives) the adjective appears in only those of two exceedingly rare vagrants, the *brown thrasher* and the *brown flycatcher Muscicapa latirostris.*

The misapprehension about the 'little brown bird' is also partly due to the fact that it is normally seen moving away from, and not approaching, the observer. The scheme of protective coloration ensures that the brightest tints are usually on the cheeks, throat, breast, and underparts of the bird. How different the same 'little brown bird' seems when seen through field-glasses or examined in the hand! The lovely carmine of the cock-linnet's forehead and breast, the buff and fawn of the stonechat – these are beauties unsuspected by those who see the birds from forty paces away. The black and white and chestnut of the male house-sparrow and the lead-blue of the dunnock have evoked surprise and admiration from many a person viewing them close at hand for the first time.

The outstanding exception is Turner's 'robin redbreast', whose coloured waistcoat has procured him his name in nearly every language, thanks to his confiding habits. In 1952 the List Sub-Committee of the B.O.U. yielded to popular sentiment and gave the name 'robin' a place side by side with 'redbreast'. The bird that will perch on the delver's spade cannot be relegated to the ruck of 'little brown birds'. Doubtless the robin's confidence and man's affection have increased *pari passu*; but it may well be supposed that the 'ruddock' was among the first of the small birds to receive a name from colour in whatever country it was found.

The comparatively infrequent occurrence of colour in the older names is yet another reminder that primitive peoples are far more interested in action than in appearance. Nouns and adjectives of colour provide no exception to the rule that the origin of a word is likely to be imbedded in a verbal root. Thus 'purple', the L. *purpureus*, which covered shades from crimson to mauve, and on occasion did duty for the contrasted ideas of gleaming white and of dark or dusky, derives, through F. and L., from Gk. *porphura*, the purple-yielding mollusc which gave the Tyrian dye – concerning which Browning enquired, 'Who fished the *murex* up?' Going back a little further in time, we find that *porphureos* was first used as an epithet for the ocean, not because it was coloured, but because it seethed and surged. The root related to the Gk., the Skt. **bhur-*, means 'to stir, to be in motion'. *Purple* is found in our bird-names as an epithet for a heron, a sandpiper, and the American gallinule *Porphyrula martinica*, recorded in the Scillies in 1958.

White (O.E. *hwīt*), the optical sensation of which corresponds to a combination of all the wave-lengths in the spectrum, is a word derived from the root **kwei-*, which implies shining, as in the Skt. *śveta*, 'white', from *śvit*, 'to shine', and in 'wheat', the shining grain or meal.

White is not the predominant colour in English bird-names. In contrast, as may be seen in the lists compiled by Dr E. O. Höhn, in the vocabularies of primitive tribes in the Arctic regions of America *white* leaves all the other colours literally in the shade. For the inhabitants of such a land as ours, where daylight is taken for granted and where green is the prevailing hue, black and red are supreme: for the Eskimo and the Hare Indian – as probably for the Lapp and the Siberian nomad – white is in the lead. Whether this is surprising when one reflects on regions deep in snow for the greater part of the year, or whether we suppose it to be a reaction against the month-long darkness, the fact remains that in the Far North of America, wherever is found a beast or bird white or even partly white, the whiteness is likely to be incorporated in its name. The majority of the 'Indian' names relate to action and habit, as 'flier' for the eagle, 'sun, looks at' for the sandhill crane; or to habitat or physique, as 'on top (sc. of the water) little' for the red-necked phalarope, 'water-fall-bird' for the harlequin-duck, 'flatbill' for the shoveler, 'having a necklace' for the killdeer plover. Onomatopoeia is well represented; and colours other than white play their part. But white is used three times as often as the names of all the other colours put together.

In contrast, the British list, with nearly 500 recognized or commonly used names, has only six names qualified by the plain adjectives *white, ivory, mealy,* or *snowy,* and hardly a dozen which are qualified by compounds such as *white-winged,* with half-a-dozen making use of *pied* or *black-and-white.* In substantive names 'white' appears only twice, viz. in *whitethroat* and *wheatear* (**O.E.** *hwīt* + *ears,* 'rump').

Mealy has the meaning of 'dusted with white powder'. Botanists use the word, as in 'mealy primrose', *Primula farinosa.* Applied to a redpoll, it hints at the appearance of the rump-feathers and other parts of the plumage. It is one of the multitude of words which the I-E. languages have from the root **mal-* (**mar-, *mri-*), 'to pound, crush, or smash', and its secondary forms such as **merd-* and **meld-.* The food of the gods is *ambrosia* – i.e. the food of the immortals, the *a-mbrotoi* (in which word the *b* eases the pronunciation of *mro-*). We *mortals* brew with *malt;* we *melt* and we *smelt.* We grind *morsels* with our *molars.* We *mollify* and we *mortify.* We shrink from *murrain* and *murder.* We pound grain in a *mortar,* or *mill* it into the *meal* which supplies the epithet for the linnet with the redpoll.

The first element in *snow-bunting, snow-goose,* and *snow-finch* alludes to habitat rather than to coloration, but leads us to the name of the snowy owl, which bred, for the first time recorded in Britain, in the Shetlands in 1967. 'Snow' (**O.E.** *snāw*) is sib to the German *Schnee,*

147

Swedish *snö*, and Russian *snieg'*, and to the Lithuanian *snigti* and Zend *snizh* ('to snow') and various other I-E. equivalents in the northern and eastern language-groups. These all keep more of the root **sneigh-* than do the Gk. and Latin, which have lost the initial *s*, as Gk. *nipha*; L. *nix, nivis*, 'snow'; Gk. *niphei* and L. *ningit*, 'it is snowing', which stand for **snipha*, etc.

For the origin of *ivory* in *ivory gull*, we look first at *ibha*, one of the many Skt. words for an elephant. This became *ebah* when borrowed by Hebrew. *Ebah* passed into Gk., and thence to Latin, prefixed by the Semitic article *el*, and became *elephas*. This article is seen also in *al-qādūs*, 'the albatross' (see Chapter IX(a)), as it is in *alkali, algebra, alcohol*, and *Alhambra*. The L. *ebur, eboris*, 'ivory', was taken more directly from *ebah*, its adjectival form *ebureus* becoming *ivurie* in O.F. and passing into M.E. as *ivorie*.

The word *red* (O.E. *rēad*) is a member of a large family derived from the root **reudh-*, 'to redden', including *rufous, ruby, rust*, the Skt. *rudhiram*, 'blood', and the Gk. *eruthros*, 'red', as well as *ruddy* and *ruddock* (O.E. *rudduc*, M.E. *ruddok*) already mentioned as a name for the robin.

Red must always have been considered the king of colours, from the day when man became vaguely, then more clearly, aware that a fluid spread over the surface of a solid – or, for the matter of that, a liquid – in some way changed it; until covering gave the sensation of colouring, and ultimately the syllable that meant 'to cover' gave birth to a word for this new discovery.

Two roots illustrate this. One is **var-*, seen in the Skt. *vṛ*, 'to cover', and *varṇa*, 'colour', and in literally *various* (L. *varius*) other words. In Latin the root takes also the form **vel-*, as in *vēlum*, 'a covering', *vēlare*, 'to cover' (whence our *veil, reveal*, etc.).

The second root, the source of *colour*, is **cal-* or **kal-* (to be distinguished from the **kal- *(kar-)* which produced the names of several birds already mentioned). In Gk. we find *kaluptein* and *kruptein* (i.e. *karuptein*), 'to hide', whence we eventually have *crypt, cryptic*, and other words such as *calyx*. In the Homeric age, beauty (*to kalon, kallos*) was considered as something external, a covering, 'skin-deep'. Latin had *cēlare*, 'to hide', and (from an older form *cēlere*) *occulere*, with derived nouns such as *cālīgo*, 'mist or darkness'; *cella*, 'a covered store, a cache'; and the pseudo-preposition *clam*, 'covertly'. From these we have many words such as *conceal, occult*, and *cellar*. Cognate with all these are the Old Irish *celim* and the O.E. *helan*, both meaning 'to hide or cover'.

Red it was that must have opened man's eyes to the phenomenon of colour. Millenniums before the use of dyes and pigments, in the hour of birth and the hour of death, in most of the crises of man's life, he was imbrued with the scarlet of his own or of another's blood. The sun rose and sank to rest in a flood of the same colour. Whether man seized his prey, or escaped from a battle or from the talons of a wild beast, or kept alive the flame of that mysterious creature, fire, he continued to leave the significance of red ever more deeply implanted in the racial memory.

Red itself occurs five times in single names of British birds. With its cognate words and *ferruginous* ('rusty-red') it occurs some 28 times in standard names. This is slightly less often than *black* and its equivalents, including *brent*; and is also roughly the frequency, as compared with blackness, in obsolete and provincial names.

Passing from red itself to different shades of it, we find the *scarlet* grosbeak taking us, through O.F. *escarlate*, to the Persian *sagalat*, 'cloth' (usually scarlet). Another form of the word, *saglatun*, is easily recognizable in the M.E. *ciclatoun*, 'rich cloth'. *Ruby* comes through O.F. and Late Latin, from L. *rubēre*, 'to be red'. The *ferruginous* of the white-eyed duck is from L. *ferrūgo*, stem *ferrūgin-*, 'iron-rust', formed from *ferrum*, 'iron', with the suffix often implying deterioration. *Ferrum* is the 'firm' stuff, the base being found also in Gk. and Skt.

The names of the unsaturated tints, *pink*, *rose*, *rosy*, and *roseate*, are taken (as are *violet*, *mauve*, and *lavender*) from names of flowers: one from the flower with *pinked* or serrated petals, and the others from the rose. The L. *rosa*, from which O.E. had *rose*, may have stood for **rhodia*, a form of the Attic Gk. *rhodon*, which represented the Aeolic Gk. *brodon* (for *wrodon*) borrowed from Armenian *ward*, 'a rose'.

Brown (O.E. *brūn*, modern German *braun*, etc.) should be a pleasing word to the zoologist, for from its earlier forms spring the names of several mammals, notably *beaver* (O.E. *beofor*, L. *fiber*, German *Biber*), formed by the reduplicated root **bhru-* 'brown', and *bear*, together with the Low German *Bruin*, a name found in *Reynard the Fox*, the 14th-century satire on mediaeval Germany, in which the characters are beasts. So also Greek had *phrunē* and *phrunos* for 'toad'. Perhaps the Hellenes, who, in the words of Professor Dawes Hicks, 'looked on Nature with a free and friendly eye', had a better outlook than the compatriots of Shakespeare who thought the toad 'ugly and venomous'. It might not be too far-fetched to imagine that the Athenians found brown shades a restful change from the intense white, purple, and blue of their seas and skies. Be that as it may, they not seldom called a girl *Phryne* – 'toad' – presumably from her having a golden-brown complexion or light brown hair. One famous Phryne, of the 4th century B.C., when arraigned on a charge of sacrilege, won the verdict by throwing off her dress and standing before her judges in nothing but her radiant beauty. It was she who was the model for the greatest work of Praxiteles, the *Venus of Cnidos*.

The oldest equivalent known for 'brown' seems to be the Skt. *babhru*, tawny, a reduplicated form of the radical word *bhru*, whence came *bhrū* and the equivalent Gk. *ophrus* and O.E. *brū* – all meaning 'eyebrow'. The radical meaning seems to be the colour of something fried (Gk. *phrugein*, L. *frīgere*, Skt. *bhrajj*, 'to roast or fry', from the root *bhleg*, 'to burn').

The *tawny* of owl and pipit is a reminder of the first great division of the Aryans. To the Teutonic peoples the root-word that gives us *tawny* denoted 'a fir-tree' (modern German *Tanne*): to some of the Celts it signified 'an oak'. From the Breton *tann* French took *tan*, 'oak-bark used in the curing of hides'; and *tanné*, 'tanned', was applied to the hue of dressed leather. In the language of heraldry it is *tenny*, one of the two rarest of the seven tinctures in the English science. In common speech we are better acquainted with *tan*.

Similarly *buff* is the colour of tanned *buffalo*-hide. The epithet is used in *buff*-breasted sandpiper, but the *buff*-backed heron (so named by Selby in 1833) is now known as 'cattle-egret'.

Comparatively few birds offer a sight of blue in their plumage. Moreover, blue *pigment* in a feather is a rarity. Generally the sensation of blueness in plumage reaches our consciousness through a sort of natural conjuring-trick, owing to the refraction of light falling on very delicately-patterned *brown* feathers. The illusion is destroyed when a 'blue' feather of this kind is held up to the eye against a strong light. It is therefore not surprising that reference to blue in substantive names is confined to the *blue*throat and the (red-flanked) *blue*tail *Tarsiger cyanurus*. *Blue* tit we have; but otherwise the adjective is found only in four compound epithets.

One theory about the origin of the M.E. *blew* is that it betokens the colour of a bruise, the result of a blow. It reached us through O.F. from O.H.G. *blāo*. Grimm connected this word and Norse cognates such as *blār*, 'livid', with the Gothic *bliggwan*, to 'strike', citing as a parallel the L. *caesius*, 'grey-blue', from *caedere*, 'to beat'. If this is correct, our *blue* and *blow*, 'a hit', and the German *blau* and *bläuen* are cognates. But *blue* is certainly connected with such words as the L. *flavus*, 'yellow', from the root **bhleg-*, 'to burn'. Another Latin word from this root is *flamma*, 'flame'; which is obvious in *flamingo*, taken from Provençal through Old Spanish *flamenco*.

Fire, found in *firecrest*, represents the O.E. *fȳr*. With its kindred, such as the German *Feuer* and Gk. *pūr*, it springs from the root **peu-*, 'to purify'.

A kind of transitional stage between *flavus* and *blao*, yellow and its complementary colour, blue, may be noted in the Old Spanish *blavo*, 'yellow-grey'.

$\overset{\displaystyle\cdots}{xiii}$ (b)

ANIMALS NAMED FROM APPEARANCE:
COLOUR (*continued*)

'*I* never saw a sunset like that, Mr Turner!'
'No, Madam? But don't you wish you could?'

THE apparent contradictions among the names of colours in the various members of any family of languages shed some light on the earlier stages of the growth of speech. Two theories may be cited which endeavour to explain the confusion. One is that the mechanism of the eye of primitive man was not sufficiently developed to allow him to discriminate among colours. Without going into technicalities we may say that the series of tiny cones of the eye which are sensitive to light allows the human brain to register the sensations of blue and yellow, while the second series is geared to the sensations of red and green. Since a young creature, from the embryo onwards, reproduces, as it grows, phases in the story of organic life, and therefore, in the final stages, phases in the story of its own species (by the evolutionary process of which it is said that 'phylogeny repeats ontology'); and since human babies, it seems, are at first colour-blind, and do not develop complete colour-discrimination until late in their second year, it has been suggested that man himself was long in developing full physical ability to distinguish colours. Proud mothers are apt to think that 'my baby' is an exception; but they ignore the baby's ability to distinguish between various degrees of brightness.

The power of speech, however, is so comparatively recent that we may discount any suggestion that it was anterior to the full development of the human retina. We are therefore driven to another hypothesis to account for man's vagueness in the naming of colours. This rests on the intimate connection between reason and speech. 'Language as we now know it,' says de Selincourt in *Pomona – The Future of English*, 'is not for communication only: it is the very framework of our thought.' Vagueness, it follows, in processes of the mental life is always correlated with vagueness in the meanings of words, even as lack of clearness of expression indicates a corresponding lack of clearness in thought. So, as Moncalm says in *The Origin of Thought and Speech*, 'Our ancestors gazed at the blue sky or the green trees as in a dream, without recognizing blue or green, as long as they lacked words to define the two colours; and some time elapsed before they particularized the colours by giving each its proper title.' And again: 'From the Sanskrit root *ghar-*, which has many different meanings, such as to heat, to melt, to drip, to burn, to shine, come not only many words (sc. meaning) heat, oven, warmth, and brightness, but also the names of many bright colours, all varying between red, yellow, green, and white. But the most striking example is afforded by the Sanskrit word *aktu*. Here we have the first instance of the uncertainty in the meanings of the names of colours which pervades all languages, and which can be terminated only by scientific definition. The word has two opposite meanings – a light tinge or ray of light, and also a dark tinge, and night. This same word in Greek, *aktis*, means a ray of light. Thus, whilst ideas are not definitely named, even the most simple, such as black and white, are not realized.'

To this may be added that experiment has shown that people who have been taught the names of various shades of grey are able to distinguish more shades than people who are unacquainted with the names. Moreover, 'memory-colour' experiments have shown that colours are perceived as remembered by the observer, not as they appear at the time. Snow, for instance, though lit up by the rays of the setting sun, or lying in the shadow cast by a wall, is almost invariably called 'white'. Coloured motion-pictures must be corrected to allow for this tendency in the observer, a tendency often indicated by comments made by laymen upon the work of artists who have reproduced in their pictures the colours in nature as they have perceived them.

It is said that Sir William Orchardson, the Academician, who had a great love for warm brown and orange tones, having finished a portrait of King Edward VII in morning-dress, was reproached rather peevishly by the king for making his black boots look yellow.

'My apologies, Sir,' was the artist's reply, 'but that is how I saw them.' This, and Turner's well-known retort to somebody who cavilled at the brilliance of his sunsets, may illustrate the essentially subjective nature of the mystery of colour.

The interdependence of precise thought and language; the infinite number of gradations of colour in nature, which render accurate description of tints almost as difficult as the description of a taste or a smell; the constant splitting up of groups of people using the same word for the same concept, and the converse process of union between groups employing different words; the comparative un-importance of colour to primitive man, whose life was essentially practical – all these are factors in the confusion of colour-names in different languages.

Perhaps we need to keep all this in proper perspective by realizing that even now the man with the richest vocabulary has names for no more than about one per cent of the 15,000 tints distinguishable by the human eye. We are content to name only seven colours in the rainbow itself. The most we can say is that we show an advance upon the writers of the sixth to fourth centuries B.C. Xenophanes clothed Iris in purple, red, and yellow; Democritus in yellow, white, and black; and Aristotle in red, yellow, and green.

*   *   *

Mankind long failed to discriminate between green and yellow, as may be gleaned from the names of these colours in the various I-E. languages. Like 'gold', 'yellow' springs from the root *ghel-, which gives us, among other words, the 'yolk' of the normal egg of every bird. Taking *yellow* (the O.E. *geolo*, M.E. *yelu* or *yelwe*) as the mean, we find on the one hand the German *gelb* (and *gold*), and L. *gilvus*, 'pale yellow'; on the other the Gk. *khlōros* (whence Aristotle's *chlōris*, possibly the greenfinch, used by Cuvier in 1800 as the generic name for that bird) and the L. *helvus*, 'yellow-green or green'. The essential meaning of all the words is provided by the Gk. *chloē*, the tender green of young plants, the colour seen when the sun shines on a field of growing wheat or through the leaves of a beech-tree. The same significance is in the L. *holus* (from an older form *helus*), 'cabbage, garden-plants'. Less obviously connected, yet still connected, with these words are *green* itself, the Skt. *harita* and L. *viridis*.

Green, so clearly a cognate of the verb to *grow*, provides the radical meaning. It was the soothing colour surrounding many of the early men from dawn to dusk. Intimately bound up with the plant-life that formed the background of their everyday view from cave or other shelter, or as they ranged in search of food, the word which they used for the varying hues of herb and foliage was taken from the root expressing the idea of growth. Yellow and green, green and yellow, typified the quiet expansion and decay of the plant, the first timid shoots, the full foliage, and the autumnal leafage.

With regard to the association of the words for yellow and blue, it is worth noting that the two colours lie on either side of green, and that an admixture of green pigment seems inseparable from blue and yellow pigments. It needs in fact a nice discernment to divide pure green from green with an infusion of yellow or of blue. It seems likely that dark blues were at first alluded to by names meaning no more than 'dark' or 'dusky', while brighter blues, untinged with red, tended to be confused with green.

The adjective *green* or *gold* or *yellow* is applied to some part of the bird's body in five of our names. In *yellowhammer* the epithet has become firmly welded to the second element of the word, as *gold* was to *finc* in Saxon times, and *grene* to *finche* by the time of Turner. In *oriole* the gold is disguised, as is the yellow colour in *serin*, *citril finch*, *citrine wagtail* and *icterine warbler*. As a separate epithet or part of an epithet *yellow* and *golden* are each used five or six times, *greenish* once, and *green* three times, though the American *green* heron is as yet only a doubtful claimant for British status.

Greenlets is a family-name, comparable with our 'leaf-warblers', given by Americans to the *Vireonidae*. Here they may be mentioned by virtue of accepted records of the red-eyed vireo, the first being from the Tusker Rock, off Greenore Point, County Wexford, in October 1951. The L. *virēre* means 'to be green', and *vireo* was a name used by Pliny for what may have been the greenfinch. To *virēre* are traceable our *vert*, *verdure*, *verdigris*, etc., the radical meaning being 'to live, to be fresh'. The red-eyed vireo (*c.* 6¼ inches from bill to tail) is one of the larger of these rather warbler-like birds, with their grey-green upper plumage and, often, spectacled or ruby eyes.

Though it is encouraging to the etymologist that *yellow* and *hammer* are still kept as separate words in the B.O.U. List of 1952, the second part of the name divorced from the first has now no special meaning for the average countryman, even if he lives in one of the valleys named from the bird – *Amberley* in Sussex and Gloucestershire or *Amberden* in Essex (*Amerdene* in 11th-century records). Skeat, in the C.E.D. says bluntly that the *h* of hammer is an 'ignorant insertion', since *ammer* answers to the O.E. *amore*, 'a small bird', and cites the

O.H.G. *amero*, the Middle Dutch *emmerick*, and the modern German *Gelbammer*, *Goldammer*, and *Emmerling*. *Gelbling*, 'little yellow one' is yet another German name for the attractive little bird, which is known by some equivalent name in practically every other European language, including Hungarian and Russian.

The German *Ammer* is the name for a bunting; *Emberiza*, the generic name given by Linnaeus, being according to von Gesner the Latinized form of the Middle German *embritz*; but the radical meaning of *amero* and *amore* seems undiscoverable. It may be, however, that they in fact denoted the yellowhammer and the cirl-bunting to our Saxon forefathers. The yellowhammer, through its brightness, song, and comparative boldness, must have claimed their attention; and no other name is known from pre-Norman times, although we must believe the northern name of 'yeorling' to be ancient, if only on the evidence of the widespread distribution of varieties of the rhyme:

'The brock and the toad and the yellow yeorling
Tak' a drap o' the deil's bluid ilka May morning.'

The 'ignorant insertion' of the *h* in 'hammer' was made long ago; for in 1544 Turner called it 'yellow ham' side by side with 'yowlryng'. By Merrett and Willughby it was called by its present name. Pennant used the same name in 1766, but in later editions of his work changed it to 'yellow bunting'. Yarrell (1843) seems to have done his best for etymology, giving 'yellow ammer' as an alternative to 'yellow bunting'.

The epithet *yellow* may be evidence that the meaning of the simple name was becoming forgotten – as when Pennant prefixed the tautological *golden* to the name of the oriole in the appendix to vol. 4 of his *British Zoology* (1776).

Oriole, like *aureole*, is from L. *aureolus*, a diminutive of *aureus*, 'golden'. Both *aurum*, 'gold' (the glowing metal) and *Aurōra*, 'the dawn' (the glowing sky) – once *ausum* and *Ausōsa* – are from the root **ush-*, 'to burn'. *Oriole* reached English through the O.F. *oriol*. In modern French the definite article has coalesced with the noun, and, the final *l* having given place to *t*, the bird's name has become *loriot*.

The name of the serin provides a puzzle. The suggestion that it is a corruption of the F. *sirène*, 'a siren', from the beauty of the bird's song, is hard to accept. W. B. Alexander wrote of that song as 'hardly

156

more than a prolonged twittering' (*in litt.*, 1947). It is more probable that 'serin', which, in the form 'seryne', can be traced back to 1530, represents a French form of a Late Latin *citrinus*, 'yellow', the colour of the citron – which, through Italian, provides the epithet for the citril finch, and, through French, that for the citrine wagtail. It is difficult to dismiss this attempt to solve the problem in view of the colour of the serin's plumage; for, though not so bright as the male oriole, he attracts the eye quite as readily as does the greenfinch. Thus it would seem that *serin* and *cedar* have a common ancestry, each springing, through the L. *citrus*, 'an orange-tree', and *cedrus*, 'a cedar', from the Gk. *kedros*. In names in various other European languages reference is made to the yellow of the plumage, but in none does there seem to be any allusion to charm of voice.

The colour lies disguised in the name of the icterine warbler *Hippolais icterina*. The Gk. *ikteros* was the name of a greenish-yellow bird; but the primary meaning was 'jaundiced'. In the Septuagint, the Greek version of the Old Testament, the word, translated as 'ague' in the Authorized Version, appears in Leviticus 26. 16:

'*Epistēsō huph' humas ton iktera sphakelizonta tous ophthalmous humōn.*'
'(If you will not hearken) I will appoint over you the burning ague that shall consume the eyes.'

In the first century A.D. Juvenal and Pliny used *ictericus* with the meaning of 'suffering from jaundice'; and Pliny, on the principle of taking a hair of the dog that bit one, gave looking at the yellow bird (*icterus*) as a cure for the disease. He added that a certain man, having gazed on the bird, was cured: 'the bird it was that died'.

Cream (in 'cream-coloured courser') derives from G. *khrisma*, 'an unguent', through F. *crème*, O.F. *chresme*, and L. *chrisma*, the consecrated oil used, e.g., in the Sacraments of Baptism and Holy Unction. The word is connected, in sense though not in form, with the *olive* and *olivaceous* in the names of three rare bird-visitors to Britain. Our 'oil' and the F. *huile* are from the older French form *olie*, which represents the L. *oleum*, 'an olive', from *olea* (Gk. *elaia*), 'an olive-tree'. *Olivaceous* seems to be merely a synonym for 'olive-coloured', 'the tint of unripe olives', i.e. 'a brown-green'. The Skt. root *li-, 'to melt', extended to the roots *lih-* and *lip-*, 'to lick' and 'to smear', gives a clue to the origin of *elaia* and of cognates such as the Gk. *lipos*, 'lard', and the O.H.G. *olea*, 'oil'.

Black, technically the absence of all colour, owing to the absence of reflected light, would appear to be another offshoot from the root **bhleg-,* 'to burn'. What is burnt may be charred until all colour is banished. Thus the *brent* or *brant* of the goose can signify 'black or dusky red'.

In substantive names black is predicated of part of the bird in *blackcap,* of the whole bird in *blackcock* (whose mate is the *greyhen*) and in *blackbird.* Altogether blackness is suggested, with the aid of *pied, sooty,* etc., in some three dozen names. These include nine substantive names preceded by the simple adjective: viz. duck, guillemot, grouse, kite, lark (temporarily under a cloud), redstart, stork, tern, and wheatear. But one more might be added unofficially, if only for the reason that it bids fair to be included in any new list that may be published. This is the name of the black woodpecker, whose plumage, apart from the crimson crest and nape of the male and his mate's more modest decoration, is indeed among the blackest of the black, with the same absence of bright reflections that characterizes the blackbird. With many happy memories of the species on the Continent, I should count it a joy* to hear its clear, fluty, unwoodpeckerlike cry, *klee-yah,* in an English wood; but, since no record of its being seen in Britain has been officially accepted, I should be apprehensive of being the sixty-fifth, or thereabouts, to have seen (or to have fancied having seen) a black woodpecker dipping across a ride, knowing that my *Martius* would almost certainly be counted as an 'escape' or as a mal-observed jackdaw or green woodpecker. Since the black woodpecker is as big as a rook, apart from the rook's longer wings, it is hard to see how any reasonable observer could be mistaken. The exaggeratedly dipping flight and the red on the head are diagnostic, except when the bird is compared with the much smaller and light-coloured yaffle. It therefore gave much pleasure to many people when R. S. R. Fitter and R. A. Richardson, in their *Pocket Guide to British Birds* (1952) included *Dryocopus martius.* This was better than leaving it to some unscrupulous person to prove that 'a live bird's a mystery, a dead one is history', by pulling a trigger to make sure that the strange bird, whether an 'escape' or not, shall at least be identified.

Bearing in mind the factors governing the bestowal of names, we cannot be surprised at the comparative newness of *blackbird.* Though

*L.C.S.

to us no name could be more obvious, to Spenser and Shakespeare the bird was the *owzel* or *owzell* (O.E. *ōsle*), a name which contains no reference to colour or the lack of it. It is true that *black bride* (which preserves the original position of the *r* shifted in *bird*) is found in *The Boke of St Alban's* (1486); but it was long before this 'obvious' name ousted the established *ouzel*, which still obtains in the north country and in the name of the blackbird's congener, the *ring-ouzel*.

The *soot* (O.E. *sōt*) of *sooty* tern and shearwater is probably from the root **sed-*, 'to sit' – being the stuff that *settles* in the chimney and elsewhere.

Coal, seen in *coal-tit* (O.E. *colmāse*) meant originally what we now call *charcoal*, not the pit-coal of modern times. It has kindred words in other Germanic languages, and is related to the Skt. causative verb *jval*, 'to make to flame'.

The *dusky* qualifying the names of Naumann's thrush and a warbler was a Norse introduction – *dusk*, itself an adjective, meaning 'obscured'. Modern Norwegian *dusk* means 'mist'. Nearer in meaning is the related L. *fuscus*, giving us *subfusc*.

Grey or *gray* (O.E. *graeg*) has cognates in other Germanic tongues, e.g. German *grau* and Swedish *grå*. It appears in *greyhen*; as an epithet for a wagtail, a plover, a phalarope, the lag-goose, and two shrikes; and in the name of the American gray-cheeked thrush *Catharus minimus*, the grey-headed wagtail, and the grey-rumped sandpiper, which was removed from the British list in 1962.

Four other adjectives are employed to denote various shades of grey, if we include the *slate-coloured* of the junco caught at the Loop Head Light in the County Clare in 1905. We have *slate* through M.E. *slat* from O.F. *esclat*, 'a slate', originating in L. *exclatare*, 'to split', *ex* ('out') and **clat-* imitative base, cf. O.L.G. *klapp*, 'a sudden loud noise' – the modern F. *éclat*.

Isabelline has been applied to a shrike and a wheatear. This shade of grey is that of soiled linen, but, like this particular wheatear, the etymology of the adjective is now on the 'doubtful' list. The legend ran that Queen Isabella of Castile, wife of Ferdinand II of Aragon, at the beginning of the siege of Granada, held by the Moors in 1491, vowed not to change her shift until the city was captured – as it eventually was in the following year, mercifully for Spain and for the Queen's personal comfort. The story has also been told *mutatis mutandis* about Isabella Clara Eugenia, Gouvernante of the Netherlands, during the investment of Ostend in 1601.

Pallid, the epithet for one species of harrier, is from L. *pallidus* (*pallēre*, 'to be pale') cognate with *pullus*, 'dark grey' and with Skt. *palita* and Gk. *polios*, 'grey', and *pellos* and *pelidnos*, 'livid'.

Glaucous (found in *glaucous* gull) came through L. from Gk. *glaukos*, which meant primarily 'bright or gleaming', and secondarily 'blue-green or blue-grey', like the sea. The Gk. adjective was akin to *glaussein*, 'to shine or to glare' – our *glass* being presumably from the same root. The bird which we call *little owl*, or sometimes 'Greek owl', the Hellenes themselves called *glaux*, from its staring yellow eyes. Owls being traditionally birds of wisdom, the little owl (to be seen on the *glaukes Laureotikai*, the coins made of silver from Mt Laurium) was the familiar of Pallas Athene, goddess of wisdom and patron deity of Athens. Formerly named, by Scopoli, *Strix noctua* (though 'night-owl' is not a particularly apposite name for so diurnal a bird), it was put with its congeners by Boie into a new genus, which he named *Athene*.

Derived from *glaux* is *glaukōpis*, Homer's favourite epithet for Athene. The exact meaning has long been debated. By derivation, it could stand for 'gleaming-' or 'grey-' or 'blue-eyed'. Even schoolboys have found 'owl-eyed' incongruous with the idea of divine beauty. 'Blue-eyed' or 'grey-eyed' seems most pleasing; but, as the owl has fierce *yellow* eyes, scholarship demands the more accurate rendering of 'flashing-eyed' for *glaukōpis Athēnē*.

Eagle (M.E. *egle*), another difficult word, finds its place among birds of sombre hue, if it is to be traced, through F. *aigle*, and L. *aquilam* to *aquilus*. This name seems to mean 'of the colour of turbid water' (*aqua*). Or was it to a sea-eagle to which the name of *aquila* was first given? *Aqua* is one of the multitude of words derived from the root *ak-*, 'to be sharp'; and, having in mind the eagle's sharp sight, sharp talons, and sharp swoop, one finds it difficult not to seek a more immediate connection between the bird's name and **ak-* than is provided by the suggestion of darkness.

To the skua belongs the distinction of having a name almost identical with its root, which is **skeu-*, 'to cover'. Our great skua *Stercorarius skua* is the mod. Icelandic *skumur*, the 'dark, or brown', gull; *skum* and similar forms being used in the Scandinavian languages for 'dark' or 'dusky'. The same root occurs in L. *obscurus* and in our own *scum* and *sky* (in the obsolete sense of 'cloud'), which are words of Norse extraction.

The *dunlin*, if not the 'bird of the sand-dunes', is 'the small brown one'. Chaucer (*P. of F.* 334) speaks of the goshawk as 'the tiraunt with his fetheres donne and greye'. The O.E. *dunn*, 'brown', could be Celtic (Welsh *dwn*), but it is probably related to O.H.G. *tusin* and back to *dusk*. It forms the base of *donkey* and of many provincial bird-names. It is found, for example, in *dunbird* (the female of the common pochard) and in *dunnock* (the hedge-sparrow); while both in Cheshire (on the border of the Celtic country) and in the north of Ireland *dun* is said to be used as a name for the knot. C. L. Hett (1899) gives *dun* as a name for the yellow wagtail.

The harlequin-duck shares with at least two other kinds of bird the distinction of being named from a parti-coloured dress. 'Pie' (M.E. *pie* or *pye*) comes through French from L. *picam*. It springs from the root **pik-* or **peig-*, which provides us with *pigment, paint, picture*, and *Picts* ('the painted folk'). Skt. *pistru*, decorated, and Gk. *poikilos*, 'variegated' (as in Sappho's *poikilothronos*, 'in a throne of many colours'), are other offshoots. Side by side with *pica* Latin had *picus*, 'a woodpecker'. The name applied equally well to the black and white and crimson of the spotted woodpeckers and to the contrasted crimson, green, and yellow of the yaffle. *Pied*, originally meaning 'variegated or parti-coloured', has tended more and more to be narrowed down to mean just 'black and white' – probably from the very general use of *piebald* to denote 'a black and white horse', in contradistinction to *skewbald*, in which is seen again the brown or murky colour which gives the skuas their name. Perhaps, too, the familiar *magpie* itself has played a part in this. From the Latin name of the bird the printers called one size of type *pica*, while the English name was stretched to cover the printer's *pie* or 'unsorted type', and the *pie* which we eat and name from its mixed contents.

The *sheld-duck* owes its name to what Hudson happily termed its 'strange guinea-pig arrangement of three colours – black, white, and red'. The omission of the second *d* in the form 'sheldrake' obscures the etymology. *Sheld* is a dialect word meaning parti-coloured (cf. M. Du. *schillede*, 'variegated') and not the same as *shield*, but indeed the duck earns its name from its bright blazonry, particularly from the red-brown patch on the white of breast and belly. This suggestion of the parti-coloured nature of a shield is paralleled by the Icelandic *skjöldöttr*, 'dappled', and *skjöldungr*, 'a sheld-drake'. The Swedish form of the word is seen in the name of the Norrland town on the Baltic coast, Örnsköldsvik, 'Eagleshield's creek', the creek of the warrior who blazoned an eagle on his shield.

It is quite possible that Christopher Swainson, in *The Folk Lore and Provincial Names of British Birds* (1886), was correct in attributing the same meaning to the first part of 'shell-apple' or 'sheld-apple', a name for the chaffinch used in the north of England. It was bracketed by Turner with 'chaffinche' and 'spink'. As to the *apple* in the name, Kirke Swann mentions *blood-olph* and *green-olph* as provincial names for bullfinch and greenfinch; plain *olph* and *alp* having been earlier names for the bullfinch, as in Chaucer's *Romaunt of the Rose*, line 658:

> 'In many places were nyghtyngales,
> Alpes, fynches, and woodwales.'*

Sheld-alp (the-bird-rather-like-a-bullfinch-with-a-coppery-breast-plate) might have been rationalized into 'shell-apple', when the significance of either element in the old name had been forgotten. (*Alp, hoop, olph*, and other varieties of the name are imitations of the soft note of the bullfinch.) But 17th- and 18th-century authors used *sheld-* or *shell-apple* as a name for the crossbill, possibly in the light of an excellent observation in R. Carew's *Survey of Cornwall* (1602). There had been, he said, in a recent autumn, an irruption of small birds with bills 'thwarted crosswise', with which 'they would cut an apple in two at one snap, eating only the kernels'.

It might be proper to include among the variegated birds the starling, though the etymology of the name seems to defy elucidation. 'Starling' is perhaps a diminutive form of O.E. *stær*, also *stærlinc*. *Stare* is still used in Ireland and parts of England. There are cognate forms in other Germanic languages (e.g. O.N. *stari* and O.H.G. *stara*), together with L. *sturnus* and Gk. *psar* (Modern Greek *psaroni*). The outstanding characteristics of the starling, apart from its skill as an imitator, are its gregarious habits, its bright sheen, and its flecked winter-plumage. The supposition that the flecks – in reality the buff tips of the feathers which become abraded to leave the dark summer-plumage in all its glory – are not obvious enough to give the bird its name is countered by the fact that the Gk. *psaros*

*'Woodwale', the golden oriole, Turner's 'witwol'.

('like a starling') meant 'spotted or flecked'. This proves little with regard to the origin of the name, but it does at least strengthen the possibility that there is an allusion to the plumage in the many cognate names in other European languages.

In discussing *sparrow* we have glanced at the prolific root **ster-* (**sper-*), 'to spread, spray, or sprinkle'. This might have been used in naming the bird whose flocks appear like a black cloud in the sky, and then dissipate like smoke, to reunite before settling on their roosting-trees or on the ground – when tree or field becomes flecked or strewn with the vociferous horde which has rained itself down. But if *starling* is an offshoot of **ster-*, it is more probably because of the flecks which sprinkle the glossy feathers when winter is over.

If this attempt to solve the problem must be discarded, there remains the even more prolific root **stā-*, to stand. One offshoot of **stā-* is our verb to *stare*, 'to keep the gaze stationary'. This acquired the secondary meaning 'to glitter', from the glittering of a staring eye. We are bound to consider the possibility that the flecked plumage and the lustre produced by the oily secretions of this particularly well-oiled species may be connected with the idea of glittering suggested by the verb to *stare*.

The *velvet* scoter, with its curiously shaped bill and large white wing-patch, owes its epithet to the soft texture of its mainly glossy black plumage. The name seems to have been first used in Fleming's *History of Animals* (1828). Willughby, 150 years previously, had suggested the suitability of *velvet* duck. *Velvet* is yet another word from the root **vel-*, 'to cover', having worked its way through O.E. and M.E. from a side-form of L. *villōsus*, 'shaggy', from *villus*, 'shaggy hair'.

Apart from the greater and lesser spotted woodpeckers (perhaps more happily called 'pied' and 'barred'), we have six *spotted* birds: crake, curlew, eagle, flycatcher, redshank, and sandpiper. A lark from beyond the Black Sea, *Melanocephala bimaculata* – the 'bimaculated', i.e. 'doubly-spotted' – has in fact been spotted only once (1962) in Britain. *Barred* can be traced to L.L. *barra*, 'a railing'. 'Bimaculated' is a word made up from L. *bi-* (the form of *bis*, 'two times', used in compounds) and the perfect participle of *maculare*, 'to stain', from *macula*, 'a spot'. *Bis*, for *dvis*, is merely our *twice* in another guise, our *two* being the equivalent of Gk and L. *duo* and Skt. *dvaɪ*. In Greek it is *dis*. The letters *b* and *v* are very near akin in sound, as may be heard in modern Castilian. The plantation-songs indicate that the Negro used to say 'berry' for 'very'. Skt. *dvis* shows how easily the Gk. and Latin became respectively *dis* and *bis*. From *maculare* we have the negative *immaculate*. *Macula* is a cognate of L. *malus*, 'bad'; Gk. *melas*, 'black'; and Skt. *malam*, 'dirt'.

*   *   *

Having dealt as fully as space allows with the etymology of the names of birds and other wild creatures, we may note that among them can be found a sprinkling of 'nature-from-nature' names, for the most part undisguised, such as *eagle-owl*, *curlew-sandpiper*, *tiger-cat*, *fox-squirrel*, and (doubly) *humming-bird hawk-moth*. There are also some which, through metaphor, enter the human world. Some men, for instance, may be *lions* in the drawing-room, but *rabbits* on the tennis-court. Among the other sex are both social *butterflies* and *shrews*. Colloquial speech and slang are rich in such metaphors. To his civilian friends the infantryman in walking-out dress was (though less commonly nowadays) a *lobster*; and a hungry *lobster* could *wolf* his *grub*.

Jenny Lind was the Swedish *nightingale*; conversely we might call the glow-worm, like Florence Nightingale, 'the Lady with the Lamp'. Idiom scarcely allows us to say that a man is a *grig*; yet we may use the simile 'as merry as a grig', whether the cricket's alternative name be onomatopoetic or a corruption of 'Greek'. So a man may run like a *hare*, drink like a *fish*, or puff like a *grampus*; and a child may sing like a *lark* – or, metaphorically, have one.

Most of the thorough-going nature-from-nature verbs are to some degree pejorative. To *ape* is hardly synonymous with to *imitate*. Good fellows, for good reasons, may change sides, but will not *rat* – a metaphor taken from rats which, understandably, try to escape from a sinking ship, as mallophaga (body-lice) crawl from a dying bird, though they are doomed soon to perish, unless they can speedily creep below the feathers of another avian host of the same species. To *crab* a suggestion implies criticism as unpleasant as the nip of the eponymous crustacean – being more than 'a mere fleabite'. To *gull* for 'to *dupe*' is now rarely heard.

Since a goat is a rather 'rare bird' on the modern farm, we may anticipate the theme of the next two chapters by citing the colloquial 'playing the giddy goat'; but note with respect the noun and verb *ram* supplied by the animal which, like the horned goat, has his place in the Zodiac; for *aries* (Latin for 'ram', 'the thruster') is yet another scion of the noble root **ar-*, and to the Romans meant both the siege-engine which knocked down the walls and its nature-derived eponym, *ram*, 'the butter'.

We now turn from the wild to the more or less tamed, lingering only to note an ingenious suggestion about the name of an occasional visitor from northern America, the red-breasted snipe or *dowicher*. It was popularly supposed that the bird had been called *deutsche* (*Schnepfe*) by the eighteenth-century 'Pennsylvania Dutch' (who were mostly Germans) because its reddish summer-plumage reminded them of the uniform of the Hessian or Hanoverian soldiers serving in the British army. But probably the cry '*do-wich-er*' first provided the name, which Webster (*Third International Dictionary*) says is of Iroquoian origin. With this may be compared the Dog-rib Indians' name for the common snipe, *iawitscho*.

$\chi i\upsilon$ (a)

WORDS FROM FAMILIAR ANIMALS

'Adam gave names to all cattle, and to the fowls of
the air, and to every beast of the field.'

Genesis 2. 20.

A FEW minutes of healthy exercise will be enough to suggest why
the root **an-* holds the notion of deep breathing found in Gk. *anemos*
and Skt. *anila*, 'wind', and L. *anima* and *animus*. These words illustrate
one constant characteristic of language – that, once a meaning has
been established, the word begins to grow and change like every
other living thing. The process is twofold: there is a gradual alteration of form, with concomitant changes of meaning.

Of *animus* the form has remained exceptionally close to the
original; but the changes of meaning have been profound. This
word (first signifying 'mind' as distinct from 'spirit') has successively
acquired the meanings of 'mental impulse, disposition, passion,
violent prejudice'. *Anima* (breath) came to mean 'breath of the
spirit' – 'soul'.

Animal in the sense of 'beast, not man' scarcely appears before the
16th century, and is not found in the A.V. of the Bible (1611).
Animalis in Latin meant 'anything alive', and had this meaning in
the first recorded example of its use in English. *Animate* (at first
meaning 'inspired') and *animalcule* are also 16th-century words. The
phrase 'animal spirits' looks back to the 'spirit' sense in *anima*, the
spirit that inspires voluntary action. The modern 'boys will be boys'
sense began in the 18th century. Our word *animus*, though it comes
from the 'disposition – passion' sense of *animus*, seems to have been
employed first in our sense of 'hostile attitude' or 'prejudice' by
Thackeray in 1840. *Equanimity* (L. *aequo animo*) and *magnanimity* were
both introduced by Renaissance authors, Latin-influenced, about
1600 – *animus* in these instances having the sense of 'spirit'. *Pusil-
lanimous*, in an Anglo-French form, had been employed by the tri-
lingual Gower in 1390.

166

From *anemos* the Hellenes made *anemōnē* – 'anemone', too lovely a name to be supplanted by the literal translation, 'wind-flower'.

Two other words which suggest the sound of breathing, and which, taken together, are at least as important to English as *animus*, are the Gk. *pneuma* and the L. *spīritus*. Originally each had the meaning 'breath'; but in our language *spīritus* has been more fruitful than *pneuma*. For this, as so often, Wyclif has been responsible. In his Bible (and all the later Bibles) *pneuma* and its equivalent in Hebrew are translated as 'spirit'. *Pneuma* has suffered an unhappy fate. Used first in the name of a disease, *pneumonia* (transliterated from Greek in Holland's version of Plutarch, 1603), it has fallen down the scale till it has reached Dunlop's Patent Pneumatic Tyre and Aldous Huxley's pneumatic young ladies. *Spirit* by contrast has given us at least a score of meanings of the word itself, closely related in their differences, and nearly all of noble or dignified significance, such as 'heavenly grace' and 'courage'. 'The Alchemist,' writes Ben Jonson in his play of that name, 'is busy with his spirits, but we'll upon him!' A modern alchemy gives us our meaning of 'hard liquor'. The parent-word, the L. *spīrare*, 'to breathe', has of course given us a great number of compounds – *conspire, conspiracy, inspire, respiration, perspire, transpire,* etc.

Domestic Animals

There is another source of nature-words so obvious that it may escape proper notice: the vocabularies gleaned from the names and characteristics of familiar animals – stock, domestic, and pets.

When fowls and even pigs were allowed to wander inside the wooden or clay-and-wattle walls of the homestead, their names, shapes, and habits were constantly in people's minds. The goat was almost as much part of the household as the dog. The fox, though not 'domestic' was never far off. He and the farmer were mutual enemies, and respected each other as such.

Words for animal characters were anthropomorphic. There was no warning voice to say that only a man could be *foxy*; that the fox could be only *fox-like*: and the ancient word *fox*, centuries before the days of polite fox-hunting, was used to describe a dozen different kinds of slyness and craftiness, wisdom and strategy. *Fox* has slid into the language by many different routes, and turns up in many different contexts, of which some are hard to explain. The *foxglove* hangs its crimson bells not for the paws of the quadruped, but for Titania and her retinue, the meaning being 'the (Little) Folk's glove'. *Fox-tail* grass is remarkably like a fox's brush. Less poetical are *fox* for a type of sword; a sickness to which beer is liable; a kind of mould; and *fox-evil* or *fox-mange* – 'alopecia' (from Gk. *alōpēx*, 'a fox'), denoting patchy baldness. One may be *foxed* by a difficulty. 'She heard a horse approaching at a foxtrot' (1888 O.E.D.) shows the way to the *fox-trot*, the dance with short-short-long steps, reminiscent of a four-legged animal trying to walk upright.

In our days perhaps only thirty per cent of the people of Britain have ever seen a fox. When the words which we have just listed were coined, he was familiar to everybody. It is this familiarity that occasions slightly less well-known animals to be described in terms of the better-known, e.g. the *fox-snake, Coluber vulpinus*; the *fox-squirrel, Sciurus cinereus*; and a bird recorded first in Britain in 1961, the *fox-sparrow, Passerella iliaca* – a big North American bunting with a long russet tail and red-brown wings, cheeks, and breast-markings, which finds its food on the forest-floor by opening its wings and kicking up the leaves and soil with both feet simultaneously in the manner of its eponymous mammal.

Sometimes the 'one animal in terms of another' explanation is not immediately recognizable. The 15th century word 'caterpillar' betokens 'a cat which is hairy' (pop. L. *catta pilōsa*). An interesting offshoot, belonging to an age before etymological self-consciousness, is *catkin*, 'a little cat'. Dr Johnson, perhaps through some philologically impossible association with *pillar*, ordained in his Dictionary that the ending should be *-ar* instead of *-er*; and no one since has dared to change it back.

A short, simple, and effective word such as *fox* lends itself to language-making. *Pig*, as forceful and even more familiar, has a still longer list of technical meanings and compounds, and is even more frequently used in proverbs. It is hard to see why one word is chosen in preference to another. The origins of *pig* are obscure; but it may be a form of O.E. *fearh*, our *farrow*, cognate with L. *porcus* (Grimm's Law helping us with the *f* for *p*). *Porcus*, through O.F. *porc*, was at the ready to give us a speakable word. In fact *pork* was tried out for *pig* from the 15th century to the 17th. It was even used for a pig-headed gentleman. 'I mean not,' said Milton, 'to dispute Philosophy with this Pork, who never used any.' But such meanings never lasted, perhaps on a sort of Principle of Linguistic Convenience, by which the Normans applied *porc* exclusively to fresh pig's-meat – a differentiation of which modern French has not made use.

On the other hand *porcus* has given us good nature-words, some of which half-conceal their origin.

> 'And each particular hair to stand on end
> Like quills upon the fretful porpentine,'

says his father's ghost to Hamlet. The origin of 'porcupine' is obvious. A Latin *porcus spīnōsus*, 'prickly pig', may be taken for granted; but some of the first recorded spellings of the words are so wild that 15th and 16th century writers made them still wilder by Guess-Etymology. *Pork despyne* is Malory's sensible version of the French equivalent; but *portpen* and Hamlet's *porpentine* suggest quill-pens. *Porpoynt, porkenpick,* and *porcupig* are also wide of the mark.

Another good *porcus* word is 'porcelain'. This is from the diminutive *porcella*, the Italian name for the Venus-shell and other species of cowrie. Porcelain has the same dense, hard, bright, polished surface as the cowrie; and there seems no necessity for looking for the connection with *porcus* beyond the fact that the shell has just the shape, and often the colour, of a recumbent piglet. (In many families *pig* is the name for the section of an orange, which has much the same shape.)

Perched on the pig-sty we may find a bird with a genuinely echoic name:

> 'While the Cock with lively din
> Scatters the rear of darkness thin
> And to the Stack, or the Barn dore,
> Stoutly struts his Dames before . . .'
>
> (Milton, *L'Allegro.*)

The cock has a particularly clear-cut character, in both appearance and manner. From the look of his spur comes the *cock* of a gun and *cock* 'a tap'. From the jerky turn of his eye and his 'stout strutting' we have *cocking a glance, cock-eyed, cock-sure, cock-a-hoop, high cockalorum, cocktail* (a cocksure, lively kind of drink), and other words and phrases. From his swaggering before his dames comes *coquette*, originally the masculine *coquet*, which we have borrowed from the

French, who have him as their totem-bird. *Cockade*, for a ribbon or badge in a cap, is from the feminine form of O.F. *coquard*, 'impudent'. Surely the Scots *cockaleekie* must mean 'chicken-broth' or, as we have heard it called in the Old Kent Road, 'fowl-soup' (spelt with a *w*, not a single *u*).

We may 'ride a cock-horse' to take us to two aspects or styles of English reflected in its treatment of the word *horse* and the use which it makes of the L. *caballus*. The tendency of Latin *c* was to become *ch* (as in *chapeau*, formed from *chape*, L.L. *cappa*): and in the Romance languages *b* was apt to become *v*. ('*Apud Hispanos*,' said the Roman, '*vivere est bibere*' – 'among the Spaniards living is drinking'.) Thus *caballus*, 'a nag', compared with *equus*, 'a race-horse', became *cheval*. *Cheval* seems to gain an aristocratic dignity not at first belonging to *caballus*, which has given us, through French, *chevalier* and *chivalry*, and, by way of Italian and French, *cavalry*, *cavalier*, and *cavalcade*. The Spanish gentleman is *un caballero*. Our *cheval-glass* is a mirror tall enough to reflect a horse, or else it is swung in a frame (cf. *clothes horse* and *easel*, from Du. *ezel*, 'donkey').

'Horse', however, has always remained doggedly plebeian, familiar, antipoetic. 'Hullo, old horse' was the greeting of Bertie Wooster and his contemporaries. 'Old cheval' would not go at all, had English chosen the alternative name. The O.E. was *hors*, which has cognates in O.H.G., L.G., and some modern Germanic tongues, e.g. the German *Ross*, which explains the Dutch loan-word *walrus*, the 'whale-horse'. These words have affinity with such words as *course*, ultimately from the supine stem of L. *currere*, 'to run'.

Here might well be brought in, not dragged in, 'I know two things about a horse; and one of them is rather coarse'. 'One of them'? Say rather a multitude. Coarseness, size, or clumsiness is evident not only in the Gaelic original of 'capercaillie' – *capullcoille*, 'horse of the woods', being the most probable guess at the derivation. (See Chapter XII.)

By the side of *horse-radish* our homely botany has *horse-tail* (*Equisetum*) and *horse-parsley* – an apt name for thrusting umbellifers, notably the greenish-yellow Alexanders, a species of *Smyrnium* which covers the upper slopes of the coast particularly thickly between Folkestone and Margate.

Slang makes frequent raids on the word, generally giving it the same kind of significance, except perhaps in the half-complimentary *horse-sense.* 'Eat like a horse' we know, and *horse-play*, and *horse-laugh.* Kipling's expression for 'to talk big' was 'to talk horse'. *Horse-kiss* is a dialect word for 'a bite', and *horse-godmother* for 'a virago, romp, or hoyden':

> 'In woman angel sweetness let me see:
> No galloping horse-godmother for me.'

A *horse-marine* is either non-existent or a clumsy person in the wrong job. From Wiltshire comes a good country crack, 'to send for a horse-ladder', i.e. to send on a fool's errand.

The *horse-latitudes* in the North Atlantic are the region of proverbial calms, where, in the days of sail, when the water-supply ran short, cattle and horses had to be jettisoned.

Further to multiply instances would be 'to flog a dead horse'.

But why – of all animals – the horse, which is beautiful, docile, discriminating, graceful, fleet, and capable of a loyalty which can summon up all the courage latent in the nervously introspective? This is one of the mysteries of the English language – and an example of its power. It will take hold of an eminently *speakable* word such as *horse*, and give it a character more suitable to its own rough sound.

Cow and *bull* words are comparatively few, despite the paramount value of the ox to our primitive pastoral ancestors, who gained from it hides for their tents, bones for needles, scrapers, and other tools, sinews for thread and for bowstrings, dung for fuel, flesh and milk for food and drink, and horn for beakers and other useful purposes.

We need, however, to keep in mind that the countryman has many other names besides *cow* and *bull*, such as *heifer*, *stot*, *stirk*, and *bullock*. The L. *vacca*, a cow, has given us *vaccine*, *vaccinate*, and *vaccination*. The derivation of *bachelor* from *baccalārius*, a Late Latin word for the owner of a small estate, is highly suspect (even though the change from *v* to *b* is common); but it is too intriguing to go without mention.

L. *bōs*, with its stem *bov-* (the Skt. and Gk. equivalents being *gaus* and *bous*) provides *bucolic* and *bovine*. It illustrates its antiquity by its pedigree, which reveals a common origin with *cow*. The word *Bovril*, unexplained and unillustrated, on every hoarding introduced the unlettered young of an earlier generation to a word which, since Norman days, has given us *beef* (O.F. *boef*, now *bœuf*). In M.E. *beef* was applied to both ox and the flesh of an ox. A derivative of the Gk. *bous* was *boubalos*, which we have noted as a name originally used for a kind of antelope (hartebeest) of which the Levitical law allowed the flesh to be eaten. This was adopted in English as *buffalo* – 'the kine, Bufalos, and bulles' which till the ground in China (1588); and 'buff' is the colour of tanned buffalo-hide. The Royal Kent Regiment, the *Buffs*, take their title from the colour of the facings of their uniform, first made from 'holland' during their long service in the Low Countries at the end of the 16th and beginning of the 17th centuries.

A less obvious descendant of *bōs* is *bugle*, formed from the diminutive *būculus*, which originally meant a wild ox, the aurochs, and then the hunting-horn which was sounded during the pursuit of the animal. The texture of the leaf of our *ox-tongue* shows the name to be perfectly apt. *Bugloss* represents the plant in which some Greek noticed an equal similarity, and united *bous* and *glōssa*. We keep *bugloss* for the boraginaceous plants with their scratchy stems and leaves, particularly the viper's bugloss, *Echium vulgare.*

'Butter' is said to be from Gk. *bouturon*, through L. *būtyron*, 'cow-cheese'. Some authorities, however, think that the word is of Scythian origin. *Butcher* first meant 'a dealer in goats or bucks' (F. *bouchier*; *bouc*), and was not connected with the eponym of Bovril.

Perhaps the animal which best illustrates the household-figure, almost the household-god, element in our domestic creatures is the dog. The affectionate observation of canine characteristics must be at least as old as Roman times; and yet there is an ambivalence in the human relationship with the dog. It depends on whether the mood is for or against – 'Love me, love my dog' or 'Give a dog a bad name'. In mediaeval times, although a dog could be a friend, it could also be a bad-luck story, a harbinger of ill. Part of the explanation lies in the significance of the phrase *dog-days*, when Sirius, the Dog-Star, first emerges from the sun's rays and becomes visible before sunrise, the season 'noted from ancient times', says the O.E.D., 'as the hottest and most unwholesome period of the year'. The actual period when Sirius 'rages' differs in England and the Mediterranean countries; but late July and early August is an approximation. This is a time of hot weather occasionally even in England: but the point is that the *dies caniculares* have from classical times been regarded as the time when dogs 'run mad'; in other words when rabies (an almost forgotten word until the scare of 1969) is supposed to be likely to manifest itself in endemic races.

Dog is completely English. First recorded in 1050, it is one of the little group of important words which are completely unknown outside our language, except when they have been borrowed from us. In French it has become *dogue*, for 'a bulldog', the meaning it probably had among the English – 'the dogged people', 'the boys of the bulldog breed'; although 'to dog (a man's footsteps)' is no more a characteristic of the bulldog than to be 'dog-tired', or the French *être d'une humeur de dogue*, i.e. to have an irascible temper.

In many oriental countries the dog is beyond the pale; in others, and in other continents, he is cherished for his meat or harnessed to a sledge or a milkcart. We do not detest him or digest him, or drive him, even in a *dog-cart*; but references to him in English are mainly derogatory, as in 'gone to the dogs', 'not a dog's chance', 'dog-eared', or in the names of plants, sometimes obsolete or provincial, such as *dog-rose*, *dog-daisy*, *dog's-chamomile*. Sometimes the suggestion is 'spurious' or 'mongrel', as in *dog-Latin* and, perhaps, *doggerel*.

As only a man can be *foxy*, so also only a human 'gay dog' can be *doggy* – 'rather too smartly dressed'. This seems to contain the sense of the quite modern slang, 'like a dog's dinner'.

The dog's big bark has been adopted as a descriptive word in the United States ('It's a *wow*'), and by Anglo-Australians, whose *wowser*, Eric Partridge thinks, is a man who says a very big *bow-wow* to very minor vices. Boswell quotes Lord Pembroke: 'Dr Johnson's sayings would not appear so extraordinary, were it not for his *bow-wow* way'. Scott, writing of Jane Austen, provides an even better quotation: 'The Big Bow-wow I can do myself like any now going; but the exquisite touch, which renders ordinary commonplace things and characters interesting, from the truth of the description and sentiment, is denied to me.'

Yet the most interesting connections of *dog* in our language are *canine*, a derivative of L. *canis*, and *hound*; both being cognate with the Gk. *kuōn*, German *Hund*, and equivalent words in other I-E. languages. The basic meaning is possibly 'to be pregnant' (cf. Gk. *kuein*). From German we have adopted *Dachshund*, 'badger-hound'.

Canis is the source of the name of the *Canaries*, *Canāria insula*, the island of those dogs whose statues still stand in the plaza of Las Palmas. Thence came *canary* wine, first mentioned in Shakespeare's

Henry IV, and the *canary* bird, first mentioned (as '*canara* bird') a few years earlier. *Canary* in the sense of 'yellow' dates from the mid-nineteenth century. The ancestral serin is a greenish-yellow bird: the bright colour of our cage-birds is a result of breeding by fanciers. The Late Latin *canīle*, 'a small house for dogs', became *chenil* in Norman-French, and, passing into M.E. as *kenel*, became our *kennel*.

The Greek *kuōn* (stem *kun-*) gives three good words: *cynic, cynosure*, and *quinsy*. The University of Wits School of Elizabethan dramatists gave *cynic* its modern meaning, though they knew well that the word referred to the Cynic School of philosophy developed by pupils of Socrates led by Antisthenes, who lectured in the gymnasium in Athens called Cynosarges, which was reserved for those of other than pure Athenian blood. As a dog of our days lives in a kennel, so the Cynic Diogenes lived in and taught from a tub.

Cynosure represents the Gk. *kunos ourā*, 'the Dog's Tail', a constellation otherwise known as Ursa Minor. It contains the Pole Star in its tail, and there shows 'a brilliancy to which all eyes are turned'. Originally the 'all eyes' were those of mariners; the modern sense dates from 1599.

The tiny flowers, touched with palest lilac, of *Asperula cyanchica* labour under the peculiar English name of *squinancywort*. *Squinancy*, a word probably known to Chaucer's Doctor of Physic, is a muddled version of the O.F. form of the Latinized Greek *kunagkē*, 'dog-throttle', a disease of the throat, i.e. tonsillitis, later further corrupted to *quinsy*. The diagnosis is apt; for the throat of the sufferer feels as if it were constricted by a dog-collar – the alternative and basic meaning of the Greek word.

Two other words remind us that dogs were behaving in character thousands of years ago. *Adulation* (L. *adūlari*, 'to flatter like a fawning dog') is admirably descriptive of the tail-wagging of a dog as it approaches its master. (But the root of the 'tail' in *adūlari* is disputed by the pundits.) *Wheedle*, a later word, may be from the German *wedeln*, 'to wag the tail', but alternatively may represent the O.E. *wǣdlian*, 'to beg' – from *wǣdl*, 'poverty'.

XIV (b)

THE TRACE OF FARM-ANIMALS

'Come uppe, Whitefoot; come uppe, Lightfoot;
Come uppe, Jetty; rise and follow,
Jetty, to the milking-shed.'

JEAN INGELOW, *High Tide on the Lincolnshire Coast.*

FARM-ANIMALS have left their own signature on the language. Though it is often difficult to decipher, the trace of it remains. (*Trace* itself is from F. *trait* – L. *tractus*, 'a drawing', from *tractare*, 'to draw forcefully along the furrow'. We have borrowed *trait* to denote 'a characteristic'.)

Crock originally meant 'an old and barren ewe'. Pigs have left their mark through *soil*, 'to dirty', via O.F. *suiller*, Rom. **suculare*, a verb formed on L. *suculus*, 'a small pig or *sus*'. 'I'm rooting for you', would once have meant, 'I am grubbing about in the dirt (e.g. of politics) for you, like a pig nosing up the ground'. *Scrophularia*, the family of plants which includes the mullein and the snapdragon, was so called because one species was thought to be beneficial in the treatment of scrofula, a form of tuberculosis of the lymph-nodes known as 'cervical lymphadenitis'. *Scrofula* comes from L. *scrōfa*, 'a breeding-sow'. Webster suggests that this may be due to 'a fanciful comparison of the glandular swellings to little pigs'; and Onions to the supposition that pigs were subject to the disease. But surely the typical neck of the sufferer from scrofula – that swelling from ear to ear – closely resembles the vast double chin of a sow, and is what must have reminded the doctors of *scrōfa*? We can see a mild example of this neck in the portraits of Dr Johnson, who suffered from this, the 'King's Evil', and was touched for it by Queen Anne. It is typical of mediaeval pharmacy that our English name for a familiar species of *Scrophularia*, 'figwort', suggests with masterly inconsistency that it was also good for haemorrhoids ('the Fig').

For a pungent example of classical wit we might take the word 'hybrid'. We now use the Gk. *hubris* as a somewhat learned term for

175

intellectual self-confidence with a touch of arrogance. In Greek the word implied 'wanton violence arising from the pride of strength or passion . . . riotousness, insolence, licentiousness'. The Romans examined the word and its related verb *hubrizein*, 'to act wantonly, etc.', and produced *hybrida*, a name for the offspring of animals of different species, and then for the child of a Roman father and an alien mother, or of a freeman and a slave. The hybridizing activities of our species of *Hieracium* (hawkweed), closely examined by our botanists, seem rather tame by comparison.

The long-established treatment and control of livestock have also left their mark. Cognates of *mutilate*, from L. *mutilare*, are the Gk. *mutilos* and *mitulos*, with Celtic relatives. The root is *mut-, 'shortened', adopted by Latin in the sense of 'dehorning' cattle.

Spoil and *despoil* (F. from L. *spoliare*) started with the sense of flaying an animal, stripping off the hide, *spolium*. (Cf. *excoriate*: Chapter XXIV.)

Control of the movements of animals is the essence of stock-management. The *pastern* of a horse meant originally the rope or cord by which a horse was hobbled. The root *pā-, 'to feed', gave Latin *pascere* and its derivative *pastūra*; the O.F. *pasture* meant the 'hobble' as well as the 'pasture'. L.L. *prominare* (F. *promener*, 'to make someone take a walk'), represents *pro* + *minare*, 'to drive forwards', from L. *minari*, 'to threaten'.

Veterinary control goes wider and much deeper. The I-E. root *wet-, a year (Skt. *vetsara*, Gk. *etos*), has entered modern English in a way which is all the more fascinating because of its indirectness. Most of the words from it are based on the notion of a *one-year*-old beast, e.g. Latin *vitulus* with diminutive *vitellus*, 'a calf'; our *wether*, 'a castrated ram'. Through French from the L.L. adjective *vitulīna* (*pellis*) we have *vellum*, 'calfskin'. A *veterinary* surgeon (1790) was originally so called because the animals in his care, at least one year old, were mature enough to be beasts of burden – were, in fact, *veterans*, 'yearlings'.

Words such as these give the farmer's-eye view, the cattle-man's view. When we see cattle now, we are usually passing them at 60 m.p.h. It takes the farmer to give us the close view, to talk of the *dewlap* of the bull, to see the drop of moisture as clear as dew on the fold of skin beneath the throat.

Thus, though we move further from living animals in our social life, they remain close to us in our language. We have fewer *farms* now, and more *firms* – terms which were interchangeable in Mediaeval Latin documents. *Farm* is the older word; *firm* is the nearer to the origin, *firmare*, which in Late Latin meant 'to confirm by one's signature'. The sense of 'signature', that brand-mark on the sheep, entered early into each of them, with the implication of 'a signed document'. The first O.E.D. entry of *farm* (1400) signified 'a firm amount payable as rent, tax, etc.' Farms did not conform to our sense of *farm* until well into the 16th century.

$\mathcal{X}i\mathcal{U}$ (c)

WORDS FROM ANIMALS OF MYTH
AND LEGEND

'Gorgons and Hydras and Chimaeras dire.'
MILTON, *Paradise Lost*, II. 628.

MYTHICAL animals such as dragons, unicorns, and wyverns were part of the furniture of the mediaeval mind, and hardly *natural* history. But mixed up with the beasts of folklore were those of the kind of legend which is more than half based on fact – creatures described by travellers and known to exist, but never seen in Britain. Always to be remembered is the vast difference in thought, belief, and method between, say, the 14th century and our own. Nowadays, if a strange animal comes into the news, a flood of articles precedes the naturalist's monograph; *Life* Magazine gives it four pages; a film-unit is sent along when the rarity is being hunted; a specimen is secured for Regent's Park. In former days things were different. The animal was *not seen*. The travellers who brought the reports, the heroes of Hakluyt, not only lived in an age before scientific training, but also knew that their descriptions would be considered plausible in proportion as they tallied with records – themselves mostly based on hearsay – from thousand-year out-of-date naturalists such as Pliny.

In the minds of ordinary people this kind of news about the unseen beasts, coupled with accounts of the 'anthropophagi and men whose heads do grow beneath their shoulders', increased the status of the story-tellers. Interest in the famous animals of literature was re-inforced, slowly at first, but ever increasingly in the 15th century, by the Wyclif Bible of 1382. So much of the original Bible seems to have been written for people with not only an awareness of animals but also a love for them. In the first full English translation was a rich reinforcement for readers among the laity who were now for the first time able to understand the Bible. Some of the animals would be strange, some familiar. A select few might have seen some of them in the royal menageries started by such monarchs as Henry I. Of lions and serpents, of the mountain-leopards of the Book of Proverbs, the reader would know something, if only from fables or from their presence in heraldic blazonry. The wild boars of Psalm LXXX most Englishmen would know very well; but of the 'pelican in the wilderness' of Psalm CII they would have been more doubtful.

The Wyclif version was often too literal a translation of the Vulgate; and, since the Latin of the Vulgate has *pelicano solitudinis*, Wyclif repeats 'pelican of wildernesse'. The use of the word in earlier English never suggests that an animal even distantly related to the pelican is being described. The Vulgate's *pelicano* is perhaps equally remote from the Hebrew word which the N.E.B. renders 'desert-owl'. The word *pelican* was adopted from Aristotle, who may have been describing a bird with a cutting beak (Gk. *pelekus*, 'axe'), such as a woodpecker (Gk. *pelekas*).

The release of the word *pelican* with the authority of the Bible brought a small spate of references, though most of them did not cite the Biblical context, but rather the legend, popularized by St Augustine, that the pelican revived her young with blood pecked from her own breast. This became part of the stock of moral tales from Natural History which reached saturation-point in Lyly's *Euphues* (1579), the style of which Shakespeare satirized in *Henry IV*. In the 15th century 'a pelican in her piety', wounding or 'vulning' her breast for the sake of her young ones, became familiar in heraldry, and the fancy was indistinguishable from fact.

One other Biblical animal should find place here, even though in the original Hebrew and Greek scriptures there is no mention of it. This is the whale – Jonah's whale. In this century, when the Bible is sometimes only indirectly part of our culture, we may find difficulty in remembering the details. Where – if it appears at all – is the word mentioned in the Bible? Not in the original account of Jonah, where what engulfed him was, in poetical symbolism, black depression through his consciousness of his disobedience to the voice of God. Here is Jonah 1. 17 in the Authorized Version:

'Now the Lord had prepared a great fish (Vulgate *grandem piscem*) to swallow up Jonah. And Jonah was in the belly of the fish three days and nights.'

No whale there! But (A.V. again) in St Matthew xii. 40 Jesus' own words are thus recorded:

'For as Jonah was three days and three nights in the whale's belly; so shall the Son of Man be three days and three nights in the heart of the earth.'

Where did the 'whale' come from? It is neither in the Hebrew of the Old Testament nor in the Greek of the New Testament, where the sense is 'sea-monster' – *kētos* – used in one place by Homer for what we call *seal*. It first appears in the Lindisfarne Gospels translation of *c.* 950. Jonah there was *on wom huales*, 'in the womb of a whale'. This is only the second recorded appearance of 'whale' in the O.E.D., the first being in Alfred (893). Wyclif (1382) has the same words as the Old Northumbrian gloss in the Lindisfarne Gospels; the A.V. only substitutes *belly* for *wom*. (*Womb* was used indiscriminately for 'belly' and 'uterus' up to, and even beyond, the time of Chaucer. More than four hundred years later another Poet Laureate, Lord Tennyson, wrote of a Spanish ship's 'having that within her womb that had left her ill-content'.)

How did 'whale' make this famous entry into our language and thought at a time when the concept 'whale' was most vague? It came through the chance use by the monks of Lindisfarne, together with the fact that it was put into the mouth of Jesus; for it was believed not only that the original Bible was inspired, but that the English translation had equal authority. All to no purpose may the Fundamentalist be told that the word translated 'day' in Genesis I meant 'epoch'. '*My* Bible,' he will answer, 'says that the world was created in seven days: and a day means twenty-four hours!' The fact that the Bible in the vernacular was a translation, and subject to human error (as witness the version which had 'green bay-*horse*' for 'bay *tree*'), was only dimly perceived.

I* am lucky enough to possess a John Kitto's *Pictorial Family Bible.* This was published in 1854. Kitto, who died in this year, was a physically handicapped workhouse-boy who became a missionary and used his knowledge of the East and the Near East when writing a Bible History for the Early Victorians. He was a deep-dyed Fundamentalist, and, believing in the literal truth of the Bible *as printed in English,* he often wrote long annotations to prove the possibility of the utterly impossible. Having worked out the date of

*S.P.

Jonah's shipwreck as 862 B.C., exactly 3,242 years after the creation of the world, he added a long footnote about the whale:

'A great deal of profane witticism has been directed against this statement about a large fish . . . It has been proved that great fishes, particularly of the shark kind, are capable of swallowing the human body entire . . . If a whale be intended, it can be supposed that the fish did not actually swallow Jonah, but detained him in its mouth. If a whale had done this, the prophet would have been less unpleasantly circumstanced than in the stomach of any fish. For the mouth of a common whale, when open, presents a cavity as large as a room, and capable of containing a ship's jolly-boat full of men . . . "Is anything too hard for the Lord?"'

Nothing better illustrates the conflict between the desire for factual truth and the desire to believe in the eternal truth of God. Many believed, as we ourselves would wish to believe, that Jonah's whale will eventually go to Paradise. In Kitto we find belief as it was in 1854, on the very threshold of the Darwinian theory of Evolution, in the very year in which Darwin began, as he wrote in his autobiography, 'to devote all my time to arranging my pile of notes, to observing and experimenting in relation to the transmutation of species'.

XV

WORDS OUT OF THE SOIL

How men may clothe the glebe with golden corn;
Under which star to plough, to train the vines;
How cattle must be bred; the livestock's needs;
The skill to share the foresight of the bees:
– These are the themes, dear Reader, of my song.
(VERGIL, *Georgic* I. 1–5.)

PLOUGHING and harrowing, threshing and sifting and grinding into meal; grazing, sheep-farming, pig-breeding, and keeping cattle from straying – such is the kaleidoscopic picture before our mental eyes when we think of farming. We may now be only 10 per cent farmers as a nation, but it is certain that every day, if not more often, we read or use a word from the vocabulary of agriculture or stock-breeding. Only last week, as it were, in the time-scale of the history of mankind, we were most of us up to the neck in the earth, sweat, and animal-smells of primitive farming. It was our life, if not our livelihood. It is therefore natural that, whether it is a novel, a news-paper, or a dictionary which claims our attention, we find agriculture as constant an element as any other.

There were no part-time gentlemen-farmers at the back of the words in question, but hardworking full-timers – all with a 'pecuniary consideration' in mind. Let us use this unpleasant phrase for a start, because it takes us back a couple of thousand years to cattle-farming. *Pecus* is Latin for 'cattle', with cognates in O.H.G., O.N., Old Saxon, and Skt. The English equivalent of *pecus* is *fee*; and the earliest meaning of *fee* is 'cattle'. Since *wild fee* meant 'deer', plain *fee* must have meant 'the livestock of a farm'. Co-existing with this sense already in King Alfred's time was the development 'movable property in general' – as in the French *meubles*, 'furniture'. The third sense, 'money', seems to be equally ancient in recorded Old English. In the same way *neat*, oxen collectively, the O.E. *nēat* (both singular and plural), was connected with *nēotan*, 'to employ', and had the secondary meaning of 'useful property'. *Pecūnia* already meant 'money' in later Latin: the use of any derivative of it is first found in *The Friar's Tale* of Chaucer:

'If any persone wolde upon hem pleyne
Ther myghte asterte hym no pecunyal peyne'.

To recapitulate: the meaning underlying *pecuniary consideration* is, '(I value my services at) so many head of cattle (the amount to be decided) when the stars are in favourable conjunction' – a mixture of good straight Latin and mediaeval astrological fuzz.

If we go back a little further, we find that our everyday language reveals even earlier farm-life beginnings. 'To colonize' and 'to cultivate' both come from the same Latin word, *colere*, the root of which implies the moving around in one place which is required for cultivation. The ancestor of our word 'ambassador', L. *ambactus*, described a man who was driven *ambi*, 'about', as a messenger or, as in Welsh *amaethwr*, 'a ploughman', 'husbandman'. The ploughman does not spend his efforts on soil that is poor (the original meaning of the L. *pauper*, from *pau-*, the equivalent of our *few* + the stem of *pario*, 'I produce'): his time is devoted to earth which has a promise of richness in the smell released by the ploughshare. This may be the first sense of yet another scion of the root *ar-*, *aroma*, which in Greek meant 'a sweet herb or spice' but was identical with another *aroma* meaning 'ploughland'. 'Ploughshare' and 'shear' are cognates, from the O.E. *scieran*, which, developing from its sense of the farmer's kind of cutting, has given us words, or is related to words, with meanings as far apart as *sheer*, *shore*, *sharp*, *shirt*, and *sharing*. The ploughman learns to keep the furrow straight; and 'learn' already has this sense planted in it. The O.E. *leornian*, 'to learn', and the parallel *lēran*, 'to teach' (whence the now provincial, 'I will learn you'), mean basically to 'lead on the way', through a *lore* which teaches you to keep the (cognate Latin) *lira*, 'furrow', straight. A man *delirious* is 'out of the furrow'. In perfectly straight line, the furrow is a 'verse', the earth turned (L. *vertere*, *versum*) in a line; from which we have a line or *verse* of poetry. If the line goes straight forward, *prō*, it is *prōversa* or *prorsa oratio*, or simply *prosa*, 'prose'.

The essential operation of the whole cycle, *sowing*, is in constant use as metaphor: and the cognates or derivatives of the word are always with us. Related to *sow* are *seed* and *saecula*, 'a generation' –

whence our *secular*, 'belonging to a generation' or 'to the world'. The L. cognate of O.E. *sāwan*, 'to sow', is *serere*, from which is derived *sēmen*. Our *seminary* school for elegant young persons represents *sēminārium*, 'a seed-plot'. From the stem of *satio*, 'a sowing', comes, via French, our 'season'.

The seed 'germinates' or 'generates', the root of each of these words being **gen-*, which has given English a great number of words, including obvious offshoots such as *gene, genetic, germ, genre, gender, genitive,* and others noted in Chapter XXV.

The L. *gens*, 'a race', originally meant a clan sharing a common ancestor; and one of a clan which was non-Roman, and therefore not one of the true-blue breed, was called in the Vulgate version of the Hebrew Bible, a *Gentile*, because he was not a Jew.

The sense of 'good stock', which gives us *genteel* (originally meaning 'well-bred') and *gentleman* and *jaunty*, has passed through the F. *gentil*. The cynical use of *genteel* was not fixed before the time of Charles Dickens.

Another *gen*-word of importance to Natural History is *general*. Latin *generalis* is the adjective of *genus*, 'class, kind, or race'. The meaning has remained constant, and has always tended to apply to the larger class, in contradistinction to the smaller. *General* for a high-ranking soldier is an ellipsis for the French *capitaine-général*, a captain at the 'head' (Latin *caput, capitis*) of powers over a wide section of his army. The importance here lies in the distinctive use of *genus* in the division of living things into groups, from the classical Latin period to the time when the science of taxonomy became more fully developed, when *genus* and *species* were accepted as denoting together absolute individuality, corresponding to Aristotle's *genos* and *eidos*. It is of great interest to find that the O.E.D. shows that the first English use of 'genus' and 'species' in the modern sense occurred in the same passage in Topsell's *Serpents* (1608):

'Because there be many kindes of Crocodiles, it is no marvel, although some have taken the word "Crocodilus" for the genus; and the several species they distinguish into the Crocodile of the Earth, and the Water.'

Let us follow a little further this sowing and generation of the seed, which has borne so much useful fruit in the English language. The first shoots must be kept clear of weeds: in fact they must be *extricated* from them. *Tricae* in Latin meant 'trifles'. Cicero speaks of domestic fusses and vexations as *domesticas tricas* (*Ad Atticum*, 10. 8): but according to Ernout this word may have originally meant 'weeds'. *Intricare*, which gives us *intricate* and *intrigue*, certainly meant 'to entangle'.

After the harvest – the O.E. *haerfest*, 'autumn', cognate with L. *carpere*, 'to pluck' (the fruit) and so with our *carping* – come the threshing and the cleaning, and, if necessary, the winnow and the sieve. All these separate processes once had a vitality and a language of their own. Then came the combine-harvester, which has put a dozen arts into the mincing machine and dropped a hundred good words into oblivion.

But the language of these old skills remains, unrecognized, in our speech. Who would connect *halo*, *area*, or *eyrie* with harvest-work? Yet all three originally described a threshing-*floor*. *Halo*, through F. and L., is from Gk. *halōs*, 'a circular threshing-floor', from which developed the sense of the disc of the sun or moon, and therefore the circle. Cicero's meanings for L. *ārea*, 'an open space', are (1) 'a site for a house', (2) 'a threshing-floor'. The Hittite *area*, 'a granary', seems to be a cognate. The question of the origin of *eyrie*, at one time more often spelt *aerie*, has been fought over with some asperity. The O.E.D. accuses one old philologist of introducing the spelling *eyrie* to fit in with his derivation from *ey*, 'an egg'. No doubt the sense of windy height has influenced the picture conjured up by the word. But the likeness to *ārea* is equally apt, and this may well be the origin. An eyrie is surely the untidiest of all nests: the eaglets stand stiffly in a welter of broken sticks and rubbish, very like a dirty threshing-floor, but with a half-eaten hare and a mess of blood thrown in. In Roman times the chaff was shaken and harassed from the wheat by a *tribulum*, 'a threshing-sledge' studded underneath with nails or sharp flints. *Tribulation* is given a new force by a realization of its original significance – something stronger than our phrase 'victim of the machine'.

To deal with the rubbish of the threshing-floor comes the *sieve* – the 'cleaning' as we now call it. Here an I-E. radical **krei-*, 'to separate', with its cognate Latin *cernere*, 'to pass through a sieve', has released groups of valuable words to illustrate in different ways the obvious metaphors for which **krei-* has been responsible. From *cernere* come *discern*, *concern*, and the curious Latin word *cernimen*, shortened to *crīmen*, an accusation requiring a sifting of judgments –

185

our *crime*. (A *criminal* is, etymologically, not necessarily a person who has committed a heinous offence, but merely 'the accused'.) From the perfect participle of *cernere, crētus*, come *discreet, discrete, secret,* and *secrete* – 'to separate' (*sē* = apart). *Secrete* gives *secretary,* originally, both in its Latin form and in English, 'a confidant'. It was a later, more Dickensian, kind of secretary, with a bunch of pens behind his ear, who gave his name to the *secretary bird,* first recorded under that name in English in 1781, the *Secretarius secretarius* of South Africa.

It is the judge who sifts the evidence, who decides for or against the accused. He is therefore a *critic* in this *crisis* of sifting; for the Gk. word *kritikos,* 'able to discern', from *krinein,* 'to judge', is cognate with *cernere.* A distant Germanic relative of these words gives us *riddle,* O.E. *hriddel,* still used to mean a sieve in Scotland and other parts of Britain, and in English everywhere in such phrases as 'riddled with holes'.

There still remains the final step in corn-farming, the action and the result of turning the grain into meal. Here our linguistic harvest is almost as rich as it is from *genus* and *cernere.* The chief sources are O.E. *melu,* 'coarsely ground grain', and L. *molere,* 'to grind into meal'. Provided that we begin with *m* and end with *l,* we can take the vowels in their due order. In Dutch *malen* is 'to grind, to whirl' – which gives us *maelstrom*; O.E. *melu* provides our *meal*; O.E. *mylen,* a *mill* (from L. *molina*) adds *mylenstān* and *mylenhwēol,* 'millstone' and 'millwheel'; and by later adoption from Latin we have *molar* tooth. From L. *mola,* 'a millstone', comes *emolument,* 'money paid to the miller for his work'. A side-shoot of the soft meal ground out by the *mola* is L. *mollis,* which has given us *mollify,* with the soft-shelled *mollusc*; and the softest, in some of the English species, of all the leaves of all the English plants is the leaf of the *mullein.* The softness of meal is recognized also in the possibly unrelated *mass,* which comes through F. and L. from Gk. *maza,* originally 'a paste of barley-flour'. The perfect fineness of flour is admirably suggested by its name, *flour* representing French *fleur de farine,* 'the flower, the best, of the wheat-meal'.

Certain details of farmland and farm-building, from an age of more primitive agriculture, stay on in our speech, although we hardly ever give them a second thought, or remember what they stand for. 'The septum', says the anatomist, 'or the membrane separating the ventricles of the heart. . . .' There are also the *nasal septum* and the *transept*, the across-division in a church. But the L. *septum*, a barrier, from *sēpīre*, to hem in, was a later word than *sēpes*, a hedge, which in fact was the parent of the verb which gives us our *sept* (part of a clan). For farms of which the boundaries were not demarcated by hedges, it was necessary to know where one property finished and the next began. This is exactly what 'finish', or the L. *finis*, first meant. (Did we not learn at school that *finis* meant 'an end' and its plural, *fines*, meant 'a boundary'?) *Fines* were indicated by fixed marks, probably by stakes driven into the ground. *Pālus*, 'a stake', which gives us, through French, *pale, palings*, and *palisade*, is closely related to *pangere, pactum*, 'to knock into the ground': and it is to this system of marking out fields and farms that we owe *pact* and *compact* and the great word *pax*, 'peace'.

Stalwart means 'foundation-worthy'; but whether it referred in Middle English to the base of a tree or to the base of a hayrick, it is derived from 14th century farming. This and the other words which we are considering belong to 'the simple scene, the rural spot' of the kind that was beginning to be applauded for its picturesqueness in the more self-conscious 18th century, but which was once an inevitable part of life no more likely to be loved than the daily walk to catch the 8.10 for Victoria.

That shed near the farmhouse was used for shoeing horses. In Mediaeval L. *angarium* was 'a blacksmith's shed', but our *hangar* is more likely to be used for aircraft. That sack full of oats was called the *haver* (oats) *sack*, although the *barn* where it was to be found was the 'barley-barn'. ('Barley', O.E. *bere* + *līc*, 'barley-like': *barn, bere* + *ern*, 'barley-storehouse'.) *Floor*, as in *bern-flōr*, originally suggested a piece of field with a roof over it.

'And his cohorts were gleaming in purple and gold,' wrote Byron; but even such a magnificently martial word as L. *cohors* meant originally 'a farm-enclosure'. The farming or the hunting sense always preceded the military sense. The ploughshare always comes before the sword.

The *crop* (the 'top', or 'ear', of the corn) of *hay*, (the *cut* grass, related to 'hack') – has bequeathed fewer words to English, except in that *grass, green*, and *grow* are background words, as it were, in the language. They spread so early from I-E. **ghra-* that it is difficult to give them a time-order. We have lost the expressive original sense of *aftermath* ('the after-mowing, the second mowing'). The figurative sense is found first in Cleveland, one of the Metaphysical Poets, in 1658 – a mid-seventeenth century 'conceit' more effective and certainly more often remembered than most:

> 'Rash Lover speak what Pleasure hath
> Thy Spring in such an Aftermath!'

Nomad is from Gk. *nemein*, 'to pasture', hence 'to find pasture', hence (but not used regularly until the 19th century) 'to live a wandering life'. *Botany* originated, by way of *botanē*, 'grass', and later 'a plant', from Gk. *boskein*, 'to graze', of which the Germanic *bush* is a cognate.

Sheep-farming has given us three words of great importance and interest. The *wool*, before shears were invented, was plucked off with an expert tug. L. *vellere*, *vulsum* was probably the technical word for this action. An Armenian cognate describes a fleece so plucked. *Signature*, mentioned in Chapter XIV(b), derives from the Late Latin *signātūra*, 'a mark of ownership on a sheep'. The Christian metaphor in 'He shall feed His flock like a shepherd' is retained in the bishop's crozier or shepherd's crook.

XVI

NATURE AS MAN SEES IT

'But Nature 'twas
Urged Man to utter various sounds of tongue,
And need and use did mould the names of things,
About in same wise as the lack-speech years
Compel young children unto gesturings,
Making them point with finger here and there
At what's before them.'

LUCRETIUS, V. 1028–32.
trans. W. W. Leonard.

IF the early history of agriculture has left its trace on our language, could not the same be said of the early history of man, or of the early history of the thought of man? Here is the threshold of a vast subject which yet may seem to be a digression. In fact it is an ingression, because the nature of man has produced the concept of universal nature, and, arising from this concept, the mind of man has gradually produced that study which we call Natural History.

Does the search for the *etymon*, the starting point of a word, reveal the evolution of human thought? Does it suggest even – late as recorded speech appears in the history of man – the first steps which differentiated human man – if there be such a category – from animal man?

Can we, in our own Indo-European mother-language, find the reflections of such a difference, or the beginning of man's unique capabilities?

Perhaps, before man spoke clearly, he was more a *pointer at* than a *speaker to*. He was the half-dumb telling the half-deaf. The I-E. root is *deik-, 'to point to, to show'. Early Greek, destined to become the first perfectly expressive language in the world's history, made direct use of the root in *deiknumi*, 'I show'. The Sanskrit cognate *diśati*, like the Germanic and the Hittite equivalents, has this meaning of 'demonstrate'. In Latin *dic-*, the meaning has already become 'say'. The sequence is 'show, display; point out by words; tell; say'.

Dĭcere with its supine *dictum* (whence our *dictate* and *dictionary*), earlier gave through *digitus*, 'the pointer', *digit* and *index*, 'the pointing finger'. *Jūdex*, our *judge* (through French), means 'the pointer at, the expounder of *jūs* the law'.

In the same way perhaps the fact that *spell* originally meant a spoken story, and had nothing to do with letters, reflects the late arrival, in human evolution, of writing.

One can point at a tree or a wound, but one cannot point at a concept. The word *idea*, now ordinarily used for *notion* ('jolly good idea'), was the one chosen by the Greeks to express the abstract concept. How was it formed? It is in fact a relative of L. *vidēre*, and Greek (w)*idein*, 'to see'. The meaning steadily evolved from the more concrete to the more abstract – 'look; semblance; form; configuration; species; kind; class; sort; nature', is the sequence. The Platonic Philosophy sense came later. In other words the human achievement of forming a 'concept' was gradual.

In the same way we can trace the simpler origins of the words *rational* and its Gallicized counterpart *reasonable*. The starting point is Latin *rēri*, *ratus*, which implies counting and calculation. *Sense* has changed all the way from *feelings* (L. *sentire*, to feel) through the *senses* to a significance so different as to be almost opposed, namely 'good judgment'. The force in *imagination*, the highest faculty of man, was originally connected with the lowlier *imitation* – the making of an *imāgo*, 'a copy, a model'.

Imagination – poetic fancy – poetry as an act of creation – these powers and faculties are named and known in language long before the parallel abilities of observation and deductive science. Yet the roots of some of the early words for 'know' suggest the sense of the power to separate, to isolate. *Science* itself comes from L. *scire* to know, and the root of this word may well be the *sci-* syllable which describes cutting, separation. Our own word *skill*, from Scandinavian, implies this power to *distinguish*.

Can we learn through etymology something of man's first thoughts about time and eternity? The old noun *world*, for instance, is puzzling. From its O.E. origins we know that it represents *wer–eld*, in other words 'man-age' (*wer* as in *werewolf*) meaning that the earth is 'as old as man'? Our words *age, eternity*, and *eon* are, respectively, Germanic, Latin, and Greek derivatives of an I-E. word, near to Greek *aei*, 'always'; and the first meaning of *aei* is 'long time', 'eternity'. The more difficult conception came later. The Greek *khronos*, 'time', however, suggests something 'wearing away' – in contradistinction to the Greek cognate of our word *life* which suggests *'sticking* to it', if we are justified in tracing it to the root **leip-*.

On this search for signs of the first recognized emergence of human faculties, it is worth looking out at the same time for evidence of the early appearance of modern human traits. The various invaders of Britain had their own race-problems. Segregation or integration? 'Who are they?' 'Where do they come from?' 'We don't like them.' Does it show a typical weakness of the English people that it was the Anglo-Saxons who said this, *of the race they invaded*? The Saxon word for a Celt was *wealh*, 'a foreigner'. Therefore (because the Celtic Britons insisted on staying put in the West Country) we have *Cornwall* and *Wales*.

How exclusively human is memory? or rather, what kind of memory belongs exclusively to humans? Clues to the answer will be found in the origin and relationships of the word. Partridge starts with the three offshoots of the supposed original thought-form from the root **smer-* – Latin *memor*, 'mindful', Greek *martur*, 'a witness' (e.g. witness of a faith), and O.E. *murnan*, 'to grieve', *mourn*. Related words all have some sense near to 'anxiety' and 'sadness'. At the apex of the tripod formed by the three offshoots – the leg of the three toes of our *pied de grue* – can be surmised a **mor-* or a **mar-* meaning, 'to be anxious, to grieve'. In other words the ability to grieve – as in the higher animals – includes the ability to remember. The dog grieves for his dead master: the eagle, grieving for his mate killed by the hunter,

> 'A great way off descries
> His huddling young left sole; at that he checks
> His pinion, and with short uneasy sweeps
> Circles above his eyry, with loud screams
> Chiding his mate back to her nest, but she
> Lies dying, with the arrow in her side;
>   . . . never more
> Shall the lake glass her, flying over it;
> Never the black and dripping precipice
> Echo her stormy scream as she sails by.'

191

The difference is that man can 'recollect the emotion in tranquillity', or can remember the emotion as fact, when no emotion is involved. Running through Greek and the Greek-influenced part of our language is the human but not exclusively human sense embodied in *idio-*: *idios*, 'personal, private, separate'; *ta idia*, 'private property'. An *idiōtēs* is 'a private person', not a *stratiōtēs*, a 'private' soldier, or public servant. We use the word rightly in *idiom, idiosyncratic*, strangely in *idiot*, in the belief that as an *idiōtēs* does not hold public office he must be incompetent – a sense which the word had already acquired in Latin. The Latin cognate is *sed*, 'but': the sceptical, self separating 'Yes, but –' of the human race; the freedom to choose, perhaps, which is embodied in the relation between O.E. *lēod* (our 'lay'), 'the people', and the cognate Latin *liber*, 'free'.

We may turn here from self to abnegation of mere self. Religious emotion, of one kind or another, has its own evolution in human history. When did this part of human life begin? Do the words help us? We know the sense of 'binding' – of *ligaments* – in this word *religion*. Cicero tried to connect its origin with *relegere* 'to re-read', but the metaphor of attachment to a different order of being, to a higher power, was slow to develop. The first meaning of the word in English expressed a 'binding by monastic vows, life in accordance with religious rule'. But this abandonment of self to the greater than self is a strong but relatively recent compulsion in the development of man.

Traces in our words of social history and custom have appeared and will appear frequently in these pages. Differences are always more striking than similarities. It is piquant to notice that *spoon* (O.E. *spōn*) originally meant 'a chip of wood', and that we seem to have returned to this with the little spoons provided with ice-cream tubs. It is amusing to find that *etiquette*, from F. *étiquette*, O.F. *estiquette*, the right practice of Order of Precedence and Good Manners, is 'the order of precedence determined by one's label or *ticket*', worn, as it were, like the right badge for the right Enclosure, not so much worn or stuck on, as impaled (the derivation-sense) by a pin, as at Ascot.

The differences go deeper. *Trade*, the word reminds us, was not a question of transatlantic telephone-calls and fleeting air-visits. *Trade* is the *trodden* route. *Trade-winds* have the same sense. *Trade* meant 'travel', and *travel*, 'hard work'. Here again the word helps.

Travel originally meant 'travail', to labour painfully, as in child-birth. Earlier still the sense was 'torment'. This is the first meaning in English (1200). But the ultimate derivation takes it one step further – back to a horrible three-staked, *tri – pālus, tripālis*, 'an instrument of torture'. It is somewhat surprising that humorous writers on the theme of British Railways have not used this derivation as a text.

Two other words suitable for texts are *church* and *mad*. 'I know it's Sunday, but need I go to church today?' To this boy *church* can be everything that is tame and dull, safe and savourless. But in the original Greek the word is derived from the dynamic word *kurios*, full of meanings such as 'lord, master, power, hero'. The terrible word *mad* may remind us of the mitigation, through centuries, of the horror of insanity. Now the pain of the word is mercifully assuaged by such thoughts as 'treatable mental illness' or 'successful analysis'. But the word first held the sense of injury. A cognate is *maim*. A root meaning *to hew* is to be supposed. The old sense of the blood-curdling irreversibility of madness is in King Lear's cry when he begins to lose his reason – 'I am cut to the brains'.

XVII

MAN AND THE NATURE OF THE STARS

'When I consider the heavens, the work of thy fingers,
the moon and the stars, which thou hast ordained –
what is man, that thou art mindful of him?'

Psalm 8. 3–4.

ANYONE who ponders on the evolution of the concept of Nature as reflected in our language is made to realize again and again that the thought of Nature as something to be enjoyed for its own sake did not exist in the minds of our ancestors. They wondered about it continually. They were obsessed by the mystery of the sun, moon, and stars. They were closely concerned with flowers and trees. They were always, like the Oldest Inhabitant, talking about the seasons and the weather. But their way of expressing their wonder might be to propitiate the god of storms by dedicating a field to his name; or to pick a bunch of Prunella because the leaves of the purple-flowered plant might cure headache or boils; or to work out a horoscope favourable to a fertile marriage between the farm-cow and the town-bull.

We use *astrology* as the name for the fortune-telling star-learning, and *astronomy* as the modern and scientific word. This, however, was not always the case. *Astronomy* in our written records (1205) preceded *astrology* by 150 years. But in 1205 the universe was still thought to be geocentric; so that *astronomer* retained the sense of the Greek bases composing it, 'an arranger'. He could not do much more than count and name the fixed pattern of stars supposed to be wheeling over his head, and affirm their grouping into what seemed in his two-dimensional view to be constellations.

There are words and phrases used today – used even in modern astronomy – which bear traces of the Ptolemaic system and remind us of the old picture of sun, moon, and planets all revolving round the earth, each in its own transparent 'crystalline sphere'. The basic meaning of *cosmos*, our word for the universe, is 'order'. In the

Gk. *kosmos* is latent the Pythagorean notion of 'the music of the spheres':

> 'There's not the smallest orb which thou beholdst
> But in his motion like an angel sings,
> Still quiring to the young-eyed cherubims.'

Ecclesiastical Latin, using the word *firmamentum*, gives evidence of the belief that the sky itself was supported by a prop of superlative firmness. Those stars which seemed to move relatively to the rest were called the *planets* (L. *planēta*, from Gk. *planētēs*, 'a wanderer'), the *stellae errantes* of the Romans. The occasional especially wondrous star with streaming 'hair' (Gk. *komē*) was a *comet*. Its appearance was a portent. The first mention in English was in the Anglo-Saxon Chronicle (1154) of the comet of 1066.

Here astrology and astronomy are linked (the words were not finally separated till the 16th century) and a generation of sceptics pays unconscious court to astrology and divination by using their language every day. *Sinister* the reader will recognize: he may himself be influenced by the extra force given to the word by older writers, who took it for granted (as the Romans did, in contrast to the Hellenes) that omens seen or heard from the left hand were unfavourable, just as those from the right hand (*dexterous*) were happy ones.

To *consider* was, as we know, supposed to mean 'to resolve a problem in terms of its horoscope'; but *desire* is a less obvious stellar word, a form of *desiderate*, meaning *de sidere*, 'without a star', with the happy outcome unfulfilled.

Today we use different *-ologies* to measure our fortunes. We speak, or used to speak, for instance, of the 'psychological moment' – a mistranslation of Bismark's *das psychologische Moment*, his phrase for the impact on the French of the bombardment of Paris, a confusion of *das Moment*, 'momentum' with *der Moment*, 'moment of time'. The sense of perfect timing is an astrological concept, and is preserved in our word *mature* (L. *mātūrus*, produced at the right moment, and therefore fully developed). 'Think before you speak' is wonderfully elaborated in the verb *contemplate*, which enshrines 'temple' – probably the precinct of a temple – with the suggestion of an augur drawing a circle with his wand in a place from which to scan the heavens.

If the omens were ill, they were called *obscene* (*obscēnus*), or *abominable* (*ab ōmine*). Yet – a reminder that one can take nothing for granted in the history of words – *abominable* did not always have an astrological meaning. It is a word whose sense has been obscured by falling between a true and a false derivation. In O.F., and in Wyclif, and up to the 17th century, the spelling was *abhominable*, falsely derived from *ab*, 'away', and *homo*, 'man'; in other words 'pervertedly inhuman'. This, with the *h*, was the spelling in Shakespeare and the Authorized Version of the Bible. Even Dr Johnson clave to the *ab homine* derivation. In *Love's Labour's Lost* the pedantic schoolmaster Holofernes reproves as unscholarly the attempt by 'rackers of ortagriphie' to remove the *h*. Though these 'rackers' finally succeeded, the meaning has never lost the fierceness which its true derivation scarcely implies. Yet *ab omine* was more fatal, because it was Fate, unalterable. Either your star was in the *ascendant* (hence 'ascendency') or it was against you (*dis-aster*). So important was the good augury, that the augur who prophesied a *fortunate* (L. *fors* = chance) future and gave a favourable forecast (L. *strēna* – whence our *strenuous*) was given a present, much as people tip the croupier for a win at Crockford's.

The star was the thing, as Napoleon believed; or it might be the planet, for we still say *jovial* (for the influence of Jupiter), and *saturnine*, and *mercurial*, as we say *lunatic* for the man who is 'moonstruck'. The star was taken in conjunction with the *hour* (*hōra*). The hour of the event was cross-fertilized, as it were, by the hour of one's birth. 'Your silence most offends me,' says Don Pedro in *Much Ado*, 'for out of question you were born in a merry hour.'

The astrological hour, the *heure*, if favourable, was *heureuse*, if not, *malheureuse*; for the French meaning was once astrological too. Shakespeare, who makes fun of astrology through the mouths of Hotspur and Edmond, allows Beatrice to give it a mocking acknowledgment in her reply to Don Pedro's question as to whether she was born under a merry planet: 'No, sure, my lord; my mother cried: but then there was a star danced, and under that was I born.'

Most Beatrices nowadays would accentuate 'star' rather than 'danced'. But everybody was born under one star or another.

XVIII

NATURE AND THE GODS

'Hath the rain a father? Or who hath begotten the
drops of dew?'

Job 38. 28.

To some of the anatomical names there is a religious background.
The broad bone which closes the pelvic girdle at the back is the *os
sacrum*. Why 'sacred'? Because it was believed to escape disintegration
after death, and therefore to form the basis of the resurrected body.
'Adam's apple' is not such a straightforward name as it seems. It
looks like pure Old Testament – the forbidden fruit stuck for ever
in the throat of man. But Arab writers, using Latin anatomical
terms, called it the *pōmum* (their name for any rounded projection)
viri, 'of man'. In Arabic, 'man' is *adam*, which, in its obviously inspired
reference to original sin, could be translated by our monastic
anatomists only as 'Adam's apple'. In the cold words of E. J. Field,
'Dissection shows that the *pōmum adami* is due to the fused anterior
margins of the thyroid laminae'.

The influence of early religion on our language is shown also in
the word *phallus* (Gk. *phallos*), which recent dictionaries include as a
synonym for (Latin) *penis*. This has been popularized through
modern psychology; while botany qualifies the musical name
Amanita by the epithet *phalloides*, 'phallus-like', for the most poisonous
of all the fungi of both Britain and America, and names the stink-
horn fungus *Ithyphallus* (Gk. *ithus*, 'erect') *impudicus* (L., 'lewd').
Phallic worship was common to many ancient religious systems. Its
traces may be seen in the carvings on our chalk-downs, and probably
in the 'Lone Man' and other granite pillars on Dartmoor and elsewhere. In ancient Greece its images were carried in processions in
the Dionysiac festivals.

If even anatomical terms are tinged with the history of religious
belief, it is not surprising that the old gods have left their mark deep
in the less scientific words of our language, whether or not they

originated in what may properly be called religion. Good and bad luck play their part, as when a man says, 'I have a hunch' (which really means that he has been lucky enough to touch a hunchback), or, 'The 15th hole has got a jinx on me: I always play it badly'. A cobalt-mine was dangerous, unlucky, 'jinxy', because of the arsenic in the ore. *Cobalt* is from the German *Kobold*, 'a goblin'. The *jinx* goes back to ancient Greece, to the time when the wryneck, *Iynx torquilla*, was associated with witchcraft. The jealous girl's 'That old hag!' takes us back a thousand years to the belief behind *hag* as a demon-woman of the hedge (O.E. *hege*). The 'mare' of 'nightmare' was a goblin who sat on the chest of a sleeper. This 'mare', 'an incubus', in the M.E. word made from O.E. *niht* + *mære*, is not the O.E. **mere*, feminine of *mearh*, 'a horse'. Skeat cites a presumed Germanic *marjan*, 'to crush'. In the French equivalent *cauchemar*, the *cauche* is not from *coucher* (L. *collocare*), but from *calcare*, 'to tread on, press down'. *Larva* was given its present meaning of 'caterpillar' or 'grub' by Ray (1691): up to that time it had the Latin sense of a disembodied spirit or spectre.

In this search for the etymology rooted in nature, one of the best fields to explore is that of primitive religion and the old gods, in the ancient time when reverence for Nature was expressed by reverence for the deities which personified Nature.

With equivalents in all the Germanic languages, the English word for the followers of the old gods was *heathen* – 'the dwellers on the heath', the outlying districts. 'Heath' was a common Germanic word found in Gothic (*haithi*), and its extended use, 'non-Christian', was also Gothic, a language from which other Christian words, such as 'church', first emerged. The use of *heathen* is a reminder that Christianity was a religion of the towns, and that the older gods retained their followers in the remoter parts of the land. In later M.E. the parallel word *pagan* (L. *pāgānus*, 'a rustic', from *pāgus*, 'a village') was also adopted. *Pāgānus* came to be applied to a civilian in contrast to *miles*, 'a soldier', later 'a soldier of Christ'.

The Germanic high gods had resounding names such as *Thor* or *Thunor*, the god of thunder, whose name we commemorate in *thorium*, the element, and *Thursday*, and in the names closely related to *thunder*, such as *astonish*, *stun*, and *blunderbuss* (Du. *donderbus*). Thunderstorms and bad weather in general are often associated, among primitive peoples, with a displeased deity. The Taino word for 'hurricane' means an evil spirit of the sea.

Dryad signifies a nymph inhabiting a tree. Gk. *drus*, 'a tree', especially an oak, came into English at the Renaissance (1555), and fitted easily, perhaps less because of the association with its cognate *Druid* than because of a shared association with tree-worship.

Often the sacred meaning is more deeply hidden because the word goes further back in time (though less far in terms of human evolution) to Greece and Rome. 'Gizzard' was originally L. *gigēria*, 'the entrails of poultry offered as sacrifice'. The *caro, carnis*, of *carnage* seems by its root to have meant a piece of flesh *cut off* in sacrificial ceremonies. *Despond* is interesting, because it was so new to our language when Bunyan introduced it in his Slough of Despond. Bunyan did not know that the word came from Latin, still less that *dēspondēre* meant 'solemnly to undertake a promise' – a vow given significance through its connection with the Gk. *spondē*, 'a wine-offering to the gods'; the plural *spondai*, 'truce', or the libations poured out by each party when the compact was made.

The classical gods have marked our language more obtrusively, though sometimes rather vaguely. 'Waft me to the arms of Morpheus' hardly means what it is meant to request; for Morpheus was not the god of sleep, but of dreams – and dreams may be bad. The sense has been affected by the derived word *morphia*. Flora and Fauna were goddesses. When volcanoes were first mentioned in English, early in the 17th century, the descriptions fitted Vulcan's smithy. A *vulcano* or 'flaming hill' it is called in 1613. To the Etruscan it meant the god of fire. Pan was supposed to be the inspirer of sudden and inexplicable fear, felt especially by travellers in remote places. 'Pannish terror' became *panic* – a valuable word to express a unique experience, but hardly the right one to use with reference to a scattering army, or in the phrase 'a panic rush for tickets for the Cup-Final'.

Orgies (Gk. plural *orgia*) were the rites connected with the cults of Demeter and of Dionysus (Bacchus), the latter involving Satyrs, Maenads, wild dances, and the tearing in pieces of animals.

That great classicist Linnaeus saw in a genus of jellyfish something like a head with snaky curls and called it *Medusa*, after the name of the chief of the three Gorgons. That was a more enthralling name than the modern scientific description 'one of the soft gelatinous discopherous hydrozoans'.

The Roman Juno, consort of Jupiter, included among her powers the faculty of memory, and among her titles 'Moneta', literally 'the Warner'. (*Monēre* (to warn), *mind*, and *memory* all derive from the root **men-*.) The temple of Juno Moneta was used as the Roman mint – *mint* being also from the same root. Financiers acknowledge the sacred nature of cash when they call it *money*. Another derivative of *monēre* is *monster*, 'a warning, an omen from Olympus'.

Yet another religious link between past and present is 'Hades'. The root word here is Gk. *aei* 'always'. It is the 'always' of Sartre's *Huit Clos* which strikes a chill into the heart.

The principal Germanic god was in O.E. *Woden*, in German *Wotan*. We speak of him when we say *Wednesday* – in a way which well illustrates the slovening of pronunciation while the earlier spelling remains nearly intact. There is an obscure dialect-word *wood*, but otherwise few traces are apparent except in place-names. The meaning of *wood* is 'mad'. In O.E. *wōdnes* was the common word for madness. In 'Woden', the Germanic Mercury and god of song, the sense of madness is inherent in that of poetry – the ancient conception of 'divine frenzy'.

Wodens are still scattered in our countryside, as in the name of the Kentish village *Woodnesborough* – pronounced 'Winsbroh' by the real countryfolk – and in the names of fields and land-marks where once were shrines. In Norse mythology Woden appears as a wanderer in disguise under the by-name of Grimr. This name is clearly preserved in those of various earthworks which seemed, in the ancient world of smallness, so big that their origin was thought to be supernatural. There is many a *Grimsdyke* in southern England, and the huge Stone Age village-enclosure, *Grimspound*, on Dartmoor, is famous.

Tiw, the god of war, is commemorated in *Tuesday*, as his equivalent, the Roman Mars, is in the French *mardi*. *Friday*, *Frige-dæg*, the O.E. translation of L. *dies Veneris*, embraces the name of *Frig*, the wife of Woden.

Bede gives in his *De Temporum Ratione* our only record of the early Saxon month-names. The ninth month was *Hāligmōnath*, 'holy month'. Two others are named respectively after the goddesses *Hrethra* and *Eostre*. We may note that *Eastry* is the name of the next village to *Woodnesborough*, mentioned above. Their churches crown the nearest hills to the west of where the Jutes must have crossed the channel – now dry land – dividing them from Thanet, where they had spent several years before venturing to the mainland of Kent. The etymology of *Eastry* is uncertain. The O.E. form *Easterege* suggests 'the eastern district'. But can the possible *Eostre-burh* or *Eostre-weoh* (shrine), matching the adjoining *Wodensburh*, be disregarded when we try to find the earlier name for the second of the two hills where the Jutes would have dedicated to their principal deities their first altars on the territory which they were about to conquer?

The rite of sacrifice, or offering to the gods, is so widespread in all religions that its exercise must have helped to bridge the worship of Woden and of the God of Abraham and Isaac. *Victim*, through French, represents the L. *victima*, 'an animal consecrated for sacrifice', having its horns bound with the *vitta* or 'fillet of ribbons' (L. *vieo*, 'I bind', from root **vē-*). The etymology, however, is not certain. Possible cognates in German and Gothic imply 'consecration' and 'holy'. According to Bede the pre-Christian and pre-classical name of the eleventh month was *Blōtmōnath* (*blōt*, 'a sacrifice'). F. M. Stenton makes a dry comment on this in *Anglo-Saxon England* (1943): 'The explanation gives what is by far the earliest reference to the practice of killing off superfluous stock for winter-food ... made, with a naive economy, into a sacrificial occasion.'

The household gods of the Romans, the Lares and Penates, have left their mark on English. The Penates were the gods of the inside of the house (*penes*, 'with'; *penitus*, 'within'). *Penetrare* has given us *penetrate*. The shrine of the household gods, the Lares, was the hearth – a fact which gives dignity and significance not only to our phrase 'hearth and home' but also to the L. name for the hearth, *focus*, and to the English sense of the word. Other derivatives suggest in various ways 'important and purposeful heat' – words such as *fuel, fusil*, and *curfew* (F. *couvrefeu*, from *couvrir* + *feu*, 'the hour for dousing the fire'), which has become current once again in these days of rioting in various parts of the world.

The influence of Christianity on the various words of proper names has been enormous; but in our everyday language its trace is notably fainter than that of the pagan influence. This is no doubt because Christianity in English came comparatively late to the language. It seems strange, for instance, that *rood* (O.E. *rōd*), formerly used for the Cross of Christ, is now hardly to be found except in *roodscreen*

and in *rood* and *rod* as measures of land. *Crux*, a support for a hori-
zontal beam, was used in Late Latin for the Holy Rood, and gave us,
through F. *croix*, *cross*. The Agony of the Cross is represented by
crucial. The Dutch typically turned the word into a naval term,
kruisen, to *cruise*, 'to sail crosswise'. Through Spanish *cruzada* comes
crusade.

Christ, the One anointed with consecrated oil or *chrism* (Gk.), has
given us, besides the obvious words, *criss-cross* (Christ-cross; the
X of the Greek capital *ch* of 'Christ') and *cretin*, the Savoyard dialect-
version of *chrétien*, a name for the congenital idiots or dwarfs once
supposed to be peculiar to certain valleys of the Alps. 'Christian'
sometimes in Shakespeare and dialect means 'human creature', in
antithesis to the brutes. 'The sense here is that these beings are really
human, though so deformed.' (O.E.D.) The first use in English
was in 1779.

We have also the *Mass* words, such as *Michaelmas*, *Christmas*, and
Lammas (*loafmass*, feast of the firstfruits, on August 1st), and the
holy words – *halibut*, holy fish for Good Friday; *hollyhock* (O.E. *hocc*,
'mallow', M.E. *holihoc*, 'holy mallow'), which was originally the name
for the marsh mallow, *Althaea officinalis*, but is now given to *A. rosea*.
There seems, from the corresponding Welsh name, to have been a
mediaeval Latin *malva benedicta*. There is evidence of some association
with St Cuthbert, but none that the plant was originally brought
from the Holy Land.

The *ladybird* is the bird of Our Lady – by whose affectionately
amused choice, no one can say. Sometimes *ladybird* meant 'sweet-
heart': the nurse addresses Juliet, 'What, lamb! What, ladybird!'

The basic names of the Deity have of course left their mark; but
in the completely English words *God* and *Lord* the influence has been
chiefly on oaths and expletives, often toned down by slight alterations. *God* gives *good-bye* ('God be with you!') and *good morning*, which
is a shortening of 'God give you good morrow!' – i.e. 'tomorrow's
morning'. The O.E.D. calls the interesting word *bigot* 'of unknown
origin', and then summarizes the theories: that, on its first appearance in France, 12th century onwards, it may have been used
abusively for 'Visigoth', the hated foreigner and heretic. To explain
its modern English 17th century sense, wishful thinking has produced the constant and dogmatic repetition of the 'By God' theory.
The 17th century was certainly an age of picturesque profanity,

perfectly preserved by the Restoration Dramatists, who use 'God take me', 'Gadswounds'. 'Gadzooks', and similar expressions, all mixed up with more friendly phrases such as 'Marry come up my dirty cousin'. (See Swift's *Polite Conversation.*)

That the sense of divinity has helped to give richness and strength to language is best shown by one word, or by two closely related words, the origins of which existed long before any written Indo-European language. The two prehistoric words, reconstructed from the bones of their various descendants, were something near to *deiwo* and *dyau*. From one flank of the pair came *Tiw*, the name of the German war-god: from the other came L. *dies*. From the central root came *dius*, which seemed to combine the three notions of divinity, the sky, and the luminous. Latin turned *dius* into *deus*, but the *di* of the alternative *dīvus* is retained in our *divine, Diana*, etc. Greek produced *Dios*, the genitive of an old form of *Zeus* and the original of the first syllable of *Jupiter* (Skt. *dyaus-pitā*). Perhaps the most numerous progeny came from the *dies* branch, which eventually gave French and English all the day words such as *jour, journey, journal, meridian,* and *diary*. 'Oggi!' is pasted across the cinema-posters in Palermo. *Hōc diē – hodiē – oggi* – today! God is Light.

Perhaps we may find here the dawn of a new kind of consciousness among the people of the Bronze Age.

xix

MEASUREMENTS FROM NATURE

Anthrōpos mētron.
Man is the measure of all things.
PYTHAGORAS.

EVERYONE knows that the old English measurement, a foot, is based on the length of the foot of a man. It is easy to imagine paleo-lithic man, a hundred thousand years ago, measuring out his own territory from cave-mouth to boundary-stick, and putting down one foot in front of the other, just like a Trollopian rector measuring out the distance between hoops on the croquet-lawn. Thus we have *foot* from 'foot'. Human anatomy was useful in early measurements. The length of an *ell* (O.E. *eln*; L. *ulna*) varies in different countries; but the length of a forearm – an *ulna* – was the best notion. *Elbow* is where the *eln* bows or bends: the Latin equivalent being *cubitum*, 'the arm lying flat'. The meaning of *cubit* evolved from 'forearm' to a linear measure of 18–22 inches, the exact length varying in different districts.

The origins of these words are natural; but what are we to say about measurements of time? There is no hour in the human anatomy. The first time-reckoning words reveal a sense of *recurring* time. The oldest meaning of L. *annus*, a year, is that of our own derivative word *annual*, in the sense of a completed period, or the first sign of some phenomenon which is recognized because it is completed.

The names of our first eight months are quite un-English, being called after Roman gods and notables. *January* seems the most aptly chosen. Janus was the god of doors, facing both ways, towards the old and the new, backwards to winter and forwards to spring. *April* is probably an exception to the god-convention. Its connection with Aphrodite is doubtful: one famous etymologist says, 'for April, see "aperient" '; suggesting that April is the month when the buds open (L. *aperire*). Our *spring* is also a measurement-word implying a re-beginning. A Skt. cognate of *summer* is *samā*, a word which implies 'season' or 'half-year', bearing the sense of a recognized recurrence. *Fall*, so wisely retained by the descendants of the emigrants who first took the word to North America, is obvious in meaning, and has the sound of the gentle dropping of the leaf in autumn. Its supplanter *autumn* may be tied to L. *augēre*, 'to increase', and signify 'the season of increase', if the old Latin etymologists were right. The much debated word *winter* may refer to the time of 'whiteness' or to the season of 'water and wetness'.

We may well wonder how the splendid trick of measurement was thought out, and to what extent the days were involved in the earliest kind of counting. The 'after many a moon' of the historical novels is a vestige of the first recognition of the fact that from new moon to new moon gave the first precise measurement of the longer periods, and that the changes in the moon supplied the first fine adjustment for periods longer than a day. Here we recall once again that in the speech of pre-historical times the words for 'moon' and 'measure' sprang from a common root. From the I-E. root **mē-* the two words (and a multitude more) have evolved in equal and parallel importance. The Gk. *mēnē*, 'moon', and *mēn*, 'month', are related to the more sophisticated *mētron*, a means of measuring, used later for the measuring of verse, and reflected in our various senses of *metre*. Latin had *mētīri*, 'to measure or mete out', and *mensis*, 'a month' (whence our *menstrual*), the Skt. form being *mās*. The Germanic variant of **mē-* is **mā-* (**mō-*), whence came our *moon* and *month* (O.E. *mōna* and *mōnath*). O.E. had also *mǣl*, a measurement, a point of time, which gives us our *mealtime*. The more ancient of our Western European names for the moon came from a root probably older than the language of the Aryans. It may have been a Mediterranean – perhaps an Egyptian – word for 'light', i.e. 'the luminous one' (and *luminous* enshrines the *lu-* of L. *lūna* and *lux* and Gk. *leukos*, and all their kindred). First man wonders at the moon: then, sensibly, he makes use of it. At what cost, or to what profit, he is extending his interest today, future generations may be able to say.

An essential process in the measurement of time is the concept of sub-division. Ernout and Meillet deal with L. *tempus* and its meaning, 'time', or, more precisely, its formation-of-time sense. They relate it to L. *templum* (our *temple*), which was originally the space cut off or marked out by the augur 'in the heavens and on earth, in which he collected and interpreted omens – hence a space consecrated to the gods'. The derivations of the less primitive words for measuring suggest 'dividing up'. The Romans had from Etruscan their word *idūs*, '*ides*', for a division of the month (Varro), the Etruscan *iduo* meaning 'to divide'. *Minute* is for the Mediaeval L. *pars minūta prīma*, 'the small part of the first degree of smallness' (*pars minūta secunda* is the 'second' degree). The division into sixty parts was borrowed from Babylon by Ptolemy (*c.* A.D. 150), who used the multiple-of-sixty method for the degrees of the circle. Its adaptation to the division of the hour began in the 13th century.

With the power of creating artificial divisions must come the power of counting them. *Mille*, L. for 'a thousand', gives us the clue to *mile*, of which the origin is *mille passūs*, with the dual and plural forms *duo mīlia, tria mīlia, passuum,* etc. Our Germanic 'thousand' (if the second syllable was originally the *hund* of 'hundred', German *hundert*, and the rest) was 'the strong hundred', 'the very big hundred'.

Era, late L. *æra*, 'number for reckoning, point from which time is reckoned', conjures up the thought of early calculations by means of *aes, aeris* (L. for 'brass') – i.e. with brass tokens or 'counters'. History has repeated itself in the slang *brass* for money, as in the schoolboy's *tin*.

When we write 'lb.' for the weight of a pound, or cash what was once equivalent to a pound sterling, or when we speak of a *lira* or of a *livre* or a *litre*, we are using words of which the origin was the machine which made possible the *calculation* (derived from L. *calculus*, 'a pebble') of weight – *libra*, 'a pair of scales'.

Pound (L. *pondo*) is cognate with L. *pondus*, 'weight', and *pendere*, 'to weigh' – especially money. For a fine measure, the seeds, or fruit, of a plant might be used as a weight. Seeds are the least variable elements in the anatomy of a plant. Three barleycorns make an inch. The *carat* of a precious stone was originally the weight in terms of the seeds from the purple pods of the algaroba or carob, the locust-tree. The long pods may be referred to in the 'locusts' eaten by St John the Baptist, though it is quite as likely that he ate the winged locusts (L. *lōcusta*, 'lobster, or locust') which are still included in the dietary of many eastern peoples. The carob-tree is known to science as *Ceratonia siliqua*, the generic name having been taken from Gk. *keration*, 'the little horn', from which, through Arabic, Spanish, and French, we have *carrot* to balance *carat*.

XX

BASIC WORDS FROM SEAFARING
AND HUNTING

'The god that hailed, the keel that sailed
are changed beyond recall,
But the robust and Brassbound Man – he is
not changed at all.'

KIPLING, Poseidon's Law.

WE still sail and we still hunt. But if the open sea must always epitomize essential wildness, and if hunting is even now a necessity of life for millions of the world's inhabitants, yet for most of us, in Britain at any rate, sailing and hunting are for pleasure, which includes the pleasure of satisfying a primal instinct. We have been engaged in both activities over a period much more than ten times as long as recorded history; and this fact we acknowledge, for the most part unconsciously, in our vocabulary.

How brisk and apt seems the word 'nautical' for naval occasions – reminding us, perhaps, of the nautical angle of the peak of a famous admiral's cap, or of hornpipes aboard H.M.S. Pinafore! Yet in fact both *nautical* and *naval* are linked at their beginnings with the most depressing of all the aspects of sea-travel, particularly in the small ships of our ancestors. From the I-E. radical **nau-*, Gk. and Sanskrit had *naus* and *nau*, and Latin *nāvis*, for 'ship'. 'Sailor' in Gk. was *nautēs*; in Latin *nāvita* (*nauta*). From Latin, through French, we have *nave* (which in a church is like a ship inverted), *navy*, *nautical*, *nautilus*, and other developments. Our *nausea* is, according to one theory, the same Latin word taken from Gk. *nausia*, which, again through French, produced, perhaps unexpectedly but certainly understandably for those who have suffered from sea-sickness, *noise*.

Words of hidden sea-faring origin include *govern*, from L. *gubernare* (through French), 'to steer, to pilot'; and the recent *cybernetics*, constructed from the Gk. cousin of *gubernare*, *kubernān*. The metaphor in *opportunity* is of a favourable wind blowing towards port. *Vogue*, of Germanic origin, reached us through Italian and French. The noun formed from F. *voguer*, 'to sail forth', meant 'the sway of a ship', derived from the earlier sense of 'sway' as power or authority. The power, not to say tyranny, of fashion is barely disguised in the modern use of the word. *Veil* came, through O.F. *veile* and the later form *voile*, from L. *vēlum*, 'a cloth', of which the first meaning was 'a sail', used to draw (*vehere*) the ship through the water. *Reveal*, 'uncover', has the same etymon.

A much more recent legacy of words comes from the Dutch wars in the 17th century. The Dutch fleet in the Medway may have been Britain's shame; but it brought us a cluster of saltily expressive sea-faring words and phrases. *Boom* (the Dutch version of O.E. *beam*, 'a tree', as in *hornbeam*), *skipper*, *dowse the glim* all have the right, manly, fresh-air tang of early naval days. *Yacht* has an unexpected connection with German *Jäger*, 'a huntsman'. The Nimrod of Elgar's *Variations* was the faithful Jaeger. *Yacht* is the Dutch word for 'hunting' and a *jaghtschip* was a ship built for the pursuit of pirates.

Even older than most of the seafaring terms are those taken from hunting. These are also more deeply embedded in the language. 'To gain', from French *gagner*, has a Germanic root meaning 'to hunt'. A *bawd*, a woman on the loose, was at first a hunting-term for a running dog. Chaucer links this word with a term taken from falconry which was first recorded in English in *The Friar's Tale*:

> 'This false theef . . .
> Had alway bawdes redy to his hond,
> As any hauk to lure in Engelond.'

The 'lure' – a bunch of feathers attached to a cord – was used in training the hawk to return to the falconer. Chaucer, the language-maker, was already using the word *metaphorically* a year or so earlier than *The Friar's Tale* (*c.* 1385). Inhabitants of Desirable Mews Flats may not always be conscious of the fact that the use of the name *Mews* suggests an effort to keep up with the royal Joneses. The 14th century Royal Mews at Charing Cross was the Royal Stables, called *Mews* because hawks used to be kept there during their moulting-period – F. *muer*, 'to moult', from L. *mūtare*, 'to change (feathers)'.

Basic words such as *shooting* (a missile) have a score of derivatives in modern English, just as the fish-hunters' *net*, passing through Latin and French, has supplied words such as *nexus, annex, connect,* and *dénouement* (unknotting). *Sleuth,* used in English from *c.* 1200, derives, through Old French, from Scandinavian *slōth,* 'the track of a deer' (our *slot*). (Strictly, *sleuth* should have *hound* hyphened to it to make our word for a 'detective'.) 'Not a *vestige*' means 'not a footprint', through French from L. *vestīgium,* itself derived from *vestigare,* 'to follow a trail' – the etymology of the verb being doubtful. The man who *stalks* a deer moves *stealthily* after it, as if to *steal* it.

Behind many of these words lies the sense of enjoyment in the hunt, or of regret for a lost way of life. An I-E. root meaning 'to desire, to want, to love' is **wen-,* which has threaded its way into every I-E. language. Its Germanic offshoots have given us a number of words such as *want* and *wish*. Coincidentally through Latin we have *Venus* and *venison.* There is no immediate connection between these two words. *Venus* is the goddess of physical desire, eminently to be hunted; *venison* is the object of another sort of chase. The two sorts of *venery* may be connected only by punning, not by etymology.

The early L. verb *lacere,* 'to entice', 'to allure', from which we have *elicit* and *delight,* had a derivative *laqueus,* 'a noose or snare'. From this word we have, through French, *lace* and *latchet,* and, through Spanish, *lasso.*

xxi

THE NATURAL HISTORY OF DISEASE
AND TREATMENT

'Honour a physician with the honour due unto him.'
Ecclesiasticus 38. 1.

A GREAT deal of old English literature is hard to understand without some knowledge of astrology, particularly when the subject-matter has anything to do with illness.

When one studies Chaucer's description of the Doctor of Physic, it is advisable to remember that the date is about 1390, and that Chaucer was a sceptic and a satirist, though a benign and affectionate one – a pre-renaissance figure, centuries ahead of his time. One must remember also that he is not satirizing astrology, a subject on which he wrote, as an expert, one of the earliest manuals in English.

Where physic and surgery were concerned, says Chaucer of his Doctor, there was no man to equal him; and he gives the reason:

'For he was grounded in astronomye.'

'In astronomy'? Astronomy and astrology were then not distinguished. The Doctor, his chronicler goes on to say, 'kept his pacients wonderly well'. How? 'In houres'. The meaning of that astounding testimonial is, 'in the astrological hours according to the best principles of astrological medicine'. In other words, instead of 'to be taken after meals', the medicine was to be taken, if the patient had been born, say, under Venus, at sunset. But this is to oversimplify the obscurely complicated, as we see from the next lines:

'Wel kowde he fortunen the ascendent
Of his ymages for his pacient.'

Nevill Coghill translated this freely as,

'He knew
The lucky hours and planetary degrees
For making charms and magic effigies.'

Put more laboriously, this would be, 'He was skilful in choosing talismans for his patient, and the times when the influence of the planets would make them work best.'

Sometimes it would be the image of the sufferer himself which the doctor would keep as a sort of personification of the modern case-history. If the patient had a pain in his side, the doctor might treat the image at the corresponding place.

Chaucer's Doctor was no quack: though in modern quackery there are still remains of this treatment by remote control.

Astrology has left its signature in our medical vocabulary. The astrologically unfavourable word *left*, unaltered from O.E., is associated with physical weakness. O.E. *lyftādl*, 'paralysis', is the earliest use of *left*, perhaps meaning 'weak' before it was applied to the weaker side of a man. *Leper*, only slightly changed in passing through Latin and French from Gk. *lepra*, might be thought to hold the same 'left-handed' sense; but *lepra* is a derivative of *lepein*, 'to peel'.

Linked with the astrological 'hours' is the Doctor of Physic's knowledge of what might be called the Theory of Flow. The Doctor

> 'knew the cause of everich maladye,
> Were it of hoot, or cold, or moyste, or drye,
> And where they engendred and of what humour.'

In the old psycho-physiology there were four 'qualities' of the body-fluids; and the rate and direction of their flow or mixing – their folding together or *complexion* (L. *plicare*, 'to fold') – determined what *humour* (L. *ūmēre*, 'to be moist') was uppermost, whether *choleric* (Gk. *kholē*, 'bile'), *melancholy* (Gk. *melas*, stem *melan-*, 'black' + *kholē*), *phlegmatic* (Gk. *phlegma*, 'phlegm'), or *sanguine* (L. *sanguis*, stem *sanguin-*, 'blood'). Here we have a group of words from the old medicine of which only *sanguine* is much changed in meaning.

The classical earliest reference to *sanguine* is Chaucer's 'of his complexioun he was sangwyn', which means that in his character the Doctor was sanguine. In other words, his disposition was made up of the hot and the moist qualities, which predominated from 6 o'clock in the evening. In the hot-and-moist man the blood prevailed over the other humours. He was *sanguineus*, ruddy of countenance, hopeful, and courageous. He fell in love frequently. Our present meaning, 'hopeful or confident with reference to some particular issue', was not established till the 18th century. 'Sanguine, groundless hopes,' wrote the Lady Elizabeth Montagu (1720–1800), 'and ... lively vanity ... make all the happiness of life.'

But students of language must be conscious that the phenomenon of Flow was the background-belief to all this. The early physiologists tried to distinguish the mysterious fluids which seemed to fill the body through channels whose anatomy, except for the veins, they were unable even vaguely to distinguish. *Panta rhei* – 'everything flows'; and the Greek verb *rhein*, 'to flow', was brought in as a sort of maid-of-all-work to describe diseases of markedly different origins. Many of them seemed to be concerned with secretions looking more or less like raw white of egg – like whey, thought the Romans and the Greeks, who used their names for whey, *serum* and the cognate *oros*, to describe the weak beef-tea in which it seemed to them that our bodies were swimming. Illnesses were 'flow', in particular the diseases which were somehow seated in the mucus that dripped from the nose of a person suffering from a cold, or from one of the two score other complaints which simulated colds. This mucus they called *rheum*. If the rheum flowed down, it was a case of 'catarrh' (Gk. *katarrhein*). If it flowed out, it pointed to 'diarrhœa' (Gk. *diarrhein*). If it was accompanied by blood, the diagnosis was a 'bloody flux, *haemorrhage*' (Gk. *haima*, 'blood' + *rhein*). The meaning of *rheum* in *rheumatism* is plain only when we understand that the pain 'was attributed to rheum flowing down from the brain and settling on the affected part'. It was believed that phlegm was secreted by the pituitary body, and that this was the origin of the nasal secretion which dripped finally down the 'philtrum', the last filter, the vertical cleft in the upper lip.

Any sample list of human diseases shows something of the picturesqueness and vigour which we associate with the medical vocabulary of English, though the words are often well-selected loans. The violent suddenness of certain ailments is embodied in the radical meaning. *Plague* represents the L. *plāga*, 'a sudden blow'. The *agra* of *podagra*, 'gout', meant 'a seizing' of the foot (Gk. *pous*, stem *pod-*). This word reached us through Latin. The sense of *impetigo* is 'attack': for this skin-trouble Latin added to *impetus* the ending attached to a number of words implying something abnormal or unpleasant, such as *rubīgo*, 'rust'; *vertīgo*; *farrāgo*; *virāgo*, 'a hell-cat of a woman'; etc. We too speak of an 'attack' of various diseases, and use *impetus* and its derivative *impetuous*.

We accept *malaria* (Italian, 'bad air'), in spite of its suggesting the wrong cause, because custom somehow makes it sound suitable and the adoption into another language obscures the meaning.

We admire the power of Greek to give dignity alike to the serious and the trivial. *Typhus* is a magnificent word to describe through *tuphos*, a cloud, the misty stupefaction of high fever. *Meteorism* is an apt word for a minor symptom. Who but the Hellenes could have invented a verb such as *meteōrizesthai*, 'to be flatulent'?

Medical pharmacy, our language tells us, was much concerned with salves and poisons. The Gk. *pharmakon*, which gave us 'pharmacy', meant 'a drug'; but earlier it had meant 'a poison'. Of the Gk. phrase *toxikon pharmakon*, for instance, the meaning is 'arrow-poison'. We have in English *toxophilite*, 'a lover of archery'; and it is interesting to reflect that remarkably few medical men realize that, when they use the phrase 'highly toxic' they are not even beginning to make sense, or would not to an ancient Greek. Poisons played a large part in mediaeval life – as a way to murder, as a method of warfare against vermin and predatory animals, and as providing the necessity for the discovery of antidotes.

Another omission is implied in names of diseases ending in *-itis*. *Neuritis*, *phlebitis*, etc. bear for the layman the sense of a disease associated with inflammation. The doctor knows better; but he does not always know that *-itis* is a Greek feminine adjectival ending used in the qualification of the feminine word *nosos*, 'a disease'. *Nephritis*, for example, is therefore the 'nephritic (disease)' i.e. 'kidney-illness'.

'That child is the bane of my life!' says the admiring mother affectionately. But she is producing from the past an ancient and terrible word. *Bane* has many I-E. cognates, which together give the force of 'death', 'murder', 'wound', and – in English especially – 'poison'. When as a boy I discovered* henbane growing under the walls of Corfe Castle, I took it for granted that the plant was always cultivated near old castles for the purpose of polishing off much more important creatures than hens. 'It *looks* evil,' I thought: but the thought was tinged with mediaevalism, the name being allowed to obstruct the clear objective view.

Hyoscyamus is the generic name of the 'pig-bean', of which literal
*S.P.

213

translation merely reinforces the sense of ugliness. In fact the flower of the henbane is the most beautiful among the *Solanaceae*, delicately veined and dim; even its greens are shadowy. The plant is certainly, and notoriously, poisonous; but if its original pre-Conquest name, *henbell*, had stuck, we might view it differently. *Bane* has stayed on, not only for the ordinary poisonous wild-flowers such as *baneberry*, but also for plants which are said to poison various animals. Our references are mostly from Herbals, in which the force of the baneful effect is unquestioningly repeated. Turner's *Herball* (1551) even extends the power of (among other plants) leopard's-bane:

'Leopardes bayne layd to a scorpione maketh hyr vtterly amased and Num.'

Those who know their British wild-plants from Bentham and Hooker will remember that there are two genera of fleabane – both composites. The first contains *Erigeron acris*, with its undistinguished and untidy bunch of low, fluffy pappus-heads, which flowers in late August. This plant is common, but unnoticed except as a fitting detail in the character of the dusty weeks of the season. Its relative has in Hooker the improbable 'popular' name of 'fleabane inule', being one of the magnificent *Inula* genus, which contains also samphire, elecampane, and ploughman's spikenard. It is a thick-charactered plant with dusky yellow flowers. Linnaeus called the smaller species of it *Inula pulicaria* (L. *pūlex, pūlicis,* 'a flea'). Species of the Order *Apocynaceae*, which includes the periwinkles and the oleanders, are called *dog's-banes*. In West Somerset a chervil has been called *rat's-bane.*

A pertinaceous pest in southern English gardens is ground-elder. But in mediaeval times, when the names of plants were forming, there were few 'weeds' which were not credited with the power to cure at least one kind of ailment. Ground-elder is so common because it was introduced as a remedy – whence its name of *goutweed.* Its by-name of *bishopsweed* must have been given at the time when the keeping of Christmas and the plum-pudding were banned by the Puritans. G. F. Scott Elliot tried to dig up an entire plant, and 'it was not until a hole about four feet deep and five feet across had been excavated that there were any signs of an end to it.'

In the Middle Ages weeds seem never to have been enjoyed for themselves, but they were respected as cures. They were *simples* –

medicines uncompounded. The juice of the plant was drunk 'straight'. Often the simple was a general nostrum, good for every complaint. *Self-heal* or *sanicle* was 'the little health-restorer'. *Valerian* stems from L. *valēre*, to be strong. L. *salvus*, 'entire, intact', gives us *Salvia*, the name of the genus of plants which, through F. *sauge*, we call *sage*. Fever, it was believed, was banished by a good *febrifuge* such as *feverfew*, an English version of the same word through Anglo-Norman. All such plants were, in one of the many changing senses of the word, *physical*.

> 'Is Brutus sick, and is it physical
> To walk unbraced and suck up the humours
> Of the dank morning?'

(Portia's question is quoted by C. S. Lewis, discussing *phusis* in his *Studies in Words*, together with the schoolboy's explanation that it meant 'sensible' as opposed to *mental* 'mad'.)

Never quite forgotten in mediaeval Medicine was the necessity of keeping in mind the possible influence of some god of Healing such as the Greek Paion, whose flower, the pæony, was the emblem of health.

There were many other plants beside the goutweed with a reputation for curing individual diseases. *Scabious* was a remedy for *scabies*. *Tormentil* was sovereign, as our forefathers would say, for the *torment* of toothache. *Prunella* (self-heal) changed from *brunella*, diminutive of Mediaeval Latin *brūnus*, 'brown', was the special remedy for throat-troubles, such as quinsy.

Naturally it is the plants with the oldest-established names – those, therefore, with the longest history – which are most likely to be connected with medical or magical properties. The lowly, common, and unromantic plants such as the buttercup were not generally considered worthy of being used as simples by the physician. A remarkable exception was *groundsel*. That name has been spelt in twenty different ways since its first appearance in the *Epinal Glossary* of *c.* 700. Spellings such as *swally* and 'grinning *swallow*' emphasize that the second element in the name is *swallow*; but not with the suggestion of the plant's being 'a swallower of ground', easily as it spreads. The *r* is an intruder in the original *gund*. *Gund* meant 'pus'; and chopped groundsel was used as a poultice, a pus-swallower, to reduce swellings.

The list could be greatly expanded; and it must be kept in mind that other natural medicinal materials besides plants were included in the mediaeval pharmacopœia. Sir Walter Raleigh wrote in 1595 of 'a kinde of green stones which the Spaniards call Piedras Hijadas, and we use for spleene stones'. What stones did he mean? The mid-18th century Chambers's Dictionary says that 'this stone applied to the reins (kidneys) is said to be a preservative from the nephritic colic'. But the plot thickens when we go back to the root of *hijadas* ('the sides'), which is found in the L. *ileum*, 'the flank, groin'. *Ileum* is a transliteration of the accusative case of Gk. *eileos*, 'an intestinal obstruction'. This derivation helps to explain *Piedras Hijadas* as stones used as remedies for pains in the side. In French this *hijadas* became *l'ejade*, which English not unnaturally regarded as *le jade* – hence our *jade*, which, on strict principles of mediaeval homeopathy carried over into the medically backward English Renaissance, first became known as the stone to cure 'the stone'.

More straightforward are two mineral cures for hangover: *amethyst*, noted in Chapter XXXI, and *soda*, the name of which we had from Med. L. *soda*, formed from L. *sodanum*, 'glasswort', a source of the mineral. It is said that the word in Arabic meant 'a splitting headache', and that the name of the pain was transferred to the plant providing the remedy.

All this substantiates our knowledge about the vagueness of anatomical and medical science during the two thousand years before Harvey discovered the circulation of the blood. What is interesting is the extent to which the older anatomy comes into our contemporary vocabulary. *Brain, spleen, liver*, and *skull* are ancient words widely established in the I-E. languages. *Liver* is cognate with *life* – perhaps suggesting early recognition of the organ's essential importance in the vitality of its possessor. The cognates of *skull* (a Norse word) suggest something thin and hard, as *Schild*, 'shield', in German, or a mussel *shell* (O.E. *sciell*). The basic sense is something split. *Lung* and *light* are Germanic cognates. The lungs are the lightest organs in the body. Akin are the Skt. *laghu*, 'not heavy', and Gk. *elakhus*, 'small'. To these may probably be added Gk. *elaphros* and L. *levis*, which have similar meanings.

A complicating factor is that in our older literature the best-known internal organs are constantly being referred to as the 'seat' of some emotion. Typical of this are the organs beneath the bosom and under the breastbone. The old technical term for 'under the breast-bone' (the ensiform cartilage) is Gk. *hupo khondria*, rather vaguely produced from *khondros*, 'a grain of corn'. We have adopted the words into our everyday language as *hypochondria*, a metaphor brilliantly apt for the morbid fears which the hypochondriac feels as being somewhere in his breast. In the days when 'under the chest bones' was taken literally, one of the organs in this region which was regarded as especially associated with strong feelings was the spleen. The moods for which the spleen was held responsible ranged from melancholy to delighted amusement. Shakespeare alone gives the word eight different senses.

Still more pertinent to a search for origins are those anatomical terms which persist although the theory which they imply has long been superseded. *Artery*, for instance, which comes into English from Greek through Latin, may derive from *airo*, 'I raise'; but ancient belief associated it with Gk. *aēr*, 'air'. To Francis Bacon, for instance, *artery* meant what *artēria* had meant to Hippocrates – 'windpipe'. At the same time the dissectors, puzzling over the fact that the arteries, unlike the veins, were devoid of blood after death, regarded them as air-ducts or conduits for the mysterious 'vital spirits'. This belief continued long after Harvey's new map of the circulation. The pulse of the radial artery at the wrist 'was thought to be due to the blood of the accompanying vein'. Plato believed that liquid passed down the trachea into the *bronchus*; accounting for the theory that the word comes from Gk. *brekhein*, 'to be moist'. Gk. *karousthai*, 'to be heavy-headed', to plunge into deep sleep, produced 'carotid', because it was said that the compression of one of these arteries (*karōtides*) produced *carus*, a 17th century medical term for 'the extremest degree of insensibility'. The long nerve from the neck to the diaphragm is called *phrenic*. The reason for this is obscure, since Gk. *phrēn* means 'mind' (the source of our *frenzy*, earlier spelt *phrenzy*). Aristotle and Hippocrates each used the name. Were they thinking of heavy breathing in times of emotional stress? Or was it because they believed that the nerve somehow connected the brain with the soul, which was sited by the anatomists in the region of the diaphragm? We can be certain that no mediaeval theorist worth his salt would say 'perhaps'.

Sometimes a relatively colourless-sounding word, a little out-of-date, perhaps, in scientific contexts, can reveal the first struggling attempts to discover the deepest secrets. One such word, created centuries before cells or hormones were thought of, goes back to the attempts to pierce the mystery of differential growth. Botany-students are familiar with the word *parenchyma* as the old common term for the softer cells of the fundamental tissues of stem, pith, or the pulp of fruit. The word is now less often used in anatomy, where the meaning has been 'the distinguishing specific tissue of a gland or organ contained within the connective tissue' (17th century and later). 'Parenchyma' was first introduced about 300 B.C., and meant literally 'something poured in beside'. It reflects the belief that the blood brought to an organ by the veins, and poured into its interstices, turned, when it congealed, into the specific substance of the organ.

In the severe pages of the anatomy-books may be seen the excitement of the valid discovery, the joy of the first clear look. The (L.) *corpus lūteum*, the greyish gland that develops in the ovarian follicles, is yellow in the cow, where it was first discovered by Regnier de Graaf (1641–1673). In de Graaf's honour, therefore, and in honour of the cow, it is called *lūteum*, 'yellow', in human anatomy as well.

Galen noted and enjoyed the (L.) *maximum mirabile*, as he called it, of the breaking-up, within the skull, of the internal carotid artery into a net-like pattern or plexus of smaller vessels. To mark Galen's wonder at this animal phenomenon (which does not, however, occur in humans), his followers called it the *rete mirabile* ('the wonderful net'.)

The ranks of the first great observers, and the discoveries named after them, seem to take on a dignity and a grandeur which make the mere recitation of the names pleasurable in a solemn way. The Spaces of Fontana, the Islets of Langerhans, the Penetrating Fibres of Sharpey – these names should ever be remembered in our flowing cups.

XXii

WORDS AND HUMAN EVOLUTION

'Nomina si nescis perit et cognitio rerum.'

LINNAEUS.

(Unless the names are known to you,
The concepts will be hazy too.)

PRESUMABLY the outstanding feature of human evolution is the ability to accelerate the evolutionary process. Relatively to the average time-scale of biological change, we have speeded things up a hundred- or a thousand-fold. Samuel Butler was surely right in regarding the saw as a new kind of hand, the microscope as a new kind of eye. The absence of vascular attachment to the human body does not make those tools different in essence from a new kind of limb. Yet how many hundreds of millions of years would it take, by normal biological processes, to evolve, say, an eye which could see the moon from the moon's own surface? How many millions to extract from the vocal chords the ordered squeaks, grunts, and hisses that form a new language? How many hundreds to produce a new word? Man evolves so quickly that the qualitative words in his language, as distinct from the quantitative, scarcely remain stable from one year to the next.

Having in mind what we said about 'idiot' in Chapter XVI, we remember from schooldays being told that, if you called Metcalf Minor a *silly idiot, silly* originally meant 'good', then 'fortunate', then 'happy', then 'innocent', then 'deserving of pity', then 'helpless', then 'weakly', then 'unsophisticated', then 'of humble origin', then 'feeble-minded', then (increasingly, from a slow start in the 16th century) 'foolish'. With *idiot* the change was more sudden. The I-E. etymon is a syllable which suggests an act of separation. Greek picked this up and soon gave it a sophisticated meaning, applicable to the man who said 'No' to public office, the man who preferred to be separate, *idio*syncratic, the natural layman. Or perhaps the 'idiot' is the man who says, 'Yes, but . . .'; for the shape of the etymon **sued* shows that by another route *id* became the Latin *sed*, 'but'. L. adopted Gk. *idiōtēs* as *idiōta* and cynicized it into 'an ignorant or simple-minded person'. By the time the word reappeared in M.F. and M.E. it was the modern *idiot* fully fledged. Why this sudden sport? A complication is that, whereas Chaucer used the modern meaning (1386), following *Cursor Mundi* (1300), Langland's use (1379) when he went forth 'as an idiot' to 'aspy after' Piers the Ploughman, infers 'ignorant', more nearly in the original sense of 'lay', 'without special knowledge'. Wyclif used the word in the same sense, which was retained in some writings until the 17th century.

What can be learnt from these words? We remember what has happened to *awful* and *amaze*, and to *idea*, which originally meant the conception of anything in its highest perfection. We remember what has happened to *tall*, of which the early meanings were 'prompt, quick, docile, tellable' (*tell* may be cognate). Afterwards it implied 'comely', 'handsome'; next 'dexterous', 'capable'; which recalls the West Country dialect *clever*, meaning 'comely' as well as 'able'. Finally, from the 16th century, *tall* has signified tall in stature. We remember *lackey*, which Shakespeare so daringly turned from a noun to a verb to describe the habit of *Iris pseudacorus* in *Antony and Cleopatra*. Derived from Arabic *al-kaid*, 'a military chief', this word may owe its fall to the end of the Moorish rule in Spain. More to the point is 'I will go presently', which should mean what it meant in Shakespeare's day and for some time afterwards – 'I will go immediately' (and even 'immediately' does not mean quite what it formerly meant).

Most of these words have gone through an obvious evolutionary process; and in almost every instance the change of meaning has been in the same direction – diminishing. *Virtue* (L. *virtus*) is a noble word for the state of true manhood. 'Female virtue' and *virtuous* are lessenings, trivializings. Does this 'semantic degradation', as it is called, illustrate a human foible, a tendency to create richly and develop cheaply?

Sir Julian Huxley describes two factors in evolution, one of which is unique, the other especially fruitful, in the human species. The first is the power to form mental concepts: the second is the development of the possibilities of cross-fertilization.

Cross-fertilization is a characteristic richly illustrated by language, and notably by the English language.

Let us consider an uninteresting-looking French word, *partenaire*. It needs no Bradley called from the grave to tell us that this word means 'partner', or that L. *pars* has something to do with it. O.E. had already dipped into Latin to take over the word *part*. One of the *pars* words, *partītio*, or, rather, *partītionem* (by the Rule of Derivation through the Accusative), produced the F. *parçon*, 'a sharing', and then *parçonier*, 'a sharer', together with the elaboration *parcener* adopted by M.E., and still kept in Legal English in the sense of 'one who shares equally with others in the inheritance of an estate'. Blending this word with 'part', still untouched since our Saxon fore-fathers borrowed it from Latin, Modern English has produced 'partner'. By yet one more process of cross-fertilization, French has used our 'partner' to produce *partenaire* – a re-importation of an export. In English natural history words the results of this dipping about are less obvious, yet they exist.

Sometimes two separate words are evolved by a Latin word's being borrowed at two different stages of its later development. The Latin (from Gk.) name for a kind of fish, *gōbio*, gave us *goby*: the M.F. development of it, *goujou*, gave us *gudgeon*. What happened to that useful Latin word *vincire*, 'to bind', and to its offspring *vincula*, 'chains'? English Flora experts will know that *Vinca* is the scientific name for the blue periwinkle. *Periwinkle* comes from Old Norman-French *pervenke* (L. *per*, an intensive prefix, with the sense of 'thoroughly' + *vincire*). Yet 'comes from' is not strictly accurate, for the form *periwinkle* is influenced by the other application of the word to the gasteropod mollusc, *Littorina littorea*. Here it is of dif-ferent derivation, probably from O.E. *pine-wincle*, which perhaps includes something of L. *pina*, 'a mussel', with English *wince*, 'a reel or winch', from the convoluted shell. (E.W.) We say 'different derivation', but here is yet another bit of inbreeding, because the *peri* of the second word is probably influenced by the *peri* of the first.

Bezantler is a fine word passing out of use because the noble creature that wears the *bezantlers* has long passed out of the view of a town-dwelling population, in England at any rate. The setting is mediaeval, with A.N. taking the place of Latin. The lowest branch of the horn of a stag is directed forwards, and lies almost before the eyes. This *ramus*, 'branch' of the horn, is *ante ocularem*, which O.F. turned into *antollier*, and M.E. into *auntelere*. (With the *aun* for *an*, cf. *aunt/tante*.) The modern German *Augensprosse* is the semantic and more easily recognizable equivalent. 'Antler' was originally used for any branch of the stag's horn; so that, to mark the difference, 'brow-antler' was used for the lower, and 'bezantler' (1598) for the upper – the first syllable standing for L. *bis*, 'twice' – i.e. 'second'. It was not until 1829 that *antler* was (popularly) used for the whole formation.

L. *fūr*, 'a thief' (whence our *furtive*), was used in Late Latin as *fūro* for a cat, 'the fish-stealer'. *Furo* was given a diminutive form, O.F. *furet*, and turned in English into 'ferret'. But it is not only the French-Latin borrowings which make new individual words. Sometimes English fertilizes itself parthenogenically, as it were, by adopting a word so deeply buried in its own past that the original meaning is lost. In O.E. the word for our *lapwing* was *hlēapwince*, which might mean 'the leap with a waver in it' (see Chapter IX(b)). This was perfectly descriptive, whereas our modern version, with its confused association of *lap* and *wing*, is less so, though not entirely off the mark. Still, *lapwing* is more speakable, with all the downright quality of a successful English word.

Many words which we take for granted and pass by without a thought are capable of illuminating the story of man's mental and emotional development. There is no mystery in the decline of *horrid* and *horrible* from the dreadful meanings which they had in the Roman poets' *horribile dictu*, or in the cry of the ghost of Hamlet's father, to their feeble sense today. This decline they share with *awful* and many another word used not only as 'wise men's counters' but also as 'the currency of fools'. What may evoke one's surprise is that the earliest meaning of L. *horridus* and *horrībilis* (from *horrēre*, 'to stand on end') should continue – like the Ghost – behind the scenes. By the Roman *horrēre* was used of human hair. *Hirsute* is probably a related word. The original sense of *horridus* was 'bristling'. Among cognates is Skt. *hrsh*, 'to bristle with fear or other deep emotion'.

The sequence of meanings in Latin itself runs from 'bristling' through 'rough, shaggy, rude, and unpolished', to 'savage and terrible'. Our *horrid* is one of the large group of classical words which arrived in English in the 16th and 17th centuries. Only word-conscious, purposely archaic writers such as Spenser and Burton used it in its first sense. Shakespeare seems to have established the English sense of 'terrible'. Sir Toby Belch 'will meditate upon some horrid message for a challenge'.

The connection between horror and bristling hair continues in poetic metaphor and folksy humour. The story which Hamlet's father could tell would make each particular hair to stand on end 'like quills upon the fretful porpentine'. The ventriloquist, 'belly-speaker', by pulling a string, makes his dummy's wig suddenly flap up erect. The ground is made ready for the 'porcupine's quills' simile either by the Gk. *kher*, 'a hedgehog', or by the L. *hirsūtus* worn down to *ēr*, which led to the longer name for the hedgehog, *ēricius*. Presuming that the Gk. *ereikē*, the bushy, bristling 'heather', does not supply the clue, we may say that French, with less than its usual ruthlessness, turned the accusative of *ēricius* into *herisson* to get its name for the hedgehog. Thereupon English, indifferent to the claims of Latin and French alike, came out with *urchin*. This word was used for a hedgehog by 1340; for a sea-urchin (on account of its spines) in Holland's translation of Pliny, 1601; and for a boy (bristling with untidy ends and importance) from 1530.

Is there somehow in all this a hint that, even during the short period of man's ability to speak an organized language, horripilation – the raising of the hair by the contraction of the cutaneous muscles of the skin, already long vestigial in our anatomy – has faded still further and been preserved in spirits, so to speak, through the medium of language?

In other words, can we find through etymology the origin of human nature? Does the connection of the word *pain* with *pāna*, 'penalty', suggest the evolving sense of guilt which man (according to Sigmund Freud, at any rate) grew to inherit? The master returns to the house after a week's absence: his dog turns circles round itself with pleasure – pure pleasure, without any feeling of wonder. Per-haps at the root of the word *wonder* is the earlier, simpler meaning, 'pleasure', that is perpetuated in the German *Wonne*. This is half guesswork; but the cognates of *threat* (O.E. *thrēat*, 'a crowd') are the German *verdriessen*, 'to vex', and the L. *trūdere*, 'to push'. 'Come on! let's crowd him!' – the physical threat came first; and not without reason has *ochlophobia*, 'the dread of crowds', always been a terrifying mental condition. To be *wicked* probably once implied to be 'weak'. In the same way, *wrong* was something 'twisted' or *wrenched*.

'Ah! human nature is always the same!' is one of the most super-ficial and inaccurate of common instances. Occasionally, however, the thread of feeling has escaped breaking. The original meaning of *banal* (1293) was 'obligatory feudal service' (O.F. from Germanic *ban*, a proclamation – cf. our 'banns of marriage ... for the first, second, and third time of asking'). The modern equivalent may be compulsory military service or compulsory games.

The meanings of certain words describing basic human activities have changed profoundly during their development. The first meaning of L. *legere*, 'to read', was 'to choose' – to choose the word. The origin of *reason* is to be found in L. *ratus*, the perfect participle of *rēri*, 'to count', 'to calculate', and (developing from the calculation of numbers or times) 'to think, to reason'. The most exclusively human power, the ability to form concepts (without which true speech is impossible, as is seen, by those who think seriously, in the indissoluble double meaning of Gk. *logos*, 'reason-speech', 'speech-reason') is described by a word originally applied to the most fundamentally animal activity of mammalian and other forms of life – *concipere*, the Latin word for 'to gather', used of a female gathering the male seed; whence *concipere semina* meant 'to conceive'. *Speak* is a Germanic equivalent of L. *spargere*, 'to strew' – 'to scatter sounds-as-words'.

The word *mark*, noted elsewhere in these pages as originally meaning 'a limit or boundary-sign', and as appearing in many of our place-names, ranges so widely through the I-E. languages that we are again and again reminded of the importance of territorial boundaries for nomadic peoples who have become settled and are not merely taking a 'rest'. As is indicated by its Gothic cognate *rasta*, 'a stage', 'the end of a day's march' (like the *stathmos* so familiar in Xenophon's *Anabasis*), 'rest' in the old days specifically suggested a resting-place for the night.

The original meaning of 'pave' is 'to tread down level' (L. *pavire*). This points to a stage in road-development only once removed from the sheep-track. A derivative may be seen in Abel Evans's epigram *On a Fat Man*:

'When Tadlow walks the streets, the paviours cry,
"God bless you, Sir!" and lay their rammers by.'

To sum up. ... But the philologist must pause over even such a trite phrase as that. Is *sum* anything to do with *summit*? In fact, yes. *Sum* represents L. *rēs summa*, the column of figures totted up – from

224

below, in the Roman fashion. We are supposed to do it the other way now: but the word remains.

How much history may be packed in a word? There is certainly one substantive which suggests the Neolithic period – *hammer*. Before the word had its present significance, its meaning in O.N. was 'rock': and probably the I-E. root was formed when such an implement was made of stone. The 'Iron' Age? *Iron* is a cognate of *ore*; and *ore* meant 'copper' or 'bronze' before it was used for 'iron'.

Two words especially suggest that the growth of an institution is implied in their names – *nobility* and *hegemony*. The L. *nōbilis* must be traced to **gno-*, the root of *noscere*, 'to know', and of a host of other words. The aristocracy of *hegemony*, 'leadership', is derived from Gk. *hēgeomai*, which is translated by its cognate, 'I seek'. Hence we have the abstract noun from the concrete *hēgemōn*, 'a guide who seeks the way, or a leader who seeks to enforce it'. Comparing with it the L. *rex, rēgis*, from *regere*, we realize that 'to guide' was an earlier conception than 'to rule', and we see, perhaps, the evolution of all government.

Two M.E. words for 'to die', *swelten* and *sterven*, have gradually dropped the sting of death from their meaning. 'I'm simply sweltering!' we say now: or 'I'm starving!' Perhaps this reflects the fact that some occasions of death are less common than they were: for *swelter* represents the M.E. *swelteren*, frequentative of *swelten* (O.E. *sweltan*), 'to die, faint, or swoon' – 'sultry' being a form of 'sweltry'; and the M.E. *sterven* meant, like O.E. *steorfan* and G. *sterben*, 'to die' (not necessarily of hunger).

We have seen that an older age of country-life and farming still haunts our vocabulary. Sometimes, more deeply hidden, are the shapes of other trades. *Normal* contains the lost meaning of 'true alignment', in the carpenter's sense; for *norma* was the Roman joiner's 'carpenter's square'. As an exact semantic parallel we might take *order*, which was originally the L. *ordo*, used in the almost universal occupation of weaving as the term for the order of the threads in the woof. Other buried words from weaving (apart from the scores spun from the root **vē-*) are *stamen* (root **stā-*), originally 'the warp, the upright threads', and *twill*, of which the meaning, 'two-threadedness', would be well-known in days when every village had its own looms, and men got their name of *Webber*, and their wives or widows or daughters their *Webster*; even as the man who dealt with mead and ale would acquire and pass on the surname of *Brewer*, whereas Mistress Margery from the same village might found a family of *Brewsters*.

Reminders of an earlier life are obvious in a word such as *window*, in which the *wind's eye* (O.N. *vindauga*) suggests a mere hole in the wall. On the other hand, the mediaeval significance of *robe* is concealed. The word is related to *robbery*, and the sense in O.F. was 'booty in the form of clothes'.

Much history may be latent in the vocabulary of Natural History itself. A well-known 'buried' example of an older attitude towards natural phenomena is *halcyon*. 'The Halcyon Days of 1911' was the title of a painting in the Royal Academy Exhibition of 1912. At the time I* did not understand the meaning of the word, though 1911 had given us one of the calmest and warmest summers of the century. Some years later I came across *halcyon* in a bird-book. It is the generic name for a group of Australian kingfishers. Its first recorded use in English as the name of this bird is in Captain Cook's *Voyages* of the years 1772–84; Cook says, 'We found the halcyon, or great kingfisher, having fine bright colours'.

Halkuōn or *alkuōn*, the Greek name for a bird identified as the kingfisher, reached Middle English through Latin. The Hellenes typically expressed their appreciation of the beauty of the bird not by exact description and study, but by giving it the dignity of a romantic but markedly impossible fable. The halcyon floated its nest on the sea, they said: meanwhile the water, by magic, was calm, serene, and sunlit. It may have been that they tried to add force to the story by putting the rough breathing (*h*) before the *a* of *alkuōn*, attaching to it the sense of *hals*, the salt sea. In its earliest form Natural History was supernatural.

*S.P.

XXiii

NATURE IN ENGLISH

'Etymological curiosity often brings us up against a
barren, unimaginative avian Adam, or again it may
unearth humour, emotion, culture, or even imagination.'

WILLIAM BEEBE, *High Jungle.*

THE vocabulary of English Nature is not only especially rich and
interesting, but also mature and deep-rooted. The reader of these
pages will know something about the time-element in our words. By
browsing here and there, if we have eyes for forms and affinities,
we may pick up on the side, as it were, a better acquaintance with
the anatomy of the language than we are likely to remember from
text-books. The ornithologically-minded reader, for instance, by
glancing at a bird flying at forty m.p.h., fifty feet above him, can
recognize it not merely as a tern, but as a Sandwich tern. It should
present no kind of difficulty for him to tell, fifty feet from the sign-
post, whether the name of the village which he is approaching is
Saxon or Scandinavian in origin.

Words and Evolution

The naturalist will immediately be aware of the way in which
words, like all forms of plant- and animal-life, are subject to 'laws'
analogous to those of Darwinian Evolution. He will notice that
languages group themselves into families or phyla; and he will find
interest in the fact that some of the parent-languages produce many
children, whereas some are barren. He will find that the tendency
of languages to become extinct as living speech was originally as
great as the tendency of new languages to make their appearance;
and that the number of languages, like the number of species of
animals and plants, tends to diminish, although the waning forms
may be artificially prolonged (as by the Northern Islands Gaelic

Society). He cannot fail to observe that some groups, such as the Chinese dialects, or the Indo-European, or the isolated Basque – that mysterious speech of the Andorrans – are so far apart as to suggest that human speech was due to spontaneous combustion, so to speak, in many different parts of the world. Other groups, however, such as the Semitic and the Egyptian, though they show differences almost as absolute, yet reveal traces of a common origin, just as the hare and the horse, or the cobra and the cockatoo, can be shown to have a common ancestor. Sometimes the connecting link is almost, though not completely, indecipherable. Semitic and Egyptian, for instance, both use grammatical gender – a peculiarity which they share with the Indo-European speech-family.

Once the primary language is established, it begins to behave on Darwinian lines. Its offspring vary from the parent, and the liveliest and most adaptable of them have the best chance of survival: errant children who go off on their own, or become marooned and form groups cut off from the main stock and create a Galápagos Island situation in which the divergent evolution is hastened. St Kilda produced not only its own wren and its own field-mouse, but, numbering the years not in tens of thousands but as a few hundreds, also its own dialect of Gaelic as well. Then, if the process is put into reverse, if communications between island and mainland are re-established, differences are rounded off by processes analogous to hybridizing. Straight out of the history of biological evolution, too, comes the fact that language and the means of recording it can grow independently of the needs of the original purpose of communication – 'dynamically', like the too-heavy armour-plating of an early Cretaceous reptile or the hypertrophy of the tusks of some forms of long-extinct elephant. Such blind-alleys of specialization, in language as in animals, are eventually closed down: the no-longer-useful becomes atrophied, and eventually lopped off. The complexity of the Chinese ideograms and the illegibility of the ornate Gothic type may serve as warnings.

Another property of words which is perhaps not so generally known to biologists is that the spoken word is as changeable and as constantly alive as protoplasm. The scientist's attitude is liable to be coloured by thinking of 'word', which is something spoken – verbal – as if it were something written. But even the written forms of English words become fixed only in the 18th century; and even when the shape of a word is fixed its meaning waxes and wanes or develops along new paths, gaining or losing force, just like a strain of bacteria or a group of trilobites.

Natural Order: Indo-European

The Indo-European family of languages (the most widespread of all language-groups) began to be so called in the early 19th century, when the affinities among its languages began to be fully apprehended. Later the name shuttled between *Indo-Germanic* and *Aryan*. (*Iran*, the ancient, and now again the modern, name for Persia, and *Aryan* come from the same original.)

The 'Natural Order' of Biology may reasonably be used as a term for the language-groups of Speech; though it may be that 'Class' would be more accurate. If 'Natural Order' fits, then it could be said that English is derived, as we have seen, from the complex Germanic family of Indo-European, which is divided into a North (Norse), an East (Gothic), and a West sub-family, which is further split into two genera, German, High and Low, and Anglo-Frisian. Anglo-Frisian produced several species, two of which hybridized to form Anglo-Saxon or Old English. From O.E., via the transitional form, Middle English, Modern English evolved as a new species, with derivative geographical sub-species, such as American English and Australian English – and 'Pidgin', which in the South Seas now has text-books of its own.

We have noted that our word *mother* is very similar to the Greek, Latin, Sanskrit, French, German, and numerous other versions, in both ancient and modern tongues, of what is obviously a basic I-E. word. *Mother*, however, might not be the best example to choose at this point, since some modern philological experts suspect that the first syllable may be onomatopoetic, echoing the sound made by the child at the breast. (*Mama* is a word for 'breast' in Egyptian and in the language of the Australian aborigines.) We might do better by considering *hundred* and some of its cognates such as Skt. *śatam*, L. *centum*, Gk. *hekaton*, Persian *sad*, Irish *céad*, Welsh *cant*, and Russian *sto*. These words give another glimpse of the early Aryans by showing that they all lived in close contact before one branch of them migrated to the north-west, and afterwards another branch to the south-west; this being substantiated by the fact that all the names of the numbers up to a hundred show a common parentage; whereas words of quite different extraction are used in different I-E. language-families for 'a thousand'.

Further knowledge can be gleaned from the word *wine* and its cognates. These latter are spread beyond the bounds of the I-E. tongues, hinting that the first form of 'wine' was adopted from an even older family of languages. We see its root *$v\bar{e}$- in words implying the notion of twisting or binding: in Skt. *veṭu*, 'a reed or flute', and *vetra*, 'a reed or rush'; L *vieo*, 'I twist', *vīmen*, 'a twig', *vītis*, 'a vine'; O.H.G. *notbendig* (Modern German *notwendig*) 'binding'; Modern German *Binse*, 'a rush', *binden*, 'to bind'; Russian *vetla*, 'a willow or osier'; and a multitude of other words including our borrowed *viburnum*. As to *wine* itself, while I was at school* my form-master revealed one mystery. He was talking about 'the lost Greek character, the digamma'. This was the double gamma, the sixth letter of the Greek alphabet, carved or written like a capital F sloping forwards, with its tail below the line. 'Probably,' he said, 'the sound was something between the sounds of *f* and *w*.' We all tried to utter the sound, and then warmly agreed that it certainly explained how, if the digamma was placed at the beginning of a word, the Greek *oinos* was a relative of the Latin *vīnum*, wine. 'You will remember,' said the master, 'that the Latin *quercus*, "an oak", and our *fir* are the same word. Well, that F-shaped letter was an Aryan letter; and the Aryan word was *forkwos*, which became *fyr* in Norse and Old English, and *quercus* in Latin, because the word was applied to the dominant tree, the most important tree in the district.'

Whatever the degree of accuracy of the details, what more striking example could there be of the use of language by a people by nature migratory?

Readers of etymological dictionaries may pick parallel cases at random. For example – the Spanish version of the dominant oak is *alcorque*, a development of *quercus* prefixed by Arabic *al*, as the name for *Quercus suber*, 'the cork-oak'. The bark of the tree, however, which we call *cork* represents the Spanish *corche* or *corcho*, from L. *corticem*, the accusative case of *cortex*, 'rind'. The root is seen also in Skt. *kart*, 'to split'.

Our *elm* is a cognate of L. *ulmus*, probably, of L. *alnus*, 'an alder'. Originally, and until the 18th century, the name was *aller*, which

*S.P.

is still a dialect-form. The *d* was inserted as a 'phonetic easement'. *Beech* is the English form of the Germanic version of the I-E. etymon *bhāgos, the Latin version of which, *fāgus*, also means 'beech'. But the Slavonic development *buzu* stands for 'elm'; and the Gk. *phēgos* for the edible oak, *Quercus aesculus*, of Southern France. Most of the cognates of *ash*, *Fraxinus excelsior* – Norse and German, Russian and Lithuanian – stand for 'ash'; but the Latin *ornus*, was used for 'the rowan, the mountain-ash'. (Here the connection is through a similar patterning of the leaflets.) The Greek cognate *oxua* meant 'a beech'.

The confusion in dialect of *holm* and *holly* (dialects still retaining the 'holly' sense of *holm*) is of somewhat different origin, and is due to the similarity of the leaves. There is a certain date, which it is fascinating to try to determine, before which plants were named more for their similarities, less for their differences. The Celtic, Norse, and Germanic languages agree about the meaning of the name of the tree which we call *yew* (O.E. *iw* – not connected with *ivy*); but the Old Slavonic form of the word, *iva*, seems to have been used for the willow. (The root *vē- keeps cropping up.)

To illustrate this theme from the names of animals is easy. To take one example: the Gk. *strouthos*, a bird's name cognate with L. *turdus*, a thrush, and therefore possibly with 'thrush' itself, was used for 'a sparrow', and also for 'an ostrich'. (Cf. Chapter IX(b).) Was this because it was the bird of interest at the moment – the most talked-of bird? Years ago I had a friend* whose household was graced by a succession of maids. Each assumed the Christian name of her predecessor, which therefore never changed. The same principle may explain the naming of *strouthos*.

The Clue of the Cognates

The great dictionary-word 'cognate' arrived fairly early in the eighteen-hundreds, the century par excellence of new philological terms. Adopted from Roman Law, in which the blood-relatives were *cognati*, it was used in 1862 or earlier to denote languages or words descended from a common ancestor. Cognates can be dramatic in their evidence of the speed and complexity of linguistic, and therefore of human, evolution.

*S.P.

In the plant-world few flowers give a clearer impression of the force of life than does the genus *Euphorbia*. Its power of adaptability allows it to range from the tree-like and majestic cactus of the desert to the obscure little petty spurge, the garden-weed which can be flicked out of the ground with one finger. Only the minute flower remains as the connecting-link to remind us of the relationship. Even so, when we are looking for the relationships among words, we may find only a couple of letters, or even just one letter, bearing the sign of an ancient common origin, and linking us with some far-distant country. Plain or concealed in *Veda, vide, view, vision, voyons!*; in *wit, wise,* and *wissen* – words found from the Ganges to the Guadalquivir – is the I-E. etymon *weid-*, which implies 'seeing', and therefore 'knowing'.

Fear does not look at first sight much like *peril*, the L. *periculum*; yet *father/pater* gives us the clue, first found by Jacob Grimm (see Chapter V). The *p* of the Indic, Hellenic, and Italic groups usually becomes *f* in the Germanic. Probably the oldest form of both *father* and *pater*, and of all their cognates, is seen in the Sanskrit *pitar-*.

The nature-names are more widely separated from the parental roots. The I-E. word for 'water' probably had *akw* as its stem. The step to L. *aqua* is straightforward; the development to French *eau* is predictable. O.E. *ēa* seems further away and looks unfamiliar, although it became the *ey* or *i* in *island* and in innumerable place-names. Celtic *au* became the Gaelic *uisge*, the important syllable being carried through to our *whisky*. Claiming relationship in the distance are *water* itself, the Slav *voda*, and the Gk. *hudōr*. (See Chapter XXV.)

A word which was perhaps old-established in Indo-European itself, a word embalming some essence basic to life, can populate half the world's languages with its offspring. The word 'life' itself, ranges widely through the Germanic tongues; but older than the root which produced 'life' is the Indo-European *gwej-* represented in both the Germanic group and in Greek and Latin. The Germanic form has given us *quick*; the Greek and Latin variations have helped us with their *bios, zōos,* and *vivus*. These words have spawned and spread until in modern English alone a hundred words, some of them relatively humble, can claim descent from the original radicals. The sense of *quick* in 'the quick and the dead' is obsolete; but it stays on in the *quick* of the nail, and in the name of the 'quick-grass', that

232

most difficult of grasses to kill, *Agropyron repens*, also called, with fifty other names, *quitch* and *couch*, each being a corruption of the original *quick*.

But why is there that *ō* in the Gk. *zōos* (meaning 'living', as in *zōon*, 'an animal', whereas *bios* covers both animal- and plant-life)? We need to look at the mysterious rules of vowel- and consonant-changes, the discovery of which occasioned modern Philology. Sometimes the gradations of widely contrasted forms make the development easier to follow. *Tears* are *lachrymose* (L. *lacrima*, 'a tear'); and both words come from the same root, **dakru-*. Ennius, the so-called Father of Latin Poetry, who died in 169 B.C., retained the archaic spelling in the epitaph which he composed for himself:

> *Nemo me dacrumis decoret, nec funera fletu:*
> (No one must tire me with tears, or honour my ashes with wailing.)

Dakru passed unchanged into Greek; and we know 'the *t* for *d* through *z*' which gave a *zahar* in O.H.G., followed by *tēar* in O.E. But where does the *l* of *lachrymose* come from? A Latin dialect turned *d* to *l* – a change which explains the connection between another pair of words, *tongue* and L. *lingua* (parent of F. *langue* and grandparent of M.E. *langage*, our 'language') which both spring from I-E. **ding-*.

Holding strictly to the rules of consonant-changes are the related *cow* and Gk. *bous*, L. *bōs*, *bovis*, and Skt. *gaus*, (stem *go*).

It is usually found that the names of male and female animals of the same species, which often seem totally different words, are in fact merely different forms of the same word that have taken different linguistic routes, e.g. *gander*, *goose*.

We have already noted the predictable consonant-change between *tooth* and its French and German equivalents *dent* and *Zahn* and all their kindred.

The I-E. etymon of *egg* and L. *ōvum* (which gives us *oval*, *oviduct*, and the rest) is **owi-*. Skt. had *andam*; Gk. *ōon*. From L. *ōvum* are derived F. *œuf*, Spanish *huevo*, etc. Gaelic, Irish, and Welsh have *ubh*, *ugh*, and *wy*; German (from O.H.G.) and Dutch (from M.L.G.) have *ei*. The O.E. form was *æg*; but English adopted the Scandinavian *egg*.

Germanic *f* for Latin *p* explains the gap between *fin* and L. *pinna*, 'a feather'; between *fish* and L. *piscis*; between *foal* and L. *pullus*, 'a young animal' (as F. *poulet*); between *foot* and Gk. *pous* and L. *pes*, with their stems *pod-* and *ped-*; between *fleece*, the feathery covering of a lamb, and *plume* (L. *plūma*, 'a feather'); and probably between the above-mentioned *foal* and Skt. *putra*, 'a son', and L. *puer*, 'a boy'.

When we first read of 'the sweetest flower that blows', we may have a vision of a rose waving about in the half-gales of an English summer. But *blow*, 'to set in motion with a current of air', and *blow*, 'to burst into flower', are two Saxon words unconnected the one with the other. If we trace the verbs back to their Germanic origins, we find for the first the O.H.G. *blahan*. Further back was the Old Teutonic *blajan*; earlier still was the ancestor which produced in Latin the *fla-* of *flare*, 'to blow'. Thus *blow* number one is linked with *inflation*. *Blow* number two, 'to blossom', on the other hand, looks back to an Old Teutonic *blojan*, with which are involved *blossom*, *bloom*, and *blade* (of grass), together with the important cognate *flo-*, which gives us and all the Romance languages forms of the L. *flōs*, *flōris*, 'flower'. No equivalent is found in classical Greek.

The history of the appearance of the word 'flower' in English is interesting. The O.E. name was *blōstma*, *blossom*: then *bloom* was adopted from the O.N. *blōm*. *Flower* was taken from *flour*, the O.F. version of L. *flōrem*, which appears in the *Ancren Riwle* as *flure*. *Blōstma* and *bloom* continued, but acquired special meanings. Neither was used for the whole plant – one of the meanings allotted to *flower*. 'Blossom,' says the O.E.D., 'suggests the promise of fruit. Cherry-trees are said to be in *blossom*, hyacinths in *bloom*.' In the Wyclif Bible the spelling is *flour*. Our modern spelling seems to belong to the Great Stabilization period of English orthography, the Restoration; whereas the form *flour* is a confusion-avoiding spelling kept for the flour which we use in making pastry, although this is the same word – the 'flower', the best part, of the meal.

Dutch words, with their strong character of linguistic independence, still maintained, have sometimes to admit connections with faraway countries. L. *ovis*, 'sheep', and English *ewe* have gone their own ways; but they have a common ancestor. Dutch *ooi* makes the link more evident.

The I-E. root **porc-* gives us our *pork* when English borrowed the French – Latin form without any of the Germanic consonant shifts – perhaps, therefore, it has stayed unchanged after five thousand years, or longer. But the *f* for *p* in the Germanic form started a big independent development which gave us *farrow* from the same root. *Fawn*, the newborn deer, has a name connected with L. *fĕtus*, 'the not-yet-born'. This was Chaucer's meaning, for 'fawn' originally meant any young animal. (Do fawns 'fawn' more than other young creatures? The verb belongs to the 14th century but is a form of O.E. *faegnian*, 'to rejoice'. Trevisa, Chaucer's contemporary, says, 'lambe ... fawneth with hys tayle when he hath founde hys moder.') The root involved here, **fē*, 'to produce offspring', must be one of the oldest in language, since it is connected with *be*. The little deer derives its name from the later form, *faon*, of the O.F. *feon*, from the (unfound) accusative of the (presumed) Late Latin **feto*. *Fetus* is a better spelling than *fætus*.

'Horse', we have explained as signifying 'runner'. It is possibly a cognate of L. *curro* – earlier *curso* – 'I run'; and has nothing to do with L. *equus* (*ecus*), which is a cognate of another, older, Saxon word, *eoh*, 'a war-horse', and has relatives in other I-E. languages. Why has 'horse' survived and *eoh* disappeared without trace? Is it not because 'horse' is the stronger word, the more eloquent and speakable? A state of general human friendliness towards the word is shown by the exceptionally large number of phrases, sayings, and plant- and animal-names attached to it. It is one of those strong monosyllabic names for animals – *sheep, swine, deer*, and the rest – which are neuter in the sense that there is no differentiating male and female forms in the inflexion of their names. As with other grammatically neuter nouns of its class, singular and plural were formerly identical. *Horse* appeared fairly early; but the uninflected plural was standard until the 17th century and later.

An *f* for *p* hidden because *s* has been added to the second word obscures the relationship between *foam* and *spume*. *Fundament* (L. *fundus*, from the I-E. root, **bhund*, gave *fundamentum*) is still more unexpectedly connected with *bottom* (O.H.G. *bodam*). As often, the Germanic version became the less polite use.

Is the *hide* of an animal the same as its *cuticle*? The root of *hide*, 'to cover', is **keudh-*; that of *hide*, 'a skin', is the related root **skeu-*. The 'skin' word has cognates in Gk. *kutos, skutos*, L. *cutis*, and throughout the Germanic group.

'Young', as a word, seems far away from 'juvenile' in spirit and atmosphere; yet each has taken a long and separate journey from the same starting-point, presumed to have been *juwungaz*. In this word we can recognize the L. *juvenis*; but to find 'young' we need the aid of a Germanic half-way stage, where *juwungaz* becomes *jungaz*.

As a final example let us take the possible origin of the name *Chiltern* – the Chiltern Hills. The word *hill* is related to the L. *celsus*, 'high', the base of which is seen in our *excel*. The parent root was probably **kel-*, 'to rise'. Another English word from this root is *holm*, 'a hill rising from the water, island'. This word, of Scandinavian origin, is found in many of our place-names, notably *Steepholm* and *Flatholm* in the Bristol Channel, and *Skokholm*, off the Pembrokeshire coast. L. *culmen* (whence our *culminate*) is a cognate. Of special interest here is the word *Celt*. This reached us through Latin; but, though Latin probably stole the word from Celtic, the root of it is the same as that of the words just cited. The Celts were the dwellers on the hills, and, in so far as much of their deep-forested Europe was concerned, the hills were often the only places for their settlements. This applies particularly to the Celts in Britain, who made their paths and raised their tumuli on the downlands – in places such as the Chilterns. Thus 'Chiltern' (O.E. *ch* representing the Latin *c*) may mean 'where the Celts live'.

XXIV

A LANGUAGE MADE FOR NATURE

'Bright-eyed Fancy, hovering o'er,
Scatters from her pictured urn
Thoughts that breathe, and words that burn.'
GRAY, *The Progress of Poetry.*

WHAT is it that makes the study of English so satisfying? Is it the complex ingredients, together with our readiness to try new things – to accept new words? Is it the refusal, or inability, to become codified, in spite of the forces of the grammarians and the style-experts, with their hopeless attempts to fix language in an un-breakable mould? Is it that English is the language not only of Chaucer and Tyndale and Shakespeare but also of – say – H. G. Wells's Mr Polly? Is it not also – if the theme of this book means anything – that, because of the exceptionally complex and rapid changes through which English has passed, the sense of the etymology of our words, even if only dimly felt, fixes an additional dimension, Time, to the words?

Description by Definition

It must have occurred to many of us that the derivation of a nature-word helps us to see the natural object more clearly, even as the power to discriminate between different shades of colour is enhanced by a knowledge of the names of the shades. A dead word can be brought to life again, just as a dead or trite quotation – a phrase, for instance, such as 'salad days' – can be restored to give us the full relish of its first meaning, if one finds the clue in the scene and context where Shakespeare created it to be spoken by Cleopatra.

Even the word *relish* which we have just used is freshened up if we think of its origin, O.F. *relaissier*, 'to leave behind', which gives us 'what is left behind', 'the lingering taste'. And even the word *clue*, in the same sentence, has more meaning when we realize that the

O.E. original, *clēowe*, meant 'a ball, a skein', a ball of thread such as was used by Theseus to find the way out of the Cretan labyrinth.

Sometimes a modern-sounding word conceals within its meaning or derivation a deeper thought, set in history. Sometimes in the description of a contemporary action can be seen the ghost of an older activity, related, yet belonging to another world.

Such a sentence as this might be found in a detective-story in *The Magnet* or *The Gem*:

'No sleuth could hope to find the vestige of a clue, hunting for his quarry in this warren of streets.'

Hunting is the theme; but the writer is of course careless of the fact that all the key-words in his sentence refer to the old days of hunting in a setting of nature. The meanings have lost their relish.

Let us put the relish back. M.E. *sleuth* is the track of an animal, a meaning preserved in the *slot* of a deer. *Vestige* is the L. *vestīgium*, 'a footprint'. *Clue* belongs to another, even earlier, sort of hunting. The meaning of *quarry* was 'certain parts of a deer placed on the hide (L. *corium*) and given to the hounds as a reward'. *Corium*, the hide – how greatly it increases the content and the force of *excoriate* when we remember that it means 'to peel off the skin' (in the use of which phrase we have probably committed tautology!).

A *warren* was originally a piece of land set aside and fenced, for the rearing of game; the root of the word being the Teutonic **war-*, 'to protect'. The scene is a place lonely and deserted, whereas the detective-story implies crowded intersections. 'As melancholy as a lodge in a warren,' says Shakespeare. Or an empty Highland hunting-lodge on a wet day? This is a perfect description of Benedict in love.

The sick stuffiness of *mawkish* takes its hue from a dialect word for *maggot*. O.E. *matha*, 'worm', is a cognate of O.N. *mathkr*, whence came M.E. *mawke*, 'a maggot', from which was derived the Scots and dialect *mawk* – which gave *mawkish*, 'maggoty', for the sickly, especially for the sickly sentimental. The word was first used in this sense in 1702.

Is there a tree in the Law Courts? Yes – when we speak of *corroborative* evidence, 'strongly supporting' evidence, with an oak (L. *rōbur* or *rōbor*) in the middle of the word; even as *robust* means 'oaken'.

Often accurate knowledge of the etymology of the name of a living thing brings that thing into mental focus. To know that L. *temptare* or *tentare* means 'to tempt or test' because it means 'to feel', or, more precisely, 'to feel experimentally', is a help towards the conception of the derived English word *tentacle*, if we must visualize the grisly 'feelers' of an octopus. New medical words making an appropriate use of Greek can be equally apt: e.g. *neurasthenia – neur-a-sthenia*, 'nerve without strength'; as can a scientific word such as *cathode – kata + hodos*, 'doorway' – the passage of the current into the negative pole.

Such derivations help us to understand mental processes. The root of *skill* is an O.N. syllable implying 'division, distinguishing'.

Indulging my youthful liking for making up words, I* invented one for the Early Morning Groan, for waking up at 4 a.m. and thinking, 'What an idiotic thing I did yesterday!' One virtually bites one's pillow with vexation. 'A pillow-bite', I called it. There is a Latin word *remordēre*, which means 'to bite again'. Its supine is *remorsum*. *Remorse!*

Peer Gynt peels the onion, takes off layer after layer, and finds nothing in the centre – the nothingness of one-ness. What rustic Roman genius of word-making first suggested *ūnio*, 'unity, the complete one-ness', for an *onion*? The word, which first appeared in the 14th century, was spelt *uniown* and *oynioun* in the Wyclif Bible.

Less obviously, our word *life* (O.E. *līf*) can be understood best by an examination of the meaning of the Gk. and Germanic cognates, which have the sense of 'to remain, to persist, to be sticky, to adhere'. Life has been defined as The Adhesive Property. 'He sticks to life', it was said (or life sticks to him), 'like a tick on a sheep' (or a kitti-wake on a rock-face, perhaps; or an old man when the world turns against him).

Names from Nature

Natural History names out of Natural History itself are not un-common. This is the simplest kind of naming, but not the oldest. The historical background is not so richly woven.

Fern is an example. Linnaeus called our species of bracken *Pteris aquilina*. This *pteris*, Gk. for 'fern', is a 'transferred application' from an original *pteron*, 'a wing or feather', from *petesthai*, 'to fly'. *Fern*,

*S.P.

the O.E. *fearn* (800), is also a member of the same large family of cognates from the root **pet-*, 'to fly', which includes Skt. *parṇam*, 'leaf, wing, feather'; L. *penna*, our (quill) *pen*; and the G. *Feder*, 'feather' or 'pen'.

On these lines are to be explained *jonquil* (1629), 'the little narcissus with *juncus*-like leaves', and *pappus* (1704), which fixes a Hellenic notion that the heads of certain *Compositae* in fruit are bearded like 'grandfather' (*pappos*). Good *campus* (L., whence the F. *champ*, 'field') produces *champignons* (mushrooms) and *champagne*. *Uvula*, late M.E., is a mediaeval Latin diminutive of *uva*, 'a grape': cf. Linnaeus' naming of the bear-berry, *Arctostaphylos uva-ursi*.

Raisin and our old botanical friend *raceme* are formed through French from L. *racemus*, 'a bunch of grapes'. *Gland* is based on the similarity of the shape of many glands to that of an *acorn* (L. *glans*, *glandis*). *Borage*, the plant with rough hair (though the L. *burra*, 'a shaggy garment', cannot be fully substantiated as its etymon) gives its name to the rough and scratchy *Boraginaceae* family. This name is more likely to be derived through F. and Spanish from the Arabic *abu-'āraq*, 'father of sweat', the plant being a sudorific. Akin to the borage is the *bugloss*, rough like the tongue of an ox (Gk. *glōssa* and *bous*), which in France is called *langue de bœuf*. English *ox-tongue* is an old botanical name for any species of borage; but in modern Botany it is used for one of the *Compositae*, that prickly old hero of dusty roadsides in August, *Helminthia echioides*.

The European root **gran-*, an offshoot of the root **ger-*, has produced two keywords, *corn* and *grain*, which have sown many nature-words in our vocabulary. From *corn* comes the *kernel* of the wheat. *Grain* gives, via Italian, *granite*, 'the many-seeded, granular, rock', and the name of that many-seeded fruit, the *pomegranate*, beside that of the more deadly fruit, the *grenade*.

In the novel, the hero's 'muscles rippled as he flexed his arms'. The ancients had a more exact, more charming, simile. The muscle moved like a mouse running under a carpet. The notion is preserved in the etymology. Gk. *mūs* for 'mouse' was later used for 'muscle' as well. In Latin *muscle* was *musculus*, 'the little mouse'.

Orchis, plural *orchises*, is a nature-from-nature word of remarkable aptness. It was Pliny the Elder (A.D. 23–79), Pliny of the Natural History, who first used a Latin transliteration of the Gk. word, *orchis*, for the plant; and Gk. *orkhis* means *testicle*. The resemblance of the orchis-tubers to testicles is close in the species belonging to the true genus *Orchis*; and so important are the forms of the tubers in classification that botanists divide the genus *Orchis* into species with round and finger-shaped tubers respectively.

The first English use of Pliny's *orchis* is to be found in Turner's *Herball* (1562). What were the plants called earlier? One can be certain that the species were very vaguely differentiated; but there are two names extant which follow Pliny's suggestion. *Dogstones* was existing in Elizabethan times at latest; and Gerard says of *Orchis spiralis* that 'some call them sweet ballocks'. This flower-name is typical of down-to-earth English appellations that have long been out of fashion. In the 14th century, however, words such as 'ballock-knife', 'a knife worn at the girdle' (O.E.D.), were used with perfect gravity by writers such as Langland. 'Peace offerings unto the Lord', says the A.V., translating Leviticus 22, should not include 'a bullock or lamb that hath anything superfluous or lacking in his parts.' In Wyclif's translation this is, 'All beeste that kitt . . . and taken away the ballokes is'.

One other reference suggests that the presence of the orchis-tubers inevitably proclaimed to the Mediaeval and Renaissance pharmacists that the plant was an aphrodisiac, 'Whyte satyrion,' says Turner, 'or, in other more unmanerly speeche, hares ballocks.' Satyrion was the satyr: *Satyrium* was the generic name given by Linnaeus to two orchid-species, which are now called by the alternative names *Goodyera repens* (creeping lady's tresses) and *Himanto-glossum hircinum* (lizard-orchis). In case anything like consistency may seem to be implied, it is worth noting that neither of these plants has the true orchis-shaped roots.

Orchid is used for any plant of the *Orchidaceae* family. The interest of the word lies in the fact that it was introduced by John Lindley in 1845. Perhaps it was the prestige of Lindley, 'the Father of Orchid-ology', which allowed this etymological blunder to be perpetuated. The original fault was that of Linnaeus, who in 1751 formed the word *Orchideae* for the Orchis family, following an earlier misrepresentation of the stem of Gk. *orkhis*, giving it a *d* which had never existed. But orchidophilists, who should really be called *orchis-ophilists*, will keep their Lindley, and will keep their *d*. Orchid is a word of personality, and will doubtless stay for ever.

Orchids are the possessors of the truest type of a nature-from-nature name, for the intense specialization of some kinds has produced exaggerated flower-forms suggesting likenesses to various animals. When I first saw a *bee-orchid*,* on the path above Folkestone Warren, I thought that there *was* a bee on the flower. The long petal of a *man-orchid* is a willowy silhouette by Max Beerbohm of Aubrey Beardsley. The *fly-* and the *spider-orchids* are quite convincing; the *lizard-* has a right dry character; the *butterfly-* is suitably flamboyant. *Cuckoo, monkey,* and *finger* all give their names to species; and the *crane-fly orchid* of North America, *Tipularia discolor,* is said to look more like a crane-fly than does a crane-fly itself.

*S.P.

XXV

NATURE HIDDEN

'If everyone had abstained from striving to penetrate
hidden things, no science would exist.'

L. NOIRÉ.

WE have considered some words born from Nature. In most of them
the nature involved has been that of a more primitive, simple, or
wild way of life. Now we will think of a few in which the debt to
nature is more direct, though often more closely concealed. Among
such are a good many whose origin in living things is forgotten all the
more completely because the meaning seems at first sight unques-
tionably man-made, if not town-bred.

Let us choose 'London cab' as an example. Taken separately or
together, the words have an urban sound: yet each started on the
margin of the jungle. *London* means 'the wild place'. Celts who found
a possible harbour in the Thames, by the two desolate gravel-hills,
called the place *lond*, 'wild'. *Cab* is an abbreviation of F. *cabriolet*,
from *cabriole*, 'a goat's skip', derived through Italian *capriola*, 'a
kid', from the accusative of L. *caper* or *capra*, 'he-goat' and 'she-goat'.
The light vehicle *capers* along.

A *carbine*, which Dr Johnson describes as 'a kind of medium
between the pistol and the musket', is the weapon of the *Carabineers*,
the regiments such as the 6th Dragoon Guards, who carried it.
Carabineer is from the early Modern French *escarbin*, 'a bearer of
plague-stricken corpses', from L. *scarabaeus*, 'a dung-beetle': for
certain species of dung-beetle not only feed on animal excreta, but
also have the habit of moulding the substance into a ball, which they
then push or otherwise manœuvre into a burrow, where they eat it
at their leisure.

Two very town-flavoured words – the first from 'up-town' New
York City – are found to be unexpectedly connected through their
origins: *kibitz* and *dupe*. In Yiddish to *kibitz* is 'to be inquisitive'.
The German original implies an inquisitive onlooker, like *Kiebitz*,

243

'a lapwing'. The lapwing, as we have noted already, has habits of anxiously wheeling about in the air, and of running fussily hither and thither while it searches for food in a field.

'For look where Beatrice, like a lapwing, runs
Close to the ground. . . .'

(Beatrice is *kibitzing*.) The American *rubber*, short for *rubberneck*, is synonymous. Rubbernecks twist their heads up and down, and from side to side, staring at what is probably not their business.

My* first sight of a hoopoe was in central France. It was sitting in the middle of a narrow road. We had to get out of the car to move it – in proof of the 'stupidity' of the bird? In French the hoopoe's onomatopoetic Latin name, *upupa*, had been shortened to *huppe*. When a man allowed himself to be cheated, he was said to be behaving in the manner of a hoopoe – *d'huppe*. He was a *dupe*.

Calendars and almanacs, marking the dividing of seasons and the reckoning of tides – nothing could seem more unnatural; and 'calendar' reflects this in its derivation. *Kalendārium* was the Romans' account-book, because interest became due on the first day of the month. Such days had to be publicly announced. They were *Kalendae*, from *kalere* or *calere*, Gk. *kalein*, 'to call, to proclaim'. The antiquity of the word is shown by the fact that it is among the very few Latin words normally spelt with an initial *k*.

Almanac is different. It is a Med. L. word supposed to come from Arabic, as is suggested by the first syllable, *al*, for 'the'. *Ma* implies 'place'. *Nakh* means 'kneeling'. It happened that when I learnt* the explanation of 'the kneeling-place' for *almanac*, I remembered what animal I had recently seen kneeling. I had just been to Morocco, and in a paddock near Fez I had seen a camel kneel down. Camels make a considerable business of this action. It was something that I had not seen previously except at Whipsnade. Now I understood the accepted explanation. The camel's 'kneeling-place' was the camp, the settled place, where the weather is predictable, where the hot season and the wet season can be recorded in the *Almanakh*.

*S.P.

Physical Roots

The phrase 'physical roots' is unlikely to occur in any textbook of philology; but it is a good heading for those signposts in our vocabulary which seem to suggest an origin in nature, in the sense that some simple physical act is implied. Anyone fond of browsing in an etymological dictionary will appreciate this.

Many words suggesting piercing, mixing, giving birth, etc. contain a distinctly echoic element: as do those beginning with the *gr* which gives us the first sound of *grudge, grouse, gruff,* and *gruesome;* or those which start with the *gl* so apposite for *glue, glebe,* and the stickiness of the cognate 'clay'. (Cf. Thoreau on Owls, Chapter XI(a).) There are the I-E. sounds of the kind that are sometimes called 'echoic'; although they do not really echo, because the acts involved are not usually associated with any particular noise. In Chapter III we tentatively called them 'fitting', which has at least the merit of not suggesting a pretentious precision for something essentially vague.

*Ak-, for example, is typical. In the primitive I-E. language it was a root meaning 'to be sharp' or 'to sharpen'; and to our ears the syllable seems to stand for the *sound* of sharpness. Is this due to association with the many words beginning with the syllable *ac*? Or to the cutting exactness of the *k* sound? If so, was it also used in language-families other than that of the Aryans? Perhaps we may think so, because in *acacia* the I-E. *ac* seems to reinforce the pointedness of the *Egyptian* name of a thorny bush or tree.

*Ak- is found in *acanthus* (1616), 'the rough and prickly flower Beares breech, called of the Latines Acanthus'. With L. *acer,* 'sharp', we remember also *acētum,* 'vinegar', and *acētābulum,* 'the socket of the hip-joint', which is well-named in the opinion of the sufferer from hip osteo-arthritis. *Acētābulum* originally meant 'vinegar-bath'. The *ache* of pain is equally reminiscent of **ak-.*

There is a parallel development from the equally powerful syllable-of-all-work, **ti-, *sti-,* or **stig-,* implying 'piercing'. *Stigma* is straight Greek. *Stick, stickleback,* and *stickle* ('a riffle in a stream', or, in dialect, 'a bristle') all derive from O.E. The Norse *steik* is a steak, roasted on a spit. But the derivatives from Latin seem to have made the longest journeys. *Stingere* and *instingere* meant 'to goad'. Cattle were sorted by pricked distinguishing marks. Animals are compulsively goaded in their behaviour by *instinct*. (The animal *Homo sapiens* is sometimes helped by instinct, and sometimes becomes *Homo insipiens* by anti-social ganging together, or by irrational fear of darkness, and so forth.)

The syllable *pu* (not the root **pū-*, 'to be rotten, to stink'; or the root **peu-*, 'to purify'; but probably found in the *pau* in L. *paucus*, etc.) provides us with many words, most of them describing the young: e.g. L. *puer* (whence our *puerile*) and *puella*, respectively 'boy' and 'girl'; *puerpera*, a woman in childbirth (whence our *puerperal* fever); *pupa, puppy, puppet*; and the delightfully apt *pupil* for the tiny image, doll-like, of oneself – or of a small schoolboy reflected when he looks his master in the eye.

*Su- is another fertility-symbol, with *sow* (pig) as its chief English example. Through French it has given us *soil*, where the sow enjoys the mud (or used to be thought to do so, before the days of scientific pig-farming), and *sully*. (See Chapter XIV(b).)

Gk. *auxein*, L. *augēre* (which gives us *auxiliary*), and English *eke* all suggest the natural process of growth or increase. An *author* (L. *auctor*) is 'an increaser', hence 'a founder', hence 'a composer of a book', or an originator of a revolution or anything else.

Augur is now considered to have nothing to do with listening to birds in order to obtain omens from their cries: the bird-watching derivation is limited to *auspices* (L. *auspex*, 'a seer', from *avis* + *specere*, 'to gaze at'). The *augurer* (L. *augur*), if he was to be respected, had to prophesy *increase*, and therefore a happy outcome. No business of import was to be undertaken without *inauguration*.

Physical Implants

Let us now glance at a few words exemplifying the way in which nature-words plant themselves, as it were, in a language, where they grow and breed – words for parts of the body, such as *foot* and *head*; features of the landscape; colours; or simple human actions.

L. *corpus*, the body itself, gives us *corpse, corpulent, corporal, corporeal*, and such refinements as the M.E. *corset*. The great date in the renaissance of science, 1660, gave us the diminutive *corpuscle*, although it was not until a hundred years later that physiology and microscopy named it for a constituent of blood. L. *caro, carnis*, 'flesh', provides a few obvious and important words, such as *carnivore* and *carnage*, with some less obvious, such as *carnation* – which is more likely to imply 'flesh-coloured' than to be a corruption of *coronation*. *Carnival* originally referred to Shrovetide, the week before Lent, a time of last-minute dissipation. The term sounds as if it meant 'farewell (L. *vale*) to flesh'; but picturesqueness must defer to truth. *Carnem levāre* in Mediaeval Latin meant 'to lighten the flesh', in preparation for the Lenten fast.

One might expect the heart, rather than the head, to be the most deeply entrenched 'physical' word in the language: but the *heart* derivatives, such as *heartiness*, are few and self-explanatory. The cognate L. *cor, cordis*, has been more useful, producing such words as *cordial, concord, discord*, and *record*; and, through French, the *courage* group.

It is in fact the *head* (O.E. *hēafod*), *caput* (L.), *kephalē* (Gk.) trinity which has been most productive linguistically. *Caput, capitis*, has given us, through French, *chief, chef, captain, kerchief, mischief*, and other words. More directly from Latin are, for instance, *capitular* and *capitulate*. In feudal times a man's *capital* was calculated by his *chattels*, i.e. his 'cattle' – the M.E. form of the word – as even today those of the Lapps who are still nomadic count their riches in terms of reindeer: and for a stranger to ask a Lapp how many reindeer he has is no more polite than to buttonhole an English stockbroker and ask what his income amounts to, a privilege reserved to H.M. Inspector of Taxes.

Feudal capital was usually confined to moveable property. *Caput* was also the source of such unrelated words as *cape*, 'a headland', and *cape*, 'a shoulder-covering' – the one through L. and Italian and F. *cap*; and the other through F. from the Late Latin *cappa*. To *caput* we owe also *biceps* and *triceps*, the 'two-headed' and the 'three-headed' muscles; and the *headlong* sense in *precipice, precipitate*, and *precipitant*. *Cadet* goes back to *capitellum*, 'the little head', the junior officer, the younger branch of the family.

The progeny of L. *oculus*, 'the eye', is fairly numerous. Besides the more obvious words there is *inoculate*, first used in the modern sense in 1722, but in M.E. employed in gardening parlance for the grafting of a bud or 'eye'. *Ogle* is from Low German (cf. Dutch *oog*, 'an eye'). *Oculus* became *œil* in French, and the pseudo-Latin *aboculus* was turned into the F. *aveugle*, 'blind', which gave English *inveigle*, signifying to allure someone who is blind to the motive.

247

L. *ōs*, *ōris*, the mouth, has helped in the formation of many words, headed by the straightforward *oral*, *orate*, *origin*, *oratorio*, etc., and including *adore*, 'to pray to', and *inexorable*, 'indifferent to prayer'. *Os* is, rather unexpectedly, the source of *usher*, through L. *ostium*, 'a river-mouth' or 'door', and *ostiārius*, 'a door-keeper', convulsively shortened in French to *huissier*, our *usher*. The Horatian *orotund* – *ore rotundo*, 'with round mouth', was first used in England in 1792.

From the second meaning of *ōs*, 'face', we have *oscillate*. *Oscillum* was 'a little face', or 'a mask'. Masks of Bacchus were hung, notably in vineyards, from trees and bushes to scare birds – and, one presumes, goats, the worst enemy of the vines – when they blew from side to side in the wind. Hence comes the unexpected connection between the *oscillations* of 'wireless' and a Bacchic rite.

L. *manus*, 'hand' (from the root **mē-*, 'to measure'), has an English cognate, the O.E. *mund*; but this has been lost, and the *manus* words have taken its place. Thus we have *manual*, *manicure*, *manipulate*, *manacle*, *emancipation*, etc., and the less obvious *manage*, 'to control by hand', and *manner*, 'a way of handling, a way of doing things'. *Manœuvre* is 'working by hand'; *manure* is 'working the soil by hand'. L. *mandare*, 'to give in hand', provides our *mandate*. The new command given by Christ to His disciples after the washing of the feet (St John 13), 'that ye love one another', has given the name *Mandate* or *Maundy* Thursday to the day of the commemorative ceremony.

Foot and L. *pēs* are cognates; but here again, except for *fetter*, the Latin influence is uppermost in English. We use *pedestal* from 1563; *pedal* – first an organ-pedal – from 1611; and *pedestrian* from 1716. *Ped-* words were adopted enthusiastically by Botany. *Pedicle* appeared in Turner's *Herball*, 1562; and *petiole* and *peduncle* a year or two after Linnaeus' first use of the word in 1753. *Pedonem*, the accusative of *pedo*, 'a splay-foot', and in Late Latin 'a foot-soldier' (cf. *foot-slogger* and *flattie*), gave *peón*, 'a servant', in Spanish; and then, via French, a *pawn* in chess. *Impedicare*, 'to entangle in a trap', gave us *impeach*. *Repudiate*, having become confused with *pudet* ('one is ashamed'), is etymologically incorrect: if it is supposed to mean 'to kick away', the spelling should be *repediate*.

By various lines of development the Greek cognate of *pes* and *foot* (*pous*, stem *pod-*) has reached us in such diverse forms as *pew* and *podagra*, and in the numerous scientific names such as *octopus*, *cephalopod* ('head-foot'), and *antipodes*.

Also of special importance in word-production are the simple things, which, rooted in language at its oldest stage, often appear above the surface in strange forms and unexpected places. *Wed-*, the root of English *water*, seems to have permeated almost all the I-E. languages. Reappearing in the O.H.G. form, it is found as *wash*; or in the Celtic form as *whisky* (*uisgebeatha*, 'water of life'); or in the Slavic *voda* 'water' and *vodka*; or, with an *n* infix, as L. *unda*, 'a wave', whence, through *undulare*, we have *undulate*. Through Gk. *hudōr* it is seen in the classical *hydra*, in the non-classical *hydrant*, and in *hydropsy*, which we have shortened to *dropsy*; and, after a High German interlude, in the less easily recognizable *otter*.

Even older is *moon*. The Gk. *mēnē* is nearer in sound that the Skt. *mās* to the I-E. root *mē-*, 'to measure'. The changes of the *moon* gave *Man* (the 'measurer', the 'thinker') his first method of measuring periods longer than a day. Latin had *mensis*, 'month', and *mētiri* (perfect participle *mensus*), 'to measure'. English has *mete, metre* (in two senses), *perimeter, menstrual, immense, dimension*, etc. Spanish *mes*, F. *mois*, and German *Monat* (all meaning 'month') are examples of the many forms which seldom disguise their origin – their awe-inspiring origin – among the Aryans.

Sometimes it is an animal that produces a litter of words; but often a plant will scatter its seeds as widely. Next-door to each other in a dictionary are *linden* and *line*. The first is an adjectival form of an old Germanic word for the lime-tree, of which the Gk. cognate *elatē* means 'silver fir'. The inner bark of either of these trees is soft and flexible. *Linden* therefore was chosen to express 'flexible', with the associated notions of 'soft, lazy, and slow'. *Lento* and *rallentando* spring to mind, *lentus* being the Italic form of German *lind*. *Relent* and *lenient* contain the same meaning. *Lithe* and *lissom* are from the Germanic branch.

Line is an older and still more productive word. The I-E. radical syllable *li* means 'flax'; and here again a plant is used to father the various *line* ('of thread') words which multiply from it. We have *linen*, *lineage*, and *lineament* (the tracing of the line of a profile), with *lint* and *linnet* (O.E. *linetwīge*, 'flax-tweaker' – to borrow James Fisher's improvement on 'flax-twister'), the little eater of seeds. A *liner* is one of a *line* of vessels.

Rose, apart from colour-derivatives, keeps itself to itself (see Chapter XIII(a)); but L. *canna*, 'the cane, the reed, the hollow tube', produces *canyon* (Sp. *cañon*) and *cannon*. The *canons* of the Church were at one time enforced not by kindness but by the rod, the symbol of authority. The other meanings of *canon* also stem from cane-rod-rule. *Canna* is probably of Arabic origin.

Finally our language is indebted to the influence of simple human activities. If we take only the Latin usages of the root **ter-*, 'to rub', as in *terere*, 'to wear away', we find the root in such words as *termite*, *tribulation*, *trite*, and *contrite* ('worn away by use or penitence';) in *terēdo*, 'the shipworm', *trituration* of the Pathology Laboratory, and *Terebratula*, the genus of fossils.

Other large groups of words are attached to L. *tangere*, 'to touch', and *tendere*, 'to stretch'; and still larger groups owe their being to the roots **sed-*, 'sit', and **stā-*, 'stand'.

Most fertile of all are the words which first described the action, complex yet almost the most fundamental for life – those relating to birth, growth, and reproduction.

At the root of *generation* is the I-E. **gen-*, found in Skt. *jana*, 'a man', and Gk. *genos* and L. *genus*, 'a race', and in a multiplicity of other words, a few of which we have noted in Chapter XV. Offspring begotten by *genus* include *engender*, and *genital*. *Generous*, when first used in English (16th century), meant 'of noble lineage'; then, for animals, 'well-bred' (17th century). The L. *genius*, signifying at first the god or spirit attendant on each individual from birth, came to mean the prevailing character of a person or of a nation (*gens*); until finally from the time of the Romantic Revival it embraced our sense of a person of unusual ability. *Genial*, originally (1566) connected with marriage and the generation of children, became later 'conducive to warmth and pleasant growth'. *Germ*, from L. *germen*, 'a sprout', meant at first 'the seed of a new organism contained in the old'; later, vaguely, the 'seed' of a disease.

Spreading and bifurcating still more widely, *gen* produced *ingenious* (meaning, till 1807, 'possessed of genius') and *ingenuous*, which originally had the sense 'of free or honourable birth'. *Engine* signified 'native wit', until the meaning of 'a product of mechanical ingenuity' became fixed. *Homogeneous* is 'all of one kind'. F. *gendarme* is difficult to understand until the word is split into *gens d'armes*. (In the old French army the bold gendarme was a horseman in full armour.)

Almost as numerous as the words in the *gen* group are the Teutonic words cognate with L. *gignere*, 'to beget'; for parallel with the Latin and Greek is the O.E. *cynn*, 'kindred, blood-relationship'. Spread through modern English are many *cynn* words. When Hamlet said, 'A little more than kin, and less than kind', he was in the presence of the king (and 'king' itself represents the O.E. *cyning*, 'a man of noble birth') who had become only too closely *akin*, related to himself, and who had too little of the *kindly*, family, feeling.

The other birth-words are almost equally productive. L. *creare* gives the fertile *create*, from which come *creature* and *creative* and all the elaborations preceded by *pro-* and *re-*. Close to *creare* is *Cĕrēs*, which we (true to Shakespeare's pun in *The Tempest*, 'Juno and Ceres whisper seriously') insist on pronouncing 'Seer-eeze', to balance our 'Ear-oss' for *Ērōs*. Ceres, daughter of *Saturn*, 'the Sower' (L. *serere*, 'to sow'), was the goddess of agriculture, of cereal crops in particular. A Latin development of *creare* was *crescere*, 'to increase' – an even more fertile word-source. Hence came *crescent*, the waxing moon. Later were added, mostly through French, *accrue*, *accretion*, *increment*, and *recruit*. The *premier crû* of the wine-list has long been anglicized. *Crew* is an increase in naval establishment.

The *New Naturalist* volumes use a birth-word, *nature*, in their title. This and a stream of other words flow from L. *nasci*, *nātus*, 'to be born'. Not all of these are immediately obvious. A *pregnant* woman is in the state 'before birth'. When Polonius says of Hamlet, 'How pregnant sometimes his answers are', the key-word is usually taken to mean 'swelling or teeming with sense'; but this is in fact another *pregnant* altogether, meaning 'weighty', from F. *preindre*, 'to press'. *Puisne* (*postea nātus*, 'born later, junior'), pronounced *puny*, as in *puisne judge*, led to *puny* itself. *Noel*, once anglicized as *Nowell*, represents *dies nātālis*, the day of the Birth of Christ, on an anniversary of which what became Natal was first sighted by Europeans. The evolution of *nātio*, 'birth', recapitulates the early social evolution of mankind. This word for 'birth' developed the sense of 'the offspring of a creature at any one time', which came to mean 'the total offspring of a clan', then of a 'people', then of a 'nation'. Would it be too much to hope that, if the word is allowed to develop naturally, *nation* will eventually mean 'mankind'?

$\mathcal{XXVI}$

NATURE LANGUAGE AND NATURAL
LAWS

'Of all the things that words do, what pleases me most
is their habit of adventure; the way they have of sitting
tight and doing nothing but their ordinary job for
centuries, and then starting out and taking quite
different work, and travelling about, changing colour
and shape as they go.'

BELLOC, *The Cruise of the Nona.*

Corruption

No sooner have words been flung into the stream of language than
they begin to change their meaning. In the 18th century this
tendency, which showed itself not least in the names of animals and
plants, was stemmed, as the rush of a river is stemmed by a weir, by
the great stabilizers of language, of whom Dr Johnson and Linnaeus
were the greatest. But nobody could halt the change in the pronunciation of words even when their form was fixed.

The term 'corruption', when applied to language, is used for any
random alteration of a word which is made without reference to its
derivation or comprehensibility. Once again it is to Chaucer that
we must turn in order to find the first use of this sense of 'corrupt' as
an adjective or a verb. In *The Man of Law's Tale*, Custance, during
one of the worst of her interminable spells of bad luck, finds herself
wrecked on the coast of Northumberland, and appeals to the
constable of the castle:

'A maner Latyn corrupt was hir speche.'

Chaucer's use of the word is scarcely pejorative; but in his time,
when exact knowledge depended upon the amount of care taken
by the scribe, 'corruption of the true text', whether the text was of
sacred or of classical origin, was still a grave offence. When we speak
of the 'corruption' not of a text but of a word, we may find it diffi-

252

cult to do so without a measure of disapproval; but often this kind of alteration is as essential to language as it is to life. Very few words of any living tongue retain their first shape. It is true that *thorn, furze,* and some other monosyllabic nature-words have lasted unchanged since Saxon times, or even longer; but they are quite exceptional.

Wearing down

'Is there anything you require, 'm?' My *friend's mother had trained her new parlourmaid to use this formula before she left the room; but the dear girl always forgot until she was almost out of sight: then she would stick her head round the door and say the words all in a burst. Her ''m' was no more than an abrupt closing of the lips after the word 'require'. 'Yes,' I thought: ' '''m" is short for "mum", which is a corruption of "mam", which is a telescoping of "madam", which was an abbreviation of "O mea domina".' This is almost as extreme an example as 'alms', which we pronounce as a monosyllable after its journey from the land of the Hellenes, where it was six-syllabled. The Greek *eleēmosunē*, 'pity', passed through Late Latin to the O.F. *almosne*, then into M.E. as *almesse*, and later to *almes*.

'*M* and *alms* are examples of 'wearing down'. Less complicated is the process of 'cutting short'. *Wig* is *periwig* diminished by more than a half. Like the *pile* of a carpet, *periwig* is to be traced to the accusative of L. *pilus*, 'a hair'. The *wig* ending is to be explained by an Italian word's entry in French – *perucca* to *peruque*. Other similar shortenings are seen in *cute* for *acute*, *squire* for *esquire*, *special* for *especial*. A more recondite example can be taken from the reflection of a character in an early-Restoration play:

'By how much is it more honourable to dye upon a sword-point than to go away in a Meagrim.'

'Meagrim' is one of thirty-four corrupt ways of spelling 'migraine', which English has adopted from French, in which was cut off the first syllable of the Gk. *hēmikrania*, 'the ache across half the head'.

The process in which only one letter or syllable is cut off is technically described as *aphaeresis* (from Gk. *aphairein*, to snatch away). For some doubtless good reason modern philologists perform this operation on the very word, and call it *aphesis*. This lopping of *S.P.

253

parts of words is a favourite habit among the language-creating but language-lazy English. Only such a word as *Shun!* for *Attention!* can be defended pragmatically. *Shun!* or the drill-sergeant's *hipe* for *arms* in 'Present arms!', 'Order arms!', etc., is the executive syllable of a word of command – which could be compared with the F. *Allez!* for the L. imperative *Ambulāte!*

Most corruptions are due to ignorance of derivation; but not Chaucer, and still less Shakespeare, ever gave much thought to this subject – which fact does not diminish by one particle the truth of Spenser's encomium of Chaucer, or of Ben Jonson's tribute to both poets in his verses *To the Memory of Shakespeare*. It is better to be a poet than a pedant.

Knowledge of other languages is no safeguard if the processes of derivation are unknown. The classical example of this truth is provided by *pediment*, a 'learned corruption' of *periment*. 'Surely it is connected with the Latin *pēs, pedis*, "a foot"?' But no: *periment* itself is a learned corruption of *pyramid*, which we probably owe to an Egyptian word that reached us through Gk. and Latin.

The majority of corruptions are a mixture of guesswork and folklore. *Albatross* (see Chapter IX(a)) is as good an example as any other.

The words sponsored by our soldiers are for the most part good attempts at words from native languages. Many of them cropped up in civilian talk, especially those from Indian dialects, until the British raj began to fade from the memory of the present generation. *Khaki* (Hindustani *khak*, 'dust') soon had its newspaper-corruption *karkee* purified. The long *a* of the languages derived from Skt. were usually pronounced *aw* by Britons in or from India; but Kipling was a good influence in the matter of spelling Urdu words containing the letter. Today some of us feel a nostalgic twinge when some middle-aged man in a *bus* (aphetic form of L. *omnibus*, 'for everyone') says *rooty* for 'bread', *mucken* for 'butter', *pozzy* for 'jam', or *bundook* for rifle. And as for *cha* . . .

The sailor is the doyen of corrupters. Seamen of many nations, as we have noted, were concerned in the change of *tortoise* to *turtle*. *Anchovy* also was twisted by them a long way out of tune. Whether a Basque word, *anchua*, or the Gk. *aphuē* was the original term, 'those rude, virile illiterates, the many-countried Mediterranean sailors, reduced *aphuē* to their needs.'

Ypres is 'Wipers' in English, and will never be anything else; and a great many more words than this have been formed through our aggressively hostile attitude towards the French language. There is no chance that the French name even for a flower will keep its pronunciation in our language for very long. *Dent-de-lion* was introduced into English near the beginning of the 16th century. For a time *pisse-en-lit* was preferred, and kept in translation as *pissabed*; but *dent-de-lion* was gradually anglicized, until by the end of the 17th century *dandelion* was the final and exclusive choice. The Germanic form of *crab* (O.E. *crabbe*) strayed into French, where it became *crevice* (the modern F. *écrevisse*). M.E. took this over, decided that the final syllable stood for *vish*, 'fish', and settled for *crayfish* (or the *crawfish* preferred by American colonists).

The boldness of corruptions helps to give English its strong quality of speakability, its foursquare solidity. *Samphire* (1545) could not be more insular for *l'herbe de St Pierre* – which could hardly be more French.

What is slightly more difficult to understand is that, until the real discovery of classical literature in the England of Colet and Erasmus, words were treated without any strictness of regard to scholarship. Chaucer's spelling of classical names always seems to us refreshingly individual – which is not surprising, since his knowledge of Greek, at any rate, was based mainly on translations into English of Arabic versions of the original language. It is therefore natural that the English names for plants, particularly, often turn out to be the Latin or Greek names adapted and put through the evolutionary mangle so vigorously that their origin is completely masked. A telling example of this is to be found in the name of a plant uncommon enough for me to have been glad* to find it, in fruit, on the shore of Balintore, near Nigg in Easter Ross. *Ligusticum scoticum*, one of the *Umbelliferae*, has delicate reddish-pink stems and very sharp fruit-ridges. It grows on sea-coasts. *Ligusticus* is the adjective of *Liguria*, and, although this particular species did not grow even as far south as Piedmont or Geneva, *Ligusticum* was accepted as the scientific name. But in the vernacular, on its way to *lovage*, *Ligusticum* was lost almost from the start. One corruption and two 'etymologizing perversions' were involved, and two separating developments were brought together again. The word was becoming

*S.P.

255

English at a time when 'love-in-a-mist', 'love-grass', 'love-in-idle-ness', and 'love-bird' were acceptable names. 'Traveller's joy' was also called 'love'. The fennel-flower was the original 'love-in-a-mist', and much more deserving of the title than our garden-flower. Any species of the unlovable parasitic dodder was a 'love-vine'.

Some of the most difficult words to explain are those which have made a sudden change for no obvious reason. *Bat*, as a name for any of our species of the order *Chiroptera*, is not particularly effective. Compared with L. *vespertilio*, 'creature of the dusk', or Norse *lether-bakke*, it is uninspiring. *Flittermouse* and the German *Fledermaus* are more amusing. The F. *chauve-souris* is more elegant than the equivalent 'bald mouse' would be in English. The main point of interest is that *bat* is a M.E. word that started as *bakke* and remained *bake or bak* till 1575, when it suddenly changed to *bat*. The *t* has stuck ever since – an unexplained sport in the evolutionary mystery.

Accidents of Meaning

Forms and meanings of words are sometimes accidental, owing to mistakes, or to 'laws' of Semantics only partly understood, or to an evolution before knowledge of etymology became an influence.

A word or phrase may be a result of the misreading of the mediaeval letter which stood for *th*, but which might be mistaken for a *y*, as it often is nowadays in such bogus archaisms as 'Ye olde Tea-shoppe'.

'To quaff' is from the German *quassen*. At some unknown date the long *s*'s – in print exactly like *f*'s without the cross-stroke – were mistaken for *f*'s.

'Forlorn hope' indicates the danger of translating from Dutch. *Verloren hoop* to the Hollander is a 'lost company' (of soldiers).

In the name 'right whale' the use of the adjective *right* accurately preserves the old sense of the word that is now obsolescent. It was an O.E. and M.E. use. Chaucer has the phrase, 'my right dochter' – 'my right daughter, treasure of my heart'. 'Justly entitled to the name' gives the sense; and in this sense the whalebone whale became *right* during the 18th century.

Guides to good English tell us to avoid tautology. We must not say, 'Everybody was unanimous', or 'horticulture of the garden'. Yet it sometimes happens, when the derivation of a word has been forgotten, that a seemingly different but synonymous term is added

256

by way of clarification. One wonders how many children have thought that 'reindeer' are so called because Father Christmas holds the reins on his sledge. Here the tautology lies in the original O.N. *hreinn* ,'reindeer' + *dȳr*, 'deer' = O.E. *dēor*, 'a beast'. *Hreinn* stood for the big species *Rangifer tarandus*; *dȳr* for the genus as a whole, like a piece of Linnaean classification turned round, with the specific epithet put before the generic name. 'Mistletoe' is the O.E. *mistiltān*: but *mistil* is already 'mistletoe', and the final syllable, *tān*, 'twig', is superfluous. Another example of an unnecessary syllable may be seen in the 16th century addition of the F. *tour* to the O.E. *nēap*, 'a turnip'. *Tour* rubs in the gratuitous information that a turnip is round. In Scotland these vegetables are usually called 'neaps', as might be expected among a people who have a rational distaste for wasting words.

Aurochs is a more precise example of tautology. The name was introduced into England from Germany in the late 18th century, when it was applied, as it should properly still be applied, to the wild ox, *Bōs ūrus*, 'described by Caesar as *ūrus*, which formerly inhabited Europe, including the British Isles, and survived until comparatively recent times . . .' The name should not be applied to the European bison. The first syllable is an ancient Germanic word for 'ox' which found its way into Greek, Latin, and O.E. (See Chapter IX(a).)

Meanings repeated, meanings unexpectedly attached, meanings which split and fly off at a tangent – all these tricks of language are well exemplified in English. How, for instance can *Argentine* and *argue* be connected? The link is in the Latin word for 'silver'. (English *silver* is O.E. *seolfor*, and has no known cognates outside Germanic and Slavonic.) 'Argent', through F. from L. *argentum*, is the heraldic white tincture. The root *arg-, 'to shine', is to be seen also in Skt. *arjuna*, 'white', and probably in *gaur*, which has the same meaning. Gk. *arguros* is 'silver'. Argentina is the land of silvery rivers, notably the Rio de la Plata ('river of silver').* It is the notion of shining clearness which is developed from the root *arg-* in the L. *arguere*, to clarify. *Argue* appears in early Modern English, and its first meanings were 'to make clear by adducing evidence', 'to prove', as in *Paradise Lost* – 'Not to know me argues yourselves unknown'.

*The Spaniards in 1513 saw it flowing through vast plains of Zephyrus lilies.

The fine old parental reproof, 'Don't argue!' contains a different, later meaning, well expressed by that excellent 18th century slang creation, *argify*. A more violent split in meaning occurred in the development of the I-E. root **kar-*, 'beloved'. Through L. *carus* (the *c* becoming *ch* in French) English gained *charity*, which was used in the early translations of the Bible as the equivalent of the Vulgate's *caritas*, the Christian 'love for one's fellow-men'. Through the Germanic *h* for *c* came O.H.G. *houra*, O.E. *hōre*, modern Eng. *whore*.

The science of Semantics has tabulated certain habits and developments of meaning. Patterns tend to repeat themselves in different languages, and at different dates.

Let us take the 'semantic parallel', as it is called. This particular pattern might help to explain the derivation of *gun*, an association of which with O.F. *engon* is improbable. Its clue is rather to be found in the tendency, perhaps almost as old as war itself, to call new and terrible weapons of war by endearing nicknames. There was 'Mons Meg' of 15th century Edinburgh. There was 'Big Bertha' of the First World War. A long cannon in Dover Castle is 'Queen Elizabeth's Pocket-pistol'. Now it is believed that *gun* itself was originally, in the early 14th century, a pet-form of *Gunnhilda*, used first as the name of a stone-throwing engine of war.

Monkey may have been the Turkish *maimun*, 'ape'. The *k* comes from a Germanic form which may conceivably have some reference to a supposed similarity between a monkey and a monk. If it has, we have our semantic parallel: the Capuchin monkey of South America.

Forest has two principal meanings: waste land and forested land. A semantic parallel is *jungle*, for the Hindi word means either a desert or a forest. This is comparable with 'heathen' and 'pagan', already noted.

Besides the parallels there are, more mysteriously, semantic opposites and contradictions. At times the 'opposites' are ironical, as a nickname such as *Shorty* for a tall man, or *Tiny* for a fat one. A less obvious example is *obese*. L. *obesus* is the past participle of *obedere*, 'to gnaw, to eat away, to thin'. One learnt dumbly at school that the meaning of L. *hospes* was both 'host' and 'guest'. That came about, we were told, because both words go back to a word of wider meaning which embraced the two senses – perhaps the term for 'hospitality'. L. *sacer* meant 'sacred'; but it carried also the sense of

258

'accursed' for the man who violated the holy. Modern French *sacré* is analogous.

Δ *for Danger*

Sometimes we fail to think about a derivation because we fancy that we know it already. Such lapses illustrate the principle of unconscious guessing. But there are danger-words, which reveal in yet another way how an origin in nature may be concealed, and accordingly passed over. We may take as examples *surround* and *miniature*. The foundation of *surround* is not *round* or *rota*, but L. *unda*, 'a wave': whence *undare*, 'to move in waves'; *superundare*, 'to overflow'; the Modern French *surrounder*; and finally, by folk-etymological association with 'round', the English word and the English meaning.

Miniature one thinks of as a 'little' picture – something to do with *minor, minimus*. But in fact the key-word is *minium*, 'red lead, vermilion'. *Minium* is a Latin borrowing from Basque, Spain being the source of red lead. *Miniature* really means 'a manuscript containing letters illuminated with red'. The word is used correctly, and for the first time, in John Evelyn's *Restoration Diary*. He speaks of 'three or four Romish breviaries, with a great deal of miniature and monkish painting and gilding'. The sense of small-scale portraits developed from the confusion with *minimus*.

A similar example is *howlet*. This looks like another version of *owlet*, but is in fact an anglicizing of F. *houlette*.

The nosegay atmosphere of 'cowslip', *Primula veris*, evaporates when we divide the word properly – *cū-slyppe* (O.E.), in other words *cow-slop*, 'cow-slobber'. There is no mistaking the German name *Kuhscheisse*, or the provincial name for the larger species of oxslip, 'bull-slop'.

XXVΙΙ

THE WORD-MAKERS

'Still are [their] pleasant voices, [their] nightingales, awake;
For Death, he taketh all away, but them he cannot take.'
CALLIMACHUS, *Heraclitus*; trans. Cory.

THERE is much we can dream, much we can imagine, much we can theorize about when we try to go back to the beginnings of Logos, in the meaning either of Reason or of Speech, which, though verbally two, are a practically inseparable unity. But it is no more difficult to write a coherent account of the creation of a galaxy than to set down the history of the very beginnings of Language, or even of the beginnings of the word-making by our Aryan ancestors.

We know that the early Aryans had a word for 'name' which became the O.E. *nama*, Icelandic *namn*, Gothic *namo*, Latin *nōmen*, Greek *onoma*, Persian *nām*, Sanskrit *nāman*, Irish *ainn*, Welsh *enw*, with similar terms in every sept of the I-E. clan; and we can find, or 'presume' a root: but, as to the how and the why of that root, the rest is silence.

We have already touched on the hints about Aryan migrations given by the divergent specific meanings acquired among the separated groups of population for words meaning 'tree'; and we can safely trace that particular word to a root **dar-*, 'to split'. But why that root should have been **dar-* and no other monosyllabic sound is out of the depth of our comprehension.

Through Homer and the Hindu Vedas we have glimpses of the Heroic Age of naming during the Myth stage of civilization; but that was only a short time ago – some three thousand years perhaps. Only when we reach the classical period do we find the first exactness.

Quite apart from the vocabularies of zoology, botany, and other special sciences, English has been gently but strongly influenced by the Hellenic word-makers, 'a handful of grey ashes, long, long ago at rest'. Comparing our language with the dialects of Sappho and

Alcaeus, to say nothing of the speech of Plato and Demosthenes, we may be proud to think that an elegy such as *Heraclitus*, from which we have just quoted, could be translated by William Cory in the 19th century into poetry as beautiful as was that of the original verses of Callimachus.

The perfect chiselling of Greek words is striking. Even the name of the humble woodworm, *thrips*, is a valuable loan to us. Greek had the outstanding ability to make words which in themselves describe detail. Latin *cardo, cardinis*, 'a hinge or pivot', from which we take *cardinal*, 'the pivot-man', *cardinal* virtues, *cardinal* numbers, etc., is represented in Greek by *krādē*, 'a waving tree-top', hinged, so to speak, on the trunk beneath it.

Our word *calm* has vague and varied senses: in Greek, compressed into the one word *kauma*, is the sense of 'the burning heat of the day, when the animals rest'. Our *sphincter* muscle is connected with the inscrutable Sphinx by the Gk. *sphiggein*, 'to bind tightly', as the Sphinx throttled those who failed to solve her riddles. But the monster's name may have been of non-Greek origin. Entomology uses it for the Family of Hawkmoths, the *Sphingidae*, in which are *Sphinx convolvuli* and *S. ligustri*, the convolvulus and privet hawkmoths; Linnaeus having fancied a resemblance between their larvae and the Egyptian 'Throttler'.

When once the period of relative exactitude had faded, the stage was set for the age of mediaevalism and the vocabularies of vagueness. This Middle Age approach continued in the words of English Natural History long after the proto-Renaissance of Chaucer's time or of the real Revival of Learning in the 16th century. Animal- and plant-names of this period are largely committed to fables, folklore, and folk-etymology. Descriptions are vague. Eyewitness accounts seem to have no standard of measurement. 'Is it in Pliny?' was the test of acceptability of a newly-observed animal.

This vagueness led to the extraordinary multiplicity both of names for one object and of objects for one name – which in turn led inevitably to Linnaeus. Our botanical and zoological nomenclatures date respectively from the publication of his *Species Plantarum* in 1753 and the fourth edition of his *Systema Naturae* in 1758: but from Francis Bacon onwards there had been natural philosophers who only just failed to forestall the master-systematist. Peter Artedi (1705–1735), who classified the Fishes, and was drowned in a Dutch canal while pursuing his favourite study, was the compatriot, friend, and collaborator of Linnaeus. Mark Catesby (c. 1680–1749) has received scarcely enough credit for what he wrote after his travels in America (1710–19 and 1722–26): 'Very few of the Birds having names assigned to them in this Country, I have called them (sc. in Latin) after English birds of the same Genus, *with an additional epithet to distinguish them.*' Catesby had made a considerable advance on Hans Sloane, who, at about the same time, was calling a Jamaican insect 'the Black-Darien-Butterfly-with-two-spots', or, more technically, '*Papilio Cartagenius nigrescens alba linea prope extremitatibus alarum*'!

In the earlier, happy-go-lucky stage of language-making a root-word for a part of the body, for instance, might develop as many meanings as it had cognates in different languages. *Heel* (O.E. *hēla*) probably came to mean 'the sinew in the hock' in Old Norse, 'hip-bone' in Latin, 'armpit' in Sanskrit, 'the part under the knee-joint' in O.H.G., and 'foot' in the dialect of the Gauls. Similarly the Swedish cognate of the 'gill' of a fish means 'jaw': further off, the Gk. *kheilos*, 'lip', is a relative. *Moth* (O.E. *moththe*) may be connected with M.H.G. *made* and O.E. *mathe*, 'maggot', and with Skt. *matkuna*, 'bug'. O.E. *cȳta*, the first English form of *kite*, is possibly (but only possibly) related to German *Kauz*, 'a screech-owl'. *Limpet* is a thinning closely connected with *lamprey*. *Panther* is the equivalent of a Skt. word for 'tiger'. Before *penguin* achieved its present meaning it was used for the great auk *Alca impennis*. It was first recorded in 1578; and for *Alca* ten years later. The Scandinavian *gairfowl*, for the great auk, had been known to us from 1549. *Auk* dates from 1580. This word, cognate with Swedish *alka*, is probably akin to *halcyon*, the not even distantly-related kingfisher (see Chapter XXII).

The mediaeval plant-names were even less precise. The O.E. *hymele* (L. *humulus*) was used without fear or favour for climbing-plants as botanically far apart as hops, convolvulus, and bryony. 'Pepper' and 'paprika' probably evolved from an Indian word from Skt. *pippala*, 'a peppercorn'. Gk. *smīlax* could be used indifferently for the holm-oak, the yew, the kidney-bean, and the bindweed. *Spikenard* was the chosen name not only for the Biblical plant, now identified as *Nardostachys jatamansi*, but also for lavender, valerian, and the rigid inule or 'ploughman's spikenard', *Inula conyza*.

We have made passing references to some of the characteristic nature-words of the great writers of the 16th century, to whom we owe a greater debt than could be expressed in many pages. Others are scattered, and continue to be scattered, in more modern books.

'Give me a good, mouth-filling oath,' says Hotspur to his refined wife: and certainly good, mouth-filling speakability seems to have offered the best of all reasons, although it may have been offered unconsciously, for the naming of Nature.

XXVIII

PRONUNCIATION AND SPELLING

'Plus ça change, plus c'est la même chose.'

W E now take a short trip up one of the side-tracks of word-evolution
– a worthwhile journey for anyone who has not made it before.

Spelling can be an important repository of the facts and details of
word-change. It can also be dangerously misleading. *Spin* and *Mister*,
for instance, announce changes from *span* and *master*. These are
straightforward records of the process which might be called
'thinning'.

Gk. *sērikos* is the adjective of *sēr*, 'a silkworm', the caterpillar of
the moth *Bombyx mori*. *Sēr* is the singular form of *sēres*, a Gk. word
for an Oriental people, perhaps Chinese, from whom silk was
obtained. How did *silk* come from *sērikos*? Perhaps, suggests Partridge, this is an instance of the well-known difficulty which the
Chinese have with the letter *r*.

A study of older spellings can give a clue to derivations which are
hidden by 'wrong division'. Words are often sliced up without the
slicer's paying any attention to their origin. *Bike* is a popular, though
hideous, English word; but it is of no help as a reminder that the
original word was *bi-cycle*. Most of the wrong divisions are concerned
with the definite or the indefinite article. We may cite *adder* again as
one of the most striking of these. The original Saxon was *nǣddre*, and
at some time in the 14th century *a nǣddre* became *an adder*. This
word is important because *nǣddre* is the Serpent, the Evil One, of the
early Christian writings. In the Rushworth Gospels, 'Ye serpents,
ye generation of vipers', is, '3e nedre, cynn uiperana'. But by the
time of the Wyclif Bible of 1382 the serpent of Genesis 3 is 'the
eddre'. 'Nedder' is still used in dialect.

Such words as this and *a newt* for *an ewte*, which we have already
mentioned, belong to the centuries of illiteracy. Some have disappeared, e.g. *a nidgit* for *an idiot*. (Does the schoolboy say 'some
ink' or 'smink'?)

264

Two English misdivisions of Dutch words are hard to recognize as such. *Daffodil* represents perhaps the Dutch *de affodil*, 'the *asphodel*' (a word from Greek). *Decoy* is produced by the running together of *de kooi*, 'the enclosure' (for trapping wildfowl); and *kooi* is ultimately traceable to L. *cavea*, 'a cave' (from *cavus*, 'hollow'). A splendid wrong division involving the indefinite article is *an umpire*, which was originally *a numpire* – the *non-pair*, the odd man out, the man standing apart from the contest.

Spelling hinders the word-genealogist in a word such as *shallow*. This, like *shoal*, 'shallow water', is from O.E. *sceald*, a component of place-names, and cognate with Gk. *skeletos*, 'dry', which gives us *skeleton* by way of *skeleton sōma*, 'a body turned hard and dry'. This at first meant a mummy, but from its earliest appearance in English in the 16th century, *skeleton* has been used in its modern sense.

Spelling is often misleading in detail. *Conger* represents the Gk. *goggros*; but Latin, influenced perhaps by *congeries*, 'a mass' (eminently suitable for a mass of writhing eels), clapped the familiar first syllable on the beginning and made it 'conger'. A Florida *key* is an island, from the Spanish *cayo* taken from Taino: but the pronunciation *key* sounds better to the average Englishman's ear, if not to the etymologist's.

Then there are the mysterious nature-words, *lamb*, *limb*, and *thumb*. It is true that we seldom think of them as mysterious, because we cannot remember the time when we did not take their silent *b*'s for granted: yet only in 'lamb' is *b* part of the original root. Our word is the same as it was in Gothic.

The *b*'s of *limb* and *thumb*, on the other hand, are more difficult to account for. *Limb* is *līm* in O.E. – a simple monosyllable peculiar to Germanic. Partridge thinks, doubtfully, that it may owe its *b* to a chance association with *limb*, 'an outside edge', found in the phrase *in limbo*. *Thumb* is the O.E. *thūma*, the *thick* finger, which causes us once again to dig down to the root **teu-* (see Chapter III), and its extension to **tubh-*, 'to swell'. Whether or not the *b* of *thumb* gives a hint about its ancestry, at least it may remind us of the vagaries in English pronunciation.

Everyone is familiar with the dropping of *h*'s (an old habit from the M.E. period until the present day), and with the aspiration of initial vowels, which was a frequent phenomenon, considered a

265

vulgarism, from the late 18th century onwards. The lady in *Roderick Random* (1771), who, according to her fiancé, 'wrote like an angel', stuck an *h* before *eyes* and *arms*, and wrote *hopjack* for *object*. One unforgettable example is the ejaculation of the supporter of Surrey cricket in 1913: "Obbes, 'Ayes, and 'Ayward – *h*all the *H*aitches is *h*out!'

The incorrect aspiration is not by any means a modern solecism. Two thousand years ago, in what might have been a playful prophetic parody of the dialect of the Cockney 'Arry – with a staggering coincidence in the names – Catullus wrote of the affected Roman Arrius:

> ' "*Ch*ommoda" dicebat, si quando "commoda" vellet
> Dicere, et "insidias" Arrius "*h*insidias".'
> ('*H*opportunities' Arrius said
> For the aitchless word of the better-bred.
> If it chanced that an ambush he was in,
> It was '*h*ambush' for him and all his kin.)

There has been a similar tendency to play about with final consonants. A habit of Modern English, 1400 onwards, has been to omit them. In the 19th century they were often restored. *Hunting*, for instance, after a long period of *huntin'* – perhaps in some social circles preserved with a certain conscious effort – is now *hunting* once more. But it was the final *t*, *d*, and *b* that seemed to be lost most easily. *Almond* and *thousand*, for example, were pronounced *almun* and *thousan*. *Egypt* was *Egip*; and Pope rhymed *sex* with *neglects*. It is known that in 1685 the *b* was lost in the pronunciation of *dumb*, *climb*, *womb*, *tomb*, and *lamb*, although in each of these words the *b* is part of the original root. These final *b*'s were never restored except in the place-name *Lambeth*, and even there probably not until the sense of the first meaning of the words *lambs' hythe* (wharf) had been forgotten. Archbishop Cranmer wrote it as *Lammeth*. *T* before another consonant was particularly likely to disappear. We still say 'gris'l', 'bris'l', 'this'l', and 'fas'n' (for 'fasten'). The *t* was taken from *colts-foot* as well, when that keen comparison between the shape of the outline of the leaf and that of the impression of the foot of a colt had been forgotten. But that particular *t* has been put back by a flower-loving and spelling-conscious generation.

The silent *b* in 'thumb' and 'limb' is a reminder that final consonants were as likely to be put in as they were to be taken away. The *swounded* and *varmint* of Dickens (for *swooned* and *vermin*) had scarcely been regarded as vulgarisms in 1700. Even Swift rhymes *vermin* with *ferment*. Probably the *b*'s of *thumb* and *limb* were temporary additions, sometimes pronounced and sometimes silent – not to be taken seriously in those orthographically light-hearted days, before our language hardened under the gaze of the great pedagogues of the 18th century.

Sometimes the spelling remained fixed over many centuries; but this does not mean that the pronunciation also remained unaltered. Consider the peaceful word *cow*, of which the cognates are touched on elsewhere in these pages. In M.E., under the influence of the spelling of French sounds, the O.E. *cū* became *cou*. This spelling, *cou* or *cow*, persisted; but the vowel-sound *oo* gradually changed into a diphthong. Early signs of this process appear in the letters of Margaret Paston (upper middle-class Norfolk) and the Cely Papers (lower middle-class Essex). The sequence from *cū* to the *cow* of contemporary 'correct' speech may be built up as follows: *-ū, -uu, -ou, -au*. (H. C. K. Wyld.) But the story is not quite as simple as that. 'What would happen if one of your new steam-engines hit a cow, Mr Stephenson?' 'It would be bad for the *coo*,' was the legendary answer; for in Northern dialects the M.E. pronunciation *coo* continued more or less unchanged. Other dialects use the diphthong, but it may vary from county to county, or from class to class. In Cockney the diphthong may be *cĕ-oo* (rather like Suffolk), *că-oo*, or even a wondrous multiple sound like *cĕ-ă-ŏ-oo*, reminiscent of those first vowel-sounds issuing from Eliza Doolittle which surprised even Professor Higgins. Another quite different diphthong can be produced by a dignified 'Oxford' intonation's lingering of the first element, *cā*, followed by an only just perceptible *oo*.

How are the older pronunciations reconstructed? Chiefly by the predictable changes in vowel- and consonant-sounds: sometimes by the rhyme (cf. Pope's *obey* and *tea*). But the best guides are contemporary spellings; even those called 'occasional spellings'; and their value is based on the proven theory that in their departures from the normal, 'spelling-mistakes' usually verge towards the phonetically accurate. 'Britten', writes the nine-year-old boy, 'was discovered by Julia Caesar.' This curious statement merely emphasizes the fact that the first *i* of 'Britain' is short, and that the second syllable has the 'obscure' relaxed vowel. Almost all of us say 'Julia Caesar'; but we get nought out of ten if we spell it so.

The work on this analysis of spelling, founded to some extent on, or parallel with, the research of Dr R. E. Zachrisson, was embodied in one of the most fascinating books on language to be published early in this century, namely *A History of Modern Colloquial English*, by Henry Cecil Wyld. (Here 'Modern' means, of course, from 1400 onwards.) In this book are many clues to the shape and pronunciation of nature-words.

The Romans, as we have noted, called the porpoise, **porcopiscis*, 'pig-fish'. The M.E. *porpeis* or *porpois* appeared in English early in the 14th century; but, though *porpoise* became the accepted form, early spellings, e.g. *porpys* in the 15th century, suggest that the French *oi* was soon lost, as it was in *turquoise* (occasional spelling, *torkes*).

'The kettle is a-biling' is good Dickensian London English. The pronunciation explains why Shakespeare in *The Rape of Lucrece* rhymes 'swine' with 'groin'. During much of the middle period of Modern English the *oi* diphthong became *ai*, although the spelling remained the same. No doubt the new spelling-pronunciations of the later 19th century, with the assistance of the new Education Acts, helped to bring *bile* back to *boil*.

Some nature-words were affected by the development of a *y*, pronounced as in 'yes', at the beginning of such words as *earth* and *herb* (where the *h* was silent), so that they might become *yearth* and *yerb*. 'The vulgar man,' wrote Lord Chesterfield in 1749, '. . . even his pronunciation . . . carries the mark of the beast. . . . He calls the earth "yearth"; and he is "obliged", not "obleeged" to you.' In fact some of these *y* pronunciations – *year* for *ear*, etc. – continued in educated speech so long that many will remember hearing them used by an older relative or friend. This *y* survives in uneducated speech in phrases such as 'this yere business'. Many of the generation born about 1850 kept the older pronunciations such as *lanskip* for *landscape* and *neighb'r'd* for *neighbourhood. Hunderd* for *hundred* is still extant.

ⅩⅩⅸ

FOLK-ETYMOLOGY

'The Frenchmen think a Pheasant to be called *Fai-
sain* because it maketh a sound man (*il fait sain*).'
THOMAS MUFFET, *Health's Improvement.*

'The grass-plot round a sundial is called "wabe", you
know, because it goes a long way before it, and a long
way behind it.'
CARROLL, *Through the Looking-glass.*

PERHAPS the most frequent cause of the corruption of words is the
general tendency to cut words short. This seems to be a special habit
of the English. We like to lop off letters and run syllables together.
This may be connected with our custom of speaking with our mouths
half-closed. Broadcasting, however, has acted as a kind of artificial
brake on the Galápagos Islands effect which develops in a migrating
race cut off from its source. The tendency of a language to produce
differences on its perimeter has been slowed down or reversed,
because there is an increasing central supply of the original stock
always available to correct eccentricities.

Another cause of corruption is what is known as 'folk-etymology'.
Folklore plays an important part in old descriptions of the habits of
animals. It has occasionally also shaped their names. *Earwig* is a
notable example. The belief that this beetle penetrated or *wiggled*
right into the head of a human being was genuine and widespread.
French uses the name *perce-oreille*, German *Ohr-wurm*. Philemon
Holland (1552–1637) translates the advice of Pliny, hard to put into
practice: 'If an earwig be gotten into the eare . . . spit into the
same, and it will come forth anon.' Even Science, through Linnaeus,
has given it the name of *Forficula auricularia.*

Not only folklore but also proverbial sayings about animals give
their colour to the language. The verb to *curry*, from Latin through
O.F. *correier*, meaning 'to comb and groom (a horse)', was borrowed
by English in the 13th century. A hundred years later English had

dipped back into French to borrow its sharp-tongued metaphorical use of the words *torcher fauvel*, 'to curry the (best) chestnut horse' – in other words, 'to butter up the most important person'. (Favel the horse was the hero, symbolizing worldly vanity, in a 14th century French satirical romance.) *Favel* of 1400 became the *curry favour* of 1510; or, more simply, in Shakespeare: 'I would curry with Master Shallow.'

This is certainly Folk-Etymology; but the phrase is misleading, because it is not only, and not particularly, the unlearned folk who like to follow their instincts where etymology is concerned. The fact that words evolved from other words, the form of which might be widely different, was a discovery of great fascination, and it was made hundreds of years before the creation in the 19th century of the science of Comparative Philology. Everybody who had a feeling for words – scholars particularly – wanted to show their skill.

Let us look again at the words *lovage* and *island*. Two efforts were made at separate times to alter the first syllable of *lovage* into *love* (successful), and the second syllable into *ache* (temporarily successful). These might be called 'folk', or at any rate be said to reflect the interest of countryfolk in love-potions.

In contrast, *island* reflects the early attempts of etymological scholarship. In the beginning King Alfred spelt this word *iland* (888), using the Saxon word *iegland* (*ieg*, 'watered place, meadow', related to *ēa*, 'water' + *land*), meaning a watery or marshy place, or a place insulated at high tide, such as Rye in the 12th century. Men spoke of being 'at the island' (*æt thǣre iege*), which became *atterīe*; and this, by wrong division, turned into 'at Rye'.

The trouble came when the first syllable of *iland* was associated with the Mediaeval French *ile*, which was derived from L. *insulam*. By this time the French scholars had got to work and begun spelling *ile* with an *s*, in evidence of their knowing something about Latin. English clerks were not going to be left out of it; so the *s* came into our *iland* too, although the word had no connection whatsoever with *insula*. Nor indeed has *insula* any connection with salt water. The derivation of *insula*, '*terra in salo*' is learned folk-etymology. The most likely derivation is *terra in solo*, 'land standing alone'.

'Debt' comes from O.F. *dette* – hence the pronunciation. *Dette*, it was discovered later, came from L. *dēbitum*. In went a *b*.

The *h* inserted in 'abhominable' (see Chapter XVII) was a straightforward mistake of derivation.

Folk-etymology, like corruption, is sometimes spoken of by philologists as if it were something to be regretted. Yet it can produce good words and fruitful notions. A few years ago my* highly educated friend Harry Longhurst was writing about the kind of plant- and soil-association often found on sandy stretches of Scottish land near the sea, as at St Andrews. 'A links,' he said, 'is so called because it is the link between land and sea.' This I shall remember and choose, and not quote documents to show that his *link* (originally of chain-mail) is something flexible, and that golf-*links* means a series of slopes. The O.E. *hlinc*, found as the second element in many place-names, is a cognate of the Scots word *law*, 'a hill', and of Gk. *klinein* and L. *clivus* and compounds of the verb *-clinare*, which together give us *declivity, incline, recline*, etc. – the root being **klei-*, which provides a multitude of words betokening sloping or bending, including our *lean*.

Occasionally the guess may at least be plausible. We may cite the name *viburnum*, known to us especially as the generic name of our tough and dusty wayfaring-tree. This could just conceivably have something to do with the laburnum of the road (*via*).

Most truly 'folk', perhaps, is the determination to turn a strange word into something more decently recognizable. A minor example of this is seen in *guinea-pig*; because the cavy, the *cabia* of the natives, did not in fact come from Guinea, but from the less familiar-sounding Guyana (earlier spelt 'Guiana').

A better, because more complicated, example is revealed by a study of *artichoke*. The original word is Arabic, *al-kharshūf*, which was transliterated into Spanish-Arabic as *al-kharstrofa*, into Italian as *arcicioffo*. This word, says the O.E.D., was much influenced, 'like other words of foreign origin, by popular etymology'. The Italian spelling, for instance, suggests the Italian *arci-*, 'chief', and *cioffo*, 'horse-collar'. More ingenious is one of the French versions, Latinized as *arti-cactus, cactus* being the Latin name of the cardoon, a plant closely allied to the artichoke, and a more distant relative of the thistle, *carduus* – which is the generic name of most of our British thistles.

Early spellings of the modern English version *artichoke*, from 1531

*S.P.

onwards, are obviously full of etymological guesses – 'archecokk', 'hortichock', 'artichoux'. Later came *hortichoke* (choking the garden) and *heartychoke* (choking the gullet, or choking over the last bit to be eaten), to exemplify the 19th century liking for punning; which may itself be considered as a form of folk-etymology, when we remember that Lewis Carroll's *burble* has become almost standard English, even if *mome* and *wabe* and other Jabberwocky words have failed to do so.

Jerusalem artichoke shows that home-bred etymologists had not yet finished with the vegetable; though it looks as if greengrocers may have been anxious to provide a high-sounding name. *Helianthus tuberosus*, the sunflower-artichoke, has of course, no connection with the other plant, except in their both being *Compositae*. The Italian name *girasole*, sarcastically holding the notion enshrined in *heliotrope*, 'turning to the sun', was transformed into the more dignified 'Jerusalem' by the Italians themselves.

A phrase which might be called 'very folk' is 'eating humble pie'. This is indeed a wise saw and common instance. *Humble-pie* is really made of *numbles*, a French word for *lumbulus*, a small cut from the lumbar or loin (F. *loigne*) part of the animal.

'Make it something we know,' is the plea, particularly if the word is not only foreign but also unpronounceable. *Puliol real* is too uncompromisingly French for us to use as our name for the pale mint, *Menthe pulegium*, which grows in damp and sandy places in late August. 'Pennyroyal' sounds much better – and better-class – especially if *puliol* has something to do with the alleged properties of the plant as a fleabane (L. *pulex*, 'a flea'). If a foreign name for an animal is involved, let us turn it into a name familiar to us!

O.F. *papegai* for 'parrot' is a promising word, even if we do not accept the etymology cited in a previous chapter. If we make it *popinjay*, at least we have in the ending the name of another kind of noisy bird which we recognize easily enough. In fact the French themselves made this alteration by tacking *gai* to the first part of the name, for the same reason.

Another rule: substitute for the obsolete word an up-to-date one! The O.E. name for the dusty labiate horehound was *hārehūne*, 'grey *hūne*'? Spanish *cucuracha* is too soft and pretty a word for the English, who accordingly turned it into *cockroach*. In the kitchen we call it *black beetle*, though beetles are coleopterous, not orthopterous.

English owes its enviable flower-name 'primrose' to this process. L. *prima*, feminine of *primus*, 'first', has a diminutive *primula*. Mediaeval French turned this into *primerole*, then into *primerose*, which we borrowed and kept.

'Learned folk-etymology' has many forms, and these are often complicated by further alterations when 'learned' forms pass into common speech. *Alligator* has become the English name for the saurians of the crocodile family which in America are called *caymans*, a Carib word borrowed by the Spaniards. 'Alligator' began as L. *lacerta*, 'lizard', which became in Spanish *lagarto*, and then (for alligator) *el lagarto de las Indias*. The first reference in English was in 1568: 'In this river we killed a monstrous lagarto or crocodile.' But soon the Spanish *el* or *al* came in, and spellings ranged from *allagarto* to *alligarte*, until *alligator* was finally chosen; perhaps because this spelling 'had a literary and etymological appearance' (O.E.D.); perhaps because of the influence of the acceptable but quite irrelevant L. *alligare*, 'to bind', which gave colour to the explanation that some of the saurians' upper and lower teeth are arranged in such a way that the jaws close like a rat-trap and *bind* their prey. The final syllable of 'alligator' was unlikely to keep its proper sound. The English like their end-syllables unstressed; so the *o* in the name had to become the 'obscure vowel'. The ending is written '-er' when representing the colloquial pronunciation of *'taters* and *tomaters*, each of which words, it may be added, also originally ended in the Spanish *o*, being derived from the Amerindian, in which the *o* was a vocal *l*.

An Aztec word, *ahuacatl*, was corrupted by the Spaniards into *avocado* ('a lawyer'); and *avocado-pear* was recorrupted by us, and for many years after the fruit was known in England it was regularly referred to as *alligator-pear*.

Some of the learned folk-etymologists seemed to want to display a knowledge of Latin. 'Gum-tree' in Malayan is *getah percha*. As if there were some mad possibility that the thought of the exuding drops of gum allied the word to L. *gutta*, 'a drop', the pundits called it *gutta-percha*. Another suspect derivation is *urtica*, the Latin name for nettle. It was used for jelly-fish and stinging plants before it became the generic name for our English nettles. 'From L. *urere*, to burn' is the original theory, repeated in the O.E.D., and we see no reason to doubt this. Wherefore the 'trunk' of an elephant? The

273

O.E.D. considers the word to be an application of *trunk* in its sense of 'a hollow tube', by analogy with the trunk of a tree (originally something cut off, 'truncated'). But other etymologists point out that F. *trompe*, 'a trumpet', came to be used of an elephant's trunk because of the resemblance in shape, and that the *k* is a purely English innovation.

> 'So thus confusion from confusion grows:
> For what else matters if 'tis said, "He knows"?'

'Wormwood, wormwood,' says Hamlet; and the text of *Hamlet* is so much better known nowadays than the characteristics of the British Flora that Hamlet's words, together with the 'gall and wormwood' of Coverdale's Bible (of which Shakespeare was probably thinking) merely suggest to most modern readers the sense of something bitter. But for Hamlet, speaking of Claudius' thoughts, and for the later Elizabethan herbalists, wormwood had a special and distinctive flavour. The genus of this English plant is *Artemisia*, and, though the four or five British species are now little noticed, this name shows the honour in which they were once held, and their association with Diana, the Healer. In the words of Trevisa (1398): 'Artemisia is callyd moder of herbes, and was somtyme halowed . . . to the goddesse that hyghte Arthemis.'

Only two English species of *Artemisia* have the stimulating bitter smell. The two darker-leaved species are scentless: the rare southernwood, *A. campestris*, and the decidedly less beautifully named *mugwort*, *A. vulgaris*, which grows muddily on riverside sites – by the Thames near London, for instance. The first syllable of *mugwort* has a Germanic etymon meaning 'fly' and cognate with *midge*. Its second name, *motherwort*, is a reminder that the plant was a 'certain cure' (all cures seemed certain in earlier days) for disturbances in the womb or difficulties in childbirth. This easy substitute for podal flexure is, says a Scots writer in 1549, 'gude for the suffocatione of any voman's bayrnis hed'.

The best cures were extracted from the two wild species of *Artemisia* – not quite hoary white like our garden-species, 'dusty miller', but mealy grey. They are *A. absinthium*, 'wormwood', and *A. maritima*, the sea-species, common for instance in the salt-marshes near Aldeburgh.

The crushed leaves of wormwood were used as a tonic. But why is it *wormwood*? The original word is Germanic. It became *weremod* or *wermod* in O.E., *Wermut* in German, and *vermouth* in French. (*A. absinthium* is used in making the apéritif.) The construction of the word looks like *wer*, 'a man', as in *werewolf*; and *mut*, 'courage' – our *mood*. *Wer* lurks in such names as *Canterbury*, the *burg* of the *Cantware*, 'Kent-men'. It has cognates in Scandinavian and Celtic languages, e.g. Welsh *gwr*; and in Skt. *vira*, 'a hero', and L. *vir*, 'a man' in contradistinction to a woman, 'a true man, a heroic man'. By attaching the *m* of the second syllable to the first, the coiner of the form *wormwood* obscured the etymology; but the two good old-established words, *worm* and *wood*, were irresistible. As a final proof of trust in the complete truth of folk-etymology, the plant was pre-scribed as a cure for worms.

Predictable changes in form

The alterations brought about by these corruptions are for the most part impossible to foresee. The final shape is a random one. But the majority of word-changes are controlled by the laws of living speech. Thus not only can earlier unrecorded forms – of O.E. or O.H.G. roots, for instance – be reconstructed with reasonable accuracy; it is also possible to predict the shape and size which a word is likely to produce in the future. Henry Sweet, the great philologist, the original of Shaw's Professor Higgins, used to discourse on the probable future pronunciation of his name. His pupil Wyld would imitate the sound of a nasalized *ing*, like 'Ingres' without the *r*, followed by *hwee*.

Predicting the pronunciation of 'Woburn'

There is a good Guide to the Duke of Bedford's *Woburn* (O.E. *wōh*, 'crooked' + *burn*, 'stream'); but possibly it does not explain why the name is pronounced *Wooburn*, in which the first syllable rhymes with 'too'.

The first phenomenon to be taken into account is that the *ā* of O.E. tended to be changed into *ō* – to become 'rounded'. Thus O.E. *hān*, *stā*, *hlāf* became *hōn*, *stōn*, *hlōf* in Middle English. We know that this process went on in Old English itself, because the O.E. *ō* had itself at an earlier stage been *ā*. A presumed primitive **gans* or **gās* (goose), for instance, became *gōs*. But sounds do not drift about without check if language is to remain intelligible; and the limiting factor is a neighbouring sound. When O.E. *ā* had become *ō*, original O.E. *ō* was pushed towards a *ū*. Thus *gōs* became 'goose', *mān* became 'moon', *wōh* became *wooh. In 'Woburn' the *ō* is retained, but the pronunciation has slipped on to the stage that we should expect to see spelt *oo*.

This picture of the shifting of long vowels is complicated by the fact that some of them were shortened at various stages in their development: as *toad* (O.E. *tāda*) in *tadpole*, *holy* (O.E. *hālig*) in *holiday*. The *ō* in some words became a rounded *ŏŏ*, in others an unrounded *ŭ*: hence the difference between *rook, book, hood,* and *flood, blood, mother*.

This then is the sequence of changes in this continuously evolving vowel, now 'fixed' (for how long?) by the modern English nature-words:

O.E. *tāda*	O.E. *mōn*	O.E. *hrōc*	O.E. *mōder*
Early M.E. *ō*	Late M.E. *ōō*	15th C. *oŏ*	Early 18th C. *ŭ*
Modern *toad*	Modern *moon*	Modern *rook*	Modern *mother*

Metathesis

Several times already we have come across examples of metathesis, the process involving the shifting of a consonant from one side to the other of an adjacent vowel. *R* is the consonant (or, rather, semi-vowel) which most frequently comes in for this treatment; and it is often difficult, even now, to be sure, when we are listening to some dialects, northern in particular, whether *r* comes before or after the full vowel in a word such as *burst* (M.E. *brest, brast*). The 15th century Paston family wrote their letters and kept their accounts in a spelling which was nearly phonetic, and therefore, it is believed, a fair copy of their pronunciation. 'Through' and 'durst' are written as *thorf* and *drust*. In the same century 'Christmas' was written *Kyrstemas*.

The metathesis of *r* has given us, as we noted earlier, a nature-word of great importance – *bird*. The *r* of the original *bridd* has for centuries flown about in the middle of the word. It is a noun which is peculiar in its individuality: there is no other Germanic form of it; and it suddenly appeared in English unrelated. The first quotation in the O.E.D. is from the *Corpus Glossary* (800). Another anomaly is that the meaning of the word sways about as unpredictably as the *r*. It ranged originally from the young of birds to the young of other animals – to 'youngster', and then to 'girl' from 1300 onwards. For a girl the term *bird* was used affectionately but respectfully, as in *Cymbeline*, 'The bird is dead that we made so much on'. The modern use of *bird* as a 'cute female' is a return to the older sense. Sixty years ago the meaning was less respectful.

The nature-meaning which is important here is the latest in the evolution of the word. Increasingly from the 13th century onwards 'bird' was used for any kind of *Avis*, whether young or not: though, as Dr Johnson was still entitled to say in his Dictionary, 'fowle is used for the larger, bird for the smaller kind of feathered animal'.

Not only *r* is metathesized. 'They wopses is awful today,' sounds as cosy as Devonshire cream-tea in the garden: but something else is in the air, because the pronunciation of *wasp*, with the *p* before the *s*, takes us floating back thousands of years. *Wæps* is the earliest O.E. form, quickly giving way to *wæsp*. It was already *vespa* in the cognate Latin; for 'wops' goes back far beyond Saxon to an ancient Germanic stem **wops-*. That was how the word was spoken in the Black Forest perhaps 3,000 years ago.

Dissimilation

Some changes are made for the sake of ease and comfort in speaking. Awkward corners are rubbed off. Sounds, particularly of foreign words in process of being ingested, are changed to fit the native tongue. Words which occasion a hold-up in the flow of speech are sometimes shortened, sometimes smoothed. English has a slight distaste for syllables which begin and end with the same explosive consonant. 'Paper', from *papyrus*, remains untouched; but, in its second meaning, *papyrus*, 'a wick' (subsequently 'a candle'), was altered to *taper*.

A perfect example of dissimilation from a native word is *lind*. *Lind* is the O.E. form of the common Germanic word for *Tilia*; and the adjectival form *linden* was later used, especially with *tree*; but something about it was unsatisfactory, and an altered form arose. Soon after Shakespeare's time the final choice was made for *lime-tree* and *lime*. (*Lime*, the fruit, was introduced at much the same time in the 17th century. The name reached us through F. and Persian from Malayan.)

The Romance languages, French particularly, use dissimilation not less frequently than does English. The Gk. *marmaros*, 'a glistening stone' (*marmairein*, 'to glisten') had as a cognate the L. *marmor*, from the accusative of which came by this process the F. *marbre*. Mediaeval English, by a characteristic change of *l* for *r*, turned this into *marbel* – *marble*.

Easing

'Easing' is a process very much like dissimilation. Children often make use of it, especially before they learn to spell. I know that I* myself always said *feeth*, because to say, for instance, 'Stop thief!' was much more difficult and tiresome. After *p* the lips are already more or less in position for the *f* sound. But I did not realize the extent to which I eased my own particular London dialect until a few years ago. Giving a lesson to my young son, I asked him to write down the name of the small animal that we had just seen in Regent's Park. I said the name; and he wrote *swirle*. His phonetic spelling revealed the extent of my 'easing' of *squirrel*.

Another good nature-word which shows this process is *spider*. The spider, as we have already noted, is 'the spinner'. The original **spinthron* had been eased in M.E. to *spithre*. This word, uncomfortable in M.E., was eased to *spider*, like the change of *murther* to *murder*.

* * *

Inchoative, intensive, frequentative, diminutive: these and other useful words are sprinkled through manuals of English. They imply affixal forms with changes in meaning. 'Inchoative' represents L. *incohare*, 'to begin'. *Alere*, 'to nourish', for instance, was turned by the addition of *-esc-* into the inchoative *alescere*, 'to begin to grow'. *Crescere*, 'to grow', is the inchoative of *creare*, 'to produce'. The moon, therefore, is truly *crescent* only when it is waxing.

Intensive forms of a word are used to increase the force. The L. verb *tangere, tactum*, 'to touch hard or sharply', having acquired such
*S.P.

additional meanings as 'blame', 'point out', 'mention', and 'value', piquantly produced from its intensive *taxare* our word *taxation*. Much as one dislikes finding oneself applying schoolmasterish corrections to Bertie Wooster, *gruntled* is not the opposite of *disgruntled*. The *t* suggests that *grunt* is a frequentative of O.E. *grūnian*, with the meaning of 'going on grounting'; in fact it is recorded as *grunnettan* and is related to *granian*, 'groan'. *Dis-* is an example of the rare intensive use of this prefix: so that *disgruntled* means 'very much inclined to utter frequent little groans' – an apt description.

Sometimes the form of one word chances to be influenced by the form of another, although there may be no etymological connection between the two. Early Modern English *gryne* suddenly became *groin* because of a supposed association with *loin*. The *n* of *bitterne* is suddenly slipped in on account of some fancied link with *erne*, eagle. In the same way – perhaps influenced by *elder/eldern* – an *n* was temporarily added to *alder*, making it *aldern*.

On occasion the contemporary word keeps the inflections and forms of the older language. The 'aldern' above may be the old adjectival form in *-en*. (Cf. 'What hempen homespuns . . .', etc.) *Aspen* was originally the adjective of *asp*, the O.E. and O.H.G. name for *Populus tremula*. Spenser first used *aspen* for the tree itself. (Spenser was a word-coiner, or, rather, a creator of old-sounding words.) Some old inflected forms stay on in the English of today. The 'mutated' plural of some words in *-u* was an unrounded vowel represented by *y*. This we retain in *mouse/mice, louse/lice*. In *women*, the plural of *woman*, the spelling is modernized, but the old pronunciation of the first syllable is retained. Of 'cow' (O.E. *cū*, plural *cȳ*; M.E. plural *ky*), our, now poetic, 'kine' looks like a double plural – the strong, with vowel-change, seemingly followed by the weak, in *-en*; but it is probably a shortening of the genitive plural *cȳna*, 'of cows'.

One influence on form which sometimes affects vocabulary comes from children – from the nursery-words such as *pussy-cat*; *Tom Tit*, for something small; *bumble-bee*, for *humble-bee*.

Nature-words have seldom had to grapple with the small group of recently-made words that come under the heading 'hybrids' – which usually means words made up of roots from two different languages, such as the Gk. and L. mongrel *television*. In Gower's edition of Fowler's *Modern English Usage*, amoral (Gk. + L.), *breath-*

alyser, and *speedometer* (whence the *o*?) are on the black-list. *Cheese-burger* and the once-recorded *gruyèreburger* might well be added.

Yet, though the special sciences of Natural History often need new words, these words are usually built up with a sense of scholarship. One nature-hybrid which has passed successfully into English is *palfrey.* The word comes straight from the O.F. *palefroi,* itself from L. *paravēredus,* 'post-horse for the lesser highways and out-of-the-way places'. The *para* is the Gk. prefix; *verēdus* is Latin, with Celtic cognates and Germanic nephews and nieces, such as German *Pferd,* 'a horse'.

DIALECT

> 'Take of English earth as much
> As either hand may rightly clutch.
> In the taking of it breathe
> Prayer for all who lie beneath,
> Not the great nor well-bespoke,
> But the mere uncounted folk
> Of whose life and death is none
> Report or lamentation.'
>   KIPLING, *A Charm.*

THE doubling up of nature-words, the constant spawning of new forms as new pockets of population are formed, the lack of a fixed standard vocabulary – these are richly illustrated when we come to examine dialects. Southern Englishmen especially are liable to underestimate the importance of dialect in our speech. Anyone born about 1900, who happens to have survived to the present day, will become conscious, when he or she returns to old holiday-haunts in the country, that most of those 'strong burrs' died out with the Old Poacher and the Public-house Saga; or, in the Home Counties at any rate, that the inflexion is tinged with some variety of London accent. Even the four principal types of Cockney seem to have been blurred or amalgamated, and to be losing their regional distinctiveness. It is all very different from the old days, when Queen Elizabeth I, for instance, was unable to understand the Devonshire accent of Raleigh, and would probably have had quite as much trouble to understand Shakespeare's Warwickshire. But the tongues of personages of much later date, whose education and birth would nowadays have moulded their speech into Standard English, were often salted with dialect. Peel had a Lancashire accent, Gladstone a 'Northern burr', and Tennyson's Lincolnshire was often playfully imitated.

But if dialects are now more hidden, students of literature are soon made aware that it was a different story in the old days: that English was quick to divide itself into five principal dialect-regions which originally followed to some extent the different peculiarities of the invading tribes of Jutes, Angles, and Saxons. For most English university-students, learning the differences among those dialects is regarded as the 'you must suffer to be beautiful' part of the English syllabus. The records of peripheral dialects are meagre, and, with few exceptions, the texts seem dry to all but specialists, for whom they have absorbing interest; and when one realized that the dominant literary dialect, the language of King Alfred, or that later form of it in which the poetry was preserved, was not the ancestor of modern Standard English – how fascinating it was!

Middle English records are more copious and varied, offering with equal hand the rich language of the West Midland *Sir Gawain and the Green Knight* and the urbanities of Kentish Gower and the civilized plenty of Chaucer, in whose tongue we begin to catch the accents of our own. A mainstream develops – a mixed dialect to which all the provinces contribute.

It is the discovery of such facts for oneself that sets one's mind off on a new train of discovery. For me* it happened during World War II, when we were living at Toppesfield in the north-east corner of Essex. Mrs Foss, our 'help', who had once migrated the fifty miles from Northamptonshire, was a tall and massive old lady who moved methodically and without haste, but got there in the end. One day I saw her slowly towering through the trees and over the lawn. Why? Of course we were short of fuel, and Mrs Foss, as she told us, had been picking up dry sticks. But what she actually said was, 'I've been gathering up they seres'. With a flash of recognition I realized that this sad autumnal figure was speaking the word of Macbeth:

> 'I have liv'd long enough; my way of life
> Is falne into the Seare, the yellow Leafe.'

O.E. *sēar* (M.E. *seare*, *seere*) has been given a reconstructed I-E. root, **sauso-*, meaning 'dry'. It has cognates in Greek and in Skt. (e.g. Skt. *śuṣ*, 'to be dry'). It has two-thirds of a column in the O.E.D., but it is there treated only as an adjective. For *sear* as a noun we have to look in Wright's *Dialect Dictionary*. Mrs Foss was talking a Midland dialect – and so was Shakespeare.

It is possible that the baffling name of the *sora* rail, a congener of

*S.P.

our corncrake – if it is not a native name – is connected with our
sere through *sorrel* (reddish-brown), which represents *sorel*, diminutive
of the O.F. *sor* (in modern French *saur*). *Hareng saur* is a smoked or
'red' herring. *Sor* was perhaps from the L.G. *soor*, 'withered'; the
Middle Dutch equivalent to *sere* being *sore*. Presumably it was from
the colour of their plumage that hawks of the first year were called
sore-hawks.

'As to the Carolina rail,' wrote Dr R. M. Mengel, Editor of *The
Auk* (*in litt.* 25.4.1965), 'Coues discussed the name in his *Key* . . . in
which he notes that the bird is also called "sora" or "soree". The
word is local and colloquial. "Soree" seems to be the older form;
it is used by Thomas Jefferson and goes back to Catesby (Vol. I, p.
19, on *Gallinula americana*, the *sorree*): but "sora" is commoner now,
though I have always heard both spoken. Origin and meaning
unknown.'

In Shakespeare dialect-reminders are plentiful. The meanings of
difficult words are sometimes revealed through the study of local
speech. Another word from *Macbeth* is *blood-boltered* (Banquo).
'Boltered' was not satisfactorily explained until it was known that
'the horses' feet were boltered with snow' is Warwickshire dialect.
From *Macbeth* also we have *brinded*, a word for *brindled* which still
survives, with Shakespeare's spelling, in dialect. 'A boy or a child?'
asks the shepherd in *A Winter's Tale*, when he finds Perdita. Here
and there, e.g. in Shropshire, *child* is still used for 'girl'. Forty years
ago the question, 'Did Bacon write Shakespeare?' was still being
discussed. The realization that there were Warwickshire words in
Shakespeare's plays seemed to serious students to make the discussion
academically out of date. But dogmatism is here quite out of place
— and will be until the publication of a full dictionary of English
spoken at the time of Shakespeare.

The impression that English dialects are disappearing is false.
The practice in some State schools of teaching a dialect-pronuncia-
tion side by side with Received Standard is restoring the status of
local speech. The science of dialect-forms is an important part of
language-studies. Phonetics are more precisely descriptive, and are
now so sophisticated that they include the colouring matter of
inflexions. There is one use for the tape-recorder.

Dialect-vocabularies are poor in abstract words and metaphors,
but well-off in similes and sayings, and rich in everyday words,

especially those connected with farm-life and animals. Dialect is therefore particularly important for nature-words.

Dialect imitative words, for instance, seem more vivid than those retained in Standard English. *Wheeple* is one of the better imitations of the cry of the lapwing. Instead of restricting themselves to *bellow* for the sound uttered by a bull, dialect-speakers will use *bawk*, *bawl*, *blare*, *blawt*, *blodder* as well.

More typically, dialects preserve the early-modern habit of multiplicity. 'In the *Dialect Dictionary* there are 1300 ways of calling somebody a fool.'

The first volume of the *Survey of English Dialects* – the Leeds Survey undertaken by Professor Harold Orton – contains in its section called 'Basic Material' the results of questionnaires carried out in the six northern counties and the Isle of Man. 'What do you call this?' would be the question. For charlock, the yellow *Brassica sinapis*, the common field-plant characterized by its hairy, lumpy pods, the answers were:

> (1) *brash-lach,*
> *brazzock,*

which were surely derived from *brassica*, Latin for 'cabbage'. The first use as a generic name was in 1832; but *brassic*, as a name for cabbage, is recorded from 1420.

> (2) *charlock,*

O.E. *cerlic*; for which O.E.D. gives also *chadlock, chedlock, cadlock, kedlock.*

> (3) *charnock,*
> *garloch,*
> *gools,*
> *wild kale,*

'kale' being the northern form of *cole*, used for several brassicas.

> (4) *katlock,*
> *kecks:*

(Is this a wild shot? 'Kecks' or 'kex' is usually kept for umbellifers.)

> (5) *mustard,*
> *runch,*
> *yellow-top,*
> *yellows.*

For *colt's-foot*, the answers included *cleat*, *foal-foot*, and two splendid extrovert corruptions of the respective English and Latin names – *coosil* and *dishilago* (*Tussilago*). Rabbit-droppings are called also rabbit *currants*, *dottles*, *partles*, *triddlings*, *dotlings*, *partnicks*, *raisins*, *trunlets*.

Here we are making particular use of that excellent and absorbing *English Dialects* by G. L. Brook, as we try to sketch a reply to the question, 'How have dialects affected our nature-words?' They have done so partly through their influence on literature, and because, from the time of Edmund Spenser onwards, some poets have liked the 'old' sound of words such as *mead* for 'field', and *merle* or *ouzel* for 'blackbird' (see Chapter XI(a)). A. E. Housman's constant use of *lad* for a boy or youth is one of the poetical uses which have helped to keep the dialect word going.

Sometimes 'wrong' usages are righted in dialect. Not seldom 'wrong division' or metanalysis is corrected, or rather the older form is preserved, so that the newt is still *evet* in dialect, and the adder is still *nadder*. Yet fresh wrong divisions are added, as *nurchin*, and the *nuncle* of Lear's Fool. *Childer* and *kye* are more correct than our double plurals, *children* and *kine*. *Foots*, *louses*, and *mouses* seem more advanced than the old vowel-change plurals that we have retained.

Dialect preserves some useful loan-words. From O.F. *araigne*, 'spider', comes *arain*: from Scandinavian come *force*, 'waterfall'; *frosk*, 'frog'; *dog*, 'dew'; *nout*, 'cattle' (from a word cognate with English *neat*). Dialect-words are apt to preserve formation-tendencies, as in *primrosen*, a weak plural from a loan-word. *Srimp* for *shrimp* represents a South Midland tendency. In *vixen* the *v* for the *f* of O.E. *fyxen* is South-Western. Corruptions, in dialect, have a kingly disregard for origins. Even the early 19th century *viaduct* has become *viaduck*, and *rumsey-voosey* (*rendez-vous*) prepares us for the shock of the 18th century *sparrow-grass* as a substitute for the earlier English from Latin from Greek from (?) Persian *asparagus*. The small, unacknowledged corruptions which we established in our childhood – such as *jommetry* and *zoo* – should be included here.

Let us add here a small collection of miscellaneous notes devoted to the differing influences of dialect on the form or meaning of the nature-words to be found in an average Standard English Dictionary.

The influence may be on form. *Hake*, the fish, is a dialect-variation of *hook* (possibly so called from the shape of its jaw, as Norwegian *hakefisk* is used for the salmon).

The original meaning of *fang*, something to seize with, literally 'a seizing', is revealed when we come across the word used in dialect as a verb; for it derives from the O.E. *fōn*, 'to seize', which has cognates in other Germanic tongues, e.g. the German *fangen*.

Dialect *rown* reminds us that the roe of a female fish was *rowne* in M.E. alongside *rowe* (cf. German *Rogen*) and that the *n* disappeared in the 18th century.

The O.E. *horte*, 'a whortleberry', still called *hurt* in Somerset and Devon, has as dialect-versions *hurtleberry* and *huckleberry*. The *berry* was tautologically added in the 16th century, when knowledge of the meaning of the original O.E. name would not have been conceivable. (Routledge.)

Sometimes dialect reminds us of a former sense of a nature-word. When Hamlet said, 'A little more than kin and less than kind', he made a good pun, for in Shakespeare's day 'kind' had a short *i*. If the words were ambiguous, they may perhaps be explained by choosing, out of all the meanings epitomized in the phrase 'out of kind', the sense of 'unnatural'. This sense is still preserved in dialect, from which we have important clues to a number of nature-words. 'Sheld', dialect for variegated or spotted, is a help towards understanding the meaning of *shelduck* (better *sheld-duck*). (See Ch. XIII(b).)

There is a Norfolk village locally called 'Crosik'. The name is spelt *Crostwick*, a folk-etymology development from an earlier *Crosthweyt* (1302). The form *Crostueit* is found in the Domesday Book, and means 'cross by the clearing'. The important word here is 'thwaite', a woodland with trees cut down, and the clue to its meaning is the dialect *thwite*, 'to cut', from O.E. *thwitan* (whence modern *whittle*). But *thwaite* does not derive from the O.E. but from the closely cognate O.N. *thveit*, 'a piece of land cut off, demarcated'. The various *thwaites* of the Northern counties mark Scandinavian settlements, which have themselves left their mark on English dialects.

The O.E. *licgan*, 'to be prostrate, to be situate' (root *legh-*), produced *leger*, 'a couch', from which came Modern English *lair*. But the cognate O.N. *latr*, a place where animals put their young, provided the good Northern dialect *laughter*, 'a place where hens put their eggs', hence 'the clutch of eggs' itself.

French dialects have given some good words to English. *Harridan* (in Dr Johnson's Dictionary 'a decayed strumpet') is probably based on F. *haridelle*, 'an old horse, old jade'. *Liana* is a form of a French dialect-word influenced in its long journey from *viburnum* by French *lier*, 'to bind'. *Moraine* (*mor*, 'a snout', and *neve*, from L. *nivem*, accusative of *nix*, 'snow') is Swiss or Savoyard French.

Schooner (1716) looks like one of our many sea-going words from Dutch; but, though the spelling is from Holland or New Holland, *scoon*, for scunning along, is Scots and Northern English. (Cf. O.N. *skunda*, 'to speed'.)

Dialect also embalms some of the famous 'old words' for animals and plants – a fact of which we were not conscious when we read Herrick's *Grace*:

> 'Here a little child I stand,
> Heaving up my either hand;
> Cold as paddocks though they be,
> Yet I lift them up to Thee . . .'

Paddock is certainly old, but *frog* is much older. The O.E. *frogga* and *frox*, were used by our forebears before the Scandinavian *paddock*. *Pad* for 'toad', and *paddock* for 'toad' or 'frog' are both M.E. words; and each still exists in dialect. *Paddock* stretches from Scotland to Kent (as in the name *Paddock Wood*); and Wright quotes its use in more compounds than the average Standard English nature-word can expect. There are *paddock-beds* for 'frog-spawn', *paddock-flowers* for 'marsh-marigolds', *paddock-spit* for 'cuckoo-spit', *paddock's pipe* for 'horsetail' (*Equisitum*), and a few more.

'Then spoke he of the mouldwarp and the ant,' says Hotspur. *Mouldwarp*, as we have noted, is from O.E., and has the meaning of 'earth-thrower', whereas the synonymous *mole* represents the M.E. *molle* or *mulle*, which may have come from a different source, e.g. Dutch: but *mouldwarp* or *mouldiwarp* still exists in dialect. The name of the spider we have also touched on. It may be added here that O.E. had, untypically, two words for spider: one of which we have retained. The other, *ātorcoppe*, 'poison-top', died out of common use in the 18th century: but forms of it are still in full use in the North. The word is recorded with a wide variety of spellings – very 'folk' – from *ottercop*, to *aftercop*. It is even used metaphorically – *nattercop* signifying a peevish person. (Wright.)

Two words used locally, notably in East Kent, are respectively mysterious and charming. *Nickypit*, with its hidden reference to Old Nick, is the term for a tiny, slowly-revolving whirlpool occasioned by a small spring beneath the more or less stagnant water of a marsh-dyke. It is supposed to be unfathomable. And of all the garden-flowers the lilac (Persian *nilak*, where *nil* = 'blue', as in the name of the Nilgiri Hills of India) surely has in *laylock* one of the most captivating dialect by-names.

XXXI

OLD AGE IS COMPLEX

'I shall indeed interpret all that I can, but I cannot
interpret all that I should wish.'

JAKOB GRIMM.

MOST of the nature-words are inspiringly old. Useful trees were
useful, strong drink could be fermented, long before there was an
Indo-European language. We find words which bear the trace of a
more ancient tongue. What could be more English and contemporary,
we think, than 'turps'? This painters' abbreviation is early 19th
century, and 'turpentine' itself is early 14th – a typically English
version of a French version of the Latin adjective formed from the
Greek *terebinthos*, 'the terebinth tree', *Pistacia terebinthus*, from which
turpentine is extracted. 'Probably pre-Greek . . . Aegean,' says
Hoffmann.

A word such as *amethyst* smuggles from Greek into English a
meaning of 'hard liquor'. When it appeared in 1290, and up to the
17th century, it was spelt *ametist*, for it came to us through French.
The surprise is that the first letter is the Greek privative *a*, betokening
'without'. The Gk. *methuein* means 'to be drunk'. *Amethystus*, as the
Romans called it, was used as a cure for hangover, and the stone
might be worn as a charm against becoming intoxicated. But *meth*
goes further back to an I-E. etymon *medhu-*, 'honey', which produced
mel in Latin and *madhu* in Sanskrit. In Celtic and Germanic languages
the syllable ends in *t* or *d*; and the English word became *mead*. It is
likely, however, that the history is more ancient. Links are surmised
with Semitic and Egyptian (as *matqa*, 'sweetness'), and with Akkadian.
Meths is from the mid-nineteenth century invention 'methylated'
spirits. *Methyl*, a new word created in the last century, is from Gk.
methu, 'wine (mead)', and *hūlē*, 'wood'.

A simpler, younger word may yet impress us more with the sense
of age, perhaps because outwardly it seems so modern – 'oscillation'.
When first I* heard the explanation of the word, it happened that I

*S.P.

289

had just been staying in Portugal, on that stretch of mountainous ground where the 'Plutonichas Rochas' have upthrust to produce those split boulders of granite on which alone the port-grape can flourish. I had seen the port-harvest from close by, with the small ceremonies of bringing in the day's crop – the tiny procession, the two-man band making a big noise; but all was seen, as it were, through the wrong end of a telescope. There was a sense of distance in space and time. There is nothing mediaeval about it all, because the age of it must be thought of in thousands, not hundreds, of years. Preserved here are the customs of wine-harvests of ancient Europe.

At last I understood 'oscillate'! Take Latin *ōs*, the mouth or face; add *-illum*, and make 'a little face' . . . the little face of the little masks . . . masks of Bacchus, which the ancients hung on the vines to frighten away the birds; they waved in the wind like the bits of crinkly paper that we put over the seedbeds; they oscillated.

In the older derivations are involved some long-established question-marks. 'Is it certain, for instance that the derivation of *swallow*, the bird, from *swallow*, the verb, is pure folk-etymology – "it swallows flies in the air!" ?' Not certain, perhaps, but it is far more probable that the *swealwe* of O.E. is an offshoot of the root **swel-*, 'to move rapidly, to swirl, to splash'. If this is so, the bird has a name indicating man's reactions to its speed, mazy flight, quick turns, and habit of skimming the surface of a pool or river.

Parakeet edges between a direct descent from *Pierrot* (diminutive of F. *Pierre*), via our 'parrot', and a connection with Italian *parrochetto*, diminutive of *parroco*, 'a cleric'. It is at any rate part of the language of pet-talk, and so its history is complicated by perversions and folk-etymology.

Berry seems straightforward, from O.E. *berige*, and continuing in parallel development with German *Beere*: yet there is a question about Celtic origin, and a suggestion by Walshe of a possible Caucasian or 'Japhetic' source.

Thoughtfully choosing his Coldwater Special, the angler may be thinking of the caddis-fly, or, if he is etymologically-minded, of whether *caddis* is connected with *Cadiz*, or *catharsis*, or even both. One explanation of the Mediaeval French *cadas*, *cadaz* origin of *caddis* and of the name of a thick woollen twill, is that the cloth, made in Provence, is associated with Cadiz. Another is that it is an O.F. word which dropped the privative *a* from the Gk. *akathartos*, 'unwashed'. Perhaps each of these possible sources contributed to the formation of the word.

> 'O for a falconer's voice
> To lure this tassel gentle back again!'

In her wistful cry Juliet calls Romeo a male falcon. Many things had happened to the pronunciation of *tercel* since Chaucer first introduced it in his *Parlement of Foules*. Shakespeare chose the version best suited to his context. *Tercel* by itself (as we noted earlier) means the male of a hawk, particularly of the peregrine falcon. Ultimately from L. *tertius*, the word must mean 'a third'. The most likely explanation is that the male of many species of birds of prey is about a third smaller than the female: but Sir Thomas Browne (*Tracts*, 1683) prefers the alternative suggestion: that when hawks lay three eggs,

'the first produceth a Female and large Hawk, the second of a midler sort, and the third a smaller Bird, Tercelline or Tassel of the Male Sex.'

Sometimes, though there may be no question-marks, the chase has been a long one for the etymologist. *Apricot*, spelt *abrecocke* in Turner's *Herball* (1551), sounds simple. The short explanation is 'from Latin *praecoquum* (sc. *malum*, fruit), "early ripe" '. This gives the gist of the matter; but the word has to be followed backwards from English to French, then to Catalan *abercoc*, previously *albercoq*, to Spanish–Arabic *al-barqoq*, and then to the Greek of Syria, which had borrowed the original Latin. *Gherkin* also has a long history, being a Dutch word borrowed from Polish, which took it from Mediaeval Greek, which had adopted it from Iran.

To discover the origin of *crimson* and *carmine* we have to seek out the pregnant female of the *kermes* insect, *Coccus ilicis*, a parasite on an evergreen-oak – once thought to be a berry – which provides a blood-red dye. *Carmine* combines the Arabic *kermes* with the L. *minium*, 'vermilion' (see Chapter XXVI). *Crimson*, which comes from the same source, has been affected in its travels by an intervening period along the trade-routes of the Byzantine Greeks, suffering such roadside accidents as the metathesis of *r*.

There are some nature-words whose histories are so complex that their origins can scarcely be summarized. Let us take three examples. Like most of the problem-words of English, they are connected with living things which, though at first local or associated with one particular country or area, have from their usefulness or picturesqueness become celebrated all over the world. They are friendly-sounding words – *rhubarb, ginger,* and *walrus.*

Rhubarb ('Rhapontick' to Culpeper, 1653) was given its *h* somewhat late in its history by a botanist who knew Greek. The plant came to us in two waves. First there were the roots produced in China and exported to Europe through the Levant from the 15th century to the 19th. Its use was 'to pour excess humours from the body'. Shakespeare speaks of it thus in *Macbeth.* The First Folio has:

> 'What Rubarb, Cyme, or what Purgatiue drugge
> Would scowre these English hence?'

English garden-rhubarbs were different species introduced in the mid-17th century, carrying an *h* in their name. This may at first have been due to association with the English word *rheum,* the generic name of both species. Later on there was an association with Gk. *rhein,* to flow. But the earlier Greek form of our word was *rhabarbaros,* which was taken either to be a barbarian word for a root, or to mean 'the barbarian root from Rha', the flowing river. Past and present etymologists who have worked on this word include Rabelais.

Ginger and *walrus* have each had monographs devoted to their histories. Even in the unexcitable O.E.D. the etymological entry for *ginger* (O.E. *gingiber,* direct from Late Latin) is relatively complicated. Latin had taken its *zingiber* from Gk. *ziggiberis,* which in turn was an adaptation of the Skt. name made up of two words meaning respectively 'horn' and 'body', the ginger rhizome being branched like antlers. A. S. C. Ross, author of a monograph on the subject, gives the lines of descent of the word by means of a diagram showing its development in sixty-three languages. 'It seems possible', he says, 'that the word reached India and China from South-East Asia.'

Walrus is dealt with by Professor V. Kiparsky in *L'histoire du Morse.* 'Morse', which appears to have its origin in Lappish, is the name by which the walrus was known in England. In *The Chronicles of England,* printed by Caxton in 1480, we find:

> 'This yere were take iiij grete fisshes bytwene Eerethe and london, that one was callyd mors marine.'

The only possible route by which *walrus* could have reached English is 'via Basque whalers in English service who had heard the word from the Lapps'. It appeared in the 18th century. The second syllable is *morse* apprehended as *ross*, a metathesized form of *horse*. The first syllable is *whale*. Hence we have 'whale-horse', and we should remember that King Alfred called the creature 'horse-whale' (*hors-hwæl*). In 1551 a modern Latin *rosmarus* was invented, and this word Linnaeus adopted for his classification.

But the essence of such discussion is of a divine lengthiness. To cut them short is like trying to condense *War and Peace* into a television-serial.

'Origin unknown'

The older English names of animals and plants are often good words as words, often picturesque, often the end of a succession of names which have never been fully accepted, but which have left their trace behind them. They are words which tend to be borrowed from, and lent to, a variety of languages; but they bear the marks of much handling; they are particularly tied up with folklore, and therefore very often with folk-etymology.

Sometimes the secret remains indecipherable. The nature-words which follow have been much discussed, but they are still of 'origin unknown'. Most of them are short, if not monosyllabic.

Ape was the general term for a member of the *Simiidae* before the equally mysterious *monkey* (see Chapter XXVI) superseded it in the 16th century, since when it has been used scientifically for a tailless Simian, or poetically and metaphorically when the resemblance to human behaviour is at issue. The word may be Celtic: there are possible Celtic cognates suggesting mimicry; but the Irish *apa* seems to have been borrowed from O.E. It may be Egyptian *aāfi*, 'ugly man'; but this is no more than a reasonable suggestion. There are Dutch, German, Russian, and Bohemian versions; but the cognates are not numerous: there are more 'collateral adoptions of an alien word along trade-routes'.

In the 16th century *cub* was used as the name for a young fox, but this sense was soon extended to the young of other animals. There is a possible connection with Icelandic *kobbi*, 'a young seal', itself a word meaning a stump or shapeless block. But once again we have to say, 'origin unknown'.

Emu, earlier *emeu*, has a complex history. It was originally the name given by natives, or by Portuguese settlers, to the cassowary of the East Indies (Purchas's *Pilgrimage*, 1611). It was next applied to the *rhea*, the American ostrich. Finally and definitively, because the bird looked like a cassowary, the name was given to the celebrated Australian *Dromaeus novae-hollandiae*, which was described soon after the colonization of New South Wales in 1788. But whence the Portuguese inherited the word, if they did inherit it, nobody knows.

Grouse is equally obscure. First recorded in 1531, it was used for the British sub-species, *Lagopus lagopus scoticus*. (See Chapter X.)

Lark and *wren* are names even more baffling for the ornithological etymologist.

For *lark* or *laverock*, Chaucer's *larke* or *laverokke*, the O.E. form was *lāferce* or *lāwerce*. This name could mean 'treason-worker'; but one hesitates to mention more than the bare possibility of our ancestors' having regarded the songster in this light. Why, we may well ask, should so harmless a bird be connected with guile or treason? If indeed there were this association of ideas, we should have to attribute it to superstition's being stronger than sentiment or aesthetic appreciation in the mental make-up of people of earlier times. Vultures and crows are protected in many countries because of their utility as scavengers – even as kites, in spite of their linen-prigging for nest-lining, were protected, or at least tolerantly regarded, in Mediaeval England: whereas, wherever the Celtic influence has prevailed, the unfortunate wren, innocent of any offence against mankind, has been persecuted throughout the centuries. We have already noted the barbarous custom among the Athenians that demanded a dead wryneck; and in Britain the corpse of a kingfisher used to play its part by being hung on a cord and spun round until, when it ceased to twirl, it came to rest with its bill pointing in the direction from which the wind was supposed to be about to blow. Nor was the lark immune from barbarity, owing to its very charm. It is not long since blinded songbirds could be seen in tiny cages in the shops of the back-street 'bird-fanciers'. We have a glimpse of the diabolical trade in *The Faerie Queene* (VII. vi. 47). There the 'darred larke' is not the 'dazzled laverock' of Alfred Noyes, soaring into the sunny sky, but a bird *dared*, 'dazed, fascinated', running up to face an imaginary rival reflected in a mirror put down by the bird-catcher and thus enticed into a snare.

Lāferce seems to be of the same stock as the generic *Alauda*, 'high songstress', the name borrowed by Latin from Celtic; the Welsh *llafaru* meaning 'to be vocal'. (Sir Richard Paget, in *Babel*, instances the widespread use of *al* to express height; the sound being produced while the tongue is strained upward to touch the palate.)

Most of our place-names referring to the bird, e.g. *Laurochebere* (now *Larkbeare*, Devon), *Lavrochestoche* (*Laverstoke*, Hants.), and a few more, are in the Domesday Book; and others – *Larkfield*, Kent, and *Lark Stoke*, Glos. – are to be found in records not much more recent.

Perhaps, by softening 'treason-worker' to 'telltale', we may think of some guilty progenitor of ours looking up at the soaring lark and imagining that it was proclaiming his crime from the very floor of heaven. Or perhaps we may allow sentiment to prevail, and soften 'treason-worker' to 'spell-binder'.

By the wren our thoughts are led to the numinous – the awe-ful. The duality of Nature, its beauty and its terror, is often reflected in man's view of supernatural beings, as in the contrasted and complementary facets of Parvati, the bride of Shiv, or in Kingsley's personification of natural law as Mrs Do-as-you-would-be-done-by and Mrs Be-done-by-as-you-did. Even so, the robin and the wren, often paired in the sayings of simple countryfolk, may be said to illustrate the dual nature of the last form taken by Pan in England. The well-loved redbreast was equated with Robin Goodfellow, and the unpopular wren with Puck – the one being representative of the benevolence of the sprite, the other of his mild malice.

Puck is the O.E. *pūca*, one of the Little People, or a goblin. *Puckeridge* ('watersprite'; *pūca* of the *ric*, 'stream'), as a name for the supposedly mischievous nightjar, or shortened to *puck*, became also a name for a disease in cattle reputed to be caused by the 'goatsucker'. It is found in the wren's by-names of Dicky Pug and Pug or Puggy Wren, which may not refer only to the bird's diminutive size.

A clue to the origin of the superstition may be found in the Scandinavian by-names which have the sense of 'hedge-sneaker' or, as we might say, 'eavesdropper'. These seem to hold the memory of the primitive belief (as may be seen in the depreciatory Egyptian hieroglyph) that small birds make mischief by telling tales of what they have heard or seen. For a base activity of this kind the wren seems well adapted by his small size and his habit of working his way along hedges. His triumphant, scolding song, as of one who has some scandal to relate, may further smirch his already tarnished reputation.

The belief that the wren played a part in Druidical rites is supported by the custom, not entirely extinct, of its being persecuted on certain days of the year in various parts of these islands where Celtic blood is still strongest, notably in some districts in Eire, in the Isle of Man, in Cornwall, and in Wales. Killing a wren, or taking a captured one from house to house, with a demand for money, was, and still is, a ceremony of Yuletide. The slaughter of wrens on St Stephen's Day has been rationalized into a memorial of the death of the first Christian martyr, or of the massacre of the Holy Innocents, but must in fact be a relic of a pre-Christian custom, rendered superficially respectable, like Yule itself, by being disguised under another name. The gosoons, while they hunt their pitiable prey among the bushes, chant:

'The wran, the wran, the king of all birds,
On St Stephen's Day was cot in the furze.'

The title of 'king' has its roots in Aristotle and Pliny, and is a part of the legend of the wren's supposed cunning. All the birds having decided that the highest flier among them should be their king, the eagle soared above the mass of them, until, when he had reached his limit in the sky, the wren, who had been hiding in the feathers of the eagle's back, fluttered above him. The birds had to adhere to their agreement; but from that day to this they have driven the wren from all open spaces and forced him to take shelter in the hedges. To the Germans he is *Zaunkönig*, 'the hedge-king', to the French *roitelet*. In Iceland he is called *musarrindill*, 'mouse-wren'.

In respect of the etymology of the M.E. *wrenne* (O.E. *wrænna*), the possibility of its being connected with *wrāne*, 'lascivious', must be mentioned; but it is hard to conjure up more than a fleeting thought of the shameless elevation of the little tail, or of the fact that the bird has a large number of offspring.

Kirke Swann, following other authors, stated without qualification that 'wren' is derived from *wrāne*; but Ekwall has shown that place-names such as *Warmfield*, *Warnham*, *Warningcamp*, and *Wrenbury*, which have been supposed to be connected with wrens, are probably derived (if not from personal names) from a probable O.E. word, *wrēna, 'a stallion'. This word has not been found, but it would correspond with words in O.H.G., Low German, and Norse. The denigrating wrēne, therefore, may be left to the lusty stallion, leaving the wren cleared of one reproach.

Yet it appears that any stick is good enough to beat the wren with. He has been credited with being a sneak, and lecherous, and full of low cunning. He was one of the first victims of our economic demoralization that led to the depreciation of our currency, through the withdrawal from circulation of the farthing that bore his image. (This attractive little coin, the wren-farthing, was minted from 1937 to 1956.) It is small wonder that the tiny bird chitters so angrily when his nest is approached; for he may well regard any larger living creature as a potential enemy. Yet not one of his friends or unfriends has been able to discover the secret of his name.

Coot poses a problem. Is the bird really the Welsh *cwtiâr*, 'short (tailed) hen'; or does the name imitate its croak?

Some of the fish-names are the most elusive. A few, such as *cod* (14th century), are known only in English. In some of them the lines of possible descent are tangled among other languages, making a kind of piscatorial *lingua franca*. Does the *haddock* of the early 14th century come from a French word, or was that word itself taken from English? There are scarcely even theories about *mackerel*. *Kipper*, originally used for 'a kippered salmon', looks less mundane in O.E. *cypera* 'a spawning salmon', but the word cannot be traced further back. There is a possibility of a relationship with 'copper' (O.E. *cyperen*, from the noun *copor*, L. *cuprum*), which is the colour of the male salmon. *Sprat* (O.E. *sprot*) may conceivably have something to do with a *young* fish, a *sprout* of a fish. Yet against this one could put one's observation that the North Sea fishermen still regard shoals of small fishes as of a separate kind, not as young ones. Certain herring-catchers of Suffolk refused to believe that whitebait are the young of herring, pointing out that they flourished in different waters!

The foregoing are but a sample of the words of which we have to call the origin unknown.

xxxii

THE WORD-ARTISTS

'Words are the only things that last for ever.'
HAZLITT, *On Thought and Action.*

IN the making and using of words the English have enough skill to save them from being shy about admitting that much of the wit in the language is borrowed. They should rather be proud that the men who have added new words to the old stock should have done it so successfully. But we may sometimes feel wistful that such words only rarely carry the signature of the inventor. The aptness of *hypochondria*, which we have already instanced – was the name at first exclusive to English? Was Dryden the first to employ it in the sense of the malaise attributed to an imaginary pain somewhere 'below the breastbone'? Sometimes, however, we can give a name to the author, whether a native or a foreigner. We know, for instance, that it was Galileo who recognized planets (Gk. *planētai*, 'planets', i.e. 'wanderers') for what they are, and that we adopted the word at the beginning of the 17th century. To Kepler, Galileo's contemporary, we are indebted for *satellite*, which he borrowed from L. *satelles*, 'an obsequious attendant on some person of importance'.

On the menu of an hotel in a small country-town used to appear 'Macedoine of Fruits'. The name of this high-class item was intended, in the original French phrase, to be a joke against Macedonia, where the races were inextricably mixed. *Barbarian* (Gk. *barbaros*) and probably also *Tartar* make fun of the efforts of foreigners to speak a language which is not their own.

Latin particularly is a source of wit in words. We have already noticed *orotund* and *pupil*. The nature-word *testicle* provides an equally imaginative example. Introduced into Late Middle English, its origin was a diminutive of L. *testis*, 'a little witness', and therefore a testament of virility.

English is witty in its adaptation of older words, as in certain descriptions of locomotion. *Canter* is described by Dr Johnson as 'the hand-gallop of an ambling horse'. There is no written record of the word before the 18th century; yet it was derived from *Canterbury*, the name of the city more renowned through Europe after the martyrdom of St Thomas Becket, than that of London itself. It must have been the leisurely top-gear of the Canterbury pilgrims, each of whom, when Chaucer made his pilgrimage, was riding some kind of animal, as the poet carefully notes. To *scamper* is by origin 'to flee from the battlefield', the Old French having tacked -*er* to the L. *ex campo* to make the verb *s'escamper* (our *scamp*). *Scut* for the tail of a rabbit could give precision to the verb *scuttle*; but, though 'scuttle' is said to be of Scandinavian origin, it is hard to connect *skott*, the O.N. word for a fox's brush, or *scut* itself, with the cognates of *scuttle* – the provincial *scuddle*, *scoot*, the bird's name *scoter*, or the ancestral O.E. *scēotan*, 'to shoot,' or 'to shoot along'.

An apt but hidden simile from nature lies in 'button' (F. *bouton*). The O.F. which gave the word to Middle English had it from O.L.G. *boton*, 'a bud'. Why *solar plexus*? Because the nerves radiate from the centre, like the beams of the sun. Some of the later nature-names take their meanings from the world of civilization. *Mimosa* (1731) may be from L. *mimus*, 'an actor'; for its leaves recoil dramatically from the touch of a finger.

There is a small group of words whose derivation bears witness to close observation by their namers. *Mountebank*, for instance, is the label of a man who has to 'mount a bench', to make room for himself, as it were, before he can drive home his point. Another good example of French extraction is *marauder*, a powerfully suggestive word for 'a scoundrel or pillager' (F. *maraud*), even if 'tom-cat' is its secondary and not its primary meaning.

The use of *supercilium*, 'the eyebrow', to suggest haughty disapproval is one of those effective Latin inventions which compress a great deal of meaning into small compass: *supercilious* well describes the look of polite surprise ... the slight lifting of the brow. The English *leer* is equally apt: we look down our cheek (O.E. *hlēor*, M.E. *lere*) when we smile in that way. Related to *stutter* was the Gk. *tuptein*, 'to push' (the tongue too hard against the cheek) – a well-observed physical detail. *Oestrus* (Gk. *oistros*), used in English from 1890 to mean 'sexual desire', caricatures this secondary meaning in the primary – the stinging gadfly that lays its eggs in the bodies of other creatures.

'The wren goes to it, and the small gilded fly
Doth lecher in my sight.'

Sometimes the wit is gently ironic. *Cosset* makes fun of the pet lamb, the 'cottage-sitter' (O.E. *cotsæta*, 'a cottar'). The derivation of *saxifrage* (L. *saxum*, 'rock' + *frangere*, 'to break') reminds one of the calm appearance of a tender shoot of thistle pushing its way through the surface of the new concrete tennis-court within seven weeks of its being laid down. No doubt some such thought as this was in the mind of the man who first called a still more delicate plant 'rock-breaker'.

In some words the irony is sharper. There may be a trace of this in the make-up of *neuter* (L. *ne uter*). There are nature-words providing charming examples. *Sultana*, the feminine of *sultan*, was taken in the eighteen-forties as the name for a new kind of *seedless* raisin. *Rumination* is a perfect word for the deliberations of those fine old characters, silent and wise, who seldom nowadays chew a quid, but metaphorically still chew its doublet, the cud (is this word nearer to Skt. *jatu*, 'resin' or *khād* 'to eat'?) in the public bar, regurgitating, the contents of the *rumen* ('gullet'). This is another brilliant Latin metaphor co-opted for English in the 16th century. Yet another is *exuberant*, 'luxuriantly fertile', or, more exactly, 'overflowing'; for in the core of the word is that great Mother-symbol, always ready to provide dinner or tea, the *uber*, 'the udder of a cow'.

Pope's famous line, 'True wit is Nature to advantage drest', could be the text for this piece of analysis. Whichever meaning of 'wit' Pope chose to use, it always, for him, stood close to poetry.

The poetry of English nature-words is often borrowed from other languages. *Pansies*, for *pensées*; *dandelion* for *dent de lion*; *forget-me-not* translated from Mediaeval F. (if not from German *Vergissmeinnicht*) are among the flowers. Some of the most felicitous borrowings were from Latin and Greek – languages which could produce words such as *vespertilio*, 'the small hunter of the evening, the bat'; or a word meaning 'dawn-singer' for the crowing cock.

Greek gave us *anemone* in 1551. It gave Middle English *onyx*, the variety of quartz likened to *onux*, 'the finger-nail', from its veined transparency. (*Nail* and L. *unguis* are cognates.) The Gk. *horizōn* was first made use of by us in Chaucer's *Troilus*: 'And whiten gan the Orisonte shene.' The word is even more majestic in the original phrase *horizōn kuklos*, 'the limiting circle'. The poetry of the sky is beautifully expressed in 'comet', *kōmētēs astēr*, 'the long-haired star', and in 'galaxy' (*galaxios kuklos*, the milky circle), to which we have already referred.

The *squirrel* (see Chapter XII(a)) carries his tail close, like a shadow; and this is almost the sense of the Greek words – *skia*, 'shadow', *oura*, 'tail' – which, with the Late Latin diminutive intervening, became, through French, our most unclassical-looking classical English word. And how easily Greek lent itself to effective late borrowings may be seen in the name for the mayfly. For this insect, which in its last metamorphosis lives 'for a day', *ephemera* is the perfect word, and *ephemerid* one of the most lovely.

If compression is the secret of true poetry, we may understand why certain Latin words have achieved their status in English. The L. *sera*, 'late evening' seems to combine the sense of 'clear and peaceful' with that of its first meaning of *serus*, 'late', still attached to it. It is almost the line, 'It was a beauteous evening, calm and free', compressed into one word.

* * *

As we have seen in earlier chapters, most distant languages contribute to Emerson's 'great English metropolitan speech'. *Tulip* is a name that seems to mingle wit with a touch of poetry, reflecting the shape, and perhaps the colour, of the Turkish *tulband*, 'a turban', which reached us through Italian and French. *Deodar*, meaning in Skt. 'tree of the gods', was introduced early in the 19th century for *Cedrus Libani deodara*. The species of cedar to which the name is given in India vary according to locality.

The poetry of the purely English nature-names is rather different. The plant-names are mixed up with a kind of animal folk-lore which seems more reminiscent of nursery-rhymes or Beatrix Potter than of poetry. Was 'Higgledy-Piggledy, my fat hen . . .' composed before or after countryfolk began using the name *fat-hen* for the white goosefoot, the *Chenopodium album* of Linnaeus?

The corruption of *folks'* to *fox* in the popular name for *Digitalis purpurea* exhibits an interest in wild-life, but is evidence of the waning of the belief in the existence of the Little People. The frequent occurrence of *hare* in plant-names points to more than affection for furry creatures. Whereas the names of the hare's-ear bugloss and the hare's-tail grass have been left in peace, attempts are sometimes made to show that the *harebell*, the 'bluebell of Scotland', should be the *hairbell*, on the ground that the flowers hang on such slender stalks. But those who first called the wild campanula *harebell* were not botanists with microscopes, but people with an eye for beauty and an interest in the wildings of the hills, even if their interest was gastronomic. They had moreover a particular feeling – a feeling of awe – for a creature which might in appearance be a hare, but in reality be a Wise Woman on her way to a meeting of her Coven. This belief was certainly not obsolete on Dartmoor a few years before the Second World War.*

Often the attraction of a name lies in its sound. Of the various developments of O.E. *wudubinde*, standard English eventually chose the dialect version *woodbine* as the most euphonious.

Sometimes enshrined in the name is a charmingly descriptive metaphor, as in *maidenhair fern*, which has unselfishly shared its epithet with the maidenhair-tree, *Gingko biloba*, that has leaves resembling the fern's in shape. Sometimes a fine metaphor is hidden. *Blizzard*, like *Blitz*, means 'a storm': *blaze* is a cognate. Flames can sound very like the hiss of heavy rain.

There are names which suggest the simplicity of poetry. *C(h)amomile*, 'apple of the ground', came, through L. and F., from Gk. *khamai*, 'on the ground' + *mēlon*, 'apple'. *Khamai* and *leōn* gave us *chameleon*, 'the grounded lion, the dwarf lion'. There is a kind of pathetic misunderstanding or poetic anthropomorphism in *primrose*, the 'rathe primrose', brave because it comes so early, like daffodils, 'before the swallow dares'. The simplest and most obvious names are probably the best. *Daisy* is an excellent word: but of course we seldom remember the meaning, because the word does not *sound* like its meaning, as *daeges ēage*, 'day's eye', did to the Saxons.

*L.C.S.

epilogue

WHILE writing this book, I have found* that pre-Elizabethan times, when most of these nature-words were born, acquired for me a strong and refreshing taste of reality. The Past is so different, yet at times it seems nearer and more comprehensible than the Present. When we try to see the sort of country that the words reveal, we get a picture of the background of a language before it began to settle, or perhaps we should say, before it exploded.

'Think of England small and white and clean . . .' It is neither clean nor particularly white, although the dirt is of a good earthy character. The sky and the hills and the shore must certainly have seemed larger, because there were no buildings taller than the stump of the church-tower to cut them to size. The villages were hamlets, and the roads the merest tracks. There were no advertisements, and no chain-stores. People were called according to their trades, in the manner of *Happy Families*: Webb the weaver, or Coward the cow-man. There were few skills unrepresented in the village. A surname – *an eek-name* they called it then, and now it has become *a nickname* – might be somewhat coarse or decidedly rude. (*Cicero* – 'chick-pea' – must have traced his descent from an ancestor with a wart; and 'Spotty-face' was a personal name in a pre-Homeric civiliz-ation.)

In Saxon and Norman England there were no street-names: people lived 'by the ford' or 'by the burnt wood'. A burned down wood was a valuable asset, because the forest was an enemy, making communications harder between one settlement and another, and harbouring the wrong kinds of neighbour, brute and human: these being disadvantages only slightly offset by the supplies of firing, of acorns as pannage for swine, and, with luck, an occasional stag or boar for meat. A fire made a potential clearing; and any sort of glade was a place to be commandeered for habitation. (A tenth of our place-names end in such a syllable as *-lay* – O.E. *lēah*, a glade, clearing, or field.) A meadow was best of all, because people could live on it, or by it; since almost everybody was a farmer, however small his holding. The enclosure or fence was one of the most im-portant things in that far-off economy; for it represented a promise, a

*S.P.

303

pact 'that this land belongs to someone' – and the animals inside it too. ('Pact', as we have noted, derives from L. *pangere, pactum*, 'to drive into the ground', e.g. a boundary-post.) Most people had animals, which wandered in and out of the house. Horses and farm-animals were man's friends; but most wild animals were his enemies. Almost anywhere in the country lambs might be carried off by wolves, or killed by ravens, which, like kites, were everywhere. There was not, nor could there be, an Anti-Blood-Sports movement, so far as hunting was concerned. Everybody hunted, though hunting pink had never been heard of, however lowly the quarry. Weather was a great topic, because everyone had an interest in the land. But there were no jokes about grumbling farmers, because every-body knew that bad weather and hard land could spell starvation, as some of our place-names remind us still. People loved and admired the birds, provided they were not birds of prey. They liked to invent, stories and 'facts' about animals, and pretty names for flowers, mixed with cruder ones for 'lords and ladies' (the wild arum) and other tough flowers which seemed too common to be pretty. The great majority of plants fell into one or the other of two classes: either they were weeds or they were remedies for gout or smallpox or quinsy. Natural History as a pursuit was a late 16th century concept; but men before that time were naturalists (and often exceedingly knowledgeable about some branches of nature) by basic necessity and the will to survive.

The language spoken by these people was much affected by the fact that for long months in the year communication with the outside world – that is to say, with the village over the hill – was difficult, and sometimes impossible. Only the priest and perhaps the doctor could read and write – and generally not very well at that. Where there was a church, the service was read in incomprehensible Latin. When the country began to open up, the Mass was celebrated every day; and some of the daily 'Hours' would be attended by such of the folk who could leave their labours for short periods. By the 14th century worldliness and 'the root of all evil' were increasingly cor-rupting the practice of the Faith: but Chaucer – no idealist – shows that there were shining examples of the best types of men in his descriptions of the Knight, the Plowman, and the Povre Persoun of a Toun.

'A Knight ther was and that a worthy man,
That fro the tyme that he first bigan
To riden out, he loved chivalrie,
Trouthe and honour, fredom and curteisie.

And though that he were worthy, he was wys,
And of his port as meeke as is a mayde.
He nevere yet no vileynye ne sayde,
In al his lyf, unto no maner wight.
He was a verray parfit, gentil knyght.'

The Plowman was the Parson's brother.

'A trewe swynkere and a good was he,
Lyvynge in pees and parfit charitee.
God loved he best, with al his hoole herte,
At alle tymes, thogh him gamed or smerte,
And thanne his neighebor right as hymselve.
He wolde thresshe, and therto dyke and delve,
For Cristes sake, for every povre wight,
Withouten hire, if it lay in his myght.'

For nearly six hundred years the 'Povre Persoun' has stood as the type of a good priest,

'That Cristes Gospel trewely wolde preche.
His parisshens devoutly wolde he teche.

Wyde was his parisshe, and houses far asonder,
But he ne lefte not for reyn ne thonder,
In siknesse nor in meschief to visite
The ferreste in his parisshe, muche and lite,
Upon his feet, and in his hand a staf.
This noble ensample to his sheepe he yaf
That first he wroghte and afterward he taughte.

(And) Cristes loore, and His Apostles twelve,
He taughte, but first he folwed it hymselve.'

The *persōna* was originally the mask worn by an actor in the Roman drama, to show which character he represented – the Runaway Slave, the Stern Parent, etc. – and, possibly by an artificial device, to increase the resonance of his voice. Hence the word came to mean 'a character', and later 'a personage'. The 'parson', was the principal personage of the village, and the one through whose lips the Gospel sounded to his people.

* * *

Yet the folk in general had little opportunity to absorb the culture of the Bible, or its powerful humanity and poetry, at first hand. This was not to become part of their lives until the Reformation and the age of the great translators. The old cults were (as they still are) hidden under the surface. Witchcraft flourished in the darkness. The name of Woden was not forgotten. Belief in the influence of the stars coloured the mind of almost everyone. There was endless rumour, but no news. The lastest sensation in the War of the Roses might filter through two years after the event.

The English thought of their language as something spoken, hardly ever as something spelt. A man who came from outside the village talked with a strange accent, and was called a foreigner (as he still is in dialects, especially those spoken on the east and south-east coasts, where for centuries – even as thirty years ago – invaders were likely to appear). We remember that the Greek *deinos* meant 'strange', and, in consequence, 'terrible': and for many years the English Litany retained the clause, 'From the fury of the Danes, good Lord, deliver us'. The strength of the insularity of our forefathers cannot cause surprise.

In those days it was often difficult to understand Grandfather, particularly if he lived across the river. To the average cultured European, English was the merest backwater; and speakers of English near the seats of power were not unconscious of the fact. There has never been a time in the past thousand years when the cultural value of French has not counted for something.

Yet underneath the surface our language was boiling. Every now and then would emerge a bubble like the surfacing of some huge animal. Chaucer was an explosion all by himself; but he came too soon to be fully recognized. There must have been others like him, who left no record but who realized with quiet excitement the possibilities of English. It was not until the 16th century that the little oil-strike became the great gusher which nobody on earth could hold down.

Such facts and many more about the English in those days are revealed when we untie those tightly-filled packets of history, the words of the English tongue.

index

INDEX

INDEX